Cultural Attractions/
Cultural Distractions

Cultural Attractions/ Cultural Distractions

Critical Literacy in Contemporary Contexts

Libby Allison, *Southwest Texas State University*
Kristine L. Blair, *Bowling Green State University*

Prentice Hall, Upper Saddle River, New Jersey 07458

Library of Congress Cataloging-in-Publication Data

Allison, Libby.
    Cultural attractions / cultural distractions : critical literacy in
contemporary contexts / Libby Allison, Kristine L. Blair.
      p. cm.
    Includes bibliographical references (p.) and index.
    ISBN 0-13-737818-1 (pbk. : alk. paper)
    1. Readers—Popular culture. 2. English language—Rhetoric
Problems, exercises, etc. 3. Critical thinking Problems, exercises,
etc. 4. Popular culture Problems, exercises, etc. 5. Report
writing Problems, exercises, etc. I. Blair, Kristine. II. Title.
PE1127.P6A48 2000
808'.0427—DC21   99-35481
                                         CIP

This book was set in 10/12 ITC Trump Medieval by Carlisle Communications, Ltd.
and was printed and bound by Hamilton Printing Co.
The cover was printed by Phoenix Color Corp.

Editor-in-chief: Leah Jewell
Managing editor: Bonnie Biller
Assistant editor: Vivian Garcia
Production liaison: Fran Russello
Editorial/production supervision: Joan Vidal/P. M. Gordon Associates, Inc.
Interior design: P. M. Gordon Associates, Inc.
Prepress and manufacturing buyer: Mary Ann Gloriande
Copy editor: Nancy Marcello
Permissions specialist: Fred Courtright
Art director: Jayne Conte
Cover designer: Joe Sengotta
Cover Art: © Anson Liaw
Director, Image Resource Center: Melinda Lee Reo
Manager, Rights & Permissions: Kay Dellosa
Image specialist: Beth Boyd
Photo researcher: Teri Stratford
Marketing manager: Sue Brekka

Printed in the United States of America
10 9 8 7 6 5 4 3 2 1

ISBN 0-13-737818-1

Prentice-Hall International (UK) Limited, *London*
Prentice-Hall of Australia Pty. Limited, *Sydney*
Prentice-Hall Canada Inc., *Toronto*
Prentice-Hall Hispanoamericana, S.A., *Mexico*
Prentice-Hall of India Private Limited, *New Delhi*
Prentice-Hall of Japan, Inc., *Tokyo*
Pearson Education Asia Pte. Ltd., *Singapore*
Editora Prentice-Hall do Brasil, Ltda., *Rio de Janeiro*

Contents

6.   LITERACIES AND LEARNING   200

Image: Thach Bui, "PC and Pixel"   200

Introduction   201

Readings:

E. D. HIRSCH, JR.: *Cultural Literacy*   203

"During the period 1970–1985, the amount of shared knowledge that we have been able to take for granted in communicating with our fellow citizens has also been declining. More and more of our young people don't know things we used to assume they knew."

Reading Reflections   210

DAVID BIANCULLI: *Teleliteracy Pretest*   210

"Are *you* teleliterate? *You Bet Your Life*—and if you just thought of Groucho Marx's quiz show of the same name, you've proven my point."

Reading Reflections   220

RODNEY D. SMITH: *The Case for Multiculturalism*   220

"Before adding this book [*The House on Mango Street* by Sandra Cisneros] to the curriculum, my colleagues and I had to overcome criticism against multiculturalism from parents, school board members, and fellow teachers. . . . If I had any doubts about the importance of multiculturalism in my classroom, Consuella eliminated them."

Reading Reflections   222

JAY DAVID BOLTER: *The Network Culture*   223

"Our culture is itself a vast writing space, a complex of symbolic structures. Just as we write our minds, we can say that we write the culture in which we live."

Reading Reflections   230

SEYMOUR PAPERT: *Obsolete Skill Set: The 3 Rs*   231

"But reading will no longer be the unique primary access road to knowledge and learning, and it should therefore no longer be the dominant consideration in the design of School."

Reading Reflections   235

EILEEN SIMPSON: *Dyslexia*   235

"It is only a slight exaggeration to say that those who learned to read without difficulty can best understand the labor reading is for a dyslexic by turning a page of text upside down and trying to decipher it."

Reading Reflections   239

MARSHA KING: *Dropout Aces GED Test, Now Dreams of College*   239

"And why do kids drop out of high school and end up on the street? For a million dif-

"Usenet, while it can be nasty, acerbic, uncaring and unsympathetic, is a truly nondiscriminatory society. It judges you only through your postings, not by what you look like, your marital status, whether you have a disability, or any of the other things that are traditionally used for discrimination."

"I personally applaud those souls on CB who, when asked 'R u m or f?' [Are you male or female?], simply answer 'yes.' "

"This isn't quite my story yet. It's the story, for now, of an elusive congeries of flesh and bytes named Mr. Bungle, and of the ghostly sexual violence he committed in the halls of LambdaMOO, and most importantly of the ways his violence and his victims challenged the thousand and more residents of that surreal, magic-infested mansion to become, finally, the community so many of them already believed they were."

Preface to Instructors

In a telling scene from the landmark study *The Machine in the Garden: Technology and the Pastoral Ideal in America*,[1] scholar Leo Marx depicts Nathaniel Hawthorne sitting in the woods near Concord, Massachusetts, in 1844, noting impressions of his surroundings, when a faint but momentous sound begins in the distance: the whistle of a locomotive streaks through the air, breaking the serenity and calm. That sound, contends Marx, is a metaphor signaling the change technology would make, by the end of the nineteenth century, on American literary history, culture, and society forever.

And so it is for many teachers in education today at the turn of the twenty-first century; the calm and quiet of our classrooms have been interrupted by an equally small but momentous sound: the clicking of computer keyboards. It is a sound that now marks the world in which our students grow up and will live, how they learn, and in essence who they are. They are no longer passive learners, sitting quietly in their seats taking notes; they are active learners, eager to see the world, to interact with others personally and online, and to learn experientially.

The sound is also the seed from which grow the images and texts in the media and technology that permeate our students' daily lives. These texts and images can blur the line between fact and fiction when intergalactic *Star Wars* weapons blast across the movie screen destroying sci-fi actors; while on the nightly news, fighter planes' laser weapons, with pinpoint accuracy, blow apart enemy targets, yet never seem to hurt real human beings. Or they can communicate values about how people resolve problems to those students whose video of choice is *Jerry Springer: Uncensored*, or they can define beauty for many women when silicon implants make the covers of most contemporary women's magazines.

Yet the sound is also the seed that enables students to research information quickly on the World Wide Web on how to support a classmate's battle with AIDS, or to hear via an audioclip famous contemporary poets read their own poetry anytime day or night, or to e-mail friends in distant lands who might otherwise be lost in their lives.

Thus the name of the book: *Cultural Attractions/Cultural Distractions: Critical Literacy in Contemporary Contexts*. We have put on the lenses of today's students looking about their world to see how to help them think, learn, and write analytically about the media and technology so influential in their lives. They are encouraged to question how these messages might present stereotypes of race, class, gender; how they represent people different from themselves; and how they influence their own concept of "self."

We neither presume to know nor present answers, because just as their world is rapidly changing, ours is also. Rather we seek to provide various situations and contexts from which to examine the messages for students to look for their own answers. But we say this without any intention of tossing out ideas that are tried-and-true to learning: reading provocative texts, questioning assumptions, and addressing those assumptions with students' own ideas. In line with a goal of a college education, we want to help students step back from what is happening immediately around them in order to think independently and assess the media and technology's influence on their lives and futures, culture, and society.

Each chapter of *Cultural Attractions/Cultural Distractions* includes a brief introduction to the theme of the chapter, images and readings from various media and technology related to the theme, and "Reading Reflections" activities specifically related to these images and readings. Then each chapter has four special sections, "Reading Reactions," "Classroom Reactions," "Media Connections," and "Community Interactions." Together all these offer students the opportunity to work out their own opinions through a variety of forums and formats, including participating in pen-and-paper classroom writing and discussion activities, studying media artifacts and researching on-line, and reaching outside the classroom into their own communities to practice being culturally literate citizens.

Because each chapter can stand on its own, teachers may want to mix and match chapters as the semester goes along. Some of the texts and images are from conventional English teaching sources, and many will be new to teachers. Teachers will find flexibility in that the writing assignments can be narrative, persuasive, and investigative, or a combination. Often students are encouraged to produce texts of their own as alternatives to the messages they see. The various writing activities can be written individually, collaboratively, and on-line. Even though each reading and activity has serious undertones for learning, we are hopeful that students will also have some fun along the way. For instance, they can create their own advertisements or take a trip to the local toy store to analyze the difference between girls' and boys' toys.

In developing the book, we want to acknowledge Vivian Garcia, our editor at Prentice Hall, who poked, prodded, and picked up the ball for us when the going got tough; the reviewers, Nedra Reynolds, Rita Eastburg, Cathryn Amdahl, and Al Maginnes; Joe and Kevin, our husbands, for their loving support throughout the years' work; and Marsha A. Groff, our friend and colleague, whose untimely death from cancer left a void in our lives that has been filled only by the lasting impression of her devotion to teaching developmental writers.

Libby Allison   Kristine L. Blair

Note

1. Leo Marx, *The Machine in the Garden: Technology and the Pastoral Ideal in America* (1964; New York: Oxford University Press, 1974).

Cultural Attractions
Cultural Distractions

Mass media violence.
Copyright B. Daemmrich/The Image Works. The Image Works is a stock agency
that features over 750,000 images ranging from traditional and contemporary
culture to family life and health care.

Is there too much violence on television? This image suggests not only that there is
but also that violence directly influences our youth. While the image of a gun pointed
at a young girl is disconcerting enough, the jaded attitude by some toward television
engendered by excessive exposure to the medium is equally disturbing.

In view of this attitude toward television violence, do you agree with the system by
which television shows are rated based on their appropriateness for children? Do television and media, in general, take enough responsibility for the material they present?

Networks assert that television violence does not affect viewers who can distinguish fiction from reality, but at the same time they charge millions of dollars for
commercial air time based on the viewer market. In light of this high cost, can
networks justify their position that they do not influence viewers?

1

Introduction

Reading and Writing the Texts of the Information Age

Cultural Attractions/Cultural Distractions is a collection of reading and writing activities presenting opportunities for you to use your writing to view and critique messages from popular culture—the mass media and popular arts—in your daily lives. This book has several goals: to acknowledge the importance of media messages in shaping and reflecting our cultural assumptions about family, others, gender, work, and life in general; to validate your expert knowledge of media culture by including opportunities to read and write about that culture; and to introduce you to the newest media and literacy technologies you may use to read, research, and produce responses to cultural messages. Indeed, *Cultural Attractions/Cultural Distractions* is designed to help you consider the ways in which messages from the mass media and the popular arts influence concepts of "self" and of group identities, such as age, gender, class, and race. As the book title suggests, these messages can be both positive and negative by presenting their assumptions about your own identities and your communities, as well as about the identities and communities of others.

Cultural Attractions/Cultural Distractions also presents opportunities to examine these media messages firsthand rather than merely respond to opinions of "experts" about these messages, which is the prevailing method for presenting cultural and media literacy. Simply put, your responding to articles about literacy is not how we believe you become more media savvy citizens. Rather, we want to involve you in actively finding and examining those messages within your own lives, within your local communities, and within your larger culture. To that end, the book focuses less on your finding the "meanings" in the articles of experts, emphasizing, instead, activities designed for you to interact with each other and community members.

Although this textbook is meant to be a starting point for thinking and writing about various cultural texts, the technologies and forums you use to express your thoughts and present your writing are changing. For that reason, many activities and projects suggest that you try new formats in addition to the tried-

and-true printed essay. These formats, such as Web pages, posters, videos, advertisements, brochures, letters, e-mail, and newsgroup posts, can be created and distributed through the very kinds of media and technology you will be studying.

Media Texts as Sites of Conflict

One approach to studying popular culture texts is for students to find and explore cultural conflicts that circulate through the mass media and the popular arts. *Cultural Attractions/Cultural Distractions* foregrounds these conflicts in several ways, addressing the following: (1) How contemporary media texts demonstrate interactions and cultural conflicts between members of different races, ethnicities, and sexes. For example, media images frequently portray the American family as white and upper middle class. We therefore ask you to observe similarities and differences between these media images and the makeup of actual families in your communities, including families of mixed races, single parents and grandparents, and gay and lesbian families. A related activity would be for you to conduct an experiment asking children to draw a family and compare their visions of a family with images of families found in advertising or other cultural texts.

(2) What contemporary texts demonstrate about individuals who cross the boundaries of long-established traditions with respect to race, gender, and ethnicity. For instance, despite cultural messages telling us that both women and men can "be all that you can be," or, in the case of women, that they've "come a long way," there remains an unwritten standard for femininity and masculinity upon which most of us are judged by others, and upon which most of us judge ourselves. For instance, Chapter 4, "Appearances versus Realities" asks you to search for media images and texts showing men being nurturing, communal, and cooperative, unlike how they have been portrayed in the past. How likely are you to find such appearances?

(3) How individuals and groups create texts that represent how they see themselves or how they think others see them. To illustrate, bell hooks' essay "Straightening Our Hair" testifies to this practice of racial and ethnic minorities being encouraged to assimilate to white standards of femininity and attractiveness. For hooks, choosing not to chemically process her hair suggests an attempt to control self-representation in ways that resist these more dominant standards.

READING CULTURAL TEXTS

Perhaps one of the most difficult challenges in studying popular culture is that many students have been discouraged from doing so by those who do not consider it worthy of academic reading and writing. One method we encourage is for you to discuss openly the biases against using popular culture in classrooms, and to discuss whether examining contemporary texts is necessary for you to be a part of a literate citizenry. For instance, examine the following list of cultural artifacts and determine which might be worthy of study.

1. The American flag
2. A *Newsweek* article
3. An MTV video
4. A famous painting, for example, the *Mona Lisa*
5. The dictionary
6. A rap album
7. Netscape Navigator
8. A crucifix
9. CK Jeans
10. A hairstyle, for example, long hair
11. *Home Improvement*
12. Barbie and Ken
13. A photo album
14. An amusement park

For example, in one of our recent class discussions, some students didn't see a photo album (item 13) as a text, but through further class debate, others were able to define the photo album as a historical narrative about family life, often compiled by a parent, who organizes it from a particular perspective with a sense of the importance of a family's history. Because such texts are important documents about what it means to be a family, you can do something similar by constructing your own collage of family images in an attempt to tell a visual story of your family rituals and histories. Related activities can be found in Chapter 3, "Family Matters." The notion of a "critical literacy" for popular culture also fits well within the discussion of different kinds of literacy found in Chapter 6, "Literacies and Learning."

Because of the importance of assessing the role that personal and social texts play in defining our world, these activities require methods of critical inquiry and innovative formats for discussing and writing about these texts, their dominant cultural assumptions, and the underlying conflicts circulating through them. To help explain and demonstrate the way in which various media circulate cultural assumptions that can cause both solidarity and conflict within and between different social groups, we have devoted the next section of this chapter to two media forums: print advertising and Internet newsgroups.

Advertising's Rhetorical and Cultural Features

Other examples of writing assignments about "texts" and cultural identity include the critique and revision of advertising images of women and men, an assignment option in Chapter 4, "Appearances versus Realities," which is profiled here.

ADVERTISING ACTIVITY

Advertising is everywhere: on billboards, radio and television, newspapers and magazines, and the Internet. Often, such ads reflect the particular goals, services, and demographic makeup of a magazine, a community, or a TV following; for example, those who watch *Home Improvement* versus those who have watched *Seinfeld*.

Your first task is to select a print or television advertisement for a product or service and then to analyze the gender images presented in the ad. Consider what these messages convey about gender roles, both in terms of competence and appearance.

You can also evaluate whether these messages are positive or negative by how they include or exclude different sexes or gender lifestyles. One of the goals in deconstructing an ad is for you then to reconstruct a more ethical, egalitarian ad image or, perhaps, to parody the advertising image.

In order to plan such an assignment, it is important for you to ask a number of questions about advertising texts in general and their ability to send powerful messages to consumers. Although many of these questions will arise during class discussion, either face to face or in e-mail chats, such an assignment could address a number of textual and cultural features with questions like the ones in the following prewriting guide.

Rhetorical Features

1. What is the context of the advertisement? What magazine is it taken from, and who is the typical reader for this magazine?
2. What is the scene of the ad? What actions are taking place, and why are they significant?
3. What is the general mood of the advertisement, and how is this mood achieved (color, text, images)?
4. What is the ratio between pictorial and printed/verbal information, and how do they work together to persuade the viewer?
5. What visual or textual symbols are found within the ad? What do they seem to stand for?
6. What is the language of the advertisement? What kinds of descriptive words are used? What is the tone of the language: serious, humorous, sexy?
7. What are the basic appeals of the ads? Some examples include logical appeals about the quality of the product, ethical appeals to authority or to the goodwill of the advertiser, emotional appeals on the basis of fear, desire to belong, desire for wealth or sexuality, and so forth.

Cultural Assumptions

1. What is the item being advertised, and what role does it play within our culture, or what image comes to mind when consumers think about the product?

2. If women or men are present within the ad, how are they portrayed? What changes if either a woman or a man is in the ad?
3. What particular groups of people are not included within the ad?
4. What values or appeals are reflected in the ad (examples may include patriotism, gender roles, family values, etc.)?
5. Offer a reaction to the ad: Why do you like it or dislike it? What are your criteria for evaluating the ad? Sample criteria might include rhetorical effectiveness, amount of information about the product, or the inclusion of diverse people and lifestyles.
6. Is there another way to advertise the product other than the ads here? Think about the possibilities for revision to be more diverse in your representation of others.

Consumer Profile for Revising Advertising Images

1. What is the product you are advertising, and who typically needs or wants this product? Try to construct a paragraph providing the basic demographic information: age, gender, race, class, and sexual orientation.
2. In what ways has this audience been invoked for previous advertisements for the product or service? What images or other communication practices have been used to establish consumer identification with the product?
3. What are the typical rhetorical appeals used for targeting this product to its audience?
4. What are some of the implied cultural assumptions behind these appeals?
5. Who might comprise alternative audiences who have typically not been targeted but could gain from personal or social use of the product?
6. In which alternative magazine or advertising forum might this ad be featured?
7. What types of visual images and scenarios could you use to target this audience in a more ethical, egalitarian manner?
8. What textual messages should be sent to the audience to promote the product or service as fairly and realistically as possible? What buzzwords or phrases will you eliminate from your text, and what language choices will you use to replace them?
9. How will your ad be better than previous ads that advertise similar products? Or how might your ad be a parody of existing advertisements?

Of course, not all questions in this guide may make their way into a writing assignment. Rather, as you begin to apply such questions to various ads, certain thematic patterns and details about the ads that support those patterns may begin to emerge, contributing to an overall focus for your written response. Recent sample projects about advertising images include an analysis and critique of the appeals in the popular Guess Jeans ads. The following excerpt is from a student project focusing on the effects of the Guess Jeans campaign on the women who view it:

> Guess advertisements are geared toward single, young, and impressionable women. These women value their appearance and find name brands vital to purchasing their clothing. The advertisements appeal to these women by implying that if they invest in Guess apparel, they will acquire these things that they desire. The woman shown in the advertising campaign has a marvelous figure and is made to resemble a Madonna-like image with her blond hair and black bra. Yet this new style created by Guess is unrealistic for women to follow. The ideal characteristics are to be thin, blond, and to have an intimidating aura. These promises made by Guess are both unrealistic and deceiving, for Guess is unfairly suggesting, through their advertisements, that consumers will obtain beauty, men, and sex.

This student writer concluded that Guess should be more realistic and use less sexualized images of women to sell its product and suggested a possible alternative of employing women with different body shapes and sizes as well as different ethnic backgrounds. Although the student did not deny the effectiveness of the campaign, she theorized that product sales could perhaps increase if "the jeans would appear as if they are for everyone instead of just a selected few" who fit the thin, blond, exotic, but unrealistic standard.

Later this same student designed an alternative ad. To avoid the typical ad tactics of Guess, she created the ad with photographs of several women of diverse body sizes and ethnic backgrounds; included were women of African American, Asian, and Hispanic descent. Stressing women's commonality and diversity, all of her "models" wore blue jeans and white T-shirts for her product, "Diversity Jeans." The slogan was "Different by Nature."

Another student who also chose Guess Jeans concentrated on how the ad campaign's consistent attention to a certain image of women can "be very damaging to a young woman's health and self-confidence" because of the implied message that women need Guess' help to feel "sexy, alluring and chic." This message says women feel both affinity and alienation, attraction and distraction. In parodying the Guess campaign, this student included a montage of Guess' hypersexualized advertising campaign, which was done as a World Wide Web document complete with visuals and links to relevant sites about Guess on-line. These types of assignments, integrating visuals and texts in rhetorically effective ways, can further extend the ideas you develop in written work.

Researching Electronic Communities

Although many typical sites of student research include workplaces, entertainment (the shopping mall, a rock concert), and home, you can also explore the process of cultural attraction and distraction found in the more recent form of media discourse—Internet newsgroups. These virtual communities, profiled in Chapter 7, "Virtual Communities/Virtual Selves," are not unlike other media in that they range from conservative to liberal in their discussions of events, issues, and even people. By being introduced to these electronic forums, you become both a participant and an observer in these new communities through sustained contact with a group to determine its social values and how these values manifest within the group's daily activities. In Usenet groups or electronic message boards, for instance, you will observe how communication fosters a sense of community as well as how power relations are played out: who speaks and who does not and what is and what is not allowable for discussion. An analysis of such electronic communities is one step in helping you recognize the textual and contextual constraints on-line, as well as in the more traditional media texts we profile within this book.

Because electronic communication is becoming such a common mode in both business and industry because of its speed and access, it is also a way for many people—be they fans of the popular television show *The X Files* or of rap artist Snoop Doggy Dog or interested in fitness groups or gay rights coalitions— to find solidarity and group identification and to resist being swayed by mainstream opinions. Despite this empowering potential, many people question the extent to which these new "virtual communities" can and do mirror traditional class, race, and other cultural hierarchies present in our "real-time" face-to-face world. To study this question, we ask you to participate in an electronic discussion group (of your choice) and spend time each week reading and responding to some of the comments and conversations there. After several weeks as participant-observers in these projects, you should be able to analyze the group for such facets as dominant and less dominant speakers, topics, values, and discourse conventions, while connecting members' observations to their own participation or lack thereof within the group. Finally, you can also comment on the ethics of the group communication practices, evaluating the level of inclusion or exclusion of varying perspectives. As with the advertising images assignment, it is important to develop a series of questions about the newsgroup to provide some possible topics to include in your written analysis. Although all the following questions may not play a role within such analyses, they can provide a wide variety of issues to draw upon as you begin to draft essay responses.

History of the Newsgroup

1. What is the genre of the newsgroup: alternative, social, and so on?
2. What purpose does the newsgroup serve?
3. How large is the group, and who is in this group?

Topics the Newsgroup Addresses

1. What topics or issues does the group consider or ignore?
2. What are allowable topics?
3. What are prohibited topics?

4. Are the topics consistent throughout time, or has there been a change in topics?
5. What constitutes validity, proof, or evidence in the forum?

Consider the difference between personal experience, scientific studies, and so forth.

Writers within the Newsgroup

1. What kind of people post within this group? (Consider professional and academic background.)
2. How does this conform to your expectations of general newsgroup membership?
3. Who are the important figures in this group?
4. Whose experience is most frequently cited?
5. What are the important key events and experiences that it is assumed members of the group already know?
6. Who tend to be the expert writers and who tend to be the novice writers?
7. Are there gender or class differences between the experts and the novices? How can you tell?

Readers within the Newsgroup

1. Who is addressed in the forum, and what are the characteristics of this assumed audience? (You might consider gender, race, class, sexual orientation, age, educational level, socioeconomic status, and so forth.)
2. What are the assumed needs of the audience?
3. To what uses are readers expected to put this information?
4. What is the audience's level of experience and knowledge of the subject matter?
5. What are the beliefs, attitudes, values, prejudices, and biases of the addressed audience?
6. How varied are the topics in relation to the audience? Is there recognition of multiple audience levels?
7. How do you fit or not fit the assumed readership? How does that affect your opinion of the newsgroup?

Style and Language

1. How formal or informal is the language used throughout the newsgroup?
2. What technical or specialized jargon is used? Who would understand such terminology?

3. What slang or buzzwords are used? Who would understand and use such language?
4. What abbreviations, for example, IMHO (in my humble opinion), exist within the forum as valid methods of communication?
5. What is the tone of most posts? What stance do writers take in relation to the audience: experts to novices, peers, and so forth?

Cultural and Multicultural Issues

1. What is the ratio of men to women represented in the texts?
2. What is the ratio between whites and ethnic minorities?
3. What are the class contexts: dinner parties, skiing outings versus fishing, bowling, and so on?
4. What are the age contexts: retirees versus young adults, Beethoven versus rock and roll?
5. What groups are missing from the forum?

Resisting and Changing the Group

1. Overall, do you believe that certain aspects of the newsgroup can be critiqued? Explain.
2. What are the benefits or risks of maintaining the current status of the group?
3. What are the benefits or risks of attempting to change the status of the group?
4. What new or previously ignored topics could be introduced in the newsgroup to construct a more diverse readership?
5. What language practices could the newsgroup employ to make readership more inclusive than exclusive?
6. How could existing topics be expanded to address points of significance to groups whose interests are represented less frequently?
7. Because the potential for changing the group forum is often limited, what alternative forums exist for the constructed readership? What issues and value systems might they offer that the current forum does not?

In many instances, gathering data about the newsgroup can lead to new knowledge about how electronic communities can serve as a microcosm of cultural assumptions and attitudes that you may see as either harmful or helpful in the construction of both a personal and social identity through the technological access to the community. For example, an analysis of newsgroups devoted to films and television shows with cult-like status, including *The Rocky Horror Picture Show*, *The X Files*, and *ER*, suggested that these groups represented electronic subcultures, and not always the type of empowering virtual community praised by writers like Howard Rheingold, author of the *Virtual Community*. As one student writer asserted:

> As part of the information superhighway, these newsgroups are supposed to bring people together from all over to share a common interest. And in an ideal world you would think they would want to educate those who tune in "about their shared interest." Obviously this is not the case. I have witnessed only reprimands and divisiveness. There is no community here. This is not another day in the neighborhood as Mr. Rodgers would say. This is a glimpse at the segregation of the cyberhood.

This student concluded with the hope that such groups, despite their growing rate on-line, did not replace face-to-face communication but extended it in more positive ways. Ultimately, such analyses of on-line communities are important to see how the same types of cultural attractions and distractions within more mainstream media might find another home on the Internet and, through the very public electronic communication forums, rapidly become an accepted part of our professional and personal lives. Although the questions we've included here are customized for readers of on-line texts, we believe such questions will help you analyze the various textual and cultural features present within all social texts you view in your personal and professional lives, be they popular or academic.

Organization of *Cultural Attractions/Cultural Distractions*

Given the book's emphasis on mass culture and its influence on the construction of social values in both global and local communities, the following issues form chapters that move from individual to social development. We begin, for example, with analysis of the relationship between self and others, family values, leading to exposure to notions of gender roles. We then move to such ethical issues facing our society as media morality, educational equity, and literacy, and culminate with the contexts in which citizens confront new cultural conflicts—virtual communities.

The media and technology range from advertising to broadcast and print news to television, music lyrics, video games, toys, and computers. In addition, there are many activities for you and your class that may call for access to computers and the Internet, but others that do not. Each chapter also includes articles with varying points of view regarding the chapter's theme and the media involved. For example, Chapter 5, "Media Morals," focuses on television, music, and the Internet, which, as types of media genres, are now subjects of controversy over their roles in shaping the habits and attitudes of children and adolescents.

Cultural Attractions/Cultural Distractions encourages you to examine varying perspectives about attractions and distractions of today's popular culture and mass-mediated messages in your personal and social lives. Yet we also encourage you to be independent thinkers and to come to your own conclusions about these messages. Each chapter includes a brief introduction to the theme of the chapter; images and readings from various media about the theme; "Reading Reflections" activities specifically related to each image and reading; and then more in-depth questions and activities relating to the chapter theme organized around the headings of "Reading Reactions," "Classroom Reactions," "Media Connections," and "Community Interactions." This allows you to work out your own opinions through a variety of forums and formats, including classroom projects, in-class writing and discussion activities, as well as library research. Media Connections range from viewing and reviewing media artifacts to researching on-line. Among other things, Community Interactions give you more opportunities to observe groups and cultures within your own communities through activities and projects ranging from interviewing teens about video games in a local arcade to photographing families in a local park to observing how people define their own families. The writing assignments, therefore, can employ your own experience as well as library research and the use of popular media as valid sources of information. Assignments can be written individually, collaboratively, and on-line, if access is available. Meanwhile, by balancing classroom and community projects and writing assignments, we hope to help you consider your own reading and writing practices in relationship with others, and at the same time turn your attention to the texts you encounter most—the ones in your daily lives.

The varying topics, readings, activities, and projects in this text are designed to fine-tune your observation, critical and cultural literacy, and communication skills in order to enhance your role as a citizen in the information age, able to question the attraction and distraction of today's media messages. Independently, not only are you able to see these texts surrounding your world, but equally important, you are also able to see *through* them.

The United Colors of Benetton ad campaign.
Photo: O. Toscani.

As a retailer of contemporary clothing, Benetton has often politicized its advertising campaign around social issues, particularly race. Yet this campaign for the spring and summer of 1991 has come under attack from media critics for promoting a more stereotypical representation of racial traits in the name of cultural diversity.

Discuss this Benetton ad and compare it to other ads featuring persons of color. Are people of color prominent in advertising? To what extent are such portrayals instances of racial harmony and inclusion (as Benetton has suggested) or just racial tokenism?

2

Ourselves and Others

In a newspaper column, "Normal Life Too Often Isn't Part of the News," journalist Susan Benesch says that although what she reports is accurate, it is not the whole picture of life in Latin America. Having recently reported about the drug-related deaths of 126 people in Medellin, Colombia, she tells us that the vast majority of the citizens in Medellin lead ordinary lives, unaffected by the violence permeating the news of their city. She advised a skeptical colleague "that he could spend months in Bogota or Medellin or elsewhere in Colombia without ever seeing a drop of blood."

Have you ever considered that the stories and images we see in America about people in other countries do not always present the whole picture? Yet these stories and images often leave lasting impressions on us. What about the stories and images on local television news, on billboards, on advertising flyers, and the like, right in our own communities of people who may look different from us in race, ethnicity, gender, age, physical abilities? What messages do these stories and images convey to us about "others"? Are they accurate or are they misleading?

The readings and activities in this chapter help you explore these questions. As you do, consider whether the messages are plainly educational or deliberately meant to persuade or perhaps even to mislead you. Who, if anyone, stands to benefit from these messages? For instance, do these messages help us understand others or do they create barriers to understanding? Do they construct an "us versus them" view of the world, or do they accurately reflect distinctions in what members of groups believe and how they live?

Other questions you'll want to consider are these: Who is the audience for the story or image? Who created it? What purpose does it serve? Finding out who the audience is and determining what the purpose is of a message help you uncover what is going on behind the scenes for any piece of writing or any media message. Keep in mind, however, there may not be any one right answer but many answers, depending on your perspective. For example, at the end of Benesch's column, she says, "I can't very well write in each of my stories: '300-million Latin Americans had a quiet, ordinary day today.' What to do?"

In considering her dilemma, you might ask, "Why would a newspaper not emphasize the stories of ordinary people's lives in other countries?" Unlike countries where the media are government-controlled, in the United States the media are profit-making businesses, and the high cost of covering international news compared to local news could preclude reporters from covering ordinary lives. On the other hand, you might address the responsibility of the media to present a fair and balanced picture for readers, and the power the media has to shape our views of the world.

These are some points that Rekha Basu raises in "Views from a Third World Journalist." She writes, "Americans tend to know less about other countries and cultures than people in other countries know about us here." She points out, as more people leave Third World countries to immigrate to the United States, there are accompanying "conflicts, jealousies, and misunderstandings." She contends that as long as the American press takes a parochial approach to news reporting not only will minorities continue to be marginalized but ultimately Americans' ability to self-govern will be jeopardized.

Basu's comments parallel those who believe an *absence* of a group or a *silence* about a group or issues within media messages or texts, in fact, says something: A particular group or issue is not worthy of attention. This theme is echoed in Dennis Overbye's "Fear in a Handful of Numbers," about how the day-to-day activities of the world's people are surely ruining the environment for our children and grandchildren. The media obviously have not done their share to help educate all people about the inherent dangers of their activities. Instead, Overbye offers, in our relations with nature, we have been operating with a "cowboy" mentality—that nature is "a vast wilderness waiting to be tamed."

Aside from considering what may not be within a media message, you will want to consider how the language in it is used to construct a reality, ranging from stereotypes and pure fantasy, to partially true, to completely accurate, or any combination of these views. For instance, in Michael Dorris' "Crazy Horse Malt Liquor and Other Cultural Metaphors," the author unpacks the discrepancy between the image portrayed on beer cans and the actual circumstances of Native American life. Also George Lakoff in "Metaphor and War" begins by saying, "Metaphors can kill," and proceeds to show how language constructed the sense of an enemy for Americans during the Gulf War. Just the name of the article by Terry Tempest Williams about the disastrous consequences from nuclear fallout she believes women in her family suffered says a great deal about how language constructs reality. "The Clan of One-Breasted Women" summons up an image of women bonding together in a world where women who have breast cancer are often seen as weak disfigured misfits.

The final selection in your readings in this chapter is a complicated and sophisticated analysis of *National Geographic*, a magazine many Americans have long accepted as an objective, scientific view of the world. In "Becoming America's Lens on the World: *National Geographic* in the Twentieth Century," Jane Collins and Catherine Lutz present an in-depth historical examination of the magazine. They discuss how its content, photography, and design have been neither objective nor scientific, but rather the outcome of political opinions of National Geographic Society board members and of political and technological trends in its 100-year history, as America grew into a world power.

When reading this selection, you may want to note how these influences on the magazine created many readers' concepts of "others," particularly those in the Third World. You can also use Collins and Lutz's analytic techniques for your own analysis of media texts.

Ultimately, the writers in this chapter critique the media's representations of people from many approaches: silences and absences; content; language; photographs and images; and layout and design of a publication. These approaches to uncovering messages to readers are to assist you in your own detective work. The questions and activities that follow are also to help you think about the reading selections, to challenge the media's messages, and to assist you in writing. As you read these selections and venture out to do the various activities, you want to keep in mind that the way the media "construct" others for us says a great deal about how they construct us for others and, perhaps, says a great deal about how we construct our own view of ourselves.

NORMAL LIFE TOO OFTEN ISN'T PART OF THE NEWS

Susan Benesch

All too often, people are willing to believe everything they read. However, as Susan Benesch points out, "What I report about Latin America is true, but it isn't the whole truth." In this column, Benesch explores the emphasis on violence in news reporting that results in a skewed American view of Latin American countries.

The St. Petersburg Times, *considered one of the best newspapers in America, has a daily circulation of more than 300,000, primarily covering the west coast of Florida. Susan Benesch was the Latin America correspondent for the* St. Petersburg Times. *Her work has also been published in* The Miami Herald.

What I report about Latin America is true, but it isn't the whole truth.

Recently, for instance, I wrote about Medellin, Colombia, a city of 2.3-million in which 126 people were killed in a long weekend. That's terrible violence, and people who read the story no doubt concluded that Medellin is very violent.

What they probably didn't realize is that at least 2-million people in Medellin—the vast majority—were not affected by the violence that weekend. It just as well might have happened in another city or on television, as far as they were concerned.

They spent Friday night watching the city's favorite soccer team on TV, and they celebrated Mother's Day on Sunday, eating big family dinners and taking peaceful walks in the park. They did not think about getting shot, any more than you think about crashing your car every time you drive it. People in Medellin are angry at foreign journalists for giving people the feeling that their city is a wasteland scattered with corpses, instead of a vibrant place with schools, churches and movie theaters.

"When has a journalist ever asked how many of us here are *alive!*" one Medellin man asked me.

Complaining that all journalists ever write about in Colombia is violence, a young man said, "the violence is true, but it's not the whole reality."

All I could reply is that it wouldn't make sense for journalists to write about all the airplanes that don't crash, for example. There is also a peculiar convention among journalists that news is bad news and writing good news is fluffy.

About a year ago I returned from a trip to El Salvador, where a war had been going on for about 10 years, and went to lunch with some friends. I told an anecdote about a wedding in El Salvador.

A woman at the table said it had never occurred to her that there were weddings in El Salvador.

I asked how she thought Salvadorans got married.

It wasn't that, she said. She had just never imagined weddings, since all she had heard about were Salvadoran guerrillas and war and death squad killings.

That was a great lesson in the flaws of foreign reporting, but I have not yet come up with a way to solve them.

If I report about something happening in a foreign country, readers assume, naturally, that what I report is typical of life in that country. But usually because of the way news is defined, what I report is exceptional, not typical.

The trouble is that many readers end up with a skewed idea of what foreign countries are like.

After reading the Medellin stories I wrote, a colleague said to me, "Colombia sounds like an interesting place. I'd like to go there sometime once it calms down a little." I explained that it would be fine to go there right now— and that he could spend months in Bogota or Medellin or elsewhere in Colombia without ever seeing a drop of blood.

I can't very well write in each of my stories: "300-million Latin Americans had a quiet, ordinary day today."

What to do?

READING REFLECTIONS

1. Benesch's column is about how news stories may not present the whole picture because they often do not present the "ordinary" news. How would you define ordinary news, and do you agree with her point?
2. Some would say Benesch's column raises the issue of how much "sensationalism" is in the presentation of news. What do you think?
3. Benesch's article states, "A woman at the table said it had never occurred to her that there were weddings in El Salvador." Taking this into consideration, can you think of an experience where you visited a place whose reality differed from the image portrayed in the media? Write a comparison or contrast of the media depiction with your experience.
4. In stating, "I can't very well write in each of my stories: '300-million Latin Americans had a quiet, ordinary day today,' " Benesch claims that everyday life isn't considered newsworthy. Do you agree with her position?
5. Benesch states that she has been unable to come up with a way to solve the "flaws of foreign reporting." Provide some possible solutions for Benesch's dilemma of writing interesting articles without leaving readers with "a skewed idea of what foreign countries are like."

VIEWS FROM A THIRD WORLD JOURNALIST

Rekha Basu

Do Americans know less about other countries and cultures than people in other countries know about us? Does the news marginalize the importance of events taking place in other areas of the world? Rekha Basu argues that the American media's unwillingness to focus on events important to minorities and immigrants can eventually alienate their own readers and viewers.

Rekha Basu's article appeared in Editor & Publisher, *a trade magazine widely read by journalists and newspaper managers throughout North America. A freelance journalist, Basu's article here is the text of a speech she presented to the New York Society of Newspaper Editors in the fall of 1989.*

As a Third World woman journalist, I have been privy to the sometimes conflicting pulls between the press and minority groups.

I have seen minorities cringe at perceived racist stereotypes in the news media, and despair at their inability to get their events covered.

I have seen colleagues in the media struggle to balance the demands of different special-interest groups. I have felt the frustration of trying to place my own stories which I thought were of broad social significance, but editors felt were of special interest only.

And I have felt indignant at what has appeared to be a white American bias to coverage of major news events.

Increasing immigration from Third World countries is subjecting the American population to rapid demographic changes. Accompanying these changes are the inevitable conflicts, jealousies and misunderstandings. The press has a crucial role to play in helping societies adjust to this influx.

I think the press also bears some responsibility for the fact that Americans tend to know less about other countries and cultures than people in other countries know about us here. Polls have found that most adult Americans do not even know which side the U.S. promotes in Nicaragua and El Salvador. Yet, my own experience has shown that a 10-year-old child in Nicaragua can give you a synopsis of U.S. foreign-policy toward Central America.

This is ironic considering the fact that America has the freest and most powerful press in the world, with a legacy of bringing down governments and exposing corruption at every level. Yet many American newspapers suffer from a parochialism that can cause them to be inward- rather than outward-looking and to feed myopia rather than countering it.

How often do we see a news story referring to a train wreck in some distant part of the world in which maybe 75 lives were lost, but the headline reads something like "Three Americans Among the Dead in Brazil Train Wreck." The message sent out is that those three American lives have greater value than the 72 others.

Or consider the occasions when a massive death toll results from internal strife in another country but the story is relegated to the back pages or given only a one-paragraph mention. Usually it is in a country in which America has no economic or political interest. Again the impression conveyed is that those thousands killed are not even worthy of prominent mention because it is just a bunch of "natives" killing each other off.

At my first newspaper job in a small upstate community, I remember being appalled because 5,000 people were killed in internal warfare in the Indian state of Assam, but the story made it only to the obituary page. When I raised this concern at an editorial meeting, one of my colleagues argued that this was a community newspaper catering to a local audience that was not concerned with infighting in rural India.

Yes, it was a community newspaper, but it was the only paper read by most of its 30,000 readers. That meant that if they did not read it there, they were unlikely to read it anywhere else.

Why should Americans know or care about what happens in a remote region of India? At the most basic level, because we are part of a global fraternity in which the same factors that give rise to strife in one part of the world are often replayed on different stages, and understanding those links helps to increase global awareness. Secondly, because these readers will be voting in national elections and are thereby in a position to influence U.S. foreign policy. Thirdly, because some of these Third World people driven from their homelands may end up as our neighbors tomorrow.

Some papers will pay more attention to such far-off events as a concession to the local immigrants from those places. The really enlightened papers, I believe, will do it regardless.

Moving closer to home, one can see the same biases at play in reporting about domestic minorities. Violent crimes against minorities in general seem to get less detailed coverage than do crimes against white people, particularly if those white people belong to a higher social class and the minorities are identified with cities. This is especially true in large cities such as New York.

For example, the news media left no stone unturned in its coverage of the brutal Central Park rape. Around the same time, a black woman in Harlem was raped and thrown off the roof of a building, and that tragedy was hardly mentioned.

Also, the Central Park coverage included numerous analyses about the socioeconomic backgrounds of the suspects and the so-called culture of poverty in the black ghetto. Those standards were not applied to coverage of the suspects in the racially motivated shooting death of a black man in Bensonhurst.

On the other hand, the press will give prominent play to someone like Al Sharpton, who had very little credibility in the black community and whose remarks only inflame racial tensions.

Mainstream newspapers have tended to patronize minority political groups by not covering them, so they end up being held less accountable for their actions.

For example, the Black and Puerto Rican Legislative Caucus tends to be one of the least scrutinized groups on the Albany political scene, either because the media do not care what the Caucus is up to or because they are afraid to treat the Caucus with the same critical eye with which they cover other political organizations.

This works to the detriment not only of the Caucus and its constituents but of the political process in general.

In light of the lack of such ongoing coverage, if a paper occasionally depict the Caucus in gross caricature, it can have the effect of being inflammatory. Likewise, we have to avoid always portraying welfare mothers in graphics as black or Hispanic, especially when that portrayal is not balanced by occasionally depicting a black woman as a brain surgeon.

I often hear minority people complain that there are not enough positive images of minorities in the media. As a journalist, I believe our job is first to tell the truth. If most members of a racial minority live in poverty, we should not only report that but probe for reasons, probe the legacy of racism, unemployment, etc. Yet we must include occasional mention of the same group's achievements and avoid depicting any minority group as monolithic in class, political perspective or concerns.

I should like to share an example of the frustration I mentioned earlier at not being able to get stories published about people considered to be marginal to American society. Over the years, I have been contacted by Indian and Pakistani immigrant women who came to the U.S. after having arranged marriages back home, and then found themselves subjected to battery and extreme cruelty by their husbands. Often these husbands had been living here longer, and in some cases they had American girlfriends or even wives on the side. Their Indian wives were multiply victimized, often being young inexperienced women away from home for the first time, with no independent incomes. Their stories were poignant, courageous and heartbreaking.

The response I got when I approached newspapers or magazines, even feminist publications, to write a story was that these women did not comprise a sizable enough part of American society. Rather than viewing the story in broad, human-interest terms, editors invariably felt such a story would be of interest only to other Indian women.

Recently, an umbrella organization of Indian associations in New York City held a first global convention of overseas Indians. It drew about 3,000 of the 12 million expatriate Indians around the world. India has the second largest population of any country, and in pockets of the United States Indians are a visible and growing presence.

The conference organizers tried hard to attract American media, but only one paper turned up the whole week. It could have been a perfect opportunity to learn something about a growing minority group that keeps largely to itself but wields a great deal of economic power and has a virtual monopoly in certain industries. If nothing else, it could have been a way to establish contacts with Indian community spokespeople for the future.

The press would do well to take the offensive rather than to cover minority groups defensively. A series of articles about a new immigrant group in the area, their concerns and contributions, can go a long way toward heading off later problems in the community. Moreover, by cultivating them early, reporters can avoid scrambling to find sources when a major news break involves that community.

Instead of seeking minority people's opinions only on minority issues, we should include them on such subjects as nuclear power, arms negotiations, biomedical research. We should take care to include minorities and women in informal street polls, and welcome the input of minority representatives on such issues as how they would like to be addressed.

It may be all the same to you whether you call a person black, Afro-American or African-American, or Asian-American or Oriental; to a reader it can mean the difference between whether the newspaper is viewed as a friend or an adversary.

It is important to hire minorities on the newsroom staff, but it is not enough if you do not benefit from their perspectives. I have had minority friends who were hired for reporting jobs simply as tokens but whose views and insights on minority affairs were not even considered.

Be prepared to offer them support when they face resistance from the established readership. I have had readers express outright anger that my funny-sounding name was appearing in their local newspaper or that I was stealing a job away from an American. As a columnist, when I write something controversial, the most frequent response from angry readers is attack upon my nationality: "What gives you the right to come to this country and criticize us?"

Indeed, if I were critical of only one group and not of others, including my own, they would have a legitimate point. However, my basic point is that minorities should be covered with the same standards you use for everyone else—not with single broad strokes, not with any special restraint, but equally thoroughly, equally critically, equally respectfully.

READING REFLECTIONS

1. Basu contends that the American press bears some responsibility for the fact that Americans "tend to know less about other countries and cultures than people in other countries know about us." Do you agree with this point?
2. What other countries, do you think, know more about us, and what factors might make this so? In what other countries might you find people who know less about us? Why might this be the case?
3. List the examples Basu includes to support her argument. Do you think her examples justify her generalizations?
4. Basu says, "I often hear minority people complain that there are not enough positive images of minorities in the media." Do you agree with her statement? Why or why not?
5. According to Basu, how can American newspapers improve their coverage of minorities?
6. What role, if any, might popular films have on other people's views of America? Do these films provide accurate depictions of American life to people in other countries? Why or why not?

FEAR IN A HANDFUL OF NUMBERS

Dennis Overbye

"To dump toxic waste in a swamp . . . is like trying to repress a bad thought or like hitting your wife every night and assuming that because she doesn't fight back you can abuse her with impunity—30 years later she sets your bed on fire."

So goes the analogy by Dennis Overbye in his cautionary tale about what is happening to the planet as we continually abuse the environment. The problem, says Overbye, "is ourselves." How can we go about changing the view that nature is there to be tamed, to be dominated, to understand that in abusing the land, we will eventually kill ourselves? How have the media dealt with the environmental crisis, and what role should they play?

Dennis Overbye, who studied physics at MIT, won an American Institute of Physics Science Writing award in 1980. His work has appeared in Time, *the* New York Times, *and* Wired *magazine. He is author of* Lonely Hearts of the Cosmos: The Story of the Scientific Quest for the Secret of the Universe.

Everybody talks about the weather, goes the saying (often wrongly attributed to Mark Twain), *but nobody does anything about it.* The word from scientists is that whoever said this was wrong. All of us, as we go about the mundane business of existence, are helping change the weather and every other aspect of life on this fair planet: Los Angelenos whipping their sunny basin into a brown blur on the way to work every morning; South Americans burning and cutting their way through the rain forest in search of a better life; a billion Chinese, their smokestacks belching blackcoal smoke, marching toward the 21st century and a rendezvous with modernization.

On the flanks of Mauna Loa in Hawaii, an instrument that records the concentration of carbon dioxide dumped into the atmosphere as a result of all this activity traces a wobbly rising line that gets steeper and steeper with time. Sometime in the next 50 years, say climatologists, all that carbon dioxide, trapping the sun's heat like a greenhouse, could begin to smother the planet, raising temperatures, turning farmland to desert, swelling oceans anywhere from four feet to 20 feet. Goodbye Venice, goodbye Bangladesh. Goodbye to millions of species of animals, insects and plants that haven't already succumbed to acid

---

Dennis Overbye, "Fear in a Handful of Numbers," *Time,* October 9, 1989, pp. 119–120. Copyright © 1989 by Dennis Overbye. Reprinted with the permission of International Creative Management.

rain, ultraviolet radiation leaking through the damaged ozone layer, spreading toxic wastes or bulldozers.

A species that can change its planet's chemistry just by day-to-day coming and going has, I suppose, achieved a kind of coming-of-age. We could celebrate or tremble. What do we do when it is not war that is killing us but progress? When it is not the actions of a deranged dictator threatening the world but the ordinary business of ordinary people? When there are no bombs dropping, nobody screaming, nothing to fear but a line on a graph or a handful of numbers on a computer printout? Dare we change the world on the basis of a wobbly line on a graph? We can change the world, and those numbers, slowly, painfully—we can ration, recycle, carpool, tax and use the World Bank to bend underdeveloped nations to our will. But the problem is neither the world nor those numbers. The problem is ourselves.

In our relations with nature, we've been playing a deadly game of cowboys and Indians. We all started as Indians. Many primitive cultures—and the indigenous peoples still clinging today to their pockets of underdevelopment—regarded the earth and all its creatures as alive. Nature was a whistling wind tunnel of spirits. With the rise of a scientific, clockwork cosmos and of missionary Christianity, with its message of man's dominion and relentless animus against paganism, nature was metaphorically transformed. It became dead meat.

The West was won, Los Angeles and the 20th century were built by the cowboy mind. To the cowboy, nature was a vast wilderness waiting to be tamed. The land was a stage, a backdrop against which he could pursue his individual destiny. The story of the world was the story of a man, usually a white man, and its features took their meaning from their relationship to him. A mountain was a place to test one's manhood; an Asian jungle with its rich life and cultures was merely a setting for an ideological battle. The natives are there to be "liberated." By these standards even Communists are cowboys.

The cowboys won—everywhere nature is being tamed—but victory over nature is a kind of suicide. The rules change when there is only one political party allowed in a country or there is only one company selling oil or shoes. So too when a species becomes numerous and powerful enough to gain the illusion of mastery. What we have now is a sort of biological equivalent to a black hole wherein a star becomes so massive and dense that it bends space and time totally around itself and then pays the ultimate price of domination by disappearing.

Modern science, a cowboy achievement, paradoxically favors the Indian view of life. Nature is alive. The barest Antarctic rock is crawling with microbes. Viruses float on the dust. Bacteria help digest our food for us. According to modern evolutionary biology, our very cells are cities of formerly independent organisms. On the molecular level, the distinction between self and non-self disappears in a blur of semipermeable membranes. Nature goes on within and without us. It wafts through us like a breeze through a screened porch. On the biological level, the world is a seamless continuum of energy and information passing back and forth, a vast complicated network of exchange. Speech, food, posture, infection, respiration, scent are but a few pathways of communication. Most of those circuits are still a mystery, a labyrinth we have barely begun to acknowledge or explore.

The great anthropologist and philosopher Gregory Bateson pointed out 20 years ago that this myriad of feedback circuits resemble the mathematical models of thinking being developed for the new science of artificial intelligence. A forest or a coral reef or a whole planet then with its checks and balances and feedback loops and delicate adjustments always striving for light and equilibrium, is like a *mind.* In this way of thinking, pollution is literal insanity (Bateson was also a psychologist). To dump toxic waste in a swamp, say, is like trying to repress a bad thought or like hitting your wife every night and assuming that because she doesn't fight back you can abuse her with impunity—30 years later she sets your bed on fire.

Some of these circuits are long and slow so that consequences may take years or generations to manifest themselves. That helps sustain the cowboy myth that nature is a neutral, unchanging backdrop. Moreover, evolution seems to have wired our brains to respond to rapid changes, the snap of a twig or a movement in the alley, and to ignore slow ones. When these consequences do start to show up, we don't notice them. Anyone who has ever been amazed by an old photograph of himself or herself can attest to the merciful ignorance of slow change, that is aging—*Where did those clothes and that strange haircut come from? Was I really that skinny?*

We weren't born with the ability to taste carbon dioxide or see the ozone layer, but science and technology have evolved to fill the gap to help us measure what we cannot feel or taste or see. We have old numbers with which, like old photographs, we can gauge the ravages of time and our own folly. In that sense, the "technological fix" that is often wishfully fantasized—cold fusion, anyone?—has already appeared. The genius of technology has already saved us. As surely as the Ghost of Christmas Future saved Scrooge by rattling the miser's tight soul until it cracked. A satellite photograph is technology, and so are the differential equations spinning inside a Cray supercomputer. There is technology in the wobbly rising trace on a piece of graph paper. There is technology in a handful of numbers.

The trick is to become more like Indians without losing the best parts of cowboys culture—rationalism and the spirit of inquiry. We need more science now, not less. How can we stretch our nerves around those numbers and make them as real and as ominous as our cholesterol readings? Repeat them each night on the evening news? We need feedback, as if we were the audience in a giant public radio fund-raising drive hitting the phones and making pledges. Like expert pilots navigating through a foggy night, we need the faith to fly the planet collectively by our instruments and not by the seat of our pants. In the West we need the faith and courage to admit the bitter truth, that our prosperity is based as much on cheap energy as on free markets. A long-postponed part of the payment for that energy and prosperity is coming due if we want to have any hope of dissuading the Chinese and the rest of the Third World from emulating us and swaddling the planet with fumes and wastes.

What if the spirit doesn't hit? We can't afford to wait if we want to survive. While we are waiting for this sea change of attitude, we could pretend—a notion that sounds more whimsical than it is. Scientists have found that certain actions have a feedback effect on the actor. Smilers actually feel happier; debaters become enamored of their own arguments; a good salesman sells himself first. You become what you pretend; that 30-ft.-long, black-tinted-glass, air conditioned limos are unfashionable because we know that real men don't need air conditioning. We can pretend that we believe it is wrong to loot the earth for the benefit of a single generation of a single species. We can pretend to care about our children's world.

The air has been poisoned before; 3 billion years ago, when the blue-green algae began manufacturing oxygen. That was the first ecological crisis. Life survived then. Life will not vanish now, but this may be the last chance for humans to go along gracefully.

READING REFLECTIONS

1. According to Overbye, what everyday actions are contributing to the deterioration of our environment? Also, provide specific examples of the deterioration.
2. Provide examples of at least three metaphors Overbye uses in his article.
3. In his article, Overbye states, "What do we do when it is not war that is killing us but progress?" Do you agree with his assertion? Write a defense or attack of his article based on your own environmental research.
4. Another statement in Overbye's article asserts that "victory over nature is a kind of suicide." How does Overbye support this stance?
5. What advice does Overbye offer to help stop pollution? Besides Overbye's suggestions, create a list of environmental reforms that can be implemented to reduce pollution.
6. One of Overbye's suggestions to raise public awareness is to "repeat deadly numbers on the news every night." Imagine you are asked to create an advertising campaign to make the public more aware of the dangers facing our environment. What types of methods, slogans, media, and the like would you employ? Write an essay detailing your campaign.
7. Overbye cites several examples of environmental neglect and abuse on our part. Using information from his article, write a letter to your local congressmember urging her or him to take actions to implement effective environmental laws.

CRAZY HORSE MALT LIQUOR AND OTHER CULTURAL METAPHORS
Michael Dorris

Have you ever witnessed a stereotypical portrayal of any given group in advertising? Dorris takes a satiric view of the less than flattering use of Native Americans to promote everything from beer to baseball. His article provides a sharp contrast of real Native Americans with their advertising counterparts.

Michael Dorris, who started his academic career as a cultural anthropologist, had a wide-ranging career from essayist, novelist, and Dartmouth professor. Dorris wrote A Yellow Raft in Blue Water *(1987), an acclaimed novel about the lives of three American Indian women. An advocate for warning labels on alcoholic beverage containers, Dorris, in his book* The Broken Cord *(1989), delves into the effects of fetal alcohol syndrome on one of his three adopted sons.*

People of proclaimed good will have the oddest ways of honoring American Indians. Sometimes they dress themselves in turkey feathers and paint—"cultural drag," my friend Duane Bird Bear calls it—and boogie on 50-yard lines.

Presumably they hope this exuberant if ethnographically questionable display will do their teams more good against opponents than those rituals they imitate and mock did for 19th century Cheyenne and Nez Perce men and women who tried, with desperation and ultimate futility, to defend their homelands from invasion.

Sometimes otherwise impeccably credentialed liberals get so swept up in honoring Indians that they beat fake tom-toms or fashion their forearms and hands into facsimiles of the axes European traders used for barter and attempt, unsuccessfully, to chop their way to victory.

Everywhere you look such respects are paid: the street names in woodsy, affluent subdivisions; mumbo-jumbo in ersatz male-bonding weekends and Boy Scout jamborees; geometric fashion statements, weepy anti-littering public service announcements. In the ever popular noble-savage spectrum, red is the hot, safe color.

For centuries, flesh and blood Indians have been assigned the role of a popular-culture metaphor for generations. Today, their evocation instantly connotes fuzzy images of Nature, the Past, Plight or Summer Camp. War-bon-neted apparitions pasted to football helmets or baseball caps act as opaque, impermeable curtains, solid walls of white noise that for many citizens block or distort all vision of the nearly two million native Americans today.

And why not? Such honoring relegates Indians to the long-ago and thus makes them magically disappear from public consciousness and conscience. What do the 300 federally recognized tribes, with their various complicated treaties governing land rights and protections, their crippling unemployment, infant mortality and teen-age suicide rates, their manifold health problems have in common with jolly (or menacing) cartoon caricatures, wistful braves or raven-tressed Mazola girls?

Perhaps we should ask the Hornell Brewing Company of Baltimore, man-ufacturers of the Original Crazy Horse Malt Liquor, a product currently dis-tributed in New York with packaging inspired by, according to the text on the back, "the Black Hills of Dakota, *steeped* [my italics] in the History of the American West, home of Proud Indian Nations, a land where imagination con-jures up images of blue clad Pony Soldiers and magnificent Native American Warriors."

Whose imagination? Were these the same blue-clad lads who perpetrated the 1890 massacre of 200 captured, freezing Dakota at Wounded Knee? Are Pine Ridge and Rosebud, the two reservations closest to the Black Hills and, co-incidentally, the two counties in the United States with the lowest per capita incomes, the Proud Nations?

Is the "steeping" a bald allusion to the fact that alcohol has long consti-tuted the No. 1 health hazard to Indians? Virtually every other social ill plagu-ing native Americans—from disproportionately frequent traffic fatalities to ar-rest statistics—is related in some tragic respect to ethanol, and many tribes, from Alaska to New Mexico, record the highest percentage in the world of ba-bies born disabled by fetal alcohol syndrome and effect. One need look no fur-ther than the Congressionally mandated warning to pregnant women printed in capital letters on every Crazy Horse label to make the connection.

The facts of history are not hard to ascertain: the Black Hills, the "paha sapa," the traditional holy place of the Dakota, were illegally seized by the Gov-ernment, systematically stripped of their mineral wealth—and have still not been returned to their rightful owners. Crazy Horse, in addition to being a patriot to his Oglala people, was a mystic and a religious leader murdered after he voluntarily gave himself up in 1887 to Pony Soldiers at Fort Robinson, Neb. What, then, is the pairing of his name with 40 ounces of malt liquor supposed to signify?

The Hornell brewers helpfully supply a clue. The detail of the logo is fo-cused on the headdress and not the face; it's pomp without circumstance, form without content. Wear the hat, the illustration seems to offer, and in the process fantasize yourself more interesting (or potent or tough or noble) than you are. Play at being a "warrior" from the "land that truly speaks of the spirit that is America."

And if some humorless Indians object, just set them straight. Remind them what an honor it is to be used.

READING REFLECTIONS

1. Dorris focuses on the text on the packaging of a beer. Because this text is an advertisement, do you think Dorris' point is significant? Why or why not?
2. What other ads or product packaging can you think of that play on certain stereotypical ideas about groups?
3. What is the significance of Dorris providing historical backgrounds for various Native American tribes?
4. Dorris says, "For centuries, flesh and blood Indians have been assigned the role of a popular-culture metaphor for generations. . . . Such honoring relegates Indians to the long-ago and thus makes them magically disappear from public consciousness and conscience." What do you think Dorris means by this statement? Do you agree? Are there other people whom we have made "magically disappear"? Who are they, and why do you think we have done this?
5. Several sporting teams use Native Americans as their mascot. Using Dorris' reasoning, compose a letter to one team's general manager requesting a mascot change.
6. What is the effect of Dorris' ironic closing statement, "And if some humorless Indians object, just set them straight. Remind them what an honor it is to be used"?

METAPHOR AND WAR

George Lakoff

The purpose of public relations is to promote an acceptable, if not desirable, view of a given event; war is not an exception. In "Metaphor and War," George Lakoff analyzes the language used in the media to describe the Gulf War. Lakoff presents the glorified war mentality that is spoonfed to the public by the government in order to win the public's approval. However, he is quick to point out that the unavoidable and tragic realities of war are all too real.

George Lakoff is a linguist whose books include Women, Fire, and Dangerous Things: What Categories Reveal about the Mind *(1987) and* More *than Cool Reason: A Field Guide to Poetic Metaphor (1989). "Metaphor and War" appeared February 1991 in the* East Bay Express, *a weekly alternative publication with about 140,000 readers for news and commentary on the arts and social and political issues for the San Francisco Bay area.*

Metaphors can kill. Secretary of State Baker sees Saddam as "sitting on our economic lifeline." President Bush sees him as having a "stranglehold" on our economy. General Schwartzkopf characterizes the occupation of Kuwait as a "rape." The President says that the US is in the Gulf to "protect freedom, protect our future, and protect the innocent," and that we must "push Saddam Hussein back." Saddam is seen as Hitler. It is vital, literally vital, to understand just what role metaphorical thought is playing in this war.

Metaphorical thought is commonplace and inescapable; in itself, it is neither good nor bad. Abstractions and enormously complex situations are routinely understood via metaphor, so it is not surprising that we use extensive, and mostly unconscious, systems of metaphor to understand the complexities and abstractions of international relations and war. The use of a metaphor, however, becomes pernicious when it hides realities in a harmful way.

It is important to distinguish what is metaphorical from what is not. Pain, dismemberment, death, starvation, and the death and injury of loved ones are not metaphorical. They are real, and in this war they are afflicting hundreds, perhaps thousands, of real human beings.

The Gulf war has been accompanied by systems of metaphor which have been used by military and foreign policy experts and by the public at large. It is important to look at these metaphor systems in order to see the realities they may be obscuring.

The State-as-Person System

In international politics, a state is usually conceptualized as a person, engaging in social relations within a world community. Its land-mass is its home. It lives in a neighborhood, and has neighbors, friends, and enemies. States are seen as having inherent dispositions: they can be peaceful or aggressive, responsible or irresponsible, industrious or lazy.

Well-being is wealth. The general well-being of a state is understood in economic terms: its economic health. A serious threat to economic health can thus be seen as a death threat. To the extent that a nation's economy depends on foreign oil, that oil supply becomes a "lifeline" (reinforced by the image of an oil pipeline).

Strength for a state is military strength.

Maturity for the person-state is industrialization. Unindustrialized nations are "underdeveloped," with industrialization as a natural state to be reached. Third World nations are thus immature children, to be taught how to develop properly or disciplined if they get out of line. Nations that fail to industrialize at a rate considered normal are seen as akin to retarded children and judged as "backward" nations.

Morality is a matter of accounting, of keeping the moral books balanced. A wrongdoer incurs a debt, and he must be made to pay. The moral books can be balanced by a return to the situation prior to the wrongdoing, by giving back what has been taken, by recompense, or by punishment. Justice is the balancing of the moral books.

War in this metaphor is a fight between two people, a form of hand-to-hand combat. Thus, the US seeks to "push Iraq back out of Kuwait" or "deal the enemy a heavy blow," or "deliver a knockout punch." A just war is thus a form of combat for the purpose of settling moral accounts.

The most common discourse form in the West where there is combat to settle moral accounts is the classic fairy tale in which people are replaced by states.

The Fairy Tale of the Just War

Cast of characters: a villain, a victim, and a hero. The victim and the hero may be the same person.

The scenario: A crime is committed by the villain against an innocent victim (typically an assault, theft, or kidnapping). The offense occurs due to an imbalance of power and creates a moral imbalance. The hero either gathers helpers or decides to go it alone. The hero makes sacrifices; he undergoes difficulties, typically making an arduous heroic journey to a treacherous terrain. The villain is inherently evil, perhaps even a monster, and thus reasoning with him is out of the question. The hero is left with no choice but to engage the villain in battle. The hero defeats the villain and rescues the victim. The moral balance is restored. Victory is achieved. The hero, who always acts honorably, has proved his manhood and achieved glory. The sacrifice was worthwhile. The hero receives acclaim, along with the gratitude of the victim and the community.

Experts in international relations have an additional system of metaphors. The principal one is Clausewitz's metaphor:

War Is Politics Pursued by Other Means

Karl von Clausewitz was a Prussian general who perceived war in terms of political cost-benefit analysis. Each nation-state has political objectives, and war may best serve those objectives. The political "gains" are to be weighed against acceptable "costs." When the costs of war exceed the political gains, the war should cease.

In Clausewitzian terms, war is justified when there is more to be gained by going to war than by not going to war. Morality is absent from the Clausewitzian equation, except when there is a political cost to acting immorally or a political gain from acting morally.

Clausewitz's metaphor only allows war to be justified on pragmatic, not moral, grounds. To justify war on both moral and pragmatic grounds, the Fairy Tale of the Just War and Clausewitz's metaphor must mesh: The "worthwhile sacrifices" of the fairy tale must equal the Clausewitzian "costs" and the "victory" in the fairy tale must equal the Clausewitzian "gains."

Clausewitz's metaphor is the perfect expert's metaphor, since it requires specialists in political cost-benefit calculation. It sanctions the use of the mathematics of economics, probability theory, decision theory, and game theory in the name of making foreign policy rational and scientific.

Clausewitz's metaphor is commonly seen as literally true, but it is, in fact, metaphorical. It uses the State-as-Person metaphor. It turns qualitative effects on human beings into quantifiable costs and gains, thus seeing political action as economics, and it sees war in terms of only one dimension of war, that of political expediency.

To bear in mind what is hidden by Clausewitz's metaphor, we should consider an alternative metaphor that is *not* used by professional strategists or by the general public to understand war as we engage in it:

War Is Violent Crime: Murder, Assault, Kidnapping, Arson, Rape, and Theft

Here, war is understood only in terms of its moral dimension, and not, say, its political or economic dimension. The metaphor highlights those aspects of war that would otherwise be seen as major crimes.

There is an Us-Them asymmetry in the public use of the War-as-Crime metaphor. The Iraqi invasion of Kuwait is reported in terms of murder, theft, and rape. The American air war or potential ground attack is never discussed in terms of murder, assault, and arson. Allied conduct of the war is seen, in Clausewitzian terms, as rational calculation, while the Iraqi invasion is discussed not as a rational move by Saddam but as the work of a madman. We see Us as rational, moral, and courageous and Them as criminal and insane.

War as a Competitive Game

It has long been noted that we understand war as a competitive game, like chess, or as a sport, like football or boxing. It is a metaphor in which there is a clear winner and loser, and a clear end to the game. The metaphor highlights strategic thinking, teamwork, preparedness, the spectators in the world arena, the glory of winning and the shame of defeat.

This metaphor is taken very seriously. There is a long tradition in the West of training military officers in team sports and chess. The military is trained to win. This can lead to a metaphor conflict, as it did in Vietnam, since Clausewitz's metaphor seeks to maximize geopolitical gains, which may or may not be consistent with absolute military victory.

The situation at present is that the public has accepted the rescue scenario of the just war fairy tale as providing moral justification. The President, for internal political reasons, has accepted the competitive game metaphor as taking precedence over Clausewitz's metaphor: If he must choose, he will go for the military win over maximizing geopolitical gains.

Throughout the congressional debate leading up to the war, and in all the expert opinion that has occupied our attention since the war began, the metaphors determining our understanding of the conflict have not been questioned.

Is Saddam Irrational?

The villain in the Fairy Tale of the Just War may be cunning, but he cannot be rational. You just do not reason with a demon, nor do you enter into negotiations with him. The logic of the metaphor demands that Saddam be irrational. But is he?

Administration policy is confused on the issue. Clausewitz's metaphor, as used by military strategists, assumes that the enemy is rational: He too is maximizing gains and minimizing costs. Our strategy from the outset has been to "increase the cost" to Saddam. That assumes he is rational and is maximizing his self-interest.

At the same time, he is being called irrational. Our fear of Iraq's possession of nuclear weapons depends on it. If Saddam is rational, he should follow the logic of deterrence. We have thousands of hydrogen bombs in warheads. Israel is estimated to have between 100 and 200 deliverable atomic bombs. The argument that Saddam and the Iraqi military would not be deterred by our nuclear arsenal and by Israel's assumes irrationality.

Saddam is certainly immoral, ruthless, and brutal, but there is no evidence that he is anything but rational. Everything he has done, from assassinating political opponents, to using poison gas against his political enemies, the Kurds, to invading Kuwait, can be seen as furthering his own self-interest.

Is Kuwait an Innocent Victim?

The classical victim is innocent. To the Iraqis, Kuwait was anything but an innocent ingenue. The war with Iran virtually bankrupted Iraq. Kuwait had agreed to help finance the war, but after the war, the Kuwaitis insisted on repayment of the "loan." Kuwaitis had invested hundreds of billions in Europe,

America, and Japan, but would not invest in Iraq after the war to help it rebuild. On the contrary, Kuwait began what amounted to economic warfare against Iraq by overproducing its oil quota to hold oil prices down.

In addition, Kuwait had drilled laterally into Iraqi territory in the Rumailah oil field and had extracted oil from Iraqi territory. Kuwait further took advantage of Iraq by buying its currency at extremely low exchange rates. Subsequently, wealthy Kuwaitis used that Iraqi currency on trips to Iraq, where they bought Iraqi goods at bargain rates. Among the things they bought most flamboyantly were liquor and prostitutes—widows and orphans of men killed in the war, who, because of the state of the economy, had no other means of support. All this did not endear Kuwaitis to Iraqis, who were suffering from over seventy percent inflation.

Moreover, Kuwaitis had long been resented for good reason by Iraqis and Muslims from other nations. Capital rich but labor poor, Kuwait imported cheap labor from other Muslim countries to do its least pleasant work. At the time of the invasion, there were 400,000 Kuwaiti citizens living in Kuwait next to 2.2 million foreign laborers who were denied rights of citizenry and treated by the Kuwaitis as lesser beings. In short, to the Iraqis and to other labor-exporting Arab countries, Kuwait is badly miscast as a purely innocent victim.

This does not in any way justify the horrors perpetrated on the Kuwaitis by the Iraqi army. But it is part of what is hidden when Kuwait is cast as an innocent victim. The "legitimate government" that we seek to reinstall is an oppressive monarchy.

Is "Victory" Possible?

In a fairy tale or a game, victory is well-defined. Once it is achieved, the story or game is over. Neither is likely to be the case in the Gulf war, since history continues.

What will constitute "victory" in this war? The President's stated objectives are total Iraqi withdrawal and restoration of the Kuwaiti monarchy. But no one believes the matter will end there, since Saddam would still be in power with a significant part of his forces intact. If, on the other hand, we conquer Iraq, wiping out its military capability, how will Iraq be governed? No puppet government that we could set up will govern effectively since it will be hated by the entire populace. Since Saddam has wiped out all opposition, the only remaining effective government for the country would be his Ba'ath party. Will it count as a victory if Saddam's friends wind up in power? If not, what other choice is there? And if Iraq has no remaining military force, how will it defend itself against Syria and Iran? It will certainly not be a "victory" for us if either of them takes over Iraq.

In all the talk about victory over Iraq, there has been little clarification about what victory would be. And if "victory" cannot be defined, neither can "worthwhile sacrifice."

The metaphors used in the West to conceptualize the Gulf crisis disregard the most powerful political ideas in the Arab world: Arab nationalism and Islamic fundamentalism. The first seeks to form a racially based all-Arab nation, the second, a theocratic all-Islamic state. Though bitterly opposed to one another, they share a great deal. Both are conceptualized in family terms, an Arab brotherhood and an Islamic brotherhood. Both see brotherhoods as more legitimate than existing states. Both are at odds with the State-as-Person metaphor, in which currently existing states are distinct entities with a right to exist in perpetuity.

Also hidden by our metaphors is perhaps the most important daily concern throughout the Arab world: Arab dignity.

Weakness is a major theme in the Arab world, and is often conceptualized in sexual terms, even more than in the West. American officials, in speaking of the "rape" of Kuwait, are conceptualizing a weak, defenseless country as female and a strong militarily powerful country as male. Similarly, it is common for Arabs to conceptualize the colonization and subsequent domination of the Arab world by the West, especially the US, as emasculation.

An Arab proverb that was reported to be popular in Iraq in the days before the war was that "It is better to be a cock for a day than a chicken for a year." The message is clear: It is better to be male, that is, strong and dominant, for a short period of time than to be female, that is, weak and defenseless, for a long time. Much of the popular support for Saddam among Arabs is due to the fact that he is seen as standing up to the US, even if only for a while, and that there is a dignity in this. If upholding dignity is an essential part of what defines Saddam's "rational self-interest," it is vitally important for our government to know this, since he may be willing to continue the war to "be a cock for a day."

The US does not have anything like a proper understanding of the issue of Arab dignity. Take the question of whether Iraq will come out of this with part of the Rumailah oil fields and two islands that would give it a port on the Gulf. From Iraq's point of view these are seen as economic necessities if Iraq is to rebuild. President Bush has spoken of this as "rewarding aggression," using a "Third-World-Countries-As-Children" metaphor, where the great powers are grown-ups who have the obligation to reward or punish children so as to make them behave properly. This is exactly the attitude that grates on Arabs, who want to be treated with dignity. Instead of seeing Iraq as a sovereign nation that has taken military action for economic purposes, the President treats Iraq as if it were a child gone bad, who has become the neighborhood bully and should be properly disciplined by the grown-ups.

The issue of the Rumailah oil fields and the two islands has alternatively been discussed in the media in terms of "saving face." Saving face is a very different concept than upholding Arab dignity and insisting on being treated as an equal, not an inferior.

Our insistence on using a State-as-Person metaphor, meanwhile, obscures the real and diverse costs of the war. The State-as-Person metaphor highlights the ways in which states act as units, and hides the internal structure of the state. Class structure is hidden by this metaphor, as are ethnic composition, religious rivalry, political parties, the ecology, the influence of the military and of corporations (especially multinational corporations).

Consider the question of our "national interest." It is in a person's interest to be healthy and strong. The State-as-Person metaphor translates this into a "national interest" of economic health and military strength. But what is in the "national interest" may or may not be in the interest of many ordinary citizens, groups, or institutions, who may become poorer as the GNP rises and weaker as the military gets stronger.

The "national interest" is a metaphorical concept, and it is defined in America by politicians and policymakers. For the most part, they are influenced more by the rich than the poor, more by large corporations than small businesses, and more by developers than ecological activists.

When President Bush argues that the war is "serving our vital national interests," he is using a metaphor that hides exactly whose interests are being served and whose are not. For example, poor people, especially blacks and Hispanics, are represented in the military in disproportionately large numbers, and in an extended ground war, they will suffer proportionally more casualties. Thus the war is less in the interest of ethnic minorities and the poor than the white upper classes.

Also hidden are the interests of the military itself, which are served when war is justified. Hopes that, after the Cold War, the military might play a smaller role have been dashed by the President's decision to go to war.

The State-as-Person metaphor has also allowed for a particularly ghoulish cost-benefit analysis about the continuing air war. There is a lot of talk about American deaths in a potential ground war as potential "costs," while Iraqi soldiers killed by the air war count as gains. The cost-benefit accounting leads us to devalue the lives of Iraqis, even when most of those actually killed are not villains at all but simply innocent draftees or reservists or civilians.

The classic fairy tale defines what constitutes a hero: it is a person who rescues an innocent victim and who defeats and punishes a guilty and inherently evil villain, and who does so for moral rather than venal reasons. But in this war, is America functioning as a hero?

It doesn't fit the profile very well.

America appears as classic hero only if you don't look carefully at how the metaphor is applied to the current situation. It is here that the State-as-Person metaphor functions in a way that continues to hide vital truths. The State-as-Person metaphor hides the internal structure of states and allows us to think of Kuwait as a unitary entity, the defenseless maiden to be rescued in the fairy tale. The metaphor hides the monarchical character of Kuwait, and the way Kuwaitis treat women and the vast majority of the people who live in their country. The State-as-Person metaphor also hides the internal structure of Iraq, and thus hides the actual people who are being killed, maimed, or otherwise harmed in this war. The same metaphor also hides the internal structure of the US, and therefore hides the fact that it is the poor and minorities who will make the most sacrifices while not getting any significant benefit from this war. And it hides the main ideas that drive Middle Eastern politics.

Metaphors can kill, and sometimes the first victim is truth.

READING REFLECTIONS

1. List the metaphors that Lakoff presents.
2. What kinds of research does Lakoff use to support his point?
3. How is this research similar to and different from the other newspaper commentaries?
4. Lakoff writes, "In international politics, a state is usually conceptualized as a person, engaging in social relations within a world community." What is the purpose of personifying a nation or a region of the world?
5. The metaphor of the fairy-tale story that Lakoff demonstrates of the Gulf War can be seen in many media representations today. Can you name some?
6. Lakoff's article bleakly ends with "Metaphors can kill, and sometimes the first victim is truth." Provide examples of the lies supported by metaphors in the Gulf War.

THE CLAN OF ONE-BREASTED WOMEN

Terry Tempest Williams

As a woman who grew up in the Mormon culture where "authority is respected, obedience is revered, and independent thinking is not," Terry Tempest Williams found herself caught between the values of the religion and the reality of the illness that had devastated many women in her family. Although Williams cannot prove there is a connection between

Terry Tempest Williams, "The Clan of One-Breasted Women," in *Refuge: An Unnatural History of Family and Place* (New York: Pantheon Books, 1991), pp. 281–90. Originally published in *Northern Lights* (January 1990). Reprinted in *Forest of Voices: Reading and Writing the Environment*, ed. Chris Anderson and Lex Runciman (Mountain View, Calif.: Mayfield, 1995), pp. 741–47. Copyright © 1990, 1991 by Terry Tempest Williams. Reprinted with the permission of Pantheon Books, a division of Random House, Inc.

the nuclear fallout in her community and the cases of breast cancer, she believes there is one, which she argues in "The Clan of One-Breasted Women." The article gives us pause to wonder how a community and a land can be considered unimportant and how women who have breast cancer often consider themselves outside the mainstream, as an "other."

Terry Tempest Williams, who writes about the environment, has a reverence for the relationship between people and the land. She has published seven books, and this selection is originally from Refuge: An Unnatural History of Family and Place, *published in 1991.*

I belong to a Clan of One-Breasted Women. My mother, my grandmothers, and six aunts have all had mastectomies. Seven are dead. The two who survive have just completed rounds of chemotherapy and radiation.

I've had my own problems: two biopsies for breast cancer and a small tumor between my ribs diagnosed as "a border-line malignancy."

This is my family history.

Most statistics tell us breast cancer is genetic, hereditary, with rising percentages attached to fatty diets, childlessness, or becoming pregnant after thirty. What they don't say is living in Utah may be the greatest hazard of all.

We are a Mormon family with roots in Utah since 1847. The word-of-wisdom, a religious doctrine of health, kept the women in my family aligned with good foods: no coffee, no tea, tobacco, or alcohol. For the most part, these women were finished having their babies by the time they were thirty. And only one faced breast cancer prior to 1960. Traditionally, as a group of people, Mormons have a low rate of cancer.

Is our family a cultural anomaly? The truth is we didn't think about it. Those who did, usually the men, simply said, "bad genes." The women's attitude was stoic. Cancer was part of life. On February 16, 1971, the eve before my mother's surgery, I accidentally picked up the telephone and overheard her ask my grandmother what she could expect.

"Diane, it is one of the most spiritual experiences you will ever encounter."

I quietly put down the receiver.

Two days later, my father took my three brothers and me to the hospital to visit her. She met us in the lobby in a wheelchair. No bandages were visible. I'll never forget her radiance, the way she held herself in a purple velour robe and how she gathered us around her.

"Children, I am fine. I want you to know I felt the arms of God around me."

We believed her. My father cried. Our mother, his wife, was thirty-eight years old.

Two years ago, after my mother's death from cancer, my father and I were having dinner together. He had just returned from St. George where his construction company was putting in natural gas lines for towns in southern Utah.

He spoke of his love for the country: the sandstoned landscape, bare-boned and beautiful. He had just finished hiking the Kolob trail in Zion National Park. We got caught up in reminiscing, recalling with fondness our walk up Angle's Landing on his fiftieth birthday and the years our family had vacationed there. This was a remembered landscape where we had been raised.

Over dessert, I shared a recurring dream of mine. I told my father that for years, as long as I could remember, I saw this flash of light in the night in the desert. That this image had so permeated my being, I could not venture south without seeing it again, on the horizon, illuminating buttes and mesas.

"You did see it," he said.

"Saw what?" I asked, a bit tentative.

"The bomb. The cloud. We were driving home from Riverside, California. You were sitting on your mother's lap. She was pregnant. In fact, I remember the date, September 7, 1957. We had just gotten out of the Service. We were driving north, past Las Vegas. It was an hour or so before dawn, when this explosion went off. We not only heard it, but felt it. I thought the oil tanker in front of us had blown up. We pulled over and suddenly, rising from the desert floor, we saw it, clearly, this golden-stemmed cloud, the mushroom. The sky seemed to vibrate with an eerie pink glow. Within a few minutes, a light ash was raining on the car."

I stared at my father. This was new information to me.

"I thought you knew that," my father said. "It was a common occurrence in the fifties."

It was at this moment I realized the deceit I had been living under. Children growing up in the American Southwest, drinking contaminated milk from contaminated cows, even from the contaminated breasts of their mother, my mother—members, years later, of the Clan of One-Breasted Women.

It is a well-known story in the Desert West, "The Day We Bombed Utah," or perhaps, "The Years We Bombed Utah,"[1] Above ground atomic testing in Nevada took place from January 27, 1951, through July 11, 1962. Not only were the winds blowing north, covering "low use segments of the population" with fallout and leaving sheep dead in their tracks, but the climate was right.[2] The United States of the 1950s was red, white, and blue. The Korean War was raging. McCarthyism was rampant. Ike was it and the Cold War was hot. If you were against nuclear testing, you were for a Communist regime.

Much has been written about this "American nuclear tragedy." Public health was secondary to national security. The Atomic Energy Commissioner, Thomas Murray, said, "Gentlemen, we must not let anything interfere with this series of tests, nothing."[3]

Again and again, the American public was told by its government, in spite of burns, blisters, and nausea, "It has been found that the tests may be conducted with adequate assurance of safety under conditions prevailing at the bombing reservations."[4] Assuaging public fears was simply a matter of public relations. "Your best action," an Atomic Energy Commission booklet read, "is not to be worried about fallout." A news release typical of the times stated,

"We find no basis for concluding that harm to any individual has resulted from radioactive fallout."[5]

On August 30, 1979, during Jimmy Carter's presidency, a suit was filed entitled "Irene Allen vs. the United States of America." Mrs. Allen was the first to be alphabetically listed with twenty-four test cases, representative of nearly 1200 plaintiffs seeking compensation from the United States government for cancers caused from nuclear testing in Nevada.

Irene Allen lived in Hurricane, Utah. She was the mother of five children and had been widowed twice. Her first husband with their two oldest boys had watched the tests from the roof of the local high school. He died of leukemia in 1956. Her second husband died of pancreatic cancer in 1978.

In a town meeting conducted by Utah Senator Orrin Hatch, shortly before the suit was filed, Mrs. Allen said, "I am not blaming the government, I want you to know that, Senator Hatch. But I thought if my testimony could help in any way so this wouldn't happen again to any of the generations coming up after us . . . I am really happy to be here this day to bear testimony of this."[6]

God-fearing people. This is just one story in an anthology of thousands.

On May 10, 1984, Judge Bruce S. Jenkins handed down his opinion. Ten of the plaintiffs were awarded damages. It was the first time a federal court had determined that nuclear tests had been the cause of cancers. For the remaining fourteen test cases, the proof of causation was not sufficient. In spite of the split decision, it was considered a landmark ruling.[7] It was not to remain so for long.

In April, 1987, the 10th Circuit Court of Appeals overturned Judge Jenkins' ruling on the basis that the United States was protected from suit by the legal doctrine of sovereign immunity, the centuries-old idea from England in the days of absolute monarchs.[8]

In January, 1988, the Supreme Court refused to review the Appeals Court decision. To our court system, it does not matter whether the United States Government was irresponsible, whether it lied to its citizens or even that citizens died from the fallout of nuclear testing. What matters is that our government is immune. "The King can do no wrong."

In Mormon culture, authority is respected, obedience is revered, and independent thinking is not. I was taught as a young girl not to "make waves"or "rock the boat."

"Just let it go—" my mother would say. "You know how you feel, that's what counts."

For many years, I did just that—listened, observed, and quietly formed my own opinions within a culture that rarely asked questions because they had all the answers. But one by one, I watched the women in my family die common, heroic deaths. We sat in waiting rooms hoping for good news, always receiving the bad. I cared for them, bathed their scarred bodies and kept their secrets. I watched beautiful women become bald as cytoxan, cisplatin and adriamycin were injected into their veins. I held their foreheads as they vomited greenblack bile and I shot them with morphine when the pain became inhuman. In the end, I witnessed their last peaceful breaths, becoming a midwife to the re-birth of their souls. But the price of obedience became too high.

The fear and inability to question authority that ultimately killed rural communities in Utah during atmospheric testing of atomic weapons was the same fear I saw being held in my mother's body. Sheep. Dead sheep. The evidence is buried.

I cannot prove that my mother, Diane Dixon Tempest, or my grandmothers, Lettie Romney Dixon and Kathryn Blackett Tempest, along with my aunts contracted cancer from nuclear fallout in Utah. But I can't prove they didn't.

My father's memory was correct, the September blast we drove through in 1957 was part of Operation Plumbbob, one of the most intensive series of bomb tests to be initiated. The flash of light in the night in the desert I had always thought was a dream developed into a family nightmare. It took fourteen years, from 1957 to 1971, for cancer to show up in my mother—the same time, Howard L. Andrews, an authority on radioactive fallout at the National Institutes of Health, says radiation cancer requires to become evident.[9] The more I learn about what it means to be a "downwinder," the more questions I drown in.

What I do know, however, is that as a Mormon woman of the fifth generation of "Latter-Day-Saints," I must question everything, even if it means losing my faith, even if it means becoming a member of a border tribe among my own people. Tolerating blind obedience in the name of patriotism or religion ultimately takes our lives.

When the Atomic Energy Commission described the country north of the Nevada Test Site as "virtually uninhabited desert terrain," my family members were some of the "virtual uninhabitants."

One night, I dreamed women from all over the world circling a blazing fire in the desert. They spoke of change, of how they hold the moon in their bellies and wax and wane with its phases. They mocked at the presumption of even-tempered beings and made promises that they would never fear the witch inside themselves. The women danced wildly as sparks broke away from the flames and entered the night sky as stars.

And they sang a song given to them by Shoshoni grandmothers:

Ah ne nah, nah
nin nah nah—
Ah ne nah, nah
nin nah nah—
Nyaga mutzi
oh ne nay—
Nyaga mutzi
oh ne nay—[10]

The women danced and drummed and sang for weeks, preparing themselves for what was to come. The would reclaim the desert for the sake of their children, for the sake of the land.

A few miles downwind from the fire circle, bombs were being tested. Rabbits felt the tremors. Their soft leather pads on paws and feet recognized the shaking sands while the roots of mesquite and sage were smoldering. Rocks were hot from the inside out and dust devils hummed unnaturally. And each time there was another nuclear test, ravens watched the desert heave. Stretch marks appeared. The land was losing its muscle.

The women couldn't bear it any longer. They were mothers. They had suffered labor pains but always under the promise of birth. The red hot pains beneath the desert promised death only as each bomb became a stillborn. A contract had been broken between human beings and the land. A new contract was being drawn by the women who understood the fate of the earth as their own.

Under the cover of darkness, ten women slipped under the barbed wire fence and entered the contaminated country. They were trespassing. They walked toward the town of Mercury in moonlight, taking their cues from coyote, kit fox, antelope squirrel, and quail. They moved quietly and deliberately through the maze of Joshua trees. When a hint of daylight appeared they rested, drinking tea and sharing their rations of food. The women closed their eyes. The time had come to protest with the heart, that to deny one's genealogy with the earth was to commit treason against one's soul.

At dawn, the women draped themselves in mylar, wrapping long streamers of silver plastic around their arms to blow in the breeze. They wore clear masks that became the faces of humanity. And when they arrived on the edge of Mercury, they carried all the butterflies of a summer day in their wombs. They paused to allow their courage to settle.

The town which forbids pregnant women and children to enter because of radiation risks to their health was asleep. The women moved through the streets as winged messengers, twirling around each other in slow motion, peeking inside homes and watching the easy sleep of men and women. They were astonished by such stillness and periodically would utter a shrill note or low cry just to verify life.

The residents finally awoke to what appeared as strange apparitions. Some simply stared. Others called authorities, and in time, the women were apprehended by wary soldiers dressed in desert fatigues. They were taken to a white, square building on the other edge of Mercury. When asked who they were and why they were there, the women replied, "We are mothers and we have come to reclaim the desert for our children."

The soldiers arrested them. As the ten women were blindfolded and handcuffed, they began singing:

> *You can't forbid us everything*
> *You can't forbid us to think—*
> *You can't forbid our tears to flow*
> *And you can't stop the songs that we sing.*

The women continued to sing louder and louder, until they heard the voices of their sisters moving across the mesa.

Ah ne nah, nah
nin nah nah—
Ah ne nah, nah
nin nah nah—
Nyaga mutzi
oh ne nay—
Nyaga mutzi
oh ne nay—

"Call for re-enforcement," one soldier said.

"We have," interrupted one woman. "We have—and you have no idea of our numbers."

On March 18, 1988, I crossed the line at the Nevada Test Site and was arrested with nine other Utahns for trespassing on military lands. They are still conducting nuclear tests in the desert. Ours was an act of civil disobedience. But as I walked toward the town of Mercury, it was more than a gesture of peace. It was a gesture on behalf of the Clan of One-Breasted Women.

As one officer cinched the handcuffs around my wrists, another frisked my body. She found a pen and a pad of paper tucked inside my left boot.

"And these?" she asked sternly.

"Weapons," I replied.

Our eyes met. I smiled. She pulled the leg of my trousers back over my boot.

"Step forward, please," she said as she took my arm.

We were booked under an afternoon sun and bussed to Tonapah, Nevada. It was a two-hour ride. This was familiar country to me. The Joshua trees standing their ground had been named by my ancestors who believed they looked like prophets pointing west to the promised land. These were the same trees that bloomed each spring, flowers appearing like white flames in the Mojave. And I recalled a full moon in May when my mother and I had walked among them, flushing out mourning doves and owls.

The bus stopped short of town. We were released. The officials thought it was a cruel joke to leave us stranded in the desert with no way to get home. What they didn't realize is that we were home, soul-centered and strong, women who recognized the sweet smell of sage as fuel for our spirits.

Notes

1. Fuller, John G., *The Day We Bombed Utah* (New York: New American Library, 1984).

2. Discussion on March 14, 1988, with Carole Gallagher, photographer and author, *Nuclear Towns: The Secret War in the American Southwest*, to be published by Doubleday, Spring, 1990.

3. Szasz, Ferenc M., "Downwind From the Bomb," *Nevada Historical Society Quarterly*, Fall, 1987 Vol. XXX, No. 3, p. 185.

(

4. Fradkin, Philip L., *Fallout* (Tucson: University of Arizona Press, 1989), 98.

5. Ibid., 109.

6. Town meeting held by Senator Orrin Hatch in St. George, Utah, April 17, 1979, transcript, 26–28.

7. Fradkin, Op. cit., 228.

8. U.S. vs. Allen, 816 Federal Reporter, 2d/1417 (10th Circuit Court 1987), cert. denied, 108 S. CT. 694 (1988).

9. Fradkin, Op. cit., 116.

10. This song was sung by the Western Shoshone women as they crossed the line at the Nevada Test Site on March 18, 1988, as part of their "Reclaim the Land" action. The translation they gave was: "Consider the rabbits how gently they walk on the earth. Consider the rabbits how gently they walk on the earth. We remember them. We can walk gently also. We remember them. We can walk gently also."

READING REFLECTIONS

1. "The Clan of One-Breasted Women" refers to breast cancer, characteristically of women, and its possible relationship with environmental problems. Are there health and environmental problems you think might be specific to one sex or the other? What are these, and what reasons do you have for thinking this might be the case? What about race-related or ethnic-related diseases? Share your thoughts about these questions with your classmates.

2. What effect does Williams' opening sentence, "I belong to a Clan of One-Breasted Women," have on you? How does her detailing her family's medical history help you better relate to her essay? Williams conveys her story through the use of imagery. Provide examples of the symbolic language used throughout the essay.

3. What examples does Williams cite to demonstrate support for nuclear testing during the 1950s? How does this attitude toward nuclear testing compare or contrast to today's views on the issue?

4. Imagine yourself as a lawyer presenting a case against the government for conducting nuclear testing in the deserts and placing citizens at risk. Write an essay using Williams' evidence—for example, statements such as "virtually uninhabited desert terrain,"—to support your case.

5. Williams writes, "Tolerating blind obedience in the name of patriotism or religion ultimately takes our lives." Write an essay citing other historical instances or current events in which following one's patriotism or religion resulted in death.

6. In her essay, Williams asserts, "To our court system, it does not matter whether the United States Government was irresponsible, whether it lied to its citizens or even that citizens died from the fallout of nuclear testing. What matters is that our government is immune." List at least three other cases where the government or a representative thereof seemed immune from punishment for lying to its citizens. Explain why you think the government was able to go unpunished for these crimes.

BECOMING AMERICA'S LENS ON THE WORLD
National Geographic *in the Twentieth Century*

Jane Collins and Catherine Lutz

No matter how fair and impartial a publication appears to be, there can al-ways be some point of contention for the careful reader. According to Jane Collins and Catherine Lutz, this is the case with National Geographic. *Over the years,* National Geographic *has helped expose millions of readers to cultures different from their own through the use of "objective" free-lance journalists and photographers. However, the magazine's view may not be as objective as it is purported to be. Collins and Lutz explore Na-tional Geographic from its origins through its current issues to illustrate where the magazine's work has gone astray from its objective philosophy.*

This article first appeared in the South Atlantic Quarterly, *an aca-demic journal with articles on the humanities, social sciences, literary criticism, and cultural theory. Anthropologists Jane Collins and Cather-ine Lutz examine* National Geographic, *a longtime staple of American reading, basing their study on extensive historical research. After ana-lyzing historical, political, and technological trends, as well as content, photographs, and graphics, the authors contend that instead of offering a scientific and objective view of the world, the magazine promotes the agenda of the National Geographic Society: an "optimistic" social evo-lutionary belief that logic and reason will drive human progress but that certain inequalities are inevitable and justifiable.*

The history of the National Geographic Society and *National Geo-graphic* magazine as generally told is an epic of success: an amateur scientific organization begun by Gardiner Greene Hubbard in 1888 goes on to become the largest scientific-educational organization in the world; a publication that started out as a "slim, dull and technical" journal for gentleman scholars evolves into a glossy magazine whose circulation is the third largest in the United States. *National Geographic's* success, in these accounts, is attributed to its editors' accurate reading of the American people and "what they want to know" about the world; to its willingness to use innovative new photo-graphic technologies; and to its ability to secure a reputation for itself as an impartial, accurate, and genteel source of information on the world and its inhabitants.[1]

Jane Collins and Catherine Lutz, "Becoming America's Lens on the World: *National Geographic* in the Twentieth Century," *South Atlantic Quarterly* 91, no. 1 (Winter 1992): 161–91. Copyright © 1992 by Duke University Press. Reprinted with the permission of the publishers.

A more complex reading of the emergence of the National Geographic Society is given by P. Pauly, who sees the possibility of such an organization as having been conditioned by several significant historical trends converging at the end of the nineteenth century.[2] These trends included the emergence of mass journalism, the development of photoengraving technology, scientific specialization, and the awakening of American interest in the rest of the world that came with the end of the Spanish American War and the United States acquisition of new territorial possessions. The convergence of these trends created the space for an organization that could effectively operate on the boundary between science and entertainment and whose subject matter was America's place in the world. . . .

The early National Geographic Society touted its research in political and economic geography as an important support for the nation in an era of new global responsibilities. It published articles on the geographic and commercial possibilities of America's new possessions, discussed the benefits of colonialism, and assigned itself the role of arbitrator in determining the proper spellings of the new parts of the world with which colonialism brought the country in contact.[3]

Encounters with newly colonized peoples, as well as an increasing flow of immigrants, required the popular American imagination to develop some way of accounting for cultural differences. Theories of polygeny and environmental determinism had offered the nineteenth-century public some straightforward ways of explaining difference. But as George Stocking has pointed out, a significant paradox emerged. To the extent that the peoples in question "remained subordinate, exploited and unfree," they challenged the "myth that 'civilization' was associated with the triumph of liberal principles and the equal freedom of all human individuals."[4]

According to Stocking, social evolutionary thinking provided the resolution of the paradox. Inequalities could be interpreted as residual effects of uneven biological or cultural development. Those whose status was unequal could be assumed to be lagging behind in the mental or moral development on which equality should be premised, and the "metaphorical extendability" of such assumptions made it possible to apply them to a wide range of situations—encompassing inequalities among nations, races, genders, and classes.

The anthropology of the late nineteenth century dedicated itself to the search for evidence of the evolutionary backwardness of subaltern peoples—inventing a wide range of biological and sociocultural indices for the purpose. From craniometry to the cataloging of marriage principles, the study of difference was directed toward the creation of hierarchy. By the first and second decades of the twentieth century, psychologists and biologists were attempting to link evolutionary schemes to abstract, yet unilinear, measures of development, such as IQ.[5] An emerging understanding of genetic principles, combined with social evolutionary thought, fueled the eugenics movement, efforts to limit immigration, and restrictive racial codes.

The National Geographic Society emerged in the midst of this context, and positioned itself as a key actor in the presentation of "backward" peoples for Western perusal. The Society's brand of evolutionism was not the pessimistic Social Darwinism of the nativist and eugenics movements—a brand of evolutionism that worried about a presumed tendency of lower classes and "primitive" peoples to outmultiply their betters. Rather, they adopted what Stocking has called a more "classical" social evolutionism: an optimistic brand of the doctrine, which focused on the "evolutionary guarantee" of progress through the increasing triumph of rationality over instinct even as it continued to justify residual inequalities of sex, class, and race.[6] *National Geographic* reinforced America's vision of its newly ascendant place in the world by showing "how far we've come." While its photographs detailed, and occasionally lingered on, one or another aspect of native life, their underlying story was always the evolutionary chronicle, with its contrastive work, its encoding of hierarchy and power relations, and its projection of an inevitable outcome. . . .[7]

The formation of the National Geographic Society reflected the tensions inherent to this larger process of professionalization of science, which were played out over a number of years in interactions between Board members and editorial staff.

The Society was formed in 1888 by Gardiner Green Hubbard, a lawyer, a member of a prominent Boston family, and a patron of science. The initial meetings, held at Washington, D.C.'s Cosmos Club, brought together thirty-three distinguished geographers, most of whom held positions in federal bureaus such as the Geological Survey, the Coast and Geodetic Survey, and the Weather Bureau. . . .

Hubbard had a history of backing "practical science," most notably in the person of Alexander Graham Bell (who married Hubbard's daughter in 1877). He gave the National Geographic Society a great deal of autonomy in the first ten years, but with the publication of the magazine left to the scientists and professionals on the Board, the content remained technical and theoretical, accessible mainly to other professionals. . . .

Change in the nature of the Society began to occur when Bell took over in 1898. Bell, a renowned and successful inventor, was trained as a teacher of speech, and saw his scientific work as a gentlemanly avocation. . . . Bell seemed much more attuned to the Society's mission to disseminate geographic knowledge than to the promotion of new research, and he believed that people would read geography only if it were light and entertaining. It was Bell who hired Gilbert Hovey Grosvenor (who later became *his* son-in-law) to help build circulation in 1899. He encouraged Grosvenor to study popular magazines of the time, particularly *Harper's* and *Century*, in order to glean ideas for the *National Geographic* magazine. He also directed him to study "popular geographers" from Herodotus to Darwin, noting that the success of such works was due to the fact that they were "accurate, eyewitness accounts; simple and straightforward."[8]

Grosvenor's first innovations were in promotion and marketing. Membership in the Society had always been by nomination. . . . He also began rejecting articles provided by the editorial committee when he found them to be too technical or difficult. . . . The increasing autonomy of the organization from its professionalized roots gave it the ability to create its peculiar and powerful position as an arbiter of national culture.

Two elements were crucial in carving out this niche. The first was the recapturing and revitalization of the declining field of natural history. If natural history was defunct as an intellectual arena by the late nineteenth century, it obtained a new lease on life through the institutions of mass culture. In Bell's and Grosvenor's hands, the magazine became such an institution. . . .

The National Geographic Society was founded within two decades after the inauguration of the American Museum of Natural History and in a period of expansion of the Smithsonian Institution. In these contexts, photographic or material traces of the colonized world were relocated to new spaces in the industrialized West. Once appropriated and transferred, they provided the materials out of which new stories about the world could be created. As James Clifford has demonstrated, collecting and display are crucial processes of Western identity formation, and cultural description itself is a form of collecting that selectively accords "authenticity" to human groups and their institutions and practices.[9] *National Geographic*, like the great natural history museums, took images of Africa, Asia, and Latin America from their historical contexts and arranged them in ways that addressed contemporary Western preoccupations.[10] The systems of classification or explanation that were chosen provided an illusion of adequate representation, and an opportunity for certain institutions of mass culture to construct stories about otherness.

Regardless of what stories were told, the very acts of collecting and presenting were significant. They created illusions of possession, of a stable and complete "humanity," and of the possibility of ordering the exotic and the foreign.[11] As Susan Stewart has forcefully argued, in collections "desire is ordered, arranged and manipulated, not fathomless. . . . Like Noah's Ark, those great civic collections, the library and the museum, seek to represent experience within a mode of control and confinement. One cannot know everything about the world, but one can at least approach closed knowledge through the collection.". . .[12]

The second element of the niche *National Geographic* carved out for itself also went against the grain of the nineteenth-century positivism. This was the attempt to combine scholarly and entertainment functions in the same institution or cultural product. The *Geographic* sought, on the one hand, to be a potent force in exploration and scientific research that was independent of national scientific organizations and their ideologies of specialized research. On the other hand, it sought to obtain the interest of large masses of people. What was to be gained by successfully achieving such a combination? First, it placed the *Geographic* in the powerful position of being both a "broker" and a maker of scientific knowledge. In the prevailing atmosphere of scientific specialization, and the denigration of amateurs and lay practitioners, *National Geographic* could fill the void between academic practitioners and the public by purveying science, while also claiming to foster and practice science in its own right. The funding and conduct of research had always been marginal to the institution's main role in popularizing and glamorizing geographic and anthropological knowledge, yet it was sufficient to establish and retain its reputation as a "*scientific* and educational organization" (emphasis ours). This made it possible for the *Geographic* to speak with the voice of scientific authority, while remaining outside and unconstrained by the scientific community.

Second, there was a tremendous flexibility to be had by playing fast and loose with the boundaries between science and entertainment. Editors concerned with market imperatives could justify photographs that glorified the exotic and ritualistic aspects of "primitive" societies, or that sensationalized head-hunting, cannibalism, mutilation, or tattoo, on the grounds that they were picturesque, or because of their role in piquing interest. Presented in a magazine that claims to present "true facts" in a judicious manner, these images were given a scholarly veneer. And readers were given reinforcement for old prejudices. Editors tended to choose photographs based on their ability to appeal to an American audience; these were then fed back to the reading public as examples of the latest, brightest scientific knowledge. In the process, the reading public's original vision of what was interesting or aesthetically pleasing about the world outside United States borders was validated, elaborated, and heightened by its presentation as scientific fact.

When a new vision of the non-Western world was called for, *National Geographic* did not have to adhere to "scientific method" in constructing it. It did not find itself constrained by scholarly opinion, but could choose images with impunity. Editors could choose a grisly photograph of a headless Ifugao warrior based on its "scientific merit"; they could justify the absence of photographs showing poverty or hunger on grounds of presenting a "positive image"; and they could appeal to aesthetics for their use of multiple photographs of attractive young women and lush landscapes. The Society's editors were attentive to both the market and the scientific community, but they were slaves to neither. They were free to construct their own particular vision of the non-Western world.

One of the topics around which the scientific halo was (and still is) placed is sexuality. In fact, nothing more defines the *National Geographic* for most older American readers than its depiction of "naked" women, with the magazine's steady inclusion of "nudity" forming a central part of the image of the non-West that it purveys. A photo of a bare-chested woman was first included in the magazine in 1903. It was accompanied by (shameless) editorial explanation. The picture, and others like it, Gilbert H. Grosvenor later said, was included in the interest of science; to exclude it would have been to give an incomplete or misleading idea of how the people being portrayed really live. This scientific purpose for use of such photos was then and is now seen as their sole purpose, with the Society taking "vehement exception to comments about the sexual attraction or eroticism of the photographs." The breast represents both a struggle against "prudery" and the pursuit of truth rather than pleasure.[13]

The centrality of a race-gender code about whose breasts to depict cannot be denied, however. With two very recent exceptions, none of the hundreds of women whose breasts have been photographed for the magazine over the last century were white; it has been reported that one bare-breasted Polynesian woman whose picture was to be included in the magazine looked "too white" to be naked and so had her skin darkened in the production process.[14] And for all its struggle against prudery, male and female genitals have been regularly airbrushed out of the picture.

The nakedness of the *Geographic*'s subjects might be seen as continuous with the nude as a perennial theme in Western "fine arts." Some of these women are posed for surveillance ("caught in the act" of their customs) and more resemble the mug shot than the oil canvas; most are rendered (through pose, lighting, etc.) in such a way as to suggest intrinsic "artfulness." "Womanliness" can then play a central role in allowing the art of photography to exist silently beneath an explicitly "scientific" agenda and thereby increase readership and further legitimate the *Geographic*'s project as one of both beauty and truth. All of this elaborate structure of signification, however, is built on a foundation of racial and gender subordination: one must first be black and female to do this kind of symbolic labor. . . .

The juxtaposition of the "West" and the "rest" was also clearly at work in the pages of *National Geographic* magazine. The non-Western world was never the only topic covered in an issue. Stories about wildlife and about life in the United States have always been featured prominently, as were more technical pieces on climate and geomorphology in the early years. The proximity of articles on the United States to articles on the non-Western world often facilitated the depiction of progress and cultural evolution. . . . The juxtaposition of articles on New Guinea rituals with articles on orderly farms in New England or shiny new factories in the South underscored evolutionary themes in the articles and photographs themselves.

The "progressive," rather than Social Darwinist, nature of the *Geographic*'s evolutionism was reflected in Grosvenor's unwillingness to publish overtly hostile or racist material. This policy was made explicit in his "seven principles," announced in an editorial in 1915:

1. The first principle is absolute accuracy. Nothing must be printed which is not strictly according to fact. . . .
2. Abundance of beautiful, instructive and artistic illustrations.
3. Everything printed in the Magazine must have permanent value. . . .
4. All personalities and notes of a trivial character are avoided. . . .
5. Nothing of a partisan or controversial nature is printed.
6. Only what is of a kindly nature is printed about any country or people, everything unpleasant or unduly critical being avoided.
7. The contents of each number is planned with a view of being timely.[15]

The avoidance of overtly critical material contributed to an impression of good sportsmanship in the evolutionary struggle. If formerly colonized peoples hadn't quite made it to the levels of "civilization" of the industrialized nations, they were not condemned; the rhetoric was one of slightly older school chums rooting them on while they gave it their best shot.

In *National Geographic's* continuing efforts to locate itself on the boundary between science and entertainment, photographs became an increasingly significant tool. . . .

By 1915, the extensive use of photographs was one of *National Geographic's* distinguishing features. Like the text, pictures were constrained by Grosvenor's principles of fairness, factual content, and positive outlook: they were to be "beautiful" (aesthetically pleasing), "artistic" (embodying certain conventions of highbrow forms of art), and "instructive" (realist in representation). The magazine relied on sharply focused, easily readable photographs to bolster its claim that it presented an unbiased, unmediated view of the world. The use of photographs that claimed (in captions and text) to represent a pre-photographic reality went hand-in-hand with the assertion that all written material was "accurate, balanced and fair." What writers accomplished by an insistently upbeat and uncomplicated style, the erasure of conflicting points of view, and the presentation of (often gratuitous) names, dates, and numbers, was reinforced by the codes of photographic realism. . . .

"Photographs were not viewed as metaphors of experience, but rather as sections of reality itself. If photographs showed gigantic trees and awe-inspiring mountains, then all the trees were gigantic and all the mountains awe-inspiring. When photographs depicted Indians as 'savages,' Indians were confirmed as savages."[16] The *Geographic* capitalized on this notion of the photograph as evidence and established itself as a source of accurate and timely information on the colonial world. . . .

The *Geographic* did not adopt such a style, but relied on technically adequate, but naive, prints from travelers. The goal of the editorial staff was to print photographs that were "straightforward." As one editor put it in 1915, *National Geographic* had discovered a "new, universal language that requires no deep study . . . one that is understood as well by the jungaleer as by the courtier; by the Eskimo as by the wild man from Borneo; by the child in the playroom as by the professor in the college; and by the woman of the household as by the hurried businessman—in short, the Language of the Photograph."[17] The implication was that the photograph was a direct transcription of a reality that was timeless, classless, and outside the boundaries of language and culture. The photographer's intent, the photographic product, and the reader's experience were assumed to be one. For this reason, photographs, unlike other cultural texts, were held to be readable by even the "simplest" among us. . . .

If the sharp focus and conventional framing of *Geographic* photographs marked them as "records," it was their replication of existing popular understandings of the third world that made them seem neutral in their presentations, and gave them the comforting feel of "commonsense" realities captured on film. In this way, the mass media's images "become mirrors, serving to reflect Americans' feelings, rather than windows to the complex, dynamic realities of foreign societies.". . .[18]

The most significant events at *National Geographic* during the 1930s turned on the adoption of color photography. . . .

Color photography inevitably changes the nature of representation. Color tends to dominate the photograph, often at the expense of line and movement. It affects the mood of the image in ways that may reinforce or contradict the shape and placement of objects. Because of its high impact, color frequently becomes a consideration in choosing an image to photograph, or selecting among images already photographed:

> Even though Kodachrome was already unnaturally bright, photographers . . . splashed the strongest possible colors in their pictures so that they would be more effective in print. One result was that the staff photographers—who were constantly being sent to colorful places to slake what was seen as the public's unquenching thirst for colorful scenes—would often find themselves needing more color to take advantage of the color film and would resort to placing the people in costume.[19]

This practice has been called the "Red Shirt School of Photography."

Color photography began to differentiate the *Geographic* in somewhat foreseeable ways from a growing tradition of photojournalism that continued to rely on black-and-white photographs well into the 1950s. It became possible to render the exotic and picturesque in ever more riveting ways, leading editors to further emphasize these traits rather than historical significance and timeliness. Pictures in *National Geographic* were increasingly seen as akin to picture postcards or snapshots taken by tourists: Guimond explains that because

> tourism is so popular and because it is considered a particularly "reliable" way to understand realities, it is not surprising that these magazines' [*Time, Life,* and *National Geographic*] articles and photo-essays are often, in effect, tourist trips with the editors, reporters and photographers acting as tour guides. . . . Similarly, many magazines, particularly the *Geographic,* heavily emphasize the exotic aspects of foreign cultures, even as they also often give their readers . . . simulated, "candid" contacts with their subjects—little conversations with (and pictures of) camel drivers, village schoolteachers, and picturesque peasants—which may occur during tourist trips.[20]

The use of color photography also highlighted the magazine's affinity to museum exhibits—with their highly framed, aestheticized "tidbits" of traditional culture—rather than to starker, more information-laden news reportage or scientific documentation. . . .

Despite the fact that the Cold War period saw the construction of bomb shelters, the stockpiling of nuclear weapons, and the McCarthy hearings, it remained a time of defiant innocence—of optimism, power, and a sense of invulnerability—for most of the American public. The *Geographic* contributed to "softening" the entrance to the nuclear age with articles such as "Nevada Learns to Live with the Atom" and "Man's New Servant, the Friendly Atom." In the meantime, the nonsocialist third world continued to be portrayed as simple, childlike and friendly—in the words of one caption, as "Paradise in Search of a Future."

Publishing at *National Geographic* was characterized by some strange lacuna in coverage during the period of the Cold War. Favorable portrayals of Eastern Bloc nations would have been unpatriotic; yet dwelling on their evils was outside editorial policy. For this reason, there was no coverage whatsoever of the Soviet Union from 1945 to 1959 (when then Vice-President Richard Nixon described his trips to the Soviet Union for *Geographic* readers, including his "kitchen confrontation" with Nikita Khruschev). China's people were a popular subject before the war, with seventy articles on the country between 1900 and 1935; they were covered only seven times in the period 1950–76, however, returning to the pages of the *Geographic* with President Nixon's visit in 1975.

Increasing educational levels and a growth in average disposable wealth also characterized the 1950s. *National Geographic* benefited from both of these trends in terms of increased readership—from one million in 1935 to two million in the early 1960s. Within the class system of the postwar period, *National Geographic* magazine was both mainstream and relatively "high culture." Because of its glossy, colorful (but never gaudy) design, its semi-official status, and its well-developed relationship to schools, it could be displayed in middle-class homes as a mark of taste and as an investment that parents could make in their children's education, akin to a set of encyclopedias, a globe, or a good dictionary.

As the United States reached the apex of its postwar power, autonomous voices from formerly colonized peoples were reaching the West in louder and more articulate forms. Independence movements and anticolonial struggles in India and Africa challenged both the philosophical basis and the on-the-ground reality of Western power. The Negritude movement in Africa and the Caribbean denied the right of the West to define third world cultural identity, and offered powerful new self-definitions. The United States was attempting to forge and solidify new economic relationships to nations of the South at a time when colonial power relations were being overturned and when evolutionist theory and its corollary—"the white man's burden"—were being contested.

The anticolonial struggles that reverberated through the social sciences—generating new forms of self-examination and challenges to extant theories—only intensified the search for order at *National Geographic*. Images of safety and stability in the third world were not abandoned. On the contrary, images of Westerners were politely removed from colonial and neo-colonial contexts, thereby allowing the magazine to avoid uncomfortable questions about the nature of their presence, to obscure the contexts and difficulties of the photographic encounter, and to create a vision of the cultures in question as hermetically sealed worlds—captured only in the sense of "captured on film." Again, the analogy to collections is instructive: "The point of the collection is forgetting—starting again in such a way that a finite number of elements create, by virtue of their combination, an infinite reverie. Whose labor made [the collection] is not the question: the question is what is inside."[21] In the heyday of colonial culture, the inclusion of Westerners in the photographs of the colonized served to establish a sort of authenticity—to demonstrate that the photographer was "really there." By the late 1960s, however, the colonial and postcolonial relationships that permitted *National Geographic* to photograph the world had become a site of struggle, and reference to them was studiously avoided.

It was also becoming evident that "home" was not exempt from the anticolonial, antiracist struggles that had been emerging in the third world. The contradictions beneath the peaceful, postwar veneer of the 1950s were revealed by the emergence of civil rights struggles. With the increasing radicalization of the movement after 1964, race and cultural difference emerged into mass culture and the media in ways that they had not since the last century—and with an intensity that far surpassed the struggles over immigration and ethnicity in the late nineteenth and early twentieth centuries. *National Geographic* did not report these issues. The struggles of the period are nonetheless part of the background to its 1950s coverage, and to the assiduous way in which the magazine averted its eyes from anything that suggested interracial or intercultural conflict. . . .

As the Vietnam War unfolded, the *Geographic* was caught in a quandary. Should it honor its tradition of upbeat, "fact-filled" war reporting? And how could it do so in an undeclared, as yet low-key war? Trusting in the past success of its war reportage, the Society began its coverage with a piece by Wilbur Garrett and Peter White in 1961, entitled "South Viet Nam Fights the Red Tide." In 1962 the Society sent photographer Dickey Chappelle to work on an article entitled "Helicopter War in South Viet Nam"—a piece that provided the first published photographs of American military personnel in action to the American public.[22]

Melville Bell Grosvenor stepped down from his positions in 1967; Melvin M. Payne took over the presidency of the Society; the editorship went to Frederick Vosburg for three years, and then to Melville's son Gilbert. Memberships had ballooned during Melville Grosvenor's tenure from 2.2 to 5.6 million. Perhaps his greatest contribution had been the hiring of a group of individuals known within the organization as "young turks"—highly acclaimed photojournalists from major midwestern newspapers who deviated strongly from the rather effete gentlemanly ethos of previous decades. This new cohort was interested in modernizing the appearance and content of the *Geographic*. They advocated more use of natural lighting in photographs, more white space in layout, and all-color issues. They also pushed for coverage of more controversial issues. Key among them was Wilbur Garrett, who was to serve as the magazine's Editor between 1980 and 1990. . . .

In this context, Grosvenor and those who supported him believed that a continuing "Pollyanna" style of reporting would make the *Geographic* look increasingly shallow and out-of-touch. They believed that the public was becoming increasingly accustomed to grisly facts and critical coverage. If *National Geographic* continued to print only kindly and noncontroversial stories, they feared the loss of two elements crucial to their prior success. First, an increasingly sophisticated public would simply find their stories uninteresting—predictable and without punch. Carefully rendered versions of the idealized and exotic third world, which had formerly piqued interest, would present little competition to stories of the real-life drama and pathos of the Vietnam War. Second, the principle of "kindliness" was found increasingly to be in conflict with the principle of "absolute accuracy." Given media attention to conflicts in places like South Africa, "noncontroversial" stories about these locations would be opened to question. As *Newsweek* noted in its coverage of the controversy, "in any other magazine the articles on South Africa, Cuba under Castro, and life in Harlem would be considered tame—if not belated—attempts to report the issues of the day."[23] *National Geographic's* claim to present a factual representation would be weakened by its studious avoidance of the conflicts and violence that were covered by other sources.

In opposition to Grosvenor's view, the ad hoc Committee established by Payne decried the "missionary instinct" of the magazine's recent coverage, arguing that "controversy is adequately covered in the daily press"; it suggested that the correct approach to coverage of controversy was to "state precisely what the current situation is, but don't take sides; you don't even quote people on either side."[24] Editors, perhaps correctly, perceived that even the recognition that multiple points of view existed made their claim to present an authoritative and objective account open to question. Coverage of social or political resistance movements not only suggested that the world was unstable, but that an omniscient, "unbiased" stance was not possible. Ultimately, the Committee asked Grosvenor for a statement that the *Geographic* would simply not cover areas or issues that were "so emotionally charged that an objective piece cannot be written." Grosvenor complied by publishing a short editorial statement in 1978 that affirmed the *Geographic's* rejection of "advocacy journalism."[25]

That such coverage already appeared naive and "storybookish" to reading audiences of the 1970s is evidenced . . . somewhat ironically, by the *National Review's* defense of the magazine's Cuba story. "*National Geographic* is not ordinarily thought of as a fellow-traveling publication. . . . Indeed, there are few more refreshing magazines, few so beautifully designed to take the reader out of himself and give him an instant vacation from politics and other humdrum distractions." If the *Geographic* flattered Cuba in the article, it was only because "the magazine flatters everyone."[26] For an enterprise that still considered itself a "scientific-educational" establishment, this defense was almost as damaging as the criticism had been: it labeled the Society's work too definitively as entertainment, if not pabulum, and damaged its claims to present a factual account of the world.

Thus, despite the Board's rebuff of Grosvenor and renunciations of "advocacy" in the editorial pages, the magazine continued to publish topical and somewhat controversial pieces. Environmental conservation has generally been seen as an important topic at *National Geographic.* Stories on environmental degradation began to be featured in 1970, and the magazine has subsequently published articles on the smuggling of endangered species, on hazardous waste, acid rain, and on the destruction of tropical rain forests. Environmental issues received significant coverage in the 1988 centennial issue. Articles on the Underground Railroad and the Vietnam War Memorial treated controversial (but now safely historical) themes.

Nevertheless, it was not long before Garrett had to go. His firing in 1990 has been interpreted as the product of long-standing ill will between Garrett and Grosvenor, who served as President of the Society during Garrett's tenure as editor.[27] But Garrett's removal also occurred during a period of market pressures: specifically, a time of declining readership and increasing production costs. Gilbert Grosvenor and the Society's Board argued that, under these circumstances, the best strategy was to pay careful attention to market research and to launch a more determined endeavor to "give the public what they want": shorter stories, fewer articles on non-American topics, and less coverage of social problems. Garrett, on the other hand, apparently preferred to "give the public what it doesn't know it wants yet"—to play a greater role in shaping public tastes, rather than simply responding to them. Garrett's activist 1970s style did not win over a Board of Trustees that welcomed the right-shifting political sands of the 1980s and 1990s. "Beauty" had to take precedence over "truth." Politeness was more marketable than "politics." And after all, the American self-identity as rational, generous, and benevolent was at stake, as it had been since the magazine's inception.

Notes

1. See Howard S. Abramson, *National Geographic: Behind America's Lens on the World* (New York, 1987); C. D. B. Bryan, *The National Geographic Society: 100 Years of Adventure and Discovery* (Washington, D.C., 1987); Tom Buckley, "With the *National Geographic* on Its Endless, Cloudless Voyage," *New York Times Magazine,* 6 September 1970; Anne Chamberlin, "Two Cheers for the *National Geographic,*" *Esquire,* December 1963; Geoffrey T. Hellman, "Geography Unshackled II." *New Yorker,* 2 October 1943; and Ishbel Ross, "Geography, Inc.," *Scribner's,* June 1938.

2. P. Pauly, " 'The World and All That Is in It': The National Geographic Society: 1888–1918," *American Quarterly* 31 (1979): 517–32.

3. Ibid., 521.

4. George W. Stocking, Jr., *Victorian Anthropology* (New York, 1987), 230.

5. See Stephen J. Gould, *The Mismeasure of Man* (New York, 1981).

6. Stocking, *Victorian Anthropology,* 233.

7. We describe the construction of cultural difference in the magazine via photographic conventions and reader response to them in a book manuscript, tentatively

titled *Reading National Geographic*. See also Catherine Lutz and Jane Collins, "The Photograph as an Intersection of Gazes: The Example of *National Geographic*, *Visual Anthropology Review* 7 (1991): 134–49; and Catherine Lutz "Intentionality, Race, and Evolutionism in Photographs of 'Non-Westerners,'" in *Culture and Intentionality*, ed. Lawrence Rosen (Cambridge, in press).

8. Abramson, *Behind America's Lens*, 48.

9. James Clifford, *The Predicament of Culture: Twentieth-Century Ethnography, Literature and Art* (Cambridge, 1988).

10. See, for example, Donna Haraway's description of how the African Hall of the Museum of Natural History encodes Western preoccupations with manhood, virile defense of democracy, and connection (or loss of connection) with nature (*Primate Visions: Gender, Race and Nature in the World of Modern Science* [New York, 1989], chap. 3).

11. Jean Baudrillard, *Le systeme des objets* (Paris, 1968).

12. Susan Stewart, *On Longing: Narratives of the Miniature, the Gigantic, the Souvenir, the Collection* (Baltimore, 1984), 163, 161, 165.

13. Abramson, *Behind America's Lens*, 141; and Bryan, *100 Years of Adventure*, 89.

14. Abramson, *Behind America's Lens*, 143.

15. Bryan, *100 Years of Adventure*, 90.

16. Christopher Lyman, *The Vanishing Race and Other Illusions: Photographs of Indians by Edward S. Curtis* (New York, 1982), 29.

17. Bryan, *100 Years of Adventure*, 133.

18. James Guimond, "Exotic Friends, Evil Others and Vice Versa," *Georgia Review* (1988): 68.

19. Bryan, *One Hundred Years of Adventure*, 294–95.

20. Guimond, "Exotic Friends," 40–41.

21. Stewart, *On Longing*, 152.

22. Fred Ritchin notes that Dickey Chappelle (who was killed covering the war in 1965) also photographed an execution during this trip that was similar to the one with which Eddie Adams riveted the American public in 1968, but that the photograph was published only in "an obscure magazine" (not *National Geographic*): "The world was not ready to see the brutality of the war, nor searching for such a symbol of it" ("The Photography of Conflict," *Aperture* 97 [Winter 1984]: 24).

23. Tony Schwartz, "The *Geographic* Faces Life," *Newsweek*, 12 September 1977.

24. Abramson, *Behind America's Lens*, 240; and Bryan, *One Hundred Years of Adventure*, 395.

25. Bryan, *One Hundred Years of Adventure*, 395–96.

26. M. J. Sobran, Jr., "Tariff on Truth," *National Review*, 13 May 1977.

27. Charles Truehart, "The Great Divide at National Geographic," *Washington Post*, 7 May 1990.

READING REFLECTIONS

1. Collins and Lutz's article is complex. To study it, you might want to break it down paragraph by paragraph. How do the concepts of audience and purpose fit into the decisions to make the publication scientific and entertaining?

2. What are the sources of Collins and Lutz's research? Are these reputable sources? How would you rate the validity of these sources?
3. Do you agree with Collins and Lutz's analysis and the way in which they did it? Explain why or why not.
4. Name other publications where this type of analysis could be done. Why can these publications be analyzed in a similar way?
5. Collins and Lutz present an analysis of everything from the photographic placement to the content of the articles in *National Geographic* as reasons to question the objectivity of this publication. Because many photographs and articles in *National Geographic* have been taken or written by freelance writers and photographers, who are not permanent staff members, do you think they have been fair to the publication in their analysis? Why or why not?

"Ourselves and Others" Activities

READING REACTIONS

1. Susan Benesch's and Rekha Basu's pieces appeared in mainstream publications, but some publications are ones where sensationalism seems to be common practice. What are some of these? Do you think you would find more "us versus them" portrayals in the sensational publications? Why or why not?
2. In analyzing any text, it is helpful to consider the audience and purpose of the message. Benesch's and Basu's pieces are both commentaries. What difference, if any, is there between commentary, newswriting, and advertising? Does considering a variety of kinds of writing affect how you feel about their representations of "others"?
3. The articles by Jane Collins and Catherine Lutz, Michael Dorris, and George Lakoff are based on how language is used in print, in ads, and on television. Brainstorm with your classmates about where you might find other texts and visuals to study.

CLASSROOM REACTIONS

1. A theme of this chapter is that language used in the media constructs certain views of the world for us, and those views can range from stereotypes and pure fantasy, to partial truths, or complete accuracies, or any combination of these views. Review at least three readings in this chapter and determine which view you think the authors are saying the media present. Share your thoughts with your classmates.

2. Dig out textbooks you have from other classes; then analyze these based on their representations of "others" in content, photographs, illustrations, and design. Did you notice any stereotypical representations? Were any groups over- or underrepresented? Compose a letter to the text's author or editor about what you have found.

3. Do you think you know someone who has been a victim of environmental pollution? Write a paragraph about the nature of this person's problem and why you think it is environmentally related. Then share it with your classmates, if you want.

MEDIA CONNECTIONS

1. Many film and television shows tell stories about people in situations where they are in places with people quite different from themselves. Sometimes these situations can be humorous and sometimes tragic. Choose a film or TV show with that sort of story and write a review for your classmates.

2. Bearing in mind Basu's statement, "I have seen minorities cringe at perceived racist stereotypes in the news," videotape the national news or your local news and make a list of men, women, and minorities that are shown and under what circumstances they are shown. Then share this with your classmates.

3. Find news stories about another country and its people from your local newspaper or national newspapers like the *Washington Post* or the *New York Times*, and then find Web pages for the particular country. Did you find differences in the way these countries are represented? Write an essay for your classmates and teachers about how you account for these differences, based on the audience and purpose of the medium or text.

COMMUNITY INTERACTIONS

1. Take a trip to your local grocery store to see if you can find products with advertisements and packaging either playing on or creating cultural metaphors which you think either misrepresent a group or accurately reflect the characteristics of a group. Write an essay for your class about what you found.

2. While you are in the grocery store, look at the tabloids along checkout counters for articles and photographs of "aliens" from other planets. How are these "others" represented? Are they friendly or not? What are their reported motives? Collect various articles about these alien sightings and visits and make a poster display or slide show presentation to your class about what you found.

3. Go to several local travel agencies, and create two vacation itineraries for a classmate for your hometown or a city in the United States with an ethnic section—one vacation should be conventional, hitting all the typical tourist spots, and the other should be a nonconventional vacation—hitting the ethnic spots or the places where the locals "hang out." Create a travel itinerary showing the difference in the two vacations.

4. Have a friend drive you around your community while you take photographs of the billboards in it. Analyze the representations of people on these signs, and make a poster display for your class about what you found.

Realities Ad.
Copyright Liz Claiborne, 1992.

"Realities": A typical American family enjoying a private moment. At least in this ad for a Liz Claiborne cologne, the presumption of what the typical family looks like seems to have changed little from the early advertisements of the 1950s. The middle-class nuclear family, according to this statement, is alive and well, despite such claims to the contrary, as President Clinton makes in his speech on media and family values, which we include in this chapter.

Given the title of this ad, why do you think the marketers decided to utilize the family image? How "real" is this family image to you? Conduct an experiment in which you ask children to draw a family. How do their images of family compare to portrayals of the Realities ad?

3

Family Matters

Ironically, what started the debate over "family values" in the early 1990s was not based on actual family life but on a television show. In 1992, television character Murphy Brown, an anchorperson for the fictional television news magazine *FYI*, decided to have the child fathered by her ex-husband. Although Murphy's decision was celebrated by the many viewers who tuned in every Monday evening during the 1992 season, Vice President Dan Quayle derided the increasing "poverty" of family values in American society, citing Murphy's "decision" as a prime-time example.

As Murphy's pregnancy has gone down in the annals of television viewing history and the show is off the air, single motherhood in the inner city approaches epidemic proportions. Recent debates about governmental support in the form of welfare suggest that although many of us can celebrate the birth of an illegitimate child to a fictional white, upper-class female, in real life the status of women and children not of Murphy's class continues to decline both socially and economically—something politicians of both parties have acknowledged. Although it is clear that the middle-class nuclear family that reigned so strongly in television shows of the 1950s, such as *Leave It to Beaver*, *Father Knows Best*, and *The Ozzie and Harriet Show*, had real-life counterparts, today's American families—consisting of single-parent families from divorce, same-sex parental figures in gay or lesbian families, and immigrant and multicultural families in America—lead many to question the traditional representations of family that political and social leaders appear to value.

Although Quayle's condemnation of Hollywood's political agenda appeared extreme in 1992, many feel that both politicians and the general public have caught up to Quayle. The most recent presidential campaign, for example, also fostered a resurgence of the family values debate, with Republican candidate Robert Dole again lamenting a lack of family values, linking its decline to the increase in violence in the media, drug addiction, and crime. Part of this concern included criticism of people such as First Lady Hillary Clinton, whose book, *It Takes a Village to Raise a Child*, stresses the role of schools, government, neighborhoods, and religious leaders in helping develop children into responsible, productive citizens. According to her book, even the best of families need help. Ironically, the family values of the Clintons themselves were under siege, as we end the twentieth century with only the second impeachment trial in our country's history for President Clinton's acknowledged sexual relationship with White House intern Monica Lewinsky and his supposed obstruction of justice in attempting to cover up the relationship. Whereas the 1868 trial of President Andrew Johnson was certainly of national interest, the investigation and trial of President Clinton became a daily media event, from the breaking of the story via the Internet, to the publication of Independent Counsel Kenneth Starr's report, to the televised coverage of the impeachment trial itself. Because of such media bombardment, parents are confronted with the questions of children about sexuality as well as morality and values, as many question the ease with which politicians embrace family values but face difficulty in living by those values. Although such questions can be difficult, it could be that the extent to which parents and children can communicate about such matters is itself an issue of family values.

In outlining this continuing debate about family values in American society, this chapter asks you to question what the word *family* means to you. What is your family unit, and how does it compare to the families you see on television or in your community? What traditions or rituals does your family engage in that are similar to or different from those of other families from different cultural backgrounds? Although other media offer images of the American family, perhaps no medium has had such an impact on shaping our attitudes and understanding of what it means to be a family as has American television. Thus one major aspect of this chapter addresses the distinction between television families and the definition of family values across a wider range of American families and cultural groups. Such images are in contrast to those of middle- and upper-middle-class families that have only recently begun to lose their stronghold on American television, with the more recent popularity of such programs as *Roseanne* and *Grace Under Fire* (both in syndication), which feature working-class families.

Just how has the representation of the family on television changed in the last thirty years? Television provides many opportunities to explore these issues through networks such as Nickelodeon or FX that offer those with a nostalgia for the nuclear family the likes of *The Patty Duke Show* or *Happy Days*. However, in keeping with social and historical changes, such nostalgia networks also chronicle the rise of single women in the 1970s in such situation comedies as *The Mary Tyler Moore Show* or its spin-off *Rhoda*, in part a result of factors such as the women's movement during the late 1960s and early 1970s. Today, it is common for networks to showcase the lives of single women, as in the series *Caroline in the City* and *Ally McBeal*, with several television series portraying young adults "living single" with friends, as in *Friends*, *Living Single*, *Melrose Place*, and *Beverly Hills 90210*.

Consider also the extent to which television now portrays more African American families, as we have seen in *The Cosby Show* during the 1980s, as well as in *Family Matters* and *The Fresh Prince of Bel Air*. This sharply contrasts to the 1950s and 1960s, a time when media portrayals of African American families were rare. Whereas some argue that the inclusion of African American families on television is progress, still others argue that vital aspects of African American culture have been made to assimilate into the prime-time culture of the American middle-class family. Meanwhile, despite the numbers of Hispanic and Asian families within the United States, little to no television representations exist in the most recent network lineups.

We hope to show from the range of readings on both sides of the issue that the debate about the role of family in American society and the image of family on American television is alive and well. For example, President Clinton associates the negative role of the media with the increasing decline in more stable family units.

Ultimately, we are both attracted to and distracted by the image of family or, as some of the readings in this chapter indicate, antifamily, we encounter on television. Whereas our attraction is based on an ideal in which few television families have problems that can't be resolved within the thirty-minute sitcom format, our distraction is based in part on the way in which media images of the family, particularly on television, differ from the models we encounter in our daily life, whether it be in our churches and synagogues or in a trip to the local grocery store. Indeed, to what extent is the traditional family unit satirized in such shows as *The Simpsons, Married . . . with Children,* or the more recent *Third Rock from the Sun?*

Yet some models of family make us uncomfortable, precisely because of our unfamiliarity with them either in the media or in real life. Even when such models find their way to both the big and the small screen, they don't always profile the rituals or struggles the characters might endure. Viewers thus empathize with the situation to an extent that we do not always find in daily life. A recent example of this occurs in the blockbuster film *The Birdcage,* in which Robin Williams and Nathan Lane portray a gay couple whose lifestyle must be camouflaged when Williams' son brings home his fiancée, the daughter of a conservative senator. The comic picture of homosexuality as portrayed in *The Birdcage* overshadows the day-to-day difficulties that real gay and lesbian couples experience. Yet such portrayals continue to cause political controversy, as evidenced when former Vice President Quayle challenged current Vice President Gore to a debate about family values in light of Gore's support for the now defunct ABC sitcom *Ellen,* which featured an openly gay leading character. To balance the media portrayal of gay and lesbian families, we profile the observations of a seven-year-old girl, who discusses the pros and cons of living in a lesbian household.

The readings in this chapter attempt to portray the conflicting attitudes about family in our society and the means through which these values tend to circulate, predominantly on television. It is true in the case of television that there have been more efforts at diversifying the family in terms of socioeconomic or marital status. But many of the images on television still reflect a dominant emphasis on a white nuclear family, despite the concern that images of the family on television are far removed from the family values of the 1950s called for by leaders like former Vice President Quayle and numerous presidential hopefuls, possibly even Elizabeth Dole, lately touted as a "family values" Republican candidate for the 2000 election.

With calls for a return to family values in both the political arena and in America's homes, it is clear that the definition of family is one of conflict in our culture and contradiction in our media. Through the inclusion of readings about Hispanic families as but one representative of the varieties of multicultural families within the larger culture, readings about caring for elderly parents, as well as readings about lesbian parenting, we also hope to show that the word *family* means different things to different people and that relying on a particular image of family as seen on television or in our own communities is not as easy or as desirable as it used to be. Regardless of the images of and debates about family we see in today's media, it is clear that issues of family matter a great deal. Thus, we ask you to question how important the role of family is in your own life, comparing your own history, values, and rituals to those of your peers and your community.

REMARKS AT THE OPENING OF SESSION I AT THE FAMILY AND MEDIA CONFERENCE IN NASHVILLE, TENNESSEE

William Jefferson Clinton

A full three years before any word of the Monica Lewinsky scandal hit the airwaves, President Clinton's address to the conference on family and media is a call to stabilize the traditional family unit in American culture. Clinton's position as president and his political position on family values enhances his credibility within his speech; however, as a historical document, its interpretation by future audiences cannot help but be ironic.

William Jefferson Clinton became the forty-second president of the United States on November 3, 1992, and was reelected for a second term in November 1996. Prior to his presidency, Clinton served as governor of Arkansas. He was born on August 19, 1946, in Hope, Arkansas. Clinton at-

William Jefferson Clinton, "Remarks at the Opening of Session I at the Family and Media Conference in Nashville, Tennessee," *Weekly Compilation of Presidential Documents* 31, no. 28 (July 17, 1995), Washington, D.C.

tended Georgetown University where he received a B.S. in International Affairs in 1968. He won a Rhodes Scholarship and studied government at Oxford. In 1973, he graduated from Yale University Law School. While at Yale, he met Hillary Rodham. They married in 1975 and had their daughter Chelsea Victoria in 1980. Clinton has also written Putting People First: How We Can All Change America, *which he co-authored with Vice President Al Gore.*

Thank you very much. I thought it might be nice to stop by here after having done my primary duty, which was delivering the soup to Mrs. Gore. [Laughter] I'm delighted to be here, Governor, Mayor, Senator, Members of Congress. To Representative Purcell and the other distinguished members of the Tennessee Legislature who are here, Dr. Erickson, and to all of you, let me say that I came here primarily to listen. And I find that I always learn a lot more when I'm listening than when I'm talking, so I will be quite brief.

I want to say a few things, however. First, I want to thank Al and Tipper Gore for their lifetime of devotion not only to their family but to the families of this State and this Nation, as manifested by this Family Reunion, the fourth such one, something they have done in a careful and sustained way. It's already been mentioned twice that Tipper has worked on the whole issue that we're here to discuss today for many, many years, never in the context of politics but always in the context of what's good for families and what we can do to move the ball forward for our children and for our future. And I think this country owes them a great debt of gratitude. And I'm glad to be here.

Secondly, I'd just like to frame this issue as it appears to me as President and as a parent. I gave a speech at Georgetown a few days ago in which I pointed out that the world in which I grew up, the world after World War II, was basically shaped by two great ideas: the middle class dream, that if you work hard you'll get ahead and your kids can do better than you did; and middle class values, that of family and community and responsibility and trustworthiness, and that both of those things were at some considerable risk today as we move out of the cold war into the global economy and the whole way we live and work is subject to sweeping challenge.

The family is the focus of both middle class dreams and middle class values, for it is the center around which we organize child rearing—our country's most important responsibility—and work. And how we work determines how we live and what will become of us over the long run.

We have seen enormous changes in both work and child rearing in the last several years. We know now that a much higher percentage of our children live in poverty, particularly in the last 10 years, even as we have a percentage of elderly people in poverty going below that of the general population for the first time in history in the last 10 years, a considerable achievement of which we ought to be proud as a country. But still, our children are becoming more and more poor.

We know that a higher percentage of our children are being born out of wedlock. What you may not know, but is worth noting, is that the number of children being born out of wedlock is more or less constant for the last few years. So we not only have too many children being born out of wedlock, we have more and more young couples where both of them are working and having careers who are deferring child bearing and, in many cases, not having children at all. I would argue that is also a very troubling thing in our country—the people in the best position to build strong families and bring up kids in a good way deciding not to do so.

We know that most children live in families where, whether they have one parent or two parents in the home, whoever their parents are in the home are also working. We know that we do less for child care and for supervised care for children as a society than any other advanced country in the world.

We know, too, that most of our parents for the last 20 years have been working a longer work week for the same or lower wages, so that while Representative Purcell here complimented the Governor on his budget because it maintained a commitment to children in terms of public investment, you could make a compelling argument that the private investment in children has been going down because most families have both less time and less money to spend on their children.

And we know that as parents spend less time with their children, by definition the children are spending more time with someone or something else, so that the media has not only exploded in its ramifications in our lives but also has more access to more of our children's time than would have been the case 20 years ago if all these technological developments had occurred when the family and our economy were in a different place. And I think we have to look at all these issues in that context.

Now, it's commonplace to say that most of us believe that there's too much indiscriminate violence, too much indiscriminate sex, and too much sort of callous degradation of women and sometimes of other people in various parts of our media today. I believe that the question is, so what? What we ought to be talking about today is, so what are we all going to do about that? Because our ability to change things, I think, consists most importantly in our ability to [take] affirmative steps.

At this talk at Georgetown, I made a commitment that I would try to set an example for what I thought our political leaders ought to be doing. We ought to have more conversation and less combat. When we criticize, we ought to offer an alternative. We ought to be thinking about the long run; these trends that we're dealing with have been developing over quite a long while now. And we ought to celebrate what is good as well as condemn what we don't like. And I think if we do those four things, then we will be able to make good decisions.

So let me just make two specific suggestions, and then I'd like to get on with listening to other people. First of all, in the spirit of alternatives and celebrating what is good, I'm for balancing the budget, but I'm against getting rid of public television or dramatically cutting it. In our family this is known as the "Leave Big Bird alone" campaign. [Laughter] I say that because we are going to have to cut a bunch of stuff folks, and we are going to have to cut a lot of things. The budget would be in balance today but for the interest we're paying on the debt run up between 1981 and 1993. Next year, interest on the debt will exceed the defense budget. This is a big problem for our families, their incomes, their living standards, their future.

But consider this. Public TV gives, on average, 6 hours of educational programming a day. Sometimes the networks have as little as a half an hour a week. Public television goes to 98 percent of our homes. Forty percent of our people don't have access to cable channels like the Learning Channel or A&E. Fourteen percent, only 14 percent of overall public television channel funding comes from Federal money, but often times in rural places, like Senator Conrad's North Dakota, over half of the money comes from the Corporation for Public Broadcasting. Sixty percent of the viewers have family incomes below $40,000. It costs you a $1.09 a year, per citizen, to fund it. And for every dollar public television and radio get from the Government, they raise $5 or $6 from the private sector. So I think that's my first suggestion.

My second suggestion relates to the presence of Senator Conrad here. If we don't believe in censorship, and we do want to tell parents that they have a responsibility, that television, to use Reverend Jackson's phrase that the Vice President mentioned, may be the third parent, but it can't be the first or the second, and that's up to the parents—if we want to say that, but we know we live in a country where most kids live in families where there's one or two parents there working and where we have less comprehensive child care than any other advanced country in the world, the question is how can we get beyond telling parents to do something that they physically cannot do for several hours a day unless they literally do want to be a home without television or monitor their kids in some other way?

There is one technological fix now being debated in the Congress which I think is very important. It's a little simple thing; I think it's a very big deal. In the telecommunications bill, Senator Conrad offered an amendment which ultimately passed with almost three-quarters of the Senate voting for it. So it's a bipartisan proposal that would permit a so-called V-chip to be put in televisions with cables which would allow parents to decide which—not only which channels their children could not watch but within channels, to block certain programming.

This is not censorship; this is parental responsibility. This is giving parents the same access to technology that is coming into your home to all the people who live there, who turn it on. So I would say when that telecommunications bill is ultimately sent to the President's desk, put the V-chip in it and empower the parents who have to work to do their part to be responsible with media. Those are two specific suggestions that I hope will move this debate forward.

Having said what I meant to say, I would like to now go on, Mr. Vice President, to hear the people who really know something about this. I want to thank you all for your care and concern. And let me echo something the Governor said:

There is a huge consensus in this country today that we need to do something that is responsible, that is constructive, that strengthens our families and gives our kids a better future, and that celebrates the fact that this is the media center of the world. And we want it to be that way 10, 20, 50 years from now. But we also want to be that way in a country that is less violent, that has a more wholesome environment for our children to grow up in, where our children are strong and taking advantage of the dominant position the United States enjoys in the world media.

Thank you very much.

READING REFLECTIONS

1. As you read through President Clinton's speech, what are some of the ways in which he establishes his credibility with his audience?
2. What aspects of television programming does Clinton praise and what aspects does he condemn?
3. Clinton claims the V-chip not to be censorship but "parental responsibility." Do you agree with his assessment?
4. According to Clinton, what cultural factors account for the decline of "strong families"?
5. What does Clinton mean when he says that the "family is the focus of both middle class dreams and middle class values"?

SEPTEMBER THONG

Katha Pollitt

"Can anything good come of Sexgate?" That's the question Katha Pollitt asks in "September Thong," in which she scrutinizes the "family values bigots" on both sides of the political spectrum. Despite her emphasis on the hypocrisy of many political leaders, including President Bill Clinton, Pollitt ultimately questions the supposed shock at Clinton's sexual liaison with Monica Lewinsky given his past history and the trend toward sex in the workplace.

Katha Pollitt's Subject to Debate *column is a regular feature of* The Nation. *An award-winning essayist and poet, Pollitt has written essays for such magazines as* The New Yorker, *the* Atlantic Monthly, *and* Harpers. *Born in New York City, she was educated at Harvard and the Columbia School of the Arts and has taught poetry at Barnard College.*

Like someone caught in one of those recurring dreams of having to retake a long-ago flunked math exam or catch a train naked without a ticket, President Clinton keeps apologizing but can't seem to get it right. But then, it's hard to sound sorry when you're really only sorry about getting caught, and when you know that in the real world, the off-camera, off-the-record world, the things you are said to have done, and have done, are not so unusual. The worst of Zippergate for Clinton, one former Democratic Party activist told me, has to be listening to all those male politicians thunder away while knowing that lots of them are up to monkey business too, and having to ask forgiveness of all those male ministers, priests and rabbis, who probably are no better than they should be either. And then there's the added torture of having to listen while former high-level staffers publicly profess themselves shocked-shocked-shocked. "What you read about the President makes it impossible to respect him," George Stephanopoulos told the *New York Post*. But Clinton's "character flaws" were already on full display in 1992, and so was "the cover-up": In the candid documentary *The War Room*, Stephanopoulos himself is shown threatening a caller who claims to have compromising information about his man.

I go to maybe four parties a year, but I've heard tons of sexual gossip about President Clinton from people who knew him at Oxford and in law school, from other reporters, from neighborhood politicos. If I am five degrees of separation from someone Monica Lewinsky used to regale with her phone messages back when the President's men were calling her a stalker and a fantasizer, how could people who actually knew him, who moved in his world and worked for him twenty-four hours a day, not know that the President was an energetic philanderer?

Now, thanks to the magic of the Internet, we have a new political term of art: the yuck factor. Kenneth Starr must be betting that "the American people," up until now surprisingly resolute defenders of the public-pubic division of presidential morality, will be grossed out by the particulars of the President's affair with Monica Lewinsky when they see them written down in gynecological black and white. Certainly, commentators have been quick to mock and deride, to profess themselves elaborately puzzled and disgusted by what Jack Newfield of the *New York Post* calls "kinky sex." Adolescent, sure, but kinky? Come on. Aren't journalists supposed to be men and women of the world? The sex acts—or, as the President would have it, nonsex acts—that are supposedly so outré are pretty tame. Not to get too clinical here, a cigar may be an unusual erotic object, but lots of people use toys, purchased or improvised, in their sex play. There's a reason you can buy a vibrator in almost every drugstore in America. Lots of people taste each other's fluids, have sex in the office while others are nearby or while talking on the phone. One friend of mine says his friend Kathy claims men in politics are especially fond of receiving oral favors during phone calls. How does Kathy know? I asked. She used to be "sort of a hooker." It's a big world.

Like the vast majority of "the American people," I'm outraged that the Starr report has publicized the intimate details of the President and Monica Lewinsky's love life. (Of course, I'm fascinated too: You'd have to go to the novels of Philip Roth to find a narrative that more skillfully reveals character through sex.) I don't want to know such things about them because I don't want people to know such things about me. It's that simple. As for sexual harassment, you'll notice nobody's talking about that anymore. The supposed rationale of this whole investigation—if Monica, then Paula—gone in the flash of a thong.

Since this knowledge has been forced upon us, though, the least we can do is resist the heaving tide of sanctimonious flotsam that is sweeping over us. In *Newsweek*, the ever-clueless Dan Quayle compares the President's affair to a high school principal sleeping with a student—never mind that the President is not a principal, the White House is not a high school and Monica Lewinsky is not a student. In the *Daily News*, Letty Cottin Pogrebin calls on Hillary Clinton to "show us how a woman of dignity responds to personal humiliation"— not by getting a divorce, a decision the entire nation could understand and many women would cheer, but by lecturing him publicly on fidelity and citing her commitment to her marriage as proof of her superior family values! This is feminism? And what about the ubiquitous handwringing about the President as a poor "role model" and fussing over how to keep the kids away from the evening news? As if ordinary people model themselves on a President. And as if the real stuff of children's nightmares, the luridly made-up face of the murdered JonBenet Ramsey, were not on display at every checkout counter.

Of course, you could say that what goes around comes around. Clinton signed the Personal Responsibility Act, which forces poor women to name the fathers of their children as a condition of receiving welfare. Where was his concern for sexual privacy then? The same bill offered states $50 million annually for classes in abstinence—not birth control, not sex ed—for poor women. Clinton signed the Defense of Marriage Act, and has presided over the ousting of record numbers of lesbians and gays from the military. He fired Joycelyn Elders for talking about masturbation. He's in a poor position to rally the forces of sexual tolerance.

Can anything good come of Sexgate? Less respect for the presidency would be nice, and never has the case for abolishing the ridiculous "job" of being First Lady looked so persuasive. Short of that, we can look forward to a grand public airing of dirty laundry that will leave family values bigots of both parties looking pretty foolish. Dan Burton, scourge of Clinton, adulterous father of an out-of-wedlock child? Helen Chenoweth, militia pinup and sexsmearer of political opponents, a fornicating would-be home-wrecker? When Bill Kristol tells CNN that Republicans are more moral than Democrats because they commit adultery with women closer to their own age, you know that the self-appointed guardians of the nation's hearths are quaking in their boots about the revelations still to come. Well, they asked for it.

READING REFLECTIONS

1. What is the Personal Responsibility Act and for what purpose does Pollitt mention it?
2. What is Pollitt's attitude toward President Clinton?
3. Based on Pollitt's editorial and other media coverage of President Clinton, how do you think such coverage has changed? Would such coverage have been possible thirty years ago?
4. On what basis does Pollitt question the supposed "shocked" reaction of both politicians and the general public about Clinton's actions?
5. Answer Pollitt's concluding question: "Can anything good come of Sexgate?"

JUST DIFFERENT, THAT'S ALL

Serena

What is a family? Serena speaks about her mother, who's "just different," in her status as a lesbian raising her daughter with an extended community of women contributing to Serena's personal development. Sensing that others are not so tolerant of her mother's chosen lifestyle, Serena challenges us to broaden our more narrow definitions of what a family is or can be.

In a sensitive, articulate response, seven-year-old Serena considers what it is like to have a lesbian mother and to live without a father figure, concluding that it's "Just Different, That's All." This narrative originally appeared in a 1990 volume titled Different Mothers and represents the changing image of the family today.

Serena, "Just Different, That's All," in *Different Mothers: Sons and Daughters of Lesbians Talk about Their Lives*, ed. Louise Rafkin (Pittsburgh: Cleis Press, 1990), pp. 549–51. Copyright © 1990 by Louise Rafkin. Reprinted with the permission of the publishers.

I'm seven and a half and I live in Albany, California. I'm about to go into second grade. I live with my mother now, but other times I've lived with lots of women. My mom's a nurse. I take kung-fu and want to be a therapist when I get older. I enjoy telling stories.

I started knowing my mother was different when I was five and I started school. A lot of people there were straight, and my mother started to talk to me about how she was different. But it wasn't until I started first grade that I really realized things. Nothing was really different, but my mom started to ask me what I felt about her being a lesbian mother, because a lot of people weren't lesbian mothers. I asked my mom what a lesbian was, and she said it was like, instead of a man and woman being together, it was two women that were in love. Then I knew what a lesbian was.

I knew it was different to be a lesbian, but it's really hard to think about. I brought this book to first grade for my sharing day. It's called *Many Mommies*. My teacher had this whole big talk about it. She talked about all different kinds of families. Then she read the book to everyone and told me it was a really great book. A couple kids said it was a good book, but no one said anything else.

Now I know a few other kids who have lesbian moms, and this makes me feel better. I know a lot of lesbian women, but not a lot of lesbian moms. Lesbian moms seem different than married women. It seems like married women get a lot more help; they don't have to work so much. Their husbands go to work and so they get to stay home with the kids. When I go to kids' houses who have a mom and a dad, it seems like they're really rich, like they have a lot of money.

Maybe it seems easier to be married, but then that might be hard because maybe straight women get in fights with their husbands a lot. My mom works all the time, and I wonder if maybe she had a husband she could stay home with me in the summer and I wouldn't have to go away to my grandparents'.

When I go to my grandparents' for the summer I get spoiled. We have ice cream all the time. But it's hard because we can't really . . . you see, my grandma and grandpa are kind of mad that my mom is not with a man and that everybody else is married. They don't even like saying the word lesbian. They don't talk about it, but my mom talks about it and she told me they didn't like it. I don't like the way they feel about her.

They feel that women should be with men. So do most of my aunts and uncles. They don't tell me this stuff, but grownups keep quiet about things like that. They don't think children should hear that kind of stuff, or maybe they don't think kids should know about different types of families. Maybe they think their family is the way all families are supposed to be. Or maybe they're embarrassed. Maybe I should send this book to the whole family!

But you know, when I was visiting my uncle, he would sit there at the dinner table and talk about business. Business, business, business. I got kind of bored talking about business at dinner. When I go out with my mom for dinner we talk about kung-fu, or sometimes we talk about my mom being a lesbian mother. It's more interesting.

I like having lots of friends who are lesbians; they take care of me and take me places. When I lived with a bunch of lesbian women, I liked coming home because there was always someone there. I have a couple of men friends who are really nice guys. Sometimes I feel like I kind of miss out on some stuff, but I like having a lesbian mother. Sometimes I like being different. Sometimes I feel special being different. Other times I wish my mom was married and that I had a dad. It depends.

It seems like everyone who has a dad also has a brother or a sister. It seems like lesbian mothers usually have one kid. But maybe it's better they only have one kid; it's less to handle. Sometimes when I want somebody to play with, I wish I had a brother or sister. Other times I'm glad I'm an only kid. There's nobody to step on my sandcastles when I make them! Maybe if I had a brother we'd fight a lot. My mom is happy she didn't have seven kids like her mom did.

I don't tell other kids about my mom. At school it kind of bothers me because when we play or tell stories, there's always a mom and a dad. There's never a mom and a mom or a dad and a dad—always just a mom and a dad. Some kids ask me who is my dad, and why I don't live with him. I don't really know how to explain it to them. I say I don't really have a dad, but then they say that's impossible. So see, it's like they don't believe me or I have to pretend I have a dad because I feel like I have to have one.

What really bothers me is when my friends come over and then they get into this whole divorce thing. They ask if my parents are divorced or what. I say yes, but then they ask me if I know my dad. So I tell them no, not really. Then they ask who he is, and what does he do, and I hate that. I really don't like it. But then they only talk about it for a couple seconds and then they want to play something. They don't want to talk about dad stuff for very long.

Sometimes I ask my mom about my dad but . . . you see, I wonder about him. I don't know where he is. I don't think my mom knows either. It's just hard to know that other kids have dads. Everybody else has a dad.

My mom has had a couple relationships with other women, but I didn't realize it at the very time. I just thought that we were sleeping over at their house, or they were sleeping over. It's really okay with me, but sometimes I like just being with her and nobody else. I like spending alone time with my mom. I like living with just my mom, but I wish it was in a house, not an apartment. In this apartment I have to be really quiet, and I don't enjoy being quiet.

When I grow up I want to live with someone; I don't know if I want to get married and I don't know if I want to have kids. It seems like you need a lot of money to have kids. Sometimes I feel strange having a lesbian mom; sometimes it's hard, and sometimes it's just different. It's good to have all kinds of families. My mom is the best mom in the world and I want that to be in this book.

READING REFLECTIONS

1. Seven-year-old Serena discusses life with her lesbian mother, pointing out pros and cons of her family situation. How similar or different do you think her childhood is to that of other children her age?

2. How did Serena start to know her mother was "different"? Is this something she should know?
3. What aspects of more traditional families does Serena claim to miss?
4. Why does Serena not want to tell others about her family situation?
5. Family units such as Serena's do not usually exist in media portrayals. What factors are keeping such portrayals off television?

TV'S ANTI-FAMILIES: MARRIED . . . WITH MALAISE

Josh Ozersky

Josh Ozersky quotes The Simpsons *creator Matt Groening who describes the show as a "mutant Ozzie and Harriet," a reference to the popular 1950s TV family with real-life couple Ozzie and Harriet Nelson and their two teenage sons. Ozersky himself terms such mutant families as represented by the Simpsons and former Fox favorite* Married . . . with Children *as "anti-families," a commentary on the role of the exalted role of the family in American media culture, all too often a picture-perfect model of perfect parents and perfect children.*

Josh Ozersky, whose work on popular culture has appeared in magazines from Seventeen *to the* Washington Times, *analyzes the range of profamily versus antifamily values on today's television, a gap between* Father Knows Best *and* The Simpsons *that represents society's ambivalence toward the status of the family. As Ozersky concludes in this article originally published in* Tikkun *magazine, such portrayals of antifamily can "undermine the stability of real families" in their ability to lower expectations of real families whose lives are meant to seem better in comparison to their television counterparts.*

It's an odd thing when a cartoon series is praised as one of the most trenchant and "realistic" programs on TV, but there you are. Never mind the Cosby-size ratings: if merchandising says anything about American culture, and it does,

Josh Ozersky, "TV's Anti-families: Married . . . with Malaise," *Tikkun* 6, no. 1 (January–February 1991): 11–14, 92–93. Copyright © 1991. Reprinted with the permission of *Tikkun: A Bimonthly Jewish Critique of Politics, Culture, and Society.* Subscriptions: $31 from *Tikkun,* 26 Fell Street, San Francisco, CA 94102.

then America was utterly infatuated with "The Simpsons" in 1990. "Utterly," because unlike other big winners in the industry such as the Teenage Mutant Ninja Turtles and the New Kids on the Block, the Simpsons graced not only t-shirts for the clamoring young, but t-shirts (and sweatshirts and posters and mugs) that went out in droves to parents, who rivaled kids for viewer loyalty.

The animated series chronicles the life of the Simpson family: father Homer, who works in a nuclear power plant and reads bowling-ball catalogs; mother Marge, with her blue beehive hairdo and raspy voice; misunderstood-bohemian daughter Lisa; baby Maggie; and bratty son Bart, the anti-everything star of the series. Bart appeals to kids, who see a flattering image of themselves, and to their parents, who, even as they identify with Bart against his lumpkin parents, enjoy Bart's caricature of their own children, with his incomprehensible sloganeering ("Don't have a cow, man!") and bad manners. Nor, tellingly, has the popularity of the show stopped with the white mainstream: a black Bart soon began to turn up in unlicensed street paraphernalia.

In the first of the unauthorized shirts, Bart was himself, only darkened. The novelty soon wore off, however, and in successive generations Bart found himself ethnicized further: "Air Bart" had him flying toward a basketball hoop exclaiming "In your face, home boy." Another shirt had Bart leering at zaftig black women, loutishly yelling "Big Ole Butt!" at their retreating figures. And in later versions, Bart has a gold tooth, a razor cut, and an angry snarl—the slogan "I got the power!" juts overhead in an oversized balloon.

The "I got the power!" Bart is barely recognizable, disfigured by rancor. But even more jarring than his appearance is his vitriol, so out of keeping with the real Bart's laid-back, ironic demeanor—an endemic condition among TV characters. The naked discontent on that shirt is jarring, disturbing. It lacks the light touch. TV does not—but then the playful suppression of unhappiness has always been one of TV's great strengths; and in its latest, ugliest form, it subtly discourages alarm at the decline of the family, its own complicity in that decline, and the resulting effects on a disintegrating society.

The success in the last few seasons of new, "anti-family" sitcoms, such as Fox's "Married . . . with Children" and "The Simpsons" and ABC's "Roseanne," began a trend that has made waves in television. "Whether it's the influence of Bart Simpson and those cheeky sitcoms from Fox," wrote *TV Guide* in September, "or ABC's artsy anti-soap 'Twin Peaks,' unconventionality is in; slick and safe are out." The "cheeky sitcoms" began that trend. "Roseanne," about an obese and abrasive proletarian mom, and "Married . . . with Children," a half hour of pure viciousness, represented along with "The Simpsons" a new development of the situation comedy, TV's definitive genre. Each program (as well as its inevitable imitators) focuses on a family marked by visual styles and characterization as bleak and miserable as those of former TV families had been handsome or cheerful.

The innovation received a lot of attention in the mass media, most of it favorable. Richard Zoglin in *Time* hailed the "real-world grit these shows provide," produced psychological authorities, and quoted Barbara Ehrenreich's wide-eyed "Zeitgeist Goddess" piece in the *New Republic*. The *New York Times*'s Caryl Rivers wrote approvingly of the new realism, although she noted perfunctorily that gays, minorities, and women were less visible than they should have been. What all sides had in common, however, was a willingness to point out the improvement over other forms of TV. "The anti-family shows aren't against the family, exactly, just scornful of the romantic picture TV has often painted of it," Zoglin pointed out. "We're like a mutant Ozzie and Harriet," Simpsons creator Matt Groening boasted in *Newsweek*, which went on to point out that the show was "hardly the stuff of Saturday-morning children's programming." "Thankfully, we are past the days of perfect Mom and all-wise Dad and their twin beds," wrote the *New York Times*'s Rivers, speaking for reviewers and feature writers everywhere. And this was prior to the advent of the "unconventional" mystery serial "Twin Peaks," which still has feature writers striving for superlatives to describe its "innovations" and "departures."

This unanimous juxtaposition of the "anti-families" to the stern TV households of yesteryear is a specious comparison designed to amuse and flatter. Not as the result of any conspiracy—writers in the commercial mass media generally write to please, and what they say is true enough if you have as your entire frame of reference the past and present of TV. But far from the "authenticity" it pretends to, the "grit" for the new shows is merely an improved artifice, a challenge only to the verisimilitude of art directors and casting companies. By pretending to realism, TV only extends its own hegemony, in which every standard of comparison points back to another sham. "Gosh," gushed *TV Guide* of Bart, "can you imagine Bud Anderson being so . . . *disrespectful* to Dad?" As if the lead of "Father Knows Best" had only recently become a figure of fun.

It is through this sort of pseudo–self-deprecation that TV tries to ingratiate itself with Americans, who in an age marked by pervasive irony want to run with the hare and hunt with the hound—to feel superior to TV and yet keep watching it. TV offers this target audience an abundance of self-images that will permit them this trick. The target viewers may be enlightened, making the "choice of a new generation" by seeing through "My Little Margie," or avant-garde, on the cutting edge, for watching "Twin Peaks," which, like "Hill Street Blues" before it, supposedly "breaks all the rules." They are in utter harmony with the very mechanics of TV production, which has no secrets from us, as we know from David Letterman's insider gags, such as the "Late Night Danger Cam."

As for discrediting paternalistic authority figures, Mark Crispin Miller has pointed out that the imperious Dads of fifties TV, now such a rich source of burlesque, were overturned by a maturing medium very early on. The "grim old abstinence" of the Puritan patriarch stood in the way of the "grim new self-indulgence" of consumer culture and was hence banished. Dads turned into "pleasant nullities," like Dick York in "Bewitched" and Timothy Busfield in "thirtysomething," or unenlightened butts of knowing and self-flattering jokes, like Archie Bunker and Homer Simpson.

The downfall of Dad, however, saw no concomitant rise of Mom or the kids. Rather, it was advertisers and corporations that benefited from the free-spending self-indulgence of all parties, liberated from patriarchal discipline. And the networks, of course, cashed in and sold advertisers airtime. In the world beyond the screen, the family has disintegrated into epidemic divorces and deteriorating marriages, latchkey children, and working parents reduced to spending "quality time" with their children, as though they were hospital visitors or the lovelorn spouses of soldiers on leave. Meanwhile, the TV world—not only in sitcoms but in endless "special reports" and talk shows and (particularly) commercials—insists again and again that we are hipper, more "open," more enlightened, and facing changing "relationships" in a new and better way. Mom, often divorced and underpaid, has her new "independence," a standard theme of programming, and Dad and the kids, faced with other losses and hardships, are offered the bold new "grittiness" of prime-time entertainment. TV has absorbed the American family's increasing sense of defeat and estrangement and presented it as an ironic in-joke.

This dynamic is seldom noted, although the mere *fact* of watching is noted by critics and commentators everywhere, and nowhere more visibly than on TV itself. The opening credits of "The Simpsons" end with the family, assembled at the end of the day, jumping mutely into fixed position on the sofa and clicking on the TV set. This absorption of criticism is and has been, except for sheer distraction, TV's greatest weapon against criticism. The transformation of the hearth into an engine of negation, after all, should have caused *some* stir. And so it would have, if TV were no more than the yammering salesman it has caricatured itself as in satirical moments. But, as Miller demonstrates, TV has never shown us TV; rather, it shows itself to us as a laughable, absurd, and harmless entity, much like the characters on its shows.

When not played for background noise—whooping Indians in older shows, unctuous game-show hosts or newsmen in newer ones—depictions of the TV set on TV itself render it invisible and omnipresent. TV itself, its conventions and production, may be the crucial point of reference for the sophisticated appeal it enjoys today, but the set as household centerpiece is seldom seen, and then only as a joke, as on "The Simpsons." Instead, the set most often poses as a portal to the outer world: hence its constant stream of images that tease us with alluring beaches, blue waters, busy city streets. Even in its living rooms, where we know its presence to be inescapable, the TV is often missing. This effect is accomplished by a simple trick of photography: when the family watches TV in "All in the Family," in "Good Times," in "Married . . . with Children," etc., the scene is shot from behind the TV set. As the family sits facing us, with the screen nowhere in sight, the illusion exists for a moment that the TV really is, if not a portal, then a mirror or reflection of us. A close look at these families, and at our own, soon banishes this impression. We are not like these TV families at all; and the TV set is obtrusive, ideological, and tendentious.

When speaking of the "anti-family" sitcoms, most of the commentators seem to have in mind "Married . . . with Children." No other show so luridly plays up the sheer negativity of the current "authenticity" trend, nor does any other show do so with such predictable regularity. The series portrays the Bundys, a lower-middle-class family with two children and a dog. Father Al (Ed O'Neill) only has "knotted bowels" to show for his life supporting the family. Peg (Katey Sagal) is Al's castrating wife. There is also the inevitable sharp-tongued teenage son, who singles out for special heckling his brainless and sleazy sister. The relentlessly ironic quality of a happy family turned thoroughly upside-down flatters the audience for their enlightenment (no "Donna Reed," this) even as it invites them to enjoy the ongoing frenzy of spite in which the show indulges. And frenzy is indeed the word. Every member of the family despises everyone else, and any given program consists of little more than continuous insults, interspersed with snide loathing or occasional expressions of despair.

FATHER (to son): Did I ever tell you not to get married?
SON: Yeah, Dad.
FATHER: Did I ever tell you not to become a shoe salesman?
SON: Yeah, Dad.
FATHER: Well, then I've told you everything I know.

This sort of resigned and paralytic discontent dominates the tone of "Married . . . with Children"; it lacks even the dim rays of hope that occasionally lifted Ralph Kramden's or Riley's gloomy existence. Every show is devoted to a new kind of humiliation: to earn extra money, Al becomes a burger-flipper; when son Bud falls victim to a practical joke perpetrated by an old flame his slutty sister Kelly comes to his defense by crucifying the girl against a locker; wife Peg belittles Al's manhood in front of strangers. Again and again, the unrelenting negativity of the show finds new ways to expand, purifying itself of any nonironic, positive content. Lovebird neighbors intended for contrast in the first season soon divorce, adding to the show's already vast reserve of bitterness. Christina Applegate, the young actress who plays Kelly, filled out during the first two years, adding a missing element of nasty prurience to the show.

The result of this hermetic exclusion of all warmth, say a number of apologists for the show, is positive: "With these new programs," says Barbara Cadow, a psychologist at USC, "we see we're doing all right by comparison." Yet at the same time, it is the very "realism" of these shows that won them praise again and again. This "realism" appeals to a cynical element in us—no one would ever admit to resembling Roseanne Barr or her family, but they are eminently "realistic" portraits of the losers next door. Roseanne Barr is shrewish and miserable to the point of self-parody, and this is seen as the great strength of her series. "Mom" (who Roseanne, it is assumed, represents) "is no longer interested in being a human sacrifice on the altar of 'pro-family' values," says Barbara Ehrenreich in the *New Republic*.

The praise of the same style of TV both for its realism and for its horrific exaggeration, while apparently contradictory, is based on a common assumption. In each case, the pervasive unhappiness and derision on TV sitcoms is assumed to be a reflection, albeit a negative one, of the unhappiness of real families. Cadow assumes that it is caricature, and Ehrenreich that it is a manifesto, but neither woman doubts that both shows offer some kind of corrective to real life for their viewers, and that this explains their popularity. This congratulatory view of hit TV shows contains a fundamental error: the old network executive's rationale that TV "gives people what they want," in response to their Nielsen-measured "choice."

The concentration of mass media into a few corporate hands invalidates that idea even more today than in the past. Given TV's entirely corporate nature, it is unreasonable to assume that the channels are referenda, since almost every channel, at least until recently, offered almost identical options. What succeeds with the public makes it, yes. But that "success" is determined by TV's agenda—which now, as always, is more than selling dog biscuits. Consumption must be encouraged psychologically; sectors and tendencies in American society have to be identified and exploited. "Since the major broadcasters are no longer winning the big numbers," observes *TV Guide*, "they're now fighting for the youthful demographics that bring in the highest revenues. That's why everyone is hyping bold, hip shows."

Of course, the success of a culture based on mass consumption depends on the creation of boundless needs; boundless needs presuppose boundless discontent. Boundless discontent must begin with the family, where social patterns are first internalized. If, latchkey in hand, TV can flatter a kinless and dispossessed child into adulthood and at the same time kid his or her parents about it, perfect consumers are thereby made. The family becomes a breeding ground for easygoing and independent citizens of the marketplace, transported beyond the inner struggle and deep feeling of family life, and bound in their place by the laws of supply and demand, consumer "choices," and a continual negation of their truest selves.

By presenting unhappy families to viewers, TV achieves many gains. First, as Cadow rightly points out, mocking the traditional family does flatter the distorted family of our times. However, this does not necessarily lift spirits. On the contrary, it lowers expectations; it stupefies discontent instead of healing it. "Married . . . with Children" is the prototype of this strategy. The petty or profound resentments of real families do not rival those of the Bundys, but then neither does their ability to punish and humiliate each other. By making our problems "seem all right by comparison," the series trivializes them rather than taking them seriously. It in fact worsens them by its counsel of despair.

Secondly, the dysfunctional TV family aids advertisers in their perennial quest for credibility by creating a supersaturated atmosphere of irony, which atrophies our ability to believe in anything. Commercials themselves work on a principle of pseudo-rebelliousness. Burger King—now officially touted by the Simpsons—proudly sports the "radical" motto, "Sometimes you've gotta break the rules." Swallowing these giant absurdities relies not on credulity, but on an ironic, self-assured disbelief. "Roseanne," with its trademark sarcasm, and "Twin Peaks," with its tongue-in-cheek grotesqueries, are good examples.

Third, and most insidious, is the stability of TV's dysfunctional families, and their passive acceptance of their fate. A successful cast is the source of "ensemble acting," which has been the formula for success for some time now on TV. Since TV characters now move in herds, they do not get divorced, move out, have devastating affairs, or anything else that would disrupt the fabric of the show's format. Implicitly, these shows assure us that family life is largely a nightmare, but one that is self-perpetuating and only requires handling with a deft, protective irony. This irony, the antithesis of deep feeling, is the essential assault on the family and on all human relationships, reducing them to problems of managerial acumen. Thus, while remaining intact in their own impoverished world, sitcom families undermine the stability of real families, discrediting the embarrassingly earnest, often abject bonds of kin while hermetically sealing themselves off from the possibility of familial collapse. And this while they consume the increasingly rare time in which American families are actually together.

"The Simpsons," the most popular of the group and certainly the least ironic and "anti-family," is TV's most effective reinforcer. This paradox begins with the fact that the show is a cartoon: with their yellow skin, bulging eyes, and comical motions, the Simpsons are funny just to look at, and hence relieve the audience of the need to continually jeer at them. The Bundy family of "Married . . . with Children," like all sitcom characters, aspire to the televisual purity of cartoon characters, but are stuck in rubbery bags of protoplasm with nothing but one-liners and a laugh track to hide behind. The Simpsons, oddly, are freer than other TV families to act human.

And so they do. There is an element of family loyalty and principle to be found in the Simpsons, often combined with witty and valid social criticism. Brother Bart and sister Lisa petulantly demand of baby Maggie to "come to the one you love most," to which the infant responds by crawling lovingly to the TV. Or again, when father Homer's sinister boss inquires disbelievingly, "You'd give up a job and a raise for your principles?" Homer responds (with almost none of the usual sitcom character's irony), "When you put it that way, it does sound far-fetched—but that's the lunk you're lookin' at!" "Hmm," the boss replies. "You're not as dumb as you look. Or sound. Or as our best testing indicates."

With pointed jokes such as these, "The Simpsons" might prompt us to conclude the same about its vast audience. The harmlessness of these jokes can be taken for granted; no one who watches TV is going to stop because they see TV criticized. We criticize it ourselves as a matter of course. On the contrary, we feel flattered, and less inclined to stop watching.

And we are that much less inclined to object to the continuing presence of unsafe workplaces, vast corporations, the therapy racket, and all the other deserving targets of the Simpsons' harmless barbs. The genial knowingness of shows like "The Simpsons" subverts criticism through an innocuous pseudo-criticism, just as the familial discontents of TV shows subvert alarm at graver discontents in real life. Criticism is further weakened by the show's irony, which although less than some other programs is still pervasive and fundamental to its humor. No one in an ironic show can get too far out of line. For example, in one episode, misunderstood Lisa meets that well-worn figure of Caucasian lore, the wise and virtuous old colored bluesman, ever ready to act as mentor to young white people in their search for self-knowledge. "The Simpsons" is far too hip to hand us such a hackneyed cliché. The Virtuous Old Blues Man is as empty a conceit as the Perfect Family—so on the show, he is named "Bleeding Gums Murphy." (Why? "I haven't brushed my teeth in thirty years, that's why.") In place of the usual soulful laments, he sings the "I Don't Have an Italian Suit Blues."

Such undercutting is typical of TV as a whole; attempts to transcend the flattened-out emotional landscape of TV are almost invariably punished by some droll comeuppance. But since as bizarre cartoons there is little need to belittle them, the Simpsons get a little more than most, and are occasionally allowed moments of earnestness unmitigated by the selfishness of "thirtysomething," the weirdness of "Twin Peaks," or the inevitable "comic relief"—the stock entrances of deadpan tots and witty oldsters, etc.—used to terminate the maudlin embraces of non-animated sitcomites. None of this is to be had on "The Simpsons," but the picture it presents is still fundamentally hopeless. The Simpsons are basically boobs, and their occasional bursts of tenderness or insight are buried under biting irony and superior, if affectionate, mockery. More than any of the other "anti-family" shows, "The Simpsons" seems to come close to our lives; more than any of the other shows, as a result, it commits us to a shared vision of pessimism and self-deprecation.

Because the TV screen is neither a mirror, reflecting ourselves paralyzed in chairs in front of it, nor a window, through which we observe the antics of distant players, it is an implicit invitation to participate in a vision of "society" largely designed to flatter us in sinister ways, manipulate our attention, and commit us to the status quo. In discrediting "yesterday's" family values in its various "breakthrough" shows (ostensibly defining "A Different World" for us, as the title of one series has it), TV seeks only to impose its own values—which is to say, the values of the marketplace. Bart Simpson, master sneerer, is the prototype of the modern series character who—by the social scripts of TV—reflects us. Small, ridiculous, and at the same time admirable for his sarcasm and enlightened self-interest, Bart is the child of the culture of TV, his parents mere intermediaries.

Paradoxically, that is why the most powerless sector of American society has adopted him, fitting him with their own wishful slogan—"I got the power!" Though black Bart's anger may be incongruous with TV, his proclamation is not, since TV is so successful an invitation to impotent posturing. At the moment, the rage of the underclass cannot be appropriated by TV, yet in black Bart, in the fatal joining of ironic hipness and earnest wrath, we see perhaps a glimpse of the future (and in fact there are already a spate of new black shows—e.g., "Fresh Prince of Bel Air," "In Living Color"), "I got the power!" says black

Bart. But in the world of the TV family, no one has power. Empty fantasies of might, like cynical, knowing giggles, are terminal symptoms of our capitulation to TV's vision.

Life outside of that vision *is* ugly and is becoming uglier as ties, familial and societal, dissolve and decay. But the only power we do have is the power of our own real selves to reject the defensive posture of materialist or ironist or cynic, and the soullessness of TV's "hip, bold," anti-life world. Bart and his aspirants exist in that world, and their example serves only to impoverish us.

READING REFLECTIONS

1. Ozersky refers to the Simpsons and the Bundys as "anti-families." What are the characteristics of these antifamilies, and how do you account for their continuing popularity with viewers? Watch an episode of one of these shows for yourself and compare your reactions to Ozersky's.
2. Taking Ozersky's article into consideration, select one of the major television networks and survey the image of the family in all its prime-time "family-oriented" television shows. Are there any "variations on a theme"? What are the differences in racial or marital status in the various programs?
3. What is Ozersky's attitude toward the antifamily?
4. According to Ozersky and others, how is consumer culture responsible for "disintegrating paternalistic authority figures"?
5. Based on Ozersky's observations, create a survey for your classmates about who is a good TV parent and why. On what criteria are such assessments based?

MY FATHER'S KEEPER

Richard Pirozzi

Richard Pirozzi's story of role reversal is not uncommon for today's middle-aged children of elderly parents, given the aging of the American population and the ways in which this factor redefines and complicates the more simplistic notion of the nuclear family in our culture.

Richard Pirozzi, "My Father's Keeper," *The Humanist* 56, no. 2 (March–April 1996): 47–48.

Richard Pirozzi is an associate professor of English and the humanities at Passaic County Community College and the author of several text-books on reading and study skills. In this "First Person" commentary from The Humanist, *Pirozzi comments on caring for his elderly father and how such care tested his patience and endurance as a son forced to become a guardian.*

We buried my mother on my twenty-fourth wedding anniversary, after her short battle with pancreatic cancer. She succumbed to the disease a few days after surgery in the early morning hours during her stay at a hospital in southern New Jersey. Although I was prepared as much as one possibly can be for the departure of a mother, I cannot make the same claim regarding the care of my 85-year-old father. That very year he had survived open-heart surgery only to lose his wife of over 50 years. His feelings for her are best expressed by the words he uttered tearfully the day she died: "I have lost everything."

In fact, my mother was the centerpiece of the entire family. At a very early age, I discovered that, if you wanted to get anything done in our house, you simply had to know just one word: *Jo.* That was what everyone called my mother instead of Josephine, which was her formal name. She did everything for my father—from serving as his personal secretary to satisfying his every need. It became so extreme that, as he watched television, he would occasionally use a bell to beckon her when he needed something, which was often. I grew up wondering if my mother was a wife or a slave left over from pre–Civil War days. Not only would she be an impossible act to follow, no one even wanted to try.

There was little time for me to grieve her loss because we were all too busy trying, unsuccessfully, to ease my father's pain. My brother, who is my only sibling, lives with his family in Georgia, so it became painfully obvious almost immediately who would be given the responsibility of looking after my father. It was both a necessary and logical arrangement because at the time he was still living in southern New Jersey, while my home was an hour away in the northern part of the state.

Caring for my father for the next three years would be an experience that had moments of hilarity, moments of frustration, and moments of great sadness. Most of the lighter times were a result of his pursuit of romance, which came as a complete shock to the rest of the family. It seems he came to the conclusion that he was irresistible to women of all ages. This phase really began right after he moved to my neighborhood in order to be closer to me. I enrolled him in the senior citizens day-care center, where he met a woman whom *he* thought was to be his next true love. It did not make a bit of difference to him that she was 40 years old and already had a boyfriend. Much to everyone's chagrin, he tried unsuccessfully to talk her out of the relationship by extolling his own unlimited virtues. It was not a coincidence that she happened to be a nurse who could provide him with the necessary medical services. His affection for her explains, in no small part, why he would often claim not to be feeling well while at the center, so that he could be sent to the nurse's office. Believe me, I received telephone calls about it.

Next on his list was a 24-year-old whom he politely told one day that her impending marriage would be over in a year because her prospective husband was not in the same league as he. (She took a chance and went through with the wedding anyway.) Virtually all of the housekeepers I hired to clean his apartment were, according to my father, desperately trying to corral him. He called them all "bimbos" and pretended to express no real interest, although he did enjoy their supposed attention. I guess he did not want to mix business with pleasure. Then he went through a series of waitresses, ranging in age from 16 to 30, before finally settling for a 70-year-old woman whom he had met at the senior citizen residence where he lived for a few months. In fact, we went on a double date with them—the highlight of which was his attempt to kiss her goodbye. The problem was that she did not realize what he was attempting to do!

As startling as these escapades were, at least they involved real people. There was the time my father, in trying to find a bathroom in a restaurant, began to have a conversation with his reflection in a full-length mirror. Because of very poor eyesight, he mistook his reflection for a lovely woman (which must explain why he had the most radiant smile on his face). I waited a moment to help him, not out of indifference or cruelty but because I had not seen him so happy in years. Love does that to people.

There were, of course, the bad times as well that go along with aging and the loss of a lifelong partner. The obvious emptiness that he experienced at major family events, the endless appointments with doctors, the various tests that needed to be taken, and the general deterioration of my father's body and mind made his final years anything but "golden." On top of all this, I came to the sad realization that, when you are old and failing, no one seems to want to be with you anymore. I will never forget how one of my father's business associates turned around and walked in the other direction when he saw him coming; how members of his family disappeared, forgetting all the things that he had done for them through the years; and how even his sons sometimes thought of our own needs over his. There was the time, for example, when he showed up at my house on New Year's Eve with his blanket because he did not want to sleep at the senior citizen residence. I had plans, so I angrily talked him into going back there to be with the other residents. Later, I found out that he had had an argument with the head nun earlier in the day. I can never forgive myself for not letting him sleep over that night. Unfortunately, there would be no chance to redeem myself, for it would be my father's last New Year's Eve.

My father was not happy at the residence because he did not like the head nun. In fact, he called her Sister Baccala to her face. (For those who do not know, *baccala* is the Italian word for dried cod fish, which has the most abominable smell.) But my father's dislike for her did not extend to the other nuns who worked there, to one of whom he proposed marriage. Apparently, he thought it was time to liberalize the rules of the Catholic church.

The end came almost three years to the day after my mother's death. Those intervening years saw a rapid decline in energy and spirit. A benign brain tumor called a meningioma took from May to September to kill my father. By that time, he was emaciated from weight loss: a mere shadow of the man I had affectionately called Charlie. But even in the final days, he managed to humor us twice more by coming out of a near comatose state to yell, "Get rid of her!" when he heard me mention one of the housekeeper's names, and by defiantly holding his mouth tightly closed so the nurse could not suction it out. He could still make us laugh even when he wasn't trying to be facetious.

Those years as my father's keeper were difficult ones which have had a lasting effect on me. Although several people were very helpful, I was primarily responsible for his well-being, serving as his part-time moving agent, financial adviser and manager, nurse, transportation planner, chauffeur, and a host of other roles. Because of his feeble condition, I was forced to do things for him that I never dreamed I would have to do, including helping him to dress and cleaning him up after the inevitable accidents in the bathroom.

The obvious role reversal bothered me a great deal then, and it still does now whenever I think about it. My patience was tried to the limit, and my emotions were on a nonstop roller-coaster. There were times when I was angry, times when I was depressed, and many times when I felt guilty for not doing more. And yet, through it all, there were still humorous moments that will stay in my memory forever. In the end, perhaps they should serve as my father's legacy.

READING REFLECTIONS

1. Why is it important to know the relationship between Richard Pirozzi's parents, which he explains at the beginning of the article?
2. In what ways does Pirozzi experience a "role reversal" in caring for his aging father?
3. Is Pirozzi's experience becoming more common in today's families?
4. How does such an example contrast with examples from your own family experience or even media examples of adult child and parent relationships?
5. Contrast Pirozzi's real experience with the portrayal of elderly parents in the media, such as Grandpa Simpson or the father character on *Frasier*. What do such portrayals suggest about the role of the senior citizens in contemporary culture?

UNITING GENERATIONS

Melinda Machado

Extended local families are common in many cultures, particularly within the Hispanic community. As the Hispanic family continues to grow and change within the larger socioeconomic and global culture, traditional closeness and importance of family are still going strong. Melinda Machado profiles a number of Hispanic families of varying lifestyles, focusing on the important role of reunions as a way of maintaining cultural and family unity.

Melinda Machado, a freelance writer based in Washington, D.C., is a regular contributor to Hispanic, *a national magazine devoted to social and economic issues facing the Hispanic community and from which this article is taken. Machado's portrayal of several Mexican American families represents both the traditional and the changing nature of today's Hispanic families as they attempt to maintain cultural unity.*

When the Vela family reunion brought relatives from almost every state and six countries together, even Elvis showed up. Michael Chapa, an Elvis impersonator who works in Los Angeles and Las Vegas, helped entertain more than 2,500 of his relatives at what is believed to be the country's largest Hispanic family reunion last summer.

Weddings, baptisms, quinceaneras, birthdays, Christmas, and other holidays are all celebrations that bring families together, strengthening the bonds of shared experiences, faith, and friendships. They are a time to honor the family, gathering relatives from near and far.

Hispanic families are finding themselves spread across the country, after moving away from the neighborhoods they grew up in, to explore education and employment opportunities. To keep distance from breaking family ties, more and more Hispanics are converging at official family reunions.

Moises "Moe" Vela Jr., who recently joined the staff of Secretary of Agriculture Mike Espy in Washington, D.C., attended the Vela family reunion at the Laguna Seca Ranch in Hidalgo County, Texas. The son of the Vela family patriarch, Macedonio Vela, founded the ranch in 1867, planting the first orange trees in the Texas Rio Grande Valley.

"This reunion gave me a sense of what the whole journey of life is about," Vela says. "Our ancestors may not be with us, but these reunions help keep their traditions alive."

Demographic studies show that Hispanic families are larger and younger than many other immigrant groups, often functioning as extended families, with grandparents, aunts, and cousins living in one house or the same neighborhood.

"What the statistics don't tell us is the closeness of the relationship. Hispanic families are very cohesive, spending much time together," says Mercedes Alvarez, vice president and associate research director for BBDO, a New York advertising agency. The agency studied Hispanic neighborhoods through a camera lens. The research found seven commonalities among all Hispanics, one of the strongest of those being the role of the family.

As youngsters in the Texas Rio Grande Valley, Dora Dominguez and her seven brothers and sisters were enveloped in a close-knit clan of *primos* and *tíos*. "But then you grow up, establish your own life, and lose track," says Dominguez, who moved to Michigan with her husband in 1969.

It was a desire to reconnect with her family while her older relatives were still alive that led Dominguez to organize the Sanchez-Zamora family reunion in Mercedes, Texas, last summer. "It became a celebration of family," she says. "We renewed our kinship, met our cousins' children, and they met ours."

Marie Brazil Lopez, of Albuquerque, New Mexico, echoed those sentiments, saying, "Family reunions are all about getting reacquainted. It's the cousins you never see. They become a postcard or a phone call." Lopez helped organize the Espinosa family reunion, celebrating her mother's side of the family.

The Vela family reunion weekend featured a golf tournament, a lunch and fashion show, a barbecue dinner, a dance, and Sunday Mass. A class in family history for children, the Vela family cookbook, and a family directory helped this extended family keep in touch and continue their family traditions.

The Espinosas held a Western celebration with a dinner, dance, and horseback riding for the kids. The Sanchez-Zamora family took over the Mercedes Civic Center for a Tex-Mex barbecue for relatives from Reynosa, Mexico, Michigan, California, and Texas. The dinner included a presentation by each family to introduce their children and describe significant events.

READING REFLECTIONS

1. According to Machado, what cultural and economic factors contribute to the importance of family in Hispanic culture?
2. How has the Hispanic family structure changed in recent years? Are such changes similar within other cultures?
3. Using Machado's article as a model for your questions, interview someone whose family structure is different than your own, an only child, or a

person with a large extended family. Are there differences in the ways such families "bond"?

4. Discuss a ritual in your family history, such as a family reunion or special holiday. How is it similar to or different from those of your classmates or of the families profiled in Machado's article?

5. How do the definitions of your classmates' families and Machado's family compare to your own? How do these competing definitions of family impact the way in which you view your own family structure?

"Family Matters" Activities

READING REACTIONS

1. Apply Josh Ozersky's definition of the antifamily to the portrayals of family in Richard Pirozzi's "My Father's Keeper" or Melinda Machado's "Uniting Generations." How do these nontraditional profiles of family compare to Ozersky's definition?

2. Based on President Clinton's speech on media and the family, what do you think he would have to say about Serena's family unit represented in "Just Different, That's All"?

3. Apply Katha Pollitt's critique of family values rhetoric to Clinton's speech. At what points would she or you find his points ironic or even hypocritical?

CLASSROOM REACTIONS

1. What does family mean to you? Describe your own family and its importance in your life. What television families do you watch regularly? Why do these particular families and their "plots" appeal to you?

2. What is the typical socioeconomic status of the television family? What are typical problems these families face each week and how are they resolved? How do these compare to problems experienced by today's families? Share your observations in a group or in an on-line dialogue with your classmates.

3. Engage in a classroom debate on the role of television in fostering or hindering family values. Use current media examples as part of your argument.

MEDIA CONNECTIONS

1. Survey the image of the American family as represented by a variety of magazines, from *Redbook* to *Good Housekeeping* to *Ebony* and *Parents Magazine.* How are the portrayals similar or different? What conclusions

can you draw about the common image of the American family in mass culture?

2. How do you think the relationship between parents and children has changed over the last thirty years? Watch a currently syndicated television show from the past, such as *Father Knows Best, The Brady Bunch*, or *Leave It to Beaver*, contrasting it to a more contemporary program, such as *Roseanne* or *Home Improvement*. What might any differences suggest about the role of parents in the lives of young people?

3. Using library resources, the Internet, or interviews, research the typical family life within a non-Western culture. What are the relationships between parents and between parents and children? How do such relationships differ from your own family relationships or those of Western cultures?

COMMUNITY INTERACTIONS

1. Go to a place of public entertainment (mall, park, stadium, or movie theater) and interview families about their last family outing. What was the typical type of activity pursued? What type of features can you observe about "typical" American family values?

2. Create a list of television families and ask people to rank them according to their favorites. What reasons do people give and what might this say about their definitions of family?

3. Interview a senior citizen, asking him or her to describe childhood memories of family. How do these memories of family rituals differ from your own, or from those of children today?

Diet Center Ad: Former Fatty Gets New Look.
Diet Center, 1993.

According to Sarah Ferguson, pitch woman for Weight Watchers, the five most flattering words someone can hear are "You've been to Weight Watchers." Unfortunately, this type of advertising responds to an ever-increasingly weight-conscious society that is searching for a quick fix for its ills. This negative advertising that encourages individuals to be dissatisfied with images of themselves if they don't conform to a societal paradigm of perfection is especially evident in the following advertisement that features before and after photos of a woman who lost 114 pounds.

Visit a local weight-loss reduction center and obtain some pamphlets about its products and promises, or speak with a customer representative. What types of images and messages exist within the promotional materials or in the representative's testimonials? What cultural assumptions about body images and appearance exist within these texts?

4

Appearances versus Realities

Even before the days of popular 1950s television shows such as *Leave It To Beaver*, with mother June Cleaver cleaning house in high heels and a pearl necklace while father Ward is away "at work," the mass media often showed specific gender images of women and men. But whether these images conform to the actual lives of women and men, then and now, is what this chapter explores. Indeed, in a 1995 *Oprah* show, Barbara Billingsley, the actress who played June Cleaver for eight years, noted the irony of playing a woman who stayed at home while being a working mother herself. Yet just as an *Oprah* episode may focus on the changing "role" of women, part of Oprah's appeal in the media has been the battle with her weight, something chronicled both in popular tabloids such as the *National Enquirer* and in the *Oprah* show itself, where Oprah often encourages others to make the same progress she has, dropping weight and toning muscle, all with the help of a personal trainer. That Oprah's body image could be the concern of the media and women alike suggests that despite the changing roles of women, our cultural acceptance of gender appearances has a way to go.

Although there have been very clear stereotypes about the image of women in society, it is equally clear from various media images of war, the old West, and today's working world, that men have also felt pressure to conform to images about what they are *supposed* to do and be, all parts of a particular gender appearance. Whether it be the influence of John Wayne's perennial tough-guy cowboy or Harrison Ford's daring Indiana Jones or Sylvester Stallone's muscle man Rambo, the common role for men has been that of a wealthy white American hero—the forever strong, decisive, in-control male. As readings by Gail Dines on black male stereotypes and Alisa Valdes on gay male appearance suggest, men from other cultural groups are negatively impacted by the predominance of this particular image of masculinity in our society. Moreover, these gender images are not just the ones we have seen on television and in the movies; they are found in all aspects of our life, from the toys we played with as children to the advertisements we consume in many popular magazines today, whether it be *GQ* or *Glamour.*

In the case of women, Katharine Greider notes that "the fashion industry is setting out to redesign the female body—from top to bottom," with such products as the WonderBra, which debuted in the United States in 1994, to buttocks enhancers, thigh tamers, and tummy terminators. In a culture that has seen such body control devices as the corset and the girdle come and go, the manufacturing and marketing of these products to women of the 1990s is discomforting, literally and figuratively, as women's bodies still require a physical disciplining. Meanwhile, for men, the image of vigor and health is one long held in our culture as a sign of virility, from the popular GI Joe to the cover of *GQ*. Although the image of women is defined primarily by external appearance, the image of men in our culture is not strictly defined by appearance but more often by activity, be it playing sports or making money. The Diet Center ad we profile captions its before-and-after photos as "Former Fatty Gets New Look," implying that the "after" look for women is a social and psychological reward for those who diet and exercise enough to conform to a thin ideal.

Thus the construction of gender is a complex personal and social process. For women it involves the use of cosmetics and clothing, and in some extreme instances, surgery, to achieve the perfect look. Whereas female plastic surgery is often done in the name of youth and beauty, male plastic surgery is often justified as a corporate necessity, to achieve a youthful, vigorous male image to compete with other executives climbing the corporate ladder. Regardless of the increasing instances of plastic surgery for men, a recent scan of cosmetic surgery advertisements in an urban yellow-page telephone directory reveals some specific assumptions about the gender of prospective clients, including the use of female images and an accompanying list of services including "breast uplift," "collagen treatments," and "nonsurgical skin peels."

Our purpose in this chapter is to present images and readings to spark your own thinking, writing, and communicating about the relationship media and technology have in constructing and reinforcing these defined appearances for men and women. Selections in this chapter question the assumptions about what women are, should be, and can be, versus what men are, should be, and can be. The questions and activities offer you opportunities to "look through" what some of these messages are telling you to believe so that you can "reconstruct" your own messages more in line with the actual lives and representations of real men and women. Our readings begin with some social commentary in unlikely forms: Lois Gould's "X: A Fabulous Child's Story" and Marge Piercy's poem "Barbie Doll," both of which question the impact traditional gender images can have on a child's personal and social development. Moving away from these fictional scenarios, we include accounts of real women's experience, such as that of bell hooks, as a contrast to traditional images of women found in the media. We also offer some recent readings on the ways in which established gender roles are changing, based on the changing goals of women and men, and the public acknowledgment of changing sexual preference and gender identity. As Diane Barthel notes, despite traditional differences between such men's and women's magazines, between a feminine model based on passivity and narcissism and a masculine model based on activity and power, the concern with appearances is becoming an all-consuming one for both women and men, as more and more ads portray men using products to attract the attention of a more independent and sexually aggressive female. While the roles may have changed somewhat from the days of June Cleaver, some would argue that the images haven't.

Although traditional gender appearances continue to circulate in our culture via the media, newer media also are helping to foster alternative gender images, including the image of cross-dressers such as RuPaul, who has made both a modeling and a television talk-show career out of an exaggerated impersonation of femininity. RuPaul's success at performing female sexuality even better than many real women in our society suggests the extent to which such gendered images of women and men can become commodities, something for people to achieve through their purchase of various products, from Rogaine, the hair-growth stimulant primarily marketed to men, or Retin-A, an acne and wrinkle eliminator marketed to women and girls.

Whether it be through the Ab-Roller or the Thigh Master, more and more media messages are encouraging both men and women to change their appearances. Yet, as an interview with plus-size model Emme, in Alex Witchel's "A Model Figure at Size 14," suggests, the standard definitions of beauty are slowly changing to account for more diverse images of women, as the fashion industry begins to market clothing lines in sizes 12 and above, the average sizes for most women in the United States. In 1997, one of the first plus-size fashion magazines, *Mode,* appeared on the scene, its plus-size models challenging narrow definitions of acceptable gender appearances.

With these conflicting images of masculinity and femininity in mind, we encourage you to analyze your own image as a man or as a woman. How does your experience match with or differ from the images and narratives presented within this chapter, or the images we commonly see in the media? In what ways do you think people have been socially conditioned to accept these particular gender standards? How might you conform to or rebel against such images? What can we do to change our own and others' perceptions of gender stereotypes in both personal and professional contexts? To help you consider these issues, we have included a series of activities both individual and collaborative, both classroom and community-based, to help you explore these appearances of femininity and masculinity and to compare and contrast them with the actual images and activities of the men and women in your own lives.

X: A FABULOUS CHILD'S STORY

Lois Gould

Have you ever been denied involvement in or been ashamed of an activity you enjoyed, based on your gender? In her essay, Gould takes a satirical look at the codes and conventions imposed by society on children of different genders by creating a fictitious child who is unaware of its gender. In doing this, she challenges gender conventions by focusing on such issues as why young girls tend to be discouraged from playing on monkey bars and mowing the lawn whereas young boys are discouraged from playing with dolls and baby carriages and vacuuming. Overall, the essay forces one to analyze the gender bias present in our everyday lives.

Lois Gould's articles have appeared in the New York Times *and she has served as an executive editor to both the* Ladies Home Journal *and* McCalls. *Her novels include* Such Good Friends *(1970),* Necessary Objects *(1972), and* La Presidenta *(1981). "X: A Fabulous Child's Story" first appeared in 1978 and provides critical commentary on society's overemphasis on a child's gender as part of his or her healthy development.*

Once upon a time, a baby named X was born. This baby was named X so that nobody could tell whether it was a boy or a girl. Its parents could tell, of course, but they couldn't tell anybody else. They couldn't even tell Baby X, at first.

You see, it was all part of a very important Secret Scientific Xperiment, known officially as Project Baby X. The smartest scientists had set up this Xperiment at a cost of Xactly 23 billion dollars and 72 cents, which might seem like a lot for just one baby, even a very important Xperimental baby. But when you remember the prices of things like strained carrots and stuffed bunnies, and popcorn for the movies and booster shots for camp, let alone 28 shiny quarters from the tooth fairy, you begin to see how it adds up.

Also, long before Baby X was born, all those scientists had to be paid to work out the details of the Xperiment, and to write the *Official Instruction Manual* for Baby X's parents and, most important of all, to find the right set of parents to bring up Baby X. These parents had to be selected very carefully. Thousands of volunteers had to take thousands of tests and answer thousands of tricky questions. Almost everybody failed because, it turned out, almost everybody really wanted either a baby boy or a baby girl, and not Baby X at all. Also, almost everybody was afraid that a Baby X would be a lot more trouble than a boy or a girl. (They were probably right, the scientists admitted, but Baby X needed parents who wouldn't *mind* the Xtra trouble.)

There were families with grandparents named Milton and Agatha, who didn't see why the baby couldn't be named Milton or Agatha instead of X, even if it *was* an X. There were families with aunts who insisted on knitting tiny dresses and uncles who insisted on sending tiny baseball mitts. Worst of all, there were families that already had other children who couldn't be trusted to keep the secret. Certainly not if they knew the secret was worth 23 billion dollars and 72 cents—and all you had to do was take one little peek at Baby X in the bathtub to know if it was a boy or a girl.

But, finally, the scientists found the Joneses, who really wanted to raise an X more than any other kind of baby—no matter how much trouble it would be. Ms. and Mr. Jones had to promise they would take equal turns caring for X, and feeding it, and singing it lullabies. And they had to promise never to hire any baby-sitters. The government scientists knew perfectly well that a baby-sitter would probably peek at X in the bathtub, too.

The day the Joneses brought their baby home, lots of friends and relatives came over to see it. None of them knew about the secret Xperiment, though. So the first thing they asked was what kind of a baby X was. When the Joneses smiled and said, "It's an X!" nobody knew what to say. They couldn't say, "Look at her cute little dimples!" And they couldn't say, "Look at his husky little biceps!" And they couldn't even say just plain "kitchy-coo." In fact, they all thought the Joneses were playing some kind of rude joke.

But, of course, the Joneses were not joking. "It's an X" was absolutely all they would say. And that made the friends and relatives very angry. The relatives all felt embarrassed about having an X in the family. "People will think there's something wrong with it!" some of them whispered. "There *is* something wrong with it!" others whispered back.

"Nonsense!" the Joneses told them all cheerfully. "What could possibly be wrong with this perfectly adorable X?"

Nobody could answer that, except Baby X, who had just finished its bottle. Baby X's answer was a loud, satisfied burp.

Clearly, nothing at all was wrong. Nevertheless, none of the relatives felt comfortable about buying a present for a Baby X. The cousins who sent the baby a tiny football helmet would not come and visit any more. And the neighbors who sent a pink-flowered romper suit pulled their shades down when the Joneses passed their house.

The *Official Instruction Manual* had warned the new parents that this would happen, so they didn't fret about it. Besides, they were too busy with Baby X and the hundreds of different Xercises for treating it properly.

Ms. and Mr. Jones had to be Xtra careful about how they played with little X. They knew if they kept bouncing it up in the air and saying how *strong* and *active* it was, they'd be treating it more like a boy than an X. But if all they did was cuddle it and kiss it and tell it how *sweet* and *dainty* it was, they'd be treating it more like a girl than an X.

On page 1,654 of the *Official Instruction Manual*, the scientists prescribed: "plenty of bouncing and plenty of cuddling, *both*. X ought to be strong and sweet and active. Forget about *dainty* altogether."

Meanwhile, the Joneses were worrying about other problems. Toys, for instance. And clothes. On his first shopping trip, Mr. Jones told the store clerk, "I need some clothes and toys for my new baby." The clerk smiled and said, "Well, now, is it a boy or a girl?" "It's an X," Mr. Jones said, smiling back. But the clerk got all red in the face and said huffily, "In *that* case, I'm afraid I can't help you, sir." So Mr. Jones wandered helplessly up and down the aisles trying to find what X needed. But everything in the store was piled up in sections marked "Boys" or "Girls." There were "Boys' Pajamas" and "Girls' Underwear" and "Boys' Fire Engines" and "Girls' Housekeeping Sets." Mr. Jones went home without buying anything for X. That night he and Ms. Jones consulted page 2,326 of the *Official Instruction Manual*. "Buy plenty of everything!" it said firmly.

So they bought plenty of sturdy blue pajamas in the Boys' Department and cheerful flowered underwear in the Girls' Department. And they bought all kinds of toys. A boy doll that made pee-pee and cried, "Pa-pa." And a girl doll that talked in three languages and said, "I am the Pres-i-dent of Gen-er-al Mo-tors." They also bought a storybook about a brave princess who rescued a handsome prince from his ivory tower, and another one about a sister and brother who grew up to be a baseball star and a ballet star, and you had to guess which was which.

The head scientists of Project Baby X checked all their purchases and told them to keep up the good work. They also reminded the Joneses to see page 4,629 of the *Manual*, where it said, "Never make Baby X feel *embarrassed* or *ashamed* about what it wants to play with. And if X gets dirty climbing rocks, never say 'Nice little Xes don't get dirty climbing rocks.' "

Likewise, it said, "If X falls down and cries, never say 'Brave little Xes don't cry.' Because, of course, nice little Xes *do* get dirty, and brave little Xes *do* cry. No matter how dirty X gets, or how hard it cries, don't worry. It's all part of the Xperiment."

Whenever the Joneses pushed Baby X's stroller in the park, smiling strangers would come over and coo: "Is that a boy or a girl?" The Joneses would smile back and say, "It's an X." The strangers would stop smiling then, and often snarl something nasty—as if the Joneses had snarled at *them*.

By the time X grew big enough to play with other children, the Joneses' troubles had grown bigger, too. Once a little girl grabbed X's shovel in the sandbox, and zonked X on the head with it. "Now, now, Tracy," the little girl's mother began to scold, "little girls mustn't hit little . . ." and she turned to ask X, "Are you a little boy or a little girl, dear?"

Mr. Jones who was sitting near the sandbox, held his breath and crossed his fingers.

X smiled politely at the lady, even though X's head had never been zonked so hard in its life. "I'm a little X," X replied.

"You're a *what?*" the lady exclaimed angrily. "You're a little b-r-a-t, you mean!"

"But little girls mustn't hit little Xes, either!" said X, retrieving the shovel with another polite smile. "What good does hitting do, anyway?"

X's father, who was still holding his breath, finally let it out, uncrossed his fingers, and grinned back at X.

And at their next secret Project Baby X meeting, the scientists grinned, too. Baby X was doing fine.

But then it was time for X to start school. The Joneses were really worried about this, because school was even more full of rules for boys and girls, and there were no rules for Xes. The teacher would tell boys to form one line, and girls to form another line. There would be boys' games and girls' games, and boys' secrets and girls' secrets. The school library would have a list of recommended books for girls, and a different list of recommended books for boys. There would even be a bathroom marked BOYS and another one marked GIRLS. Pretty soon boys and girls would hardly talk to each other. What would happen to poor little X?

The Joneses spent weeks consulting their *Instruction Manual* (there were 249½ pages of advice under "First Day of School"), and attending urgent special conferences with the smart scientists of Project Baby X.

The scientists had to make sure that X's mother had taught X how to throw and catch a ball properly, and that X's father had been sure to teach X what to serve at a doll's tea party. X had to know how to shoot marbles and how to jump rope and, most of all, what to say when the Other Children asked whether X was a Boy or a Girl.

Finally, X was ready. The Joneses helped X button on a nice new pair of red-and-white checked overalls, and sharpened six pencils for X's nice new pencilbox, and marked X's name clearly on all the books in its nice new bookbag. X brushed its teeth and combed its hair, which just about covered its ears, and remembered to put a napkin in its lunchbox.

The Joneses had asked X's teacher if the class could line up alphabetically, instead of forming separate lines for boys and girls. And they had asked if X could use the principal's bathroom, because it wasn't marked anything except BATHROOM. X's teacher promised to take care of all those problems. But nobody could help X with the biggest problem of all—Other Children.

Nobody in X's class had ever known an X before. What would they think? How would X make friends?

You couldn't tell what X was by studying its clothes—overalls don't even button right-to-left, like girls' clothes, or left-to-right, like boys' clothes. And you couldn't guess whether X had a girl's short haircut or a boy's long haircut. And it was very hard to tell by the games X liked to play. Either X played ball very well for a girl, or else X played house very well for a boy.

Some of the children tried to find out by asking X tricky questions, like "Who's your favorite sports star?" That was easy. X had two favorite sports stars: a girl jockey named Robyn Smith and a boy archery champion named Robin Hood. Then they asked, "What's your favorite TV program?" And that was even easier. X's favorite TV program was "Lassie," which stars a girl dog played by a boy dog.

When X said that its favorite toy was a doll, everyone decided that X must be a girl. But then X said that the doll was really a robot, and that X had computerized it, and that it was programmed to bake fudge brownies and then clean up the kitchen. After X told them that, the other children gave up guessing what X was. All they knew was they'd sure like to see X's doll.

After school, X wanted to play with the other children. "How about shooting some baskets in the gym?" X asked the girls. But all they did was make faces and giggle behind X's back.

"How about weaving some baskets in the arts and crafts room?" X asked the boys. But they all made faces and giggled behind X's back too.

That night, Ms. and Mr. Jones asked X how things had gone at school. X told them sadly that the lessons were okay, but otherwise school was a terrible place for an X. It seemed as if Other Children would never want an X for a friend.

Once more, the Joneses reached for their *Instruction Manual.* Under "Other Children," they found the following message: "What did you Xpect? *Other Children* have to obey all the silly boy-girl rules, because their parents taught them to. Lucky X—you don't have to stick to the rules at all! All you have to do is be yourself. P.S. We're not saying it'll be easy."

X liked being itself. But X cried a lot that night, partly because it felt afraid. So X's father held X tight, and cuddled it, and couldn't help crying a little, too. And X's mother cheered them both up by reading an Xciting story about an enchanted prince called Sleeping Handsome, who woke up when Princess Charming kissed him.

The next morning, they all felt much better, and little X went back to school with a brave smile and a clean pair of red-and-white checked overalls.

There was a seven-letter-word spelling bee in class that day. And a seven-lap boys' relay race in the gym. And a seven-layer-cake baking contest in the girls' kitchen corner. X won the spelling bee. X also won the relay race. And X almost won the baking contest, except it forgot to light the oven. Which only proves that nobody's perfect.

One of the Other Children noticed something else, too. He said: "Winning or losing doesn't seem to count to X. X seems to have fun being good at boys' skills *and* girls' skills."

"Come to think of it," said another one of the Other Children, "maybe X is having twice as much fun as we are!"

So after school that day, the girl who beat X at the baking contest gave X a big slice of her prizewinning cake. And the boy X beat in the relay race asked X to race him home.

From then on, some really funny things began to happen. Susie, who sat next to X in class, suddenly refused to wear pink dresses to school any more. She insisted on wearing red-and-white checked overalls—just like X's. Overalls, she told her parents, were much better for climbing monkey bars.

Then Jim, the class football nut, started wheeling his little sister's doll carriage around the football field. He'd put on his entire football uniform, except for the helmet. Then he'd put the helmet *in* the carriage, lovingly tucked under an old set of shoulder pads. Then he'd start jogging around the field, pushing the carriage and singing "Rock-a-bye Baby" to his football helmet. He told his family that X did the same thing, so it must be okay. After all X was now the team's star quarterback.

Susie's parents were horrified by her behavior, and Jim's parents were worried sick about his. But the worst came when the twins, Joe and Peggy, decided to share everything with each other. Peggy used Joe's hockey skates, and his microscope, and took half his newspaper route. Joe used Peggy's needlepoint kit, and her cookbooks, and took two of her three baby-sitting jobs. Peggy started running the lawn mower, and Joe started running the vacuum cleaner.

Their parents weren't one bit pleased with Peggy's wonderful biology experiments, or with Joe's terrific needlepoint pillows. They didn't care that Peggy mowed the lawn better, and that Joe vacuumed the carpet better. In fact, they were furious. It's all that little X's fault, they agreed. Just because X doesn't know what it is, or what it's supposed to be, it wants to get everybody *else* mixed up, too!

Peggy and Joe were forbidden to play with X any more. So was Susie, and then Jim, and then *all* the Other Children. But it was too late; the Other Children stayed mixed up and happy and free, and refused to go back to the way they'd been before X.

Finally, Joe and Peggy's parents decided to call an emergency meeting of the school's Parents' Association, to discuss "The X Problem." They sent a report to the principal stating that X was a "disruptive influence." They demanded immediate action. The Joneses, they said, should be *forced* to tell whether X was a boy or a girl. And then X should be *forced* to behave like whichever it was. If the Joneses refused to tell, the Parents' Association said, then X must take an Xamination. The school psychiatrist must Xamine it physically and mentally, and issue a full report. If X's test showed it was a boy, it would have to obey all the boys' rules. If it proved to be a girl, X would have to obey all the girls' rules.

And if X turned out to be some kind of mixed-up misfit, then X should be Xpelled from the school. Immediately!

The principal was very upset. Disruptive influence? Mixed-up misfit? But X was an Xcellent student. All the teachers said it was a delight to have X in their classes. X was president of the student council. X had won first prize in the talent show, and second prize in the art show, and honorable mention in the science fair, and six athletic events on field day, including the potato race.

Nevertheless, insisted the Parents' Association, X is a Problem Child. X is the Biggest Problem Child we have ever seen!

So the principal reluctantly notified X's parents that numerous complaints about X's behavior had come to the school's attention. And that after the psychiatrist's Xamination, the school would decide what to do about X.

The Joneses reported this at once to the scientists, who referred them to page 85,759 of the *Instruction Manual.* "Sooner or later," it said, "X will have to be Xamined by a psychiatrist. This may be the only way any of us will know for sure whether X is mixed up—or whether everyone else is."

The night before X was to be Xamined, the Joneses tried not to let X see how worried they were. "What if . . . ?" Mr. Jones would say. And Ms. Jones would reply, "No use worrying." Then a few minutes later, Ms. Jones would say, "What if . . . ?" and Mr. Jones would reply, "No use worrying."

X just smiled at them both, and hugged them hard and didn't say much of anything. X was thinking. What if . . . ? And then X thought: No use worrying.

At Xactly 9 o'clock the next day, X reported to the school psychiatrist's office. The principal, along with a committee from the Parents' Association, X's teacher, X's classmates, and Ms. and Mr. Jones, waited in the hall outside. Nobody knew the details of the tests X was to be given, but everybody knew they'd be *very* hard, and that they'd reveal Xactly what everyone wanted to know about X, but were afraid to ask.

It was terribly quiet in the hall. Almost spooky. Once in a while, they would hear a strange noise inside the room. There were buzzes. And a beep or two. And several bells. An occasional light would flash under the door. The Joneses thought it was a white light, but the principal thought it was blue. Two or three children swore it was either yellow or green. And the Parents' Committee missed it completely.

Through it all, you could hear the psychiatrist's low voice, asking hundreds of questions, and X's higher voice, answering hundreds of answers.

The whole thing took so long that everyone knew it must be the most complete Xamination anyone had ever had to take. Poor X, the Joneses thought. Serves X right, the Parents' Committee thought. I wouldn't like to be in X's overalls right now, the children thought.

At last, the door opened. Everyone crowded around to hear the results. X didn't look any different; in fact, X was smiling. But the psychiatrist looked terrible. He looked as if he was crying! "What happened?" everyone began shouting. Had X done something disgraceful? "I wouldn't be a bit surprised!" muttered Peggy and Joe's parents. "Did X flunk the *whole* test?" cried Susie's parents. "Or just the most important part?" yelled Jim's parents.

"Oh, dear," sighed Mr. Jones.

"Oh, dear," sighed Ms. Jones.

"*Sssh,*" ssshed the principal. "The psychiatrist is trying to speak."

Wiping his eyes and clearing his throat, the psychiatrist began, in a hoarse whisper. "In my opinion," he whispered—you could tell he must be very upset— "in my opinion, young X here . . ."

"Yes? Yes?" shouted a parent impatiently.

"*Sssh!*" ssshed the principal.

"Young *Sssh* here, I mean young X," said the doctor, frowning, "is just about . . ."

"Just about *what?* Let's have it!" shouted another parent.

" . . . just about the *least* mixed-up child I've ever Xamined!" said the psychiatrist.

"Yay for X!" yelled one of the children. And then the others began yelling, too. Clapping and cheering and jumping up and down.

"*SSSH!*" SSShed the principal, but nobody did.

The Parents' Committee was angry and bewildered. How *could* X have passed the whole Xamination? Didn't X have an *identity* problem? Wasn't X mixed up at *all*? Wasn't X *any* kind of a misfit? How could it *not* be, when it didn't even *know* what it was? And why was the psychiatrist crying?

Actually, he had stopped crying and was smiling politely through his tears. "Don't you see?" he said. "I'm crying because it's wonderful! X has absolutely no identity problem! X isn't one bit mixed up! As for being a misfit—ridiculous! X knows perfectly well what it is! Don't you, X?" The doctor winked, X winked back.

"But what *is* X?" shrieked Peggy and Joe's parents. "*We* still want to know what it is!"

"Ah, yes," said the doctor, winking again. "Well, don't worry. You'll all know one of these days. And you won't need me to tell you."

"What? What does he mean?" some of the parents grumbled suspiciously.

Susie and Peggy and Joe all answered at once. "He means that by the time X's sex matters, it won't be a secret any more!"

With that, the doctor began to push through the crowd toward X's parents. "How do you do," he said, somewhat stiffly. And then he reached out to hug them both. "If I ever have an X of my own," he whispered, "I sure hope you'll lend me your instruction manual."

Needless to say, the Joneses were very happy. The Project Baby X scientists were rather pleased, too. So were Susie, Jim, Peggy, Joe, and all the Other Children. The Parents' Association wasn't, but they had promised to accept the psychiatrist's report, and not make any more trouble. They even invited Ms. and Mr. Jones to become honorary members, which they did.

Later that day, all X's friends put on their red-and-white checked overalls and went over to see X. They found X in the back yard, playing with a very tiny baby that none of them had ever seen before. The baby was wearing very tiny red-and-white checked overalls.

"How do you like our new baby?" X asked the Other Children proudly.

"It's got cute dimples," said Jim.

"It's got husky biceps, too," said Susie.

"What kind of baby is it?" asked Joe and Peggy.

X frowned at them. "Can't you tell?" Then X broke into a big, mischievous grin. "*It's a Y!*"

READING REFLECTIONS

1. Why do you think Gould wrote this in the form of a children's story?
2. Who has the most difficulty accepting X as a genderless baby? Why? Does X's gender or lack of one dictate how people treat X?
3. Visit a local toy store and survey the various toys marketed. What toys seem to be aimed at little boys and what toys seem to be aimed at little girls? How do you know? What are the assumptions about the social roles of boys and girls?
4. Select a children's book from your local library and analyze the role of gender within the story. Compare the book's structure to Gould's story, noting the ways in which Gould both conforms to and resists this genre.
5. Gould wrote the story of Baby X in 1978. To what extent has the androgyny she advocates become more common and accepted in today's culture?

BARBIE DOLL

Marge Piercy

Our images of ourselves are shaped in part by what others say about us. In her poem, Piercy details the feelings of a young girl who is made aware of her "thick legs and fat nose" by a classmate. The poem demonstrates that despite the girl's other talents and accomplishments, she defines herself by that one painful criticism. The tragic outcome of her damaged self-esteem is a lesson for all women who have ever defined themselves by a real or perceived physical shortcoming.

Marge Piercy has made a career of turning poetry into social commentary in such collections as Circles on the Water *(1982) and* To Be of Use *(1973). Piercy's "Barbie Doll" is a powerful statement about the price of beauty and conformity in our culture, utilizing a cultural icon to which people of all ages can relate, precisely because of Barbie's timeless and unchanging qualities.*

This girlchild was born as usual
and presented dolls that did pee-pee
and miniature GE stoves and irons
and wee lipsticks the color of cherry candy.
Then in the magic of puberty, a classmate said:
You have a great big nose and fat legs.

She was healthy, tested intelligent,
possessed strong arms and back,
abundant sexual drive and manual dexterity.
She went to and fro apologizing.
Everyone saw a fat nose on thick legs.

She was advised to play coy,
exhorted to come on hearty,
exercise, diet, smile and wheedle.
Her good nature wore out
like a fan belt.
So she cut off her nose and her legs
and offered them up.

In the casket displayed on satin she lay
with the undertaker's cosmetics painted on,
a turned-up putty nose,
dressed in a pink and white nightie.
Doesn't she look pretty? everyone said.
Consummation at last.
To every woman a happy ending.

READING REFLECTIONS

1. Why does Piercy select Barbie as the subject of her poem?
2. How important do you think Piercy feels Barbie is in our cultural history?
3. Has Barbie changed much over the years? What appearances and occupations has Barbie recently had? Considering Piercy's poem, why do you think these changes have taken place?
4. Is Piercy's poem still relevant given the changes in today's Barbie?
5. What was your favorite game or toy as a child? What were the rules for playing? Discuss what cultural assumptions about society and gender were implied by your favorite toy and game, and how your childhood games and toys have socialized you either positively or negatively, or both. What cultural assumptions about society and gender does Piercy seem to attribute to Barbie?

STRAIGHTENING OUR HAIR

bell hooks

For the most part, the typical standard of beauty for a woman in America, reinforced by a dominant white society, consists of long blonde hair and blue eyes. In her essay, hooks explains that despite the dominant white message of what defines a woman's beauty in our society, different standards of beauty do exist. By refusing to straighten her hair, hooks fights racial oppression and embraces her natural self. In calling for other black women to stop straightening their hair, she encourages them to follow suit.

bell hooks has become a powerful voice within the American academy about the role of race, gender, and class, connecting her experiences as an academic to her impoverished beginnings as a child growing up in the South in such books as Ain't I a Woman: black women and feminism *(written while hooks was an undergraduate at Stanford) and* Teaching to Transgress *(1995). "Straightening Our Hair," originally published in 1988 as a column for* Z Magazine, *is an example of hooks' ability to connect personal experience and political issues.*

On Saturday mornings we would gather in the kitchen to get our hair fixed, that is straightened. Smells of burning grease and hair, mingled with the scent of our freshly washed bodies, with collard greens cooking on the stove, with fried fish. We did not go to the hairdresser. Mama fixed our hair. Six daughters—there was no way we could have afforded hairdressers. In those days, this process of straightening black women's hair with a hot comb (invented by Madame C. J. Waler) was not connected in my mind with the effort to look white, to live out standards of beauty set by white supremacy. It was connected solely with rites of initiation into womanhood. To arrive at that point where one's hair could be straightened was to move from being perceived as child (whose hair could be neatly combed and braided) to being almost a woman. It was this moment of transition my sisters and I longed for.

Hair pressing was a ritual of black women's culture—of intimacy. It was an exclusive moment when black women (even those who did not know one another well) might meet at home or in the beauty parlor to talk with one another, to listen to the talk. It was as important a world as that of the male barber shop—mysterious, secret. It was a world where the images constructed as barriers between one's self and the world were briefly let go, before they were made again. It was a moment of creativity, a moment of change.

I wanted this change even though I had been told all my life that I was one of the "lucky" ones because I had been born with "good hair"—hair that was fine, almost straight—not good enough but still good. Hair that had no nappy edges, no "kitchen," that area close to the neck that the hot comb could not reach. This "good hair" meant nothing to me when it stood as a barrier to my entering this secret black woman world. I was overjoyed when mama finally agreed that I could join the Saturday ritual, no longer looking on but patiently waiting my turn. I have written of this ritual: "For each of us getting our hair pressed is an important ritual. It is not a sign of our longing to be white. There are no white people in our intimate world. It is a sign of our desire to be women. It is a gesture that says we are approaching womanhood . . . Before we reach the appropriate age we wear braids, plaits that are symbols of our innocence, our youth, our childhood. Then, we are comforted by the parting hands that comb and braid, comforted by the intimacy and bliss. There is a deeper intimacy in the kitchen on Saturdays when hair is pressed, when fish is fried, when sodas are passed around, when soul music drifts over the talk. It is a time without men. It is a time when we work as women to meet each other's needs, to make each other feel good inside, a time of laughter and outrageous talk."

Since the world we lived in was racially segregated, it was easy to overlook the relationship between white supremacy and our obsession with hair. Even though black women with straight hair were perceived to be more beautiful than those with thick, frizzy hair, it was not overtly related to a notion that white women were a more appealing female group or that their straight hair set a beauty standard black women were struggling to live out. While this was probably the ideological framework from which the process of straightening black women's hair emerged, it was expanded so that it became a real space of black woman bonding through ritualized, shared experience. The beauty parlor was a space of consciousness raising, a space where black women shared life stories—hardship, trials, gossip; a place where one could be comforted and one's spirit renewed. It was for some women a place of rest where one did not need to meet the demands of children or men. It was the one hour some folk would spend "off their feet," a soothing, restful time of meditation and silence. These positive empowering implications of the ritual of hair pressing mediate but do not change negative implications. They exist alongside all that is negative.

Within white supremacist capitalist patriarchy, the social and political context in which the custom of black folks straightening our hair emerges, it represents an imitation of the dominant white group's appearance and often indicates internalized racism, self-hatred, and/or low self-esteem. During the 1960s black people who actively worked to critique, challenge, and change white racism pointed to the way in which black people's obsession with straight hair reflected a colonized mentality. It was at this time that the natural hairdo, the "afro," became fashionable as a sign of cultural resistance to racist oppression and as a celebration of blackness. Naturals were equated with political militancy. Many young black folks found just how much political value was placed on straightened hair as a sign of respectability and conformity to societal expectations when they ceased to straighten their hair. When black liberation struggles did not lead to revolutionary change in society the focus on the political relationship between appearance and complicity with white racism ceased and folks who had once sported afros began to straighten their hair.

In keeping with the move to suppress black consciousness and efforts to be self-defining, white corporations began to acknowledge black people and most especially black women as potential consumers of products they could provide, including hair-care products. Permanents specially designed for black women eliminated the need for hair pressing and the hot comb. They not only cost more but they also took much of the economy and profit out of black communities, out of the pockets of black women who had previously reaped the material benefits. . . . Gone was the context of ritual, of black woman bonding. Seated under noisy hair dryers black women lost a space for dialogue, for creative talk.

Stripped of the positive binding rituals that traditionally surrounded the experience, black women straightening our hair seemed more and more to be exclusively a signifier of white supremacist oppression and exploitation. It was clearly a process that was about black women changing their appearance to imitate white people's looks. This need to look as much like white people as possible, to look safe, is related to a desire to succeed in the white world. Before desegregation black people could worry less about what white folks thought about their hair. In a discussion with black women about beauty at Spelman College, students talked about the importance of wearing straight hair when seeking jobs. They were convinced and probably rightly so that their chances of finding good jobs would be enhanced if they had straight hair. When asked to elaborate they focused on the connection between radical politics and natural hairdos, whether natural or braided. One woman wearing a short natural told of purchasing a straight wig for her job search. No one in the discussion felt black women were free to wear our hair in natural styles without reflecting on the possible negative consequences. Often older black adults, especially parents, respond quite negatively to natural hairdos. I shared with the group that when I arrived home with my hair in braids shortly after accepting my job at Yale my parents told me I looked disgusting.

Despite many changes in racial politics, black women continue to obsess about their hair, and straightening hair continues to be serious business. It continues to tap into the insecurity black women feel about our value in this white supremacist society. Talking with groups of women at various college campuses and with black women in our communities there seems to be general consensus that our obsession with hair in general reflects continued struggles with self-esteem and self-actualization. We talk about the extent to which black women perceive our hair as the enemy, as a problem we must solve, a territory we must conquer. Above all it is a part of our black female body that must be controlled. Most of us were not raised in environments where we learned to regard our hair as sensual or beautiful in an unprocessed state. Many of us talk about situations where white people ask to touch our hair when it is unprocessed then show surprise that the texture is soft or feels good. In the eyes of many white folks and other non-black folks, the natural afro looks like steel wool or a helmet. Responses to natural hairstyles worn by black women usually reveal the extent to which our natural hair is perceived in white supremacist culture as not only ugly but frightening. We also internalize that fear. The extent to which we are comfortable with our hair usually reflects on our overall feelings about our bodies. In our black women's support group, *Sisters of the Yam*, we talk about the ways we don't like our bodies, especially our hair. I suggested to the group that we regard our hair as though it is not part of our body but something quite separate—again a territory to be controlled. To me it was important for us to link this need to control with sexuality, with sexual repression. Curious about what black women who had hot-combed or had permanents felt about the relationship between straightened hair and sexual practice I asked whether people worried about their hairdo, whether they feared partners touching their hair. Straightened hair has always seemed to me to call attention to the desire for hair to stay in place. Not surprisingly many black women responded that they felt uncomfortable if too much attention was focused on their hair, if it seemed to be too messy. Those of us who have liberated our hair and let it go in whatever direction it seems fit often receive negative comments.

Looking at photographs of myself and my sisters when we had straightened hair in high school I noticed how much older we looked than when our hair was not processed. It is ironic that we live in a culture that places so much emphasis on women looking young, yet black women are encouraged to change our hair in ways that make us appear older. This past semester we read Toni Morrison's *The Bluest Eye* in a black women's fiction class. I ask students to write autobiographical statements which reflect their thoughts about the connection between race and physical beauty. A vast majority of black women wrote about their hair. When I asked individual women outside class why they continued to straighten their hair, many asserted that naturals don't look good on them, or that they required too much work. Emily, a favorite student with very short hair, always straightened it and I would tease and challenge her. She explained to me convincingly that a natural hairdo would look horrible with her face, that she did not have the appropriate forehead or bone structure. Later she shared that during spring break she had gone to the beauty parlor to have her perm and as she sat there waiting, thinking about class reading and discussion, it came to her that she was really frightened that no one else would think she was attractive if she did not straighten her hair. She acknowledged that this fear was rooted in feelings of low self-esteem. She decided to make a change. Her new look surprised her because it was so appealing. We talked afterwards about her earlier denial and justification for wearing straightened hair. We talked about the way it hurts to realize connection between racist oppression and the arguments we use to convince ourselves and others that we are not beautiful or acceptable as we are.

In numerous discussions with black women about hair one of the strongest factors that prevent black women from wearing unprocessed hairstyles is the fear of losing other people's approval and regard. Heterosexual black women talked about the extent to which black men respond more favorably to women with straight or straightened hair. Lesbian women point to the fact that many of them do not straighten their hair, raising the question of whether or not this gesture is fundamentally linked to heterosexism and a longing for male approval. I recall visiting a woman friend and her black male companion in New York years ago and having an intense discussion about hair. He took it upon himself to share with me that I could be a fine sister if I would do something about my hair (secretly I thought mama must have hired him). What I remember is his shock when I calmly and happily asserted that I like the touch and feel of unprocessed hair.

When students read about race and physical beauty, several black women describe periods of childhood when they were overcome with longing for straight hair as it was so associated with desirability, with being loved. Few women had received affirmation from family, friends, or lovers when choosing not to straighten their hair and we have many stories to tell about advice we receive from everyone, including total strangers, urging to understand how much more attractive we would be if we would fix (straighten) our hair. When I interviewed for my job at Yale, white female advisers who had never before commented on my hair encouraged me not to wear braids or a large natural to the interview. Although they did not say straighten your hair, they were suggesting that I change my hairstyle so that it would most resemble theirs, so that it would indicate a certain conformity. I wore braids and no one seemed to notice. When I was offered the job I did not ask if it mattered whether or not I wore braids. I tell this story to my students so that they will know by this one experience that we do not always need to surrender our power to be self defining to succeed in an endeavor. Yet I have found the issue of hairstyle comes up again and again with students when I give lectures. At one conference on black women and leadership I walked into a packed auditorium, my hair unprocessed wild and all over the place. The vast majority of black women seated there had straightened hair. Many of them looked at me with hostile contemptuous stares. I felt as though I was being judged on the spot as someone out on the fringe, an undesirable. Such judgments are made particularly about black women in the United States who choose to wear dreadlocks. They are seen and rightly so as the total antithesis of straightening one's hair, as a political statement. Often black women express contempt for those of us who choose this look.

Ironically, just as the natural unprocessed hair of black women is the subject of disregard and disdain we are witnessing return of the long dyed, blonde look. In their writing my black women students described wearing yellow mops on their heads as children to pretend they had long blonde hair. Recently black women singers who are working to appeal to white audiences, to be seen as crossovers, use hair implanting and hair weaving to have long straight hair. There seems to be a definite connection between a black female entertainer's popularity with white audiences and the degree to which she works to appear white, or to embody aspects of white style. Tina Turner and Aretha Franklin were trend setters; both dyed their hair blonde. In everyday life we see more and more black women using chemicals to be blonde. At one of my talks focusing on the social construction of black female identity within a sexist and racist society, a black woman came to me at the end of the discussion and shared that her seven-year-old daughter was obsessed with blonde hair, so much so that she had made a wig to imitate long blonde curls. This mother wanted to know what she was doing wrong in her parenting. She asserted that their home was a place where blackness was affirmed and celebrated. Yet she had not considered that her processed straightened hair was a message to her daughter that black women are not acceptable unless we alter our appearance or hair texture. Recently I talked with one of my younger sisters about her hair. She uses bright colored dyes, various shades of red. Her skin is very dark. She has a broad nose and short hair. For her these choices of straightened dyed hair were directly related to feelings of low self-esteem. She does not like her features and feels that the hairstyle transforms her. My perception was that her choice of red straightened hair actually called attention to the features she was trying to mask. When she commented that this look receives more attention and compliments, I suggested that the positive feedback might be a direct response to her own projection of a higher level of self-satisfaction. Folk may be responding to that and not her altered looks. We talked about the messages she is sending her dark-skinned daughters—that they will be most attractive if they straighten their hair.

A number of black women have argued that straightened hair is not necessarily a signifier of low self-esteem. They argue that it is a survival strategy; it is easier to function in this society with straightened hair. There are fewer hassles. Or as some folk stated, straightened hair is easier to manage, takes less time. When I responded to this argument in our discussion at Spelman by suggesting that perhaps the unwillingness to spend time on ourselves, caring for our bodies, is also a reflection of a sense that this is not important or that we do not deserve such care. In this group and others, black women talked about being raised in households where spending too much time on appearance was ridiculed or considered vanity. Irrespective of the way individual black women choose to do their hair, it is evident that the extent to which we suffer from racist and sexist oppression and exploitation affects the degree to which we feel capable of both self-love and asserting an autonomous presence that is acceptable and pleasing to ourselves. Individual preferences (whether rooted in self-hate or not) cannot negate the reality that our collective obsession with straightening black hair reflects the psychology of oppression and the impact of racist colonization. Together racism and sexism daily reinforce to all black females via the media, advertising, etc. that we will not be considered beautiful or desirable if we do not change ourselves, especially our hair. We cannot resist this socialization if we deny that white supremacy informs our efforts to construct self and identity.

Without organized struggles like the ones that happened in the 1960s and early 1970s, individual black women must struggle alone to acquire the critical consciousness that would enable us to examine issues of race and beauty, our personal choices, from a political standpoint. There are times when I think of straightening my hair just to change my style, just for fun. Then I remind myself that even though such a gesture could be simply playful on my part, an individual expression of desire, I know that such a gesture would carry other implications beyond my control. The reality is: straightened hair is linked historically and currently to a system of racial domination that impresses upon black people, and especially black women, that we are not acceptable as we are, that we are not beautiful. To make such a gesture as an expression of individual freedom and choice would make me complicit with a politic of domination that hurts us. It is easy to surrender this freedom. It is more important that black women resist racism and sexism in every way; that every aspect of our self-representation be a fierce resistance, a radical celebration of our care and respect for ourselves.

Even though I have not had straightened hair for a long time, this did not mean that I am able to really enjoy or appreciate my hair in its natural state. For years I still considered it a problem. (It wasn't naturally nappy enough to make a decent interesting afro. It was too thin.) These complaints expressed my continued dissatisfaction. True liberation of my hair came when I stopped trying to control it in any state and just accepted it as it is. It has been only in recent years that I have ceased to worry about what other people would say about my hair. It has been only in recent years that I could feel consistent pleasure washing, combing, and caring for my hair. These feelings remind me of the pleasure and comfort I felt as a child sitting between my mother's legs feeling the warmth of her body and being as she combed and braided my hair. In a culture of domination, one that is essentially anti-intimacy, we must struggle daily to remain in touch with ourselves and our bodies, with one another. Especially black women and men, as it is our bodies that have been so often devalued, burdened, wounded in alienated labor. Celebrating our bodies, we participate in a liberatory struggle that frees mind and heart.

READING REFLECTIONS

1. Why would hooks and other young African American girls want to straighten their hair?
2. What did it mean for hooks to have "good hair," and how did she feel about this judgment?

3. What cultural assumptions about beauty would lead to this activity? Provide examples of these cultural assumptions from hooks' essay.
4. How does hooks typify the response to "natural" hairstyles worn by African American women?
5. Select two fashion magazines, one aimed at a mainstream audience and one aimed at an African American audience to note similarities and differences in the presence and portrayal of African American women to both audiences. What might hooks have to say about such portrayals?

KING KONG AND THE WHITE WOMAN
Hustler Magazine *and the Demonization of Black Masculinity*

Gail Dines

The demonization by the media of black men as rapists and murderers has been well documented by scholars interested in film, television, and rap music. Recently, a number of researchers have turned their attention to pornography, "specifically, how the codes and conventions of this genre (re)construct the Black male body, especially the penis, as dangerous and as a threat to White male power." For Gail Dines, the use of cartoons in Hustler *magazine is a way of making such a threat comical to white males, further enabling cultural stereotypes about black men as well as white women.*

Gail Dines is an associate professor of sociology at Wheelock College in Boston. She is co-editor of Gender, Race, and Class in the Media, *and is co-author of the forthcoming book,* Pornography: The Production and Consumption of Inequality. *She lectures across the country on pornography and media and has written numerous articles on the topic of pornography.*

From the box-office success of *The Birth of a Nation* in 1915 to the national obsession with O. J. Simpson, the image of the Black man as the spoiler of White womanhood has been a staple of media representation in this country.

Gail Dines, "King Kong and the White Woman: *Hustler Magazine* and the Demonization of Black Masculinity," *Violence against Women* 4, no. 3 (June 1998): 291–307. Copyright © 1998 by Sage Publications. Reprinted with the permission of Sage Publications, Inc.

The demonization by the media of Black men as rapists and murderers has been well documented by scholars interested in film (Carby, 1993; Guerrero, 1993; Mercer, 1994; Snead, 1994; Wiegman, 1993; Winston, 1982), news (Entman, 1990; Gray, 1989), and rap music (Dyson, 1993; Rose, 1994). Although this image stands in sharp contrast to the feminized Uncle Tom that was popular in early Hollywood films, both images serve to define Black men as outside the normal realm of (White) masculinity by constructing them as "other" (Wiegman, 1993). Although both the Uncle Tom and the sexual monster continue to define the limits of Black male representation in mainstream media, the latter image dominates and, according to Mercer (1994), serves to legitimize racist practices, such as mass incarceration of Black men, police brutality, and right-wing government policy.

Recently, scholars have turned their attention to pornography (Cowan & Campbell, 1994; Forna, 1992; Mayall & Russell, 1993; Mercer, 1994) and specifically how the codes and conventions of this genre (re)construct the Black male body, especially the penis, as dangerous and as a threat to White male power. The focus of this research tends to be poorly produced, hard-core pornography movies that are relegated to the shelves of adult-only stores because of their close-up shots of erect penises, ejaculation, and vaginal, anal, and oral penetration. What tends to be ignored in these studies is the content of the mass-produced, mass-circulated pornography magazines that, because they can be purchased in bookstores, newsstands, and airport terminals, have a much larger audience.

Of the hundreds of mass-produced, mass-distributed pornography magazines, the three best sellers are *Playboy, Penthouse,* and *Hustler* (Osanka, 1989). Although these three magazines are often lumped together, they differ markedly in the type of world that they construct. *Playboy* and *Penthouse,* in their pictorials, cartoons, advertisements, and editorials, depict a Whites-only world, a world so affluent and privileged that Blacks are excluded by invisible market forces. Indeed, even the White working class is invisible in the *Playboy* world of expensive clothes, gourmet restaurants, and well-appointed homes. *Hustler,* however, in its pictorials, "beaver hunts" (explicit snapshots of readers' wives and girlfriends), advertisements, and editorials, constructs a world populated by working-class Whites who live in trailer homes, eat in fast-food restaurants, and wear ill-fitting clothes. Although Blacks are absent from most sections of the magazine, they appear regularly in caricatured form in the cartoons, where they are depicted as competing with White men for the few sexually available White women. *Hustler* cartoons depict a world filled with seething racial tensions brought about by the Black man's alleged insatiable appetite for White women. The competition between Black and White men and the ultimate victory of the Black man is the source of much humor in *Hustler* cartoons and serves to visually illustrate to the mainly White, working-class male readership what happens if Black masculinity is allowed to go uncontained. *Hustler* is by no means the first mass-distributed medium to visually depict the ultimate White fear; indeed, *The Birth of a Nation* and *King Kong*

(1933) played similar roles. Only in *Hustler*, it is the White man who loses, as evidenced in his failure to win back the girl. This article will examine how *Hustler* draws from past regimes of racial representation and articulates a more contemporary myth of Black masculinity that, having been allowed to run amok because of liberal policies, has finally rendered White men impotent, both sexually and economically.

From *The Birth of a Nation* to *Black Studs*

Theorists such as Wiegman (1993) and Snead (1994) have traced back to the late 19th century the beginnings of the image of the Black man as a sexual monster, as the product of a White supremacist ideology that saw the end of slavery as bringing about an unleashing of animalistic, brute violence inherent in African American men. D. W. Griffith's *The Birth of a Nation* (1915), was, without question, the first major mass circulation of this image in film and was to become the blueprint for how contemporary mass media depict Black men.

The notion of the Black man as a sexual monster has been linked to the economic vulnerability that White working-class men feel in the face of a capitalist economy over which they have little power. Guerrero (1993), in his discussion of the emergence of this new stereotype in the novels of Thomas Dixon, suggests that the economic turmoil of the postbellum South served to undermine the white southern man's role as provider for his family; thus he sought to inflate his depreciated sense of manhood by taking up the honorific task of protecting White womanhood against the newly constructed specter of the "brute Negro." (p. 12)

This encoding of the economic threat in a sexual context is, according to Snead (1994), the principal mechanism of cinematic racism, and is one of the subplots of the enormously successful *King Kong* movie (renamed *King Kong and the White Women* in Germany). Arguing that "in all Hollywood film portrayals of blacks . . . the political is never far from the sexual" (p. 8), Snead links the image of King Kong rampaging through the streets of Manhattan with a defenseless White woman clutched to his body, to the increasing economic emasculation of White men in the Depression years and the growing fear that Black migration from the South had reduced the number of jobs available to working-class Whites. King Kong's death at the end of the movie remasculinizes the White man, not only through his conquest of the Black menace but also through regaining the woman. In this way, representations of Black men and White men are not isolated images working independently, but rather "correlate . . . in a larger scheme of semiotic valuation" (Snead, p. 4). Thus, the image of the Black man as a sexual savage serves to construct White male sexuality as the protector of White womanhood, as contained, and, importantly, as capable of intimacy and humanity.

In her analysis of Black and White masculinity in Hollywood movies, Jones

(1993) argues that although Black and White actors are increasingly portrayed in terms of a violent masculinity, for White actors this violence is tempered by his sexually intimate scenes with a White woman. These scenes assure the audience that for all his violence, the White man is still capable of bonding with another human being and of forming relationships. For Black actors, however, this humanizing quality is absent, and thus he can only be defined in terms of his violence. The problem with these types of representations is that, according to Jones, "they suggest that there are fundamental differences in the sexual behavior of Black men and White men and are ultimately indicative of the psychic inferiority of the Black man" (p. 250) and the superiority of White masculinity.

Hard-core pornography similarly depicts Black men as more sexually dehumanized than White men. This seems surprising because in pornography, all participants, men and women, are reduced to a series of body parts and orifices. However, studies that compare the representation of White men and Black men in pornography (Cowan & Campbell, 1994; Mayall & Russell, 1993) have found that it is Black male characters who are granted the least humanity and are most lacking in the ability to be intimate. Moreover, in movies and magazines that feature Black men, the focus of the camera and plot is often on the size of his penis and his alleged insatiable sexual appetite for White women. Movies with titles such as . . . *Black Stallions on Top* . . . and *Black Studs*, draw attention to the Black male body and in particular the penis, a rare occurrence in pornography targeted at heterosexual men. Movies such as *The Adventures of Mr. Tootsie Pole* (Bo Entertainment Groups) feature a Black man and a White woman on the cover. In *Black Studs* (Glitz Entertainment), three White women are shown having sex with three Black men.

The image of the Black man as sexually aggressive is a regular cartoon feature in *Hustler*, one of the best-selling hard-core porn magazines in the world (Osanka, 1989). Cartoons that have as their theme the sexual abuse of White women by Black men began appearing in the late 1970s, and by the mid-1980s, *Hustler* was running an average of two to three such cartoons an issue. *Hustler* was by no means the first to produce such an image, but it is probably the first mass-distributed cultural product (albeit in caricatured form) to visually depict an enormous Black penis actually doing severe physical damage to the vagina of a small White woman.

That these types of images have been marginalized in the debate on pornography is problematic, especially in light of the international success of *Hustler* magazine. Much of the analysis of pornography has focused on the ways the text works as a regime of representation to construct femininity and masculinity as binary opposites. This type of theorizing assumes a gender system that is race-neutral, an assumption that cannot be sustained in a country where "gender has proven to be a powerful means through which racial difference has historically been defined and coded" (Wiegman, 1993, p. 170). From the image of the Black woman as Jezebel to the Black man as savage, mainstream White representations of Blacks have coded Black sexuality as deviant, excessive, and a threat to the White social order. In *Hustler* sex cartoons, this threat is articulated par excellence in caricatured form and serves to reaffirm the racist myth that failure to contain Black masculinity results in a breakdown of the economic and social fabric of White society.

"F*** You if You Can't Take a Joke": Marketing the *Hustler* Cartoon

In the history of American mass media, cartoons have been a major forum for the production and reproduction of racist myths. From the prestigious *Harper's Weekly* of the late 1900s to contemporary Disney cartoons, Blacks have been caricatured as savages, animals, and lazy servants. Cartoons, with their claim to humor, have been especially useful vehicles for the expression of racist sentiments that might otherwise be considered unacceptable in a more serious form. Indeed, in his award-winning documentary *Ethnic Notions* (1987), Marlon Riggs shows how the cartoon image of Blacks has changed little from the beginning of the century to the more contemporary versions, whereas other media forms were forced, in the post–civil-rights era, to encode the racist myths in a more subtle manner.

The *Hustler* cartoons that have as their theme the Black man as the spoiler of White womanhood are an outgrowth of the portrait caricatures that originated in Italy at the end of the 16th century. These portrait caricatures, with their distinctive technique of "the deliberate distortion of the features of a person for the purpose of mockery" (Gombrich, 1963, p. 189), became very popular across Europe and were adapted in the middle of the 19th century by cartoonists who used similar methods of distortion against anonymous members of recognizable social groups, rather than well-known individuals. Gombrich, in his celebrated essay on caricatures, argues that the power of this visual technique is that the distorted features come to stand as symbols of the group and are thought to say something about the essential nature of the group as a whole. The Black male cartoon character in *Hustler* is caricatured to the point that his penis becomes the symbol of Black masculinity and his body the carrier of the essential nature of Black inferiority.

It is not surprising, therefore, that the only place where Blacks appear with any regularity in *Hustler* is the cartoon. To depict Black men as reducible to their penis in the more serious sections of the magazine might open *Hustler* up to charges of racism as well as the regular criticisms it receives from women's groups regarding the openly misogynist content. Indeed, the cartoon has become the only place where *Hustler*'s claim to being the most outrageous and provocative sex and satire magazine on the shelves is realized. Although Larry Flynt (publisher and editor of *Hustler*) regularly criticizes *Playboy* and *Penthouse* for being too soft and for "masquerading the pornography as art" (Flynt, 1983, p. 5), *Hustler*'s own pictorials tend to adopt the more soft-core codes and conventions (young, big-breasted women bending over to give the presumed male spectator a clear view of her genitals and breasts), rather than the hard-core ones that specialize in rape, torture, bondage, bestiality, defecation, and incest. However, these hard-core themes regularly appear in the cartoons, together with cartoons . . . [depicting] Black men raping, mutilating, and pimping White women.

One of the main reasons for the hard-core content of the cartoons is that *Hustler* has to be careful not to alienate its mainstream distributors with pictorials or articles that might be classed as too hard-core, thus relegating the magazine to the porn shops, a move that would severely limit its sales. (*Hustler*'s success is mainly due to its ability to gain access to mass distribution outlets in the United States and Europe.) On the other hand, *Hustler* also has to keep its promise to its readers to be more hard-core or else it would lose its readership to the more glossy, expensively produced soft-core *Playboy* and *Penthouse*. Toward this end, *Hustler* relies on its cartoons to make good on its promise to its readers to be "bolder in every direction than other publications" (Flynt, 1988, p. 7), while keeping the pictorials within the limits of the soft-core genre.

Flynt regularly stresses that the cartoons' boldness is not limited to sexual themes, but extends to their political content. Indeed, in his editorials, Flynt (1983) regularly stresses that "We are a political journal as well as a sex publication" (p. 5). In an editorial responding to critics of *Hustler* cartoons titled "Fuck You if You Can't Take a Joke," Flynt (1988) tells his readers that his critics are not upset with the sexual content of the magazine but, rather, with his satire that carries "the sting of truth itself" (p. 7). Flynt continues by arguing that he will not allow his critics to censor what is, in effect, the political content of his magazine, because "Satire, both written and visual, has . . . been the only alternative to express political dissent" (p. 7).

A strategy that Flynt has used to promote the cartoons to the readers is to elevate the long-standing cartoon editor of *Hustler*, Dwaine Tinsley, to a present-day major satirist. The creator of the "Chester the Molester" cartoon (a White, middle-aged pedophile who appeared monthly until Tinsley was arrested on child sexual abuse charges in 1989) and some of the most racist cartoons, Tinsley is described by *Hustler* editors as producing "some of the most controversial and thought-provoking humor to appear in any magazine" ("Show and Tell," 1983, p. 7) and, in some cases, cartoons that are "so tasteless that even Larry Flynt has had to think twice before running them" ("Tinsley in Review," 1983, p. 65). We are, however, reassured by Hustler that the tastelessness will continue, as "Larry is determined not to sell out and censor his creative artists" (p. 65) because satire "is a necessary tool in an uptight world where people are afraid to discuss their prejudices" ("Show and Tell," 1984, p. 9).

Thus, *Hustler* does not position itself simply as a sex magazine, but also as a magazine that is not afraid to tell the truth about politics. This linking of the sexual with the political makes *Hustler* cartoons a particularly powerful cultural means for the production and reproduction of racist ideology, for, as Snead (1994) argues, "It is both as a political and as a sexual threat that Black skin appears on screen" (p. 8). On the surface, these cartoons seem to be one more example of *Hustler*'s outrageous sexual humor, the Black man with the huge penis being equivalent to the other sexually deviant (White) cartoon characters. However, *Hustler*'s depictions of Black men are actually part of a much larger regime of racial representation, beginning with *The Birth of a Nation* and continuing with Willie Horton, which makes the Black man's supposed sexual misconduct a metaphor for the inferior nature of the Black "race" as a whole.

Black Men and White Women: The White Man under Siege

During the 1980s, Hustler featured the work of four cartoonists: Collins, Decetin, Tinsley, and Trosley. Surprisingly, although these cartoonists had very distinct styles, they all used a similar caricatured image of a Black man with an enormous muscular body, an undersized head (signifying retardation), very dark skin, and caricatured lips. The striking feature of this caricature is that the man is drawn to resemble an ape, an image that, according to Snead (1994), has historical and literary currency in this country. Pointing to *King Kong* as a prime example of this representation, Snead argued that "a willed misreading of Linnaean classification and Darwinian evolution helped buttress an older European conception . . . that blacks and apes, kindred denizens of the 'jungle,' are phylogenetically closer and sexually more compatible than blacks and whites" (p. 20). Black film critics have long argued that the *King Kong* movie and its sequels played a major role in the sexual demonization of Black masculinity because the ape—the carrier of blackness—was depicted as out of White control, resulting in the stalking and capturing of a White woman.

Whereas the original Kong lacked a penis, the *Hustler* version has, as his main characteristic, a huge black penis that is often wrapped around the "man's" neck or sticking out of his trouser leg. The penis, whether erect or limp, visually dominates the cartoon and is the focus of humor. This huge penis is depicted as a source of great pride and as a feature that distinguishes Black men from White men. For example, in one cartoon, a Black man and a White man are walking next to a fence. The White man makes a noise by dragging a stick along the fence, while the Black man does the same using his large penis, which is much bigger than the stick. The Black man, who is walking behind the White man, is snickering at the White man's stick (*Hustler*, February 1989, p. 95). . . .

Whereas the *King Kong* movies left to the imagination what would happen to the White woman if Kong had his way, Hustler provides the mainly White readership with detailed images of the violence Black men are seen as capable of doing to White women's bodies. In many of the cartoons, the theme of the joke is the severely traumatized vagina of the White sexual partner. In one cartoon, a naked White woman is sitting on a bed, legs open, and her vagina has red stars around it, suggesting pain. . . .

In *Hustler* cartoons, the White man is constructed as anything but the protector of White womanhood. He is a lower working class, middle-aged man whose flabby body is no match for the muscular, enormous Black body. In stark contrast to the big Black penis is the small-to-average White penis that is rarely erect and never threatening to White women. On the contrary, the size of the White man's penis is a source of ridicule or frustration to his sex partner (who is always White). Rather than showing empathy, the woman is constantly poking fun at his manhood by searching for it with magnifying glasses or binoculars. One cartoon, for example, has a White couple in bed, with the woman under the covers gleefully shouting, "Oh, I found it" (*Hustler*, May 1992, p. 10). The man is clearly embarrassed and is covering up his penis. Other cartoons show the White man endlessly searching pornography shops for penis enlargers (presumably the same enlargers that can be mail-ordered from the ads in the back of *Hustler*).

The small penis would seem to be one of the reasons why White male cartoon characters, in contrast to Black male cartoon characters, have trouble finding willing sex partners. His sexual frustration leads him to seek female surrogates in the form of dolls, bowling balls, children, chickens, and skulls. The Black man, however, appears to have no problem attracting a bevy of young, White women. When the White man does find a willing sex partner, she tends to be middle-aged, overweight, and very hairy. The Black man's White sexual partner is, however, usually thin, attractive, and lacks body hair. This is a very unusual female image in *Hustler* cartoons and suggests that the Black man is siphoning off the few sexually available, attractive women, leaving the White man with rejects. . . .

Because of the lack of willing sex partners, the White man is often reduced to paying for sex. However, once again, Black men have the upper hand because almost all the pimps in *Hustler* cartoons are Black. These Black men have, however, traded in their large penises for big Cadillacs, heavy gold jewelry, and fur coats, riches no doubt obtained from White johns. The prostitutes are both Black and White, but the johns are almost always depicted as White. Many of the cartoons have as their theme the White man trying to barter down the Black pimp, with the Black pimp refusing to change the price. The power of the Black man is now absolute—not only can he get his pick of attractive White women, he also controls White prostitutes, leaving the White man having to negotiate to buy what he once got for free.

Not only is the Black man draining the White man's access to women, he is also draining his pocket in the form of welfare. The Black man is shown as deserting his family and numerous unkempt, diseased children, leaving the welfare system to pick up the tab. One cartoon features a Black woman surrounded by children and saying to a White interviewer, "Yes, we does [sic] believe in Welfare" (*Hustler*, December 1992, p. 47). Another example is a cartoon advertising different dolls. The first doll, called "Beach Darbie," is a Barbie look-alike in a bathing costume. The second doll, also Darbie, is dressed in a white jacket and is called "Ski Darbie." The third doll is an overweight White woman with bedroom slippers and a cigarette hanging out of her mouth; she is called "Knocked-Up Inner-City Welfare Darbie." In each hand she has a Black baby (*Hustler*, December 1992, p. 107).

In *Hustler* cartoons, Black men have precisely the two status symbols that White men lack: big penises and money. The White man's poor sexual performance is matched by his poor economic performance. Reduced to living in trailer homes, poorly furnished apartments, or tract houses, the *Hustler* White male cartoon character is clearly depicted as lower working class. His beer gut, stubble, bad teeth, and working man's clothes signify his economic status and stand in sharp contrast to the signifiers of power attached to the image of the Black man.

A New Ending to an Old Story

The coding of Black men as sexual and economic threats takes on a contemporary twist in *Hustler*, as this threat cannot be easily murdered as in *King Kong*, but rather is now uncontainable and returns month after month to wreak havoc on White women's bodies and the White men's paychecks. This new ending changes the relationship between the binary representations of Black and White masculinity. In his analysis of the racial coding of masculinity in cinema, Snead (1994) argues that "American films . . . have always featured . . . implicit or explicit correlations between the debasement of Blacks and the elevation and mythification of Whites" (p. 142). In *Hustler* cartoons, both Black and White men are debased, the former for being hypermasculine and the latter for not being masculine enough.

As the target audience of *Hustler* is White men, it seems surprising that the cartoons regularly ridicule White men for being sexually and economically impotent and for failing to contain the Black menace. However, when class is factored into the analysis, it becomes apparent that it is not White men as a group who are being ridiculed. The debasement of White masculinity in *Hustler* cartoons is played out on the caricatured flabby, unkempt body of the lower working-class White man, a class that few Whites see themselves as belonging to, irrespective of their income. Thus, in between the hypermasculinity of the Black man and the undermasculinized White lower working-class man, is the reader inscribed in the text who can feel superior to both types of "deviants." The reader is invited to identify with what is absent in the cartoons, a "real man" (*Hustler*'s first issue ran an editorial that introduced the magazine as one for "real men") who turns to *Hustler* because it is, according to its editors, "truly the only magazine that deals with the concerns and interests of the average American."

The reader, constructed as the average American, is, as *Hustler* is careful about pointing out, not the same as the cartoon characters. In an editorial praising Tinsley, the editors wrote, "Dwaine Tinsley is not a black, a Jew, a wino, a

child molester, or a bigot. But the characters in his cartoon are. They are everything you have nightmares about, everything you despise" (p. 6). Thus, in coded
terms, *Hustler* provides distance between the reader and the cartoon characters, who are either lower class (Black, wino, child molester, bigot) or the elite
(Jew), by leaving open the middle class, the category in which most White
Americans situate themselves (Jhally & Lewis, 1992).

The lower class, sexually impotent White man in *Hustler* cartoons is,
thus, not an object of identification, but rather of ridicule, and serves as a piti-
ful example of what could happen if White men fail to assert their masculinity
and allow the Black man to roam the streets and bedrooms of White society.
The *Hustler* White male cartoon character thus stands as a symbol of the devastation that Blacks can cause, a devastation brought about by bleeding-heart
liberals who mistakenly allowed Blacks too much freedom. Just as Gus (the
Black, would-be rapist) in *The Birth of a Nation* is an example of what might
happen when Blacks are given their freedom from slavery (a dead White woman
being the end result), the *Hustler* Black man is an example of what could happen if Black men are not contained by White institutional forces, such as the
police and the courts. Whereas *The Birth of a Nation* and *King Kong* were, according to Snead (1994), the past's nightmare visions of the future, *Hustler's*
representation of Black men can be seen as the current nightmare vision of the
future, because it "re-enacts what never happened, but does so in an attempt to
keep it from ever happening" (p. 148).

By making the White man the loser, *Hustler* departs from the traditional
racial coding of masculinity and provides a different ending to the nightmare
vision of Black men taking over. This ending is, however, not simply restricted to the pages of *Hustler*; rather, it is articulated in the numerous news
stories on welfare cheats, inner-city violence, and reverse discrimination.
The White man is, according to the media, fast becoming the new minority
who has to support Black families in the inner city and give up his job to an
unqualified Black person because of past oppression. The White man is under
siege and unless he fights back, he will lose his masculine status as bread-
winner. The absence in *Hustler* cartoons of elite Whites as exploiters of poor
Whites firmly positions the Black man as the other who is the source of White
male discontent. Given the current economic conditions, which include
falling wages, downsizing, and off-shore production, the average White man
(along with everyone else who is not a member of the economic elite) is experiencing increasing levels of discontent and, as in previous periods of economic decline, it is the Black population that is demonized and scapegoated
as the cause of the economic woes.

Although the racial codings of masculinity may shift, depending on the
socioeconomic conditions, from the feminized Uncle Tom to the hypermas-
culinized "buck," Black masculinity continues to be represented as deviant. It
is this constructed, deviant status that continues to legitimize the oppression
and brutality that condemns young Black men to a life on the margins of society and makes them the convenient scapegoat for the economic and social up-

heaval brought about by global capitalism and rightwing government policies. Although this article has foregrounded *Hustler* cartoons, the regime of racial representation discussed continues to inform most mainstream media content and contributes to the commonsense notion that Black culture, not White supremacy, is the source of racial strife in America.

References

The biggest, blackest cock ever. (1983, November). *Hustler*, p. 6.

Carby, H. (1993). Encoding White resentment "Grand Canyon"—A narrative. In C. McCarthy & W. Crichlow (Eds.), *Race, identity and representation in education* (pp. 236–247). New York: Routledge.

Cowan, G., & Campbell, R. (1994). Racism and sexism in interracial pornography: A content analysis. *Psychology of Women Quarterly, 18,* 323–338.

Dyson, M. (1993). Reflecting Black: African-American cultural criticism. Minneapolis: University of Minnesota Press.

Entman, R. (1990). Modern racism and the image of Blacks. *Critical Studies in Mass Communication, 7,* 332–345.

Flynt, L. (1983, November). The politics of porn. *Hustler*, p. 5.

Flynt, L. (1988, July). Fuck you if you can't take a joke. *Hustler*, p. 7.

Forna, A. (1992). Pornography and racism: Sexualizing oppression and inciting hatred. In C. Itzin (Ed.), *Women, violence and civil liberties: A radical new view* (pp. 102–112). Oxford, UK: Oxford University Press.

Gombrich, E. (1963). *Meditations on a hobby horse.* London: Phaidon.

Gray, H. (1989). Television, Black Americans and the American dream. *Critical Studies in Mass Communication, 6,* 376–385.

Guerrero, E. (1993). *Framing blackness: The African American image in film.* Philadelphia: Temple University Press.

Jhally, S., & Lewis, J. (1992). *Enlightened racism: The Cosby Show, audiences, and the myth of the American dream.* Boulder, CO: Westview.

Jones, J. (1993). The construction of Black sexuality: Towards normalizing the Black cinematic experience. In M. Diawara (Ed.), *Black American cinema* (pp. 247–256). New York: Routledge.

Mayall, A., & Russell, D. (1993). Racism in pornography. In D. Russell (Ed.), *Making violence sexy: Feminist views on pornography* (pp. 167–177). New York: Teachers College Press.

Mercer, K. (1994). *Welcome to the jungle: New positions in Black cultural studies.* New York: Routledge.

Osanka, E. (1989). *Sourcebook on pornography.* Lexington, MA: Lexington Books.

Riggs, Marlon (Producer & director). (1987). *Ethnic Notions* [Documentary]. San Francisco: California Newsreel.

Rose, T. (1994). *Black noise: Rap music and Black culture in contemporary America.* Hanover, NH: University of New England Press.

Show and tell. (1983, November). *Hustler*, p. 7.

Show and tell. (1984, July). *Hustler*, p. 9.

Snead, J. (1994). *White screen, Black images: Hollywood from the dark side.* New York: Routledge.

Tinsley in review. (1983, November). *Hustler,* p. 65.

Wiegman, R. (1993). Feminism, "The Boyz," and other matters regarding the male. In S. Cohan & I. R. Hark (Eds.), *Screening the male: Exploring masculinities in Hollywood cinema* (pp. 173–193). New York: Routledge.

Winston, M. (1982). Racial consciousness and the evolution of mass communication in the United States. *Daedalus,* 4, 171–182.

READING REFLECTIONS

1. Why does Dines cite the O. J. Simpson case at the beginning of the article?
2. According to Dines, what socioeconomic factors have contributed to the stereotype of the black male as "monster"?
3. What is the presumed relationship between the white and the black male as portrayed by cartoons in *Hustler* magazine?
4. How does such a relationship reflect cultural racism in Dines' view, and how is that racism supposedly reflected in other media forms?
5. Test Dines' theory of cultural racism by watching a television crime drama and analyzing the roles of male characters.

LOOKING GOOD, FEELING SCARED

Alisa Valdes

Whereas people would most likely associate eating disorders and distorted body images with women, these same people wouldn't think to also associate it with the gay male community where looking good has become a means of conveying that one is a desirable and healthy sexual partner. In her article, Valdes concentrates on the image of the homosexual male in light of the AIDS epidemic and its impact on the self-image of the gay male community.

Alisa Valdes is a staff writer for the Boston Globe, *whose articles often cover Hispanic issues, personality profiles, and theater and music reviews. Here she writes of the connection between bodybuilding and self-esteem for many gay men and the impact the AIDS crisis has had on the "perfect body" obsession by profiling personal trainer and model Greg Cloutier.*

The skin on his legs is shaved smooth. It stretches over the furrows between his muscles and he could be an anatomy textbook: quadriceps, gluteus, hamstrings, soleus, gastrocnemius. They are legs with the look and feel of a pink boulder on a Provincetown beach, washed clean and sanded to perfection.

You wouldn't know it to look at him, but Greg Cloutier, 30, personal trainer and bodybuilder, was an asthmatic kid who always sat out of gym class in school, an aspen of a boy with a willow walk, teased by everyone. Faggot. You skinny little fag. Even before he knew he was gay, they seemed to know. Even before he knew to like himself, they seemed to hate. Their words were like needles, and his self-esteem was a fragile balloon floating him through a world that wanted to down him at every turn.

When he was a junior, Cloutier joined the tennis team at his high school in Dennisport and realized he was athletic, and that as an athlete people left him alone. But it wasn't until he was 21 that Cloutier began to work out seriously— as a professional bodybuilder. He pumped up and his world changed, because no one mocks the jagged side of a mountain.

If he stopped working out today, however, Cloutier says he wouldn't let himself leave the house. "If I had to stop exercising, my perception would be that it would change my social life," Cloutier said. "It probably wouldn't, but I would think it did. I'd be thinking, like, I can't go to the beach because I don't look as good as I used to. Even though I'd know it would be wrong, I'd believe it anyway."

Body-image problems and obsessive-compulsive eating and exercise disorders have been well-documented among women. But the same issues have also long plagued segments of the gay male community. Now, as Gay Men's Health Crisis reports that the average 20-year-old gay man in the United States stands a 50 percent chance of contracting the AIDS virus in his lifetime (men over 45 have a 65 percent chance), the need many gay men feel to look strong and healthy has become tacitly synonymous with being acceptable as a sexual partner. As Brian Rosenberg, the Living Well Series coordinator at the Fenway Community Health Center and a gay advocate, said: "Body image is the hottest topic in the gay community right now."

Cloutier's day at the Metropolitan Health Club in Boston's South End, where he has worked as a personal trainer for 11 years, begins at 4:45 a.m. He's been up since 4, and for breakfast he had a dry bagel, nonfat yogurt with extra protein powder and half a Power Bar. There are few cars on Columbus Avenue, so the only noise is the jangling of the keys to the Met as he opens the door, and then locks it behind him.

One hour, 15 minutes. This is the time Cloutier has alone in the Met, the basement gymnasium beneath Club Cafe, with the exposed rock walls. It is time to lift without members gawking, time to concentrate. It's been like this for years, working hard for a perfect body. Cloutier has been featured in "pretty boy" calendars, in underwear ads, in the black-and-white photo book "Sleeping Beauties." One hour, 15 minutes now, and it's not enough. There will be two more hours of working out at World Gym in Weymouth, where he lives, this afternoon.

Even though it's impossible to change your form one day to the next, when Cloutier wakes up depressed and looks in the mirror he sees someone who isn't there: Where there is a sculpted, strong, positively beautiful man, Cloutier sees someone "flabby and not muscular at all." This type of distorted perception is called body dysmorphic disorder (anorexia, in which people starve themselves under the illusion that they are grossly overweight, and bulimia, where people binge and purge under the same illusion, are both forms of BDD). This perception of self throws Cloutier into a tailspin of self-doubt and extra exercise that can last for days, until he talks to a friend or a client and they remind him that looks aren't everything and that even if they were, he looks great.

Cloutier is aware of what happens to him, not in denial like he used to be. He wants to help other men not be like him, and also to lead them on the path toward being like him. It's awkward. They flock to him because he looks perfect and has the tools to teach them to be perfect, too. He makes $40 an hour to help them—that's about $80,000 a year. Yet he doesn't feel perfect, and he doesn't want them to value themselves the way he did, or the way the modeling industry did: "from the neck down." He said he wants them "to know they have positive attributes other than their bodies."

"Once you get into obsessing on your appearance you can't escape it," Cloutier said. "You start to think it's all you have going for you, and you want people to recognize that you're intelligent and you want them to take you seriously. I wish I had gone through more school and not made education second to bodybuilding."

Even though he says he is aware of the shallowness of this, Cloutier's body fat is the same as it was when he was modeling—close to none. "I'm obsessive," he explained. "I can't just have low body fat, I have to have none." He wants to break away, but he can't. He tells himself his goal is peace of mind and inner serenity, but he still worries that he is flabby.

It's hard to track down studies on people like Cloutier. Most of the research on body image has focused on women in general and only on men if they were in psychiatric hospitals. However, what little research has been done on men in general and body image indicates that gay men are more likely to feel bad about their bodies than straight men are.

"There is evidence that groups who receive sexual objectification from men—straight women and gay men—tend to be more unhappy with their bodies," said Peter Kassel, a psychologist at Beth Israel Hospital who specializes in gay men and body image. "Those groups that don't view themselves as sexual objects for men—lesbians and straight men—tend to be more comfortable with their bodies as gay men are."

By 6 a.m., members are already lined up outside the Met. Cloutier doesn't want them to know that he's in here at 4:45, because many of them would join him if they could.

While the Met shies away from being known as a "gay gym"—this reputation has hurt the gym in the past, says Caleb Davis, the owner—many of the clients are gay men, including all of Cloutier's clients today.

Cloutier's first client is Robby, then John, then "Brad," then Jimmy, then Charles, then Chris and then Franco, who calls to cancel, which gives Cloutier some extra time to work out. They are all unhappy with their present bodies.

Chris is short and strong, shaped like the Tasmanian devil, and does pull-ups from his fingertips like he's erasing a chalkboard. During his session, the song blares over the speakers: What is love? Baby don't hurt me, don't hurt me no more. Cloutier stands beneath, ready to catch him if he falls. Chris is an accountant with a gold earring in each ear—one hoop, one stud. He thinks of competing in bodybuilding, but says that he thinks he is "too small and skinny."

"I'd like 20 more pounds of muscle," he says later, looking in the mirror. "I've always wanted to be bigger, but I guess that doesn't come very easily to me."

He starts bicep curls under the watch of Cloutier's gentle green eyes. The blue veins in his forearms rise into a relief map, and the song changes: Everybody's freeeeeeee to feel good.

Chris says that he thinks gay men spend more time worrying about their appearance than straight men do, himself included. "For homosexuals one big difference is that you can see someone and say 'I want him' and you can also say 'I want to look like him.' It sets up a rivalry that straight people don't have to worry about. That's part of it."

Charles, a 35-year-old hairstylist and colorist, spends his session with Cloutier concentrating on his pecs and offers the following explanation for his own need to look good: "Women are much more generous with men than men are with women or men," he said, wiping his brow. "A woman will say, 'Oh, I like him because he's so nice or he's this and he's that,' where a man will say, 'Oh, she's cute, or he's cute.' Two men together make it even worse. You have to look good."

Kassel, who teaches at Harvard, takes the analysis a step further. He says that women—who have traditionally held little power in society—are more apt to judge a potential partner based on social status, money or power; men, on the other hand, have long been free to choose a partner based on appearance only. The song goes on: Everybody's freeeeeeee to feel good.

"There's no way to emerge from the task of coming into being a gay person without significant scars to a person's self-esteem," said Kassel. Usually these scars manifest themselves in three ways: a sense of isolation, constant feelings of rejection and a sense of not belonging. It is precisely these feelings, he says, that drive so many gay men to dissatisfaction with their bodies.

Jimmy spends his session with Cloutier working on his lower body—squats, leg curls. He's 36, a hairdresser and a former drug addict who says he works out "to look and feel the best I possibly can," though he monitors his diet carefully and hopes to get bigger and stronger and leaner.

"Diet is 90 percent of this," Cloutier says. "No amount of working out can make up for a poor diet."

Jimmy looks at Cloutier in the mirror and raises one eyebrow. "Maybe so, but I refuse to eat baby food."

Cloutier looks embarrassed for a moment and then explains: "I carry baby food with me, vegetables. It's low-fat, convenient and nutritious."

Lunch is coming up, and Cloutier will eat a small can of tuna fish, plain; pita bread, dry; and baby food peas. He doesn't eat cheese, ever, or any added fats. The only dairy he allows himself is skim milk, nonfat yogurt and nonfat cottage cheese. He drinks something called Critical Mass several times a day for extra protein so that his muscles "won't eat themselves." For dinner he will have brown rice and steamed vegetables, possibly boiled chicken.

Does he ever binge? Does ice cream call to him in the middle of the night? "No, not really. Besides, there are fat-free, sugar-free frozen yogurts on the market now, so you can always satisfy those urges without the negative side effects."

"You just stop craving it after a while," Jimmy added, pushing red-faced out of one last squat. "But if I want something, I usually have it, even just a little."

Cloutier smiles, in his professional trainer mode. All of the self-doubt he seemed to feel earlier about his obsession with his body, all the wishing he had gone to college instead of to the gym, all his hopes that people would judge him for his soul instead of his beauty, all of that has gone out the window and now he is proud. He flip-flops like this, between guilt and satisfaction. It's hard to keep up.

"I know I'm extreme," he says. "But I guess I consider myself a role model for these guys."

Jimmy has lost 20 pounds and a serious gut since he started working out with Cloutier, but no one mentions that at the gym except for Cloutier, and even then in whispers no one else can hear: You're looking good since you took that weight off. Keep it up. At the Met memorial service announcements are posted next to signs for apartments to rent. Since AIDS, it's taboo to tell a man that he has lost weight.

"No one says you look thinner anymore, or you've lost weight," said Cloutier, who himself is HIV negative and lives with his partner. "It implies that the guy looks sick, and no one wants that. Instead, you say, 'Oh, you look leaner' or 'more muscular.' Never 'thinner.' It's tough. Even though I'm negative, I still start to worry when I get a short haircut and someone says to me, 'Oh, you look thinner.' It's like I think, what are they thinking? Do they think I have it?"

Rosenberg, the Living Well Series coordinator at the Fenway health center, is convinced that the AIDS epidemic has taken the issues many gay men have with body image and made them even worse.

"As the crisis booms, there's even more of an emphasis on looking good," he said in an interview after a panel discussion on HIV and body image at the center. A roomful of HIV-positive men listened to the panelists, one of them raising his hand at the end to say that going into the Randolph Country Club with an IV bag and his lesions showing was the most revolutionary act he'd ever done. Seems no one wanted to see him there, because he looked sick. Some went so far as to ask him to leave, he said.

Rosenberg said that body image can also play a large role in negotiating safe-sex decisions: "If you're small and thin and you get together with a bigger, stronger man, and he doesn't want you to use a condom, you probably won't have the self-esteem to insist."

Rosenberg looks something like your best friend's big brother, square jaw, rosy cheeks, broad shoulders, like someone on a prep school soccer team. He is HIV positive. "Today it's ridiculous, but many men think that if you look good maybe you're HIV negative. But men can look great and have no T-cells at all," he said.

All of this bothers men like panelist and Provincetown-based AIDS activist Victor D'Lugan. Partly it's the sores that cover his body and hide his needs and his soul from the world. Mostly it's the hypocrisy of the men he used to love who no longer see him as a sexual being, condom or no condom. He's simply not acceptable. Not at parties, not on the beach. Not since the lesions. "And one of them," he said, "is an AIDS educator. He knows better."

The beautiful ideal, canonized by Calvin Klein, lived by Greg Cloutier, has become a requirement in many gay circles since the rise of the AIDS epidemic. Take the fabled "Underwear Parties" of the South End, where large groups of beautifully sculpted young men—wearing only $15 Calvin Klein underwear and colorful beads—do hallucinogenic drugs and dance in close, damp groups.

"The Oh Boy parties in LA and the Underwear Parties in the South End have criterium for entry," says Boston-based writer and gay activist Michael Bronski, who publishes regularly in *Out* magazine and other gay publications. "You can call them up on the phone and say, 'Well, I'm young and attractive and I went to a good school.' But if you say, 'I have lesions all over my chest, will that be a problem?' you can bet that the conversation will end pretty soon after that."

"Where are all the sick men?" D'Lugan asks. "What happens when we start to waste and our lesions start to show? We stop going outside, that's what happens. We wear turtlenecks."

At the beginning of May, Michael Walker died. He was one of the most popular personal trainers at the Metropolitan gym—outgoing, vivacious, friendly and beautiful. He was careful about what he ate. Lifted like a maniac. But as his sickness progressed, Michael, unlike the men who wear long-sleeved shirts and pants on the P-town beach in the summer, made an effort to show up for work with his lesions like proud tattoos.

"He didn't want to be ashamed of what was happening to him," said Caleb Davis, owner of the Met. "He was very upfront about it."

So Michael continued to train people as he himself wasted. And the clients were polite. "Everyone loved him," said Cloutier. "They didn't really talk about it, but they were nice to him."

When Cloutier talks about his friend and colleague, it is only a week after his death. Yet there is a certain blankness in his eyes, the tired eyes of someone who has lived through a war.

"In the gay community, you just see so many of your friends dying that it becomes different, somehow. You start to expect it," he explained.

Michael's memorial service was in June. It was a perfect summer Saturday—Provincetown, Commercial Street, happy couples with their fat-free, sugar-free frozen yogurt cones dripping over their hands, golden retrievers restless for water. The Unitarian Universalist meeting house was white in the sun, green lawn stretched to the street, the steeple like a finger pointing in the direction of a thousand souls.

Inside, John Thomas, a close friend of Walker's and a composer, performed music he had written that Walker had requested be played at the service. The whole memorial service was like this, planned by the man it was held for.

Walker is the 15th close friend Thomas has had taken by AIDS. Thomas was the one to go through Walker's closets in his mother's house when she said she couldn't bear to see the clothes anymore. As he went through the rugby shirts, holding each one up to the mirror, he remembered how great they looked on his friend, the friend he watched move away from worry about wasting from AIDS to an eventual peace with what was happening to his once perfect body.

"Michael was amazing," Thomas said. "He was so wrapped up in his fears in the beginning of what would happen to his body. He used to pray, 'Please God, nothing above the neck.' But as it progressed, all of his fear disappeared. The sicker he looked, the less he seemed like someone with a disease and the more he embraced life.

"I came out of the closet in the late '70s, and at the time being thin was in. And then it changed quite radically when it became associated with sickness. I saw an incredible rush to the gym, and I'd say that even more gay men bought into the buff body image than before, as if that could keep the disease at bay. It's sad, because what a lot of gay men are in denial about is looks-ism. This obsession with physical beauty is really sad, because it discounts so many other equal human beings in our life, as if the only way in which to know someone is through hormones. It's choosing one door out of the four doors to the soul. I really miss Michael. I miss talking to him about this stuff."

Not everyone in the gay community agrees that gay men are more obsessed with their appearance than straight men, however.

"I'm hesitant to say gay male culture is obsessed with youth and beauty," said Bronski, the writer. "There is certainly a part of gay male culture that is obsessed, but I think there's a little bit of a homophobic strain in that critique of gay male culture."

Kassel agreed that body-image problems are worse for men in general than the public acknowledges, especially with the rise in images like a perfectly sculpted Marky Mark in his underwear.

"I don't think this is just about gay men," Kassel said. "Men as objects of desire is a relatively new concept in our culture, so we'll see where Marky Mark in his briefs takes straight men.

"But is the worry equally spread? No. I think gay men have a particular vulnerability to experience dissatisfaction with their bodies that is slightly elevated above straight men. But of course, this is all very dicey and controversial."

Back at the Met, the house music vibrates the mirrors that are on every wall. Men watch themselves curl and pump and flex and crunch. There is sweat, and there is a need so great that it fills the room like a dream no one can shake.

Cloutier trains his client, and it's hard to locate on his face the sentence he spoke moments before: "Physical beauty is just a Band-Aid for the real situation for all of us, which is low self-esteem and shyness. As gay men, we grow up feeling inadequate. Beauty is like a suit of armor that holds off the feelings of inadequacy for a while. But they always come back."

The need is a ghost who whispers the words of one exercise-obsessed man: "I don't work out so that someone will worship me; I work out so that I'll be good enough to worship someone else."

Cloutier, who trains straight clients and gay clients, male and female, said he firmly believes that gay men have much lower self-esteem about their bodies than do straight men.

"Women and gay men say the same things to me," he said. "That they'll never be good enough. Straight men never say that. They're already ahead in life because they've been on top of the world since they were little boys and everything they did was congratulated. Gay men always feel they have to try harder to measure up. They don't just have to be in shape, they have to be really in shape. Just like women, they learn from early on that the better they look, the more attention they will get. The pretty little girl always gets noticed."

READING REFLECTIONS

1. Based on Valdes' interviews with gay men, how has the emphasis on the gay male body changed within the past decade?
2. How is the concern with appearance within the gay community both a personal and a social one, according to Valdes?
3. Is there such a thing as a "gay appearance"? To what extent is such an appearance portrayed in advertising, television, or film? Use specific examples to make your point. Is there any evidence in Valdes' article of a gay appearance?
4. How might such appearances conform to the appearances that are portrayed in Valdes' article? Are there portrayals that work against this image?
5. As evidenced in Valdes' article, in what ways is the gay male concern with body image similar to the concern women have with body image? What accounts for these concerns?

THE SHAPE OF THINGS TO COME

Katharine Greider

Women's fashion history has boasted a number of body-shaping devices that range from corsets and control top pantyhose to padded pants and push-up bras. With the emergence of the Wonderbra fad, Katharine Greider explores this dangerous trend in fashion that teaches women to hate their bodies and remedy their faults with any number of shapewear designs that provide them with the means to alter their unsatisfactory body shapes.

A writer living in New York, Katharine Greider's articles have appeared in Self, Harper's Bazaar, *and* Mother Jones. *In this 1995 article from* In These Times, *Greider questions attitudes about the female body that contribute to the development and marketing of shapewear such as the Wonderbra.*

Last May, after an impressive promotional buildup, the first batch of Wonderbras arrived at Macy's Manhattan store in an armored truck. A caravan of guards and a large brass band bore an oversized box of the cleavage-enhancing brassieres through the store's Broadway entrance and along its main corridor, finally reaching the appointed place for the ribbon-cutting. There, a set of twins—one sporting a Wonderbra, the other not—showed customers what a little engineering could do. "It was a whole cloak-and-dagger kind of thing," recalls Carolyn Moss, fashion director of the ready-to-wear department at Macy's.

Like the toys advertised in the comic books you read as a kid, the Wonderbra fascinates partly because of the sheer implausibility of its purportedly miraculous properties. Like x-ray glasses and Sea Monkeys, these fussy undergarments with their fantastical names—Gossard's Super-Uplift, It Must Be Magic—promise more than they can possibly deliver. Yet there is a part of you that half believes the promises anyway.

When, my curiosity piqued, I finally tried one on, there was no magic about it. I felt like one of those calendar dogs who stare forlornly into the camera, solemn in their mortification at being posed in a sailor suit or some such atrocity. The Wonderbra did not give me cleavage. It only protruded ridiculously from my chest, as stiff and crusty as the spun sugar on an old wedding cake.

Why, then, have the Wonderbra and its bust-enhancing ilk been such a sensation? As the Intimate Apparel Council's Dotti Keagy points out, push-ups offer

---

Katharine Greider, "The Shape of Things to Come," *In These Times,* May 1, 1995, pp. 14–16. Reprinted with the permission of *In These Times,* a bi-weekly newsmagazine published in Chicago.

a safe alternative to breast implants, "the look without the surgery." But this doesn't explain why the busty "look" so appeals in the first place. "I think women feel freer to have a more overt expression of their femininity than many have in the last two decades," a spokeswoman for Maidenform suggests. "I think, as women enter the workforce in greater and greater numbers and at every level, that changes the kind of clothing people feel comfortable wearing." The new suits for fall are tight and curvy, just the thing to wear over bust-enhancing undergarments—and they, too, it is said, are an expression of women's newfound freedom. "Thank God it's perhaps the end of the politically correct era," Christian Lacroix recently told one fashion mag. "At last everyone can be him- or herself."

Despite media reports of feverish women descending on Wonderbra displays, the bra's success is more a testimony to clever packaging than a response to clamorous demand. Many of the very same bras that are making news today have been available for years. A company called Gossard has been peddling the Wonderbra in Europe and the United Kingdom without much fanfare since the '60s. Gossard sells the bra under license from a company that joined with Sara Lee Foundations, the bra's current maker. "The padded push-up has always been around," says Karyn Monget of *Women's Wear Daily*. "[Sara Lee] just had the megabucks to promote it."

In 1994, the year of the Wonderbra's U.S. debut, Sara Lee Foundations increased its ad budget by 40 percent. The company's PR people skillfully whipped up media hype—the bra was thrice mentioned by name in *People* magazine—with carefully staged publicity stunts. Other companies, sensing a great opportunity, threw their own bras in the ring. Neiman-Marcus played videos in their stores instructing customers on how to wear cleavage-enhancing bras. Victoria's Secret and others introduced their own versions or stepped up promotional efforts for already existing product lines—see, for example, Maidenform's current "Lift your Spirits" sweepstakes.

Recently, the Council of Fashion Designers of America honored Wonderbra's maker for its impressive contribution to American fashion. "To those of us in the fashion industry," said the council's gleeful announcement, "the success of the Wonderbra made sense. Designers had returned to glamour on the runways, with a focus on cleavage. Suddenly, corsets were back. Women realized that their bodies could have shape again." Or, rather, that they could *be* shaped and reshaped with each new fashion season.

No one was more excited by this prospect than the makers and sellers of intimate apparel, whose business had been relatively lackluster. In October 1993, 14.4 percent of the total spent on bras in department stores went for push-ups; a year later, that percentage had risen to 20.6 percent, according to the NPD Group, a market research firm in Port Washington, N.Y. The total amount spent on bras increased 18 percent from 1991 to 1994, jumping from $2.4 billion to $2.9 billion. Maidenform reports that its old cleavage enhancers have been selling at five times the usual rate since the inception of Wonderbra Madness.

It was writer Sarah Mower who touched off the Wonderbra's ascension to greatness. She casually mentioned the bra in a 1991 article in *British Vogue* after discovering one in a dusty corner of a British lingerie shop. "It had such a fabulously kitschy name: The Gossard Wonderbra. Perfect!" Mower later wrote. "I amused myself mildly with the thought of giving the Wonderbra some sort of second outing. . . . Anyway, I'm over that now."

But it was too late to put the genie back in the bottle. At the end of 1993, Gossard's license to make the bra lapsed and Sara Lee snapped it back up, launching a series of risqué ads featuring a very bosomy model wearing only a bra and panties, with the tag lines "Look me in the eyes and tell me you love me," "Or are you just glad to see me?" and other such teasers. Gossard struck back with a new push-up of its own; a British ad for that bra showed a woman pulling tissue from another's brassiere. "Knocks the stuffing out of ordinary bras," the ad's text read. The Bra Wars, as Mower called them, were on.

The advertisers were prepared for controversy. "We expect some adverse comment," one account director told *Adweek*, "for the simple reason that there are a minority who mistake sexy for sexist." To defuse feminist objections, the ad firm that put together the U.K.'s Wonderbra campaign stressed the fact that the ads were designed by women.

American ads have certainly exploited the less-than-subtle suggestion that gentlemen prefer boobs. But they have also taken pains to present push-ups as an emblem of the modern woman's freedom to be her sexy, feminine self. In a Wonderbra ad, a model thrusts her snowy bosom at the camera, a come-hither glint in her eyes; the tag line reads, "Who cares if it's a bad hair day?" But Maidenform reassures customers, "No matter what they think, you wear it for the lift it gives your spirits." Another push-up bra bears the label: "You'll feel self-confident, in control, sexy, beautiful." Leaving aside whether or not these bras actually produce cleavage, much less self-confidence, the general message is that the two go together.

Women wear bras all day, every day, and what they want more than anything is not cleavage but comfort. In a survey conducted by EDK Associates, a market analysis firm specializing in female consumers, 36 percent of women said buying lingerie is a "sexy pick-me-up," but nearly all said they would choose comfort over sexiness. Seventy-eight percent said their first consideration is comfort, even when dressing for a night on the town. More than half of the women surveyed said they thought bra ads were sexist, and three-quarters thought the ads sold sexiness from a male point of view.

Nevertheless, complaints about the bra have been few. Perhaps that's because the bras haven't become a required element of the feminine uniform; on the contrary, push-up bras are still something of a novelty. Women can ignore them with impunity or buy them simply for the fun of it. Women's magazines have certainly devoted attention to the trend, but have leavened their coverage with a sense of the absurd. "When you take off this bra, you hang up your boobs," one *Mirabella* tester wisecracked about an $80 lace number.

The apparel industry is less inclined to joke. The plan now is to strike while the iron is hot with "bustier and corset looks, long-line Merry Widows for hip control and novelty items such as push-up bras with padded straps to define the shoulders," according to a recent story in the March issue of

Women's Wear Daily. That harmless little Wonderbra "didn't just create wonderful numbers" for its makers, says Roberta Elins of New York's Fashion Institute of Technology. "They created a category, one that's not been around for a long time, and that is seemingly expanding to other body parts." The category is called shapewear: underwear that reconfigures the body.

I have seen the future—and friends, it is scary: pantyhose that, in the slightly abashed words of their promoter, "lift and separate" the buttocks. "As women (and men!) celebrate the return of femininity in all its glory, Vanity Fair Intimate Legwear emerges as a beautiful complement to nature" that "does for the derriere what the push-up bra did for the bustline," trumpets one press release. "No one has focused on bottoms, with the Wonderbra and all of the bust-boosting hype," designer Nancy Ganz complained to *Women's Wear Daily.* "We now need to get the interest going in bottoms."

If push-up bra ads have tried to get across the idea that larger-than-life breasts are the ideal, makers and marketers of shapewear will have to push a far nastier message about women's bodies: that our butts and thighs and bellies are ugly. To remedy this, we will be offered underthings touted as "liposuction without the surgery," products with trademarked names like Tummy Terminator, Thigh Tamer and Waist Eliminator (really). Even the traditional home of comfort-first underwear, Jockey For Her, introduced a "Sculptures Bodyshaping Collection" in March. "From daringly bare nightwear to the retro-revival day dress, slip into the season's shapely styles without a care—or another trip to the gym!" shrieks Jockey's promotional release.

I asked Ethel Klein, president of EDK Associates, if clever marketing can get American women to wear body-shapers. Her reply: "Not if they're not comfortable." Whatever manufacturers may claim about the new stretch fabrics, that which moves flesh to where it does not incline to go eventually causes discomfort if not outright pain. The Fashion Institute's Elins guesses older women who remember girdles will resist, though the young may be convinced of their novelty. "I think whether a woman will buy something that is not comfortable has a lot to do with her age and her politics—her feminist politics," she says.

Not long ago I visited the lingerie department at Macy's to look for a sign or, perhaps, to divine a mood. The corset shop I had read about—it opened last fall—was nowhere to be found, and as yet, there wasn't much in the way of shapewear.

I located the Wonderbra and a few other push-ups displayed together in a small section of their own. There a couple furtively fingered the cups of the Wonderbras, whispered, and slunk back and forth to the dressing room. A British woman read the slogan on the wall—"one *little* push"—and joked to her friend, "Couldn't they make it one big push for me?" "Oh, you poor girl," the friend murmured fondly.

Then two young American women zeroed in on the new Wonderbra swimwear with obvious interest. They pulled at the stretchy fabric and squeezed the padding at the bust. "Look at that *print*," one said in disgust. "I might as well buy a one-piece girdle, 'cause that's what they look like," the other replied. And off they went, as briskly and purposefully as they had come.

READING REFLECTIONS

1. What, according to Greider, is the dominant message behind the current marketing of "shapewear"?
2. As per Greider's article, what do today's lingerie products have in common with the corsets of yesteryear?
3. Greider analyzes the mass-marketing campaign of the Wonderbra and other body-shaping devices to today's women. Survey a series of such advertisements within several fashion magazines, and analyze the cultural assumptions about the female body that make such products marketable.
4. The manufacturers of the Wonderbra accuse critics of not being able to distinguish between "sexy" and "sexist." Based on Greider's article, do you see this as a valid argument?
5. If 78 percent of women contend that they would choose "comfort over sexiness" in their lingerie purchases, and that half of women surveyed said bra ads were sexist, how do you account for the popularity of the Wonderbra? What do you think Greider would say?

A MODEL FIGURE AT SIZE 14

Alex Witchel

In a time of anorexic models sporting the heroin-chic look, Emme is the exception to the rule. Her full-figured body and defiance of the standard size 6 or below of most models has made her a realistic model for the average woman, who wears a size 14. Emme's high self-esteem and practical attitude toward accepting different body types is a lesson that is too slow in coming for the fashion industry.

Alex Witchel frequently writes about the fashion industry for the New York Times Magazine, Vogue, *and* Mademoiselle. *In this syndicated article from the* New York Times *News Service, Witchel profiles the skyrocketing career of plus-size model Emme and the development of designer marketing campaigns for the "average" woman, whom statistics report as a size 14, rather than the traditional size 6 still common to most fashion magazines.*

New York—The moment came, as it inevitably does. She stood, turned, and started to walk. Her lime green T-shirt tucked into her form-fitting pants, she lifted her head and smiled. The men had left the restaurant by now. The women had not. In front of her, they smiled back. Behind her, their eyes followed her pants, amply filled by a pair of hips as broad as her shoulders. Some looked concerned. Some looked relieved. All looked at their plates.

Emme Aronson was going to the ladies' room, and at 5 foot 11, 190 pounds, she's hard to miss. Emme (pronounced like Emmy), as she is known professionally, is the world's leading model for plus sizes, which means size 12 and above. And that means 60 per cent of the women in this country. Emme herself wears a 14 or 16 and a size 11 shoe. Though her agency, Ford Models, would not divulge her exact earnings, it did say that Emme is the top moneymaker in her division worldwide.

Most women would kill to have Emme's face, with her great bones and wide eyes, recently on a billboard display in Times Square for Liz Claiborne's plus-size line, Elisabeth. Just as many would kill to have her confidence.

"I try and wear clothes that are tighter," she said. "This is just another body type; it's not slovenly. I have great proportion."

Does she also have cellulite? "Of course," she said easily. "And I have a gut. But when you look at everyone else, they have one, too. So, instead of standing in front of the mirror saying, 'You look horrible,' I don't stay away from bikinis. The last time I went to the beach I wore a thong. Sometimes I go a little overboard to get to a balanced place. It's all attitude. I'm never going to be size 10, 150 pounds again. But if I feel great, that's more attractive than trying to cover up with a towel."

It's also attractive to eat with a woman who admits to an appetite. When the waitress at Park Avalon, on Park Avenue South, described the day's specials, Emme's response was "Mmmmmmmm." First she ordered a glass of chardonnay, followed by an appetizer of a swordfish hand roll with tabbouleh and an entree of crab cakes. She doesn't pick. She eats.

"I stopped dieting," she said. "I've changed my psyche, my self-esteem, the 'good girl, bad girl' thing. If you cheat on your husband or commit murder, that's bad. A cookie is just a cookie. I got tired of fighting myself every step of the way. I live my life now. I don't get crazy."

Emme, 33, shares her philosophy in her new book, *True Beauty: Positive Attitudes and Practical Tips From the World's Leading Plus-Size Model* (Putnam, $23.95), written with Daniel Paisner.

Mode, a new fashion magazine for plus sizes, published its premiere issue last month. "We could not have done this magazine five years ago," said Julie Lewit-Nirenberg, who created it with Nancy Nadler LeWinter. "It was all polyester then, and muumuus. Now, designers and manufacturers have recognized that this is not a niche market but the majority of American women, Versace, Givenchy, Emanuel, and Dana Buchman are all doing collections now for sizes 14 to 24."

But Alan Millstein of the Fashion Network Report, a newsletter for the retail industry, finds that change has been slow in coming. "There is still enormous prejudice among retailers when it comes to plus sizes," he said. "Those customers pay higher prices for their clothes than other women do, and there is rarely a sale in those departments because the stores know they're dealing with desperadoes."

"But," he added, "Conde Nast and Hearst are also at fault. In those fashion magazines with their descriptive patter of 'young,' 'thin,' 'waif,' 'chic,' and their obsession with articles on diets and diet aids, the large woman hasn't got a fighting chance."

That's an opinion Emme shares. "The diet industry is a $33-billion-a-year business with a 98 per cent failure rate," she said. "We've fallen into a whole system where we want to be accepted and seen as attractive. Those are basic needs, and who knows that better than advertisers? I don't promote obesity and I don't promote anorexia. We should all have more compassion for our differences. We don't have to be the same to be accepted."

This was a lesson she learned early. Emme, whose name originally was Melissa Miller, was raised by her mother in Manhattan after her parents' divorce. (Her mother called her 'M,' which turned into Emme.) When she was 5, her mother married a man named Bill (Emme won't reveal his full name), and they moved to Saudi Arabia, where he taught music at a junior high school. Like her father, who is deceased, Bill was a large man, 6 foot 6, weighing more than 300 pounds. Along with his own weight, he was obsessed with Emme's.

In her book, she tells the story of Bill's instructing her at age 12 to strip down to her underwear while he took a black marker and drew circles on her outer thighs, hips, stomach, and arms to highlight where she needed to lose weight. She scrubbed them off, or thought she did, put on her bathing suit, and went out for a swim. But when she got to the pool, one of the boys started pointing and laughing at the marks that stayed behind.

"After that, I didn't allow myself to feel," she said. "A few years ago I went into therapy and said, 'I'm angry, and I need to know why.' "

She had enough reasons to choose from. Besides her stepfather and the weigh-ins he subjected her to, there was the death of her mother from cancer at 39, when Emme was 15. Her mother had had two more children with Bill: Melanie, now 24, a plus-size model at the Wilhelmina agency, and Chip, 26, a Wall Street trader and part-time plus-size model himself.

Emme says she is close to both of them, though she no longer speaks to her stepfather.

Part of the healing process was demystifying food. "I eat desserts when I feel like it," she said. "Yesterday, I had a Hershey bar with almonds. I was in the mood. I've allowed myself everything for so long I don't have to overdo it because I haven't had it. I eat pizza, goat cheese, french toast, waffles, omelets, roast potatoes. I don't eat a lot of meat because it hurts my stomach. But when I need to eat it, I do."

Well! To become a model and be able to eat normal amounts of food and not only that, but also to be 33, when most models are considered ancient, is truly remarkable. Then again, their faces don't have as much padding.

Not that she has time for more. Besides a full modeling schedule, she is the spokeswoman for both Liz Claiborne's Elisabeth line and for Playtex's new full-figured lingerie, Body Language. She is also in demand on the lecture circuit.

"I have a deep concern for women who wear size 14 and above," she said. "They have no voice. My book and my talks are vehicles to say, 'You're not alone.' Women who've read the book call me and cry. It's the first time they're hearing a positive, nonbashing message."

Emme hears one all the time, from her husband of seven years. Phillip Aronson, whom she knew at Syracuse. The couple live in Bergen County, N.J., and he works in New York as a creative vice president for the Aronson Group, his family's advertising agency. He is 5 foot 11, the same height as his wife, but at 155 pounds, he is 35 pounds lighter. He told *People* magazine, which included Emme in its 50 Most Beautiful People in the World issue of 1994, "When I'm tired, she can give me a piggyback ride."

Emme said happily: "He's been such an inspiration to me. He really stands up for what I'm doing. And we plan to have a family in the next couple of years."

READING REFLECTIONS

1. In his chronicle of the life of plus-size model Emme, Witchel quotes the co-editor of the newest plus-size fashion magazine, *Mode*, who notes that such a publication would not have been possible five years previous. Why do you think this is so?
2. How does the emergence of *Mode* conflict with other images of women, such as the Wonderbra campaign discussed in Greider's article?
3. How are the goals of the Wonderbra campaign and the magazine *Mode* similar or different?
4. What are some of the reasons Emme has "stopped dieting"? To what extent is dieting expected of both women and men in our culture?
5. In what ways is Emme's story of self-acceptance an unusual one for women of all body sizes?

A GENTLEMAN AND A CONSUMER

Diane Barthel

---

*How has advertising changed in regard to its treatment of male con-
sumers? Barthel's article takes a look at the pressure placed on men, usually reserved for women, to conform to notions of style imposed on them
by the advertising world. Increasingly, men have become more self-
conscious of their appearance. This trend is evidenced by the rise of male-
oriented fashion magazines, such as* GQ, M Magazine, YMF, *and* Young
Black Male, *as well as by advertisements that heavily promote the importance of one's appearance. The question, however, is whether or not
men are buying it.*

*Diane Barthel is a professor of English at Temple University and the
author of* Putting On Appearances: Gender and Advertising *(1988), an
analysis of how gender is defined through advertising images. Her excerpt from this book, "A Gentleman and a Consumer," examines the
evolving image of men and definition of masculinity as advertisers market appearances and appearance-based products to male audiences.*

There are no men's beauty and glamour magazines with circulations even
approaching those of the women's magazines. The very idea of men's beauty
magazines may strike one as odd. In our society men traditionally were supposed to make the right appearance, to be well groomed and neatly tailored.
What they were *not* supposed to do was to be overly concerned with their appearance, much less vain about their beauty. That was to be effeminate, and not
a "real man." Male beauty was associated with homosexuals, and "real men"
had to show how red-blooded they were by maintaining a certain distance from
fashion.

Perhaps the best-known male fashion magazine is *GQ* founded in 1957
and with a circulation of 446,000 in 1986. More recently, we have seen the
launching of *YMF* and *Young Black Male*, which in 1987 still [had] few advertising pages. *M* magazine, founded in 1983, attracts an audience "a cut above"
that of *GQ*.[1]

Esquire magazine, more venerable (founded in 1933), is classified as a general interest magazine. Although it does attract many women readers, many of
the columns and features and much of the advertising are definitely directed

---

Diane Barthel, "A Gentleman and a Consumer," in *Putting On Appearances: Gender and Advertising* (Philadelphia: Temple University Press, 1988), pp. 169–83.

toward attracting the attention of the male readers, who still make up the overwhelming majority of the readership.

The highest circulations for men's magazines are for magazines specializing either in sex (*Playboy*, circulation 4.1 million; *Penthouse*, circulation nearly 3.8 million; and *Hustler*, circulation 1.5 million) or sports (*Sports Illustrated*, circulation 2.7 million).[2] That these magazines share an emphasis on power—either power over women or over other men on the playing field—should not surprise. In fact, sociologist John Gagnon would argue that sex and sports now represent the major fields in which the male role, as defined by power, is played out, with physical power in work, and even in warfare, being less important than it was before industrialization and technological advance.[3]

If we are looking for comparative evidence as to how advertisements define gender roles for men and women, we should not then see the male role as defined primarily through beauty and fashion. This seems an obvious point, but it is important to emphasize how different cultural attitudes toward both the social person and the physical body shape the gender roles of men and women. These cultural attitudes are changing, and advertisements are helping to legitimate the use of beauty products and an interest in fashion for men, as we shall see. As advertisements directed toward women are beginning to use male imagery, so too advertisements for men occasionally use imagery resembling that found in advertisements directed toward women. We are speaking of two *modes*, then. As Baudrillard[4] writes, these modes "do not result from the differentiated nature of the two sexes, but from the differential logic of the system. The relationship of the Masculine and the Feminine to real men and women is relatively arbitrary."[5] Increasingly today, men and women use both modes. The two great terms of opposition (Masculine and Feminine) still, however, structure the forms that consumption takes; they provide identities for products and consumers.

Baudrillard agrees that the feminine model encourages a woman to please herself, to encourage a certain complacency and even narcissistic solicitude. But by pleasing herself, it is understood that she will also please others, and that she will be chosen. "She never enters into direct competition. . . . If she is beautiful, that is to say, if this woman is a woman, she will be chosen. If the man is a man, he will choose his woman as he would other objects/signs (HIS car, HIS woman, HIS eau de toilette)."[6]

Whereas the feminine model is based on passivity, complacency, and narcissism, the masculine model is based on exactingness and choice.

> All of masculine advertising insists on rule, on choice, in terms of rigor and inflexible minutiae. He does not neglect a detail . . . It is not a question of just letting things go, or of taking pleasure in something, but rather of distinguishing himself. To know how to choose, and not to fail at it, is here the equivalent of the military and puritanical virtues: intransigence, decision, "virtus."[7]

This masculine model, these masculine virtues, are best reflected in the many car advertisements. There, the keywords are masculine terms: *power*, *performance, precision.* Sometimes the car is a woman, responding to the touch and will of her male driver, after attracting him with her sexy body. "Pure shape, pure power, pure Z. It turns you on." But, as the juxtaposition of shape and power in this advertisement suggests, the car is not simply other; it is also an extension of the owner. As he turns it on, he turns himself on. Its power is his power; through it, he will be able to overpower other men and impress and seduce women.

> How well does it perform?
> How well can you drive? (Merkur XR4Ti)

> The 1987 Celica GT-S has the sweeping lines and aggressive stance that promise performance. And Celica keeps its word.

> Renault GTA:
> Zero to sixty to zero in 13.9 sec.
> It's the result of a performance philosophy where acceleration and braking are equally important.
> There's a new Renault sports sedan called GTA. Under its slick monochromatic skin is a road car with a total performance attitude. . . . It's our hot new pocket rocket.

In this last example, the car, like the driver, has a total performance attitude. That is what works. The slick monochromatic skin, like the Bond Street suit, makes a good first impression. But car, like owner, must have what it takes, must be able to go the distance faster and better than the competition. This point is explicitly made in advertisements in which the car becomes a means through which this masculine competition at work is extended in leisure. Some refer directly to the manly sport of auto racing: "The Mitsubishi Starion ESI-R. Patiently crafted to ignite your imagination. Leaving little else to say except . . . gentlemen, start your engines." Others refer to competition in the business world: "To move ahead fast in this world, you've got to have connections. The totally new Corolla FX 16 GT-S has the right ones." Or in life in general. "It doesn't take any [Japanese characters] from anyone. It won't stand for any guff from 300ZX. Or RX-7. Introducing Conquest Tsi, the new turbo sport coupe designed and built by Mitsubishi in Japan." Or Ferrari, which says simply, "We are the competition." In this competition between products, the owners become almost superfluous. But the advertisements, of course, suggest that the qualities of the car will reflect the qualities of the owner, as opposed to the purely abstract, apersonal quality of money needed for purchase. Thus, like the would-be owner, the BMW also demonstrates a "relentless refusal to compromise." It is for "those who thrive on a maximum daily requirement of high performance." While the BMW has the business attitude of the old school ("aggression has never been expressed with such dignity"), a Beretta suggests what it takes to survive today in the shark-infested waters of Wall Street. In a glossy three-page cover foldout, a photograph of a shark's fin cutting through indigo waters is accompanied by the legend "Discover a new species from today's

Chevrolet." The following two pages show a sleek black Beretta similarly cutting through water, and, presumably, through the competition: "Not just a new car, but a new species . . . with a natural instinct for the road . . . Aggressive stance. And a bold tail lamp. See it on the road and you won't soon forget. Drive it, and you never will."

And as with men, so with cars. "Power corrupts. Absolute power corrupts absolutely" (Maserati). Not having the money to pay for a Maserati, to corrupt and be corrupted, is a source of embarrassment. Advertisements reassure the consumer that he need not lose face in this manly battle. Hyundai promises, "It's affordable. (But you'd never know it.)"

> On first impression, the new Hyundai Excel GLS Sedan might seem a trifle beyond most people's means. But that's entirely by design. Sleek European design, to be exact.

Many advertisements suggest sexual pleasure and escape, as in "Pure shape, pure power, pure Z. It turns you on." Or "The all-new Chrysler Le Baron. Beauty . . . with a passion for driving." The Le Baron may initially suggest a beautiful female, with its "image of arresting beauty" and its passion "to drive. And drive it does!" But it *is* "Le Baron," not "La Baronness." And the advertisement continues to emphasize how it "*attacks* [emphasis mine] the road with a high torque, 2.5 fuel-injected engine. And its turbo option can blur the surface of any passing lane." Thus the object of the pleasure hardly has to be female if it is beautiful or sleek. The car is an extension of the male that conquers and tames the (female) road: "Positive-response suspension will calm the most demanding roads." The car becomes the ultimate lover when, like the Honda Prelude, it promises to combine power, "muscle," with finesse. Automobile advertisements thus play with androgyny and sexuality; the pleasure is in the union and confusion of form and movement, sex and speed. As in any sexual union, there is ultimately a merging of identities, rather than rigid maintenance of their separation. Polymorphous perverse? Perhaps. But it sells.

Though power, performance, precision as a complex of traits find their strongest emphasis in automobile advertisements, they also appear as selling points for products as diverse as shoes, stereos, and sunglasses. The car performs on the road, the driver performs for women, even in the parking lot, as Michelin suggests in its two-page spread showing a male from waist down resting on his car and chatting up a curvaceous female: "It performs great. And looks great. So, it not only stands out on the road. But in the parking lot. Which is one more place you're likely to discover how beautifully it can handle the curves" (!).

As media analyst Todd Gitlin points out, most of the drivers shown in advertisements are young white males, loners who become empowered by the car that makes possible their escape from the everyday. Gitlin stresses the advertisements' "emphasis on surface, the blankness of the protagonist; his striving toward self-sufficiency, to the point of displacement from the recognizable world."[8] Even the Chrysler advertisements that coopt Bruce Springsteen's "Born in the USA" for their "Born in America" campaign lose in the process the original political message, "ripping off Springsteen's angry anthem, smoothing it into a Chamber of Commerce ditty as shots of just plain productive-looking folks, black and white . . . whiz by in a montage-made community." As Gitlin comments, "None of Springsteen's losers need apply—or rather, if only they would roll up their sleeves and see what good company they're in, they wouldn't feel like losers any longer."[9]

This is a world of patriarchal order in which the individual male can and must challenge the father. He achieves identity by breaking loose of the structure and breaking free of the pack. In the process he recreates the order and reaffirms the myth of masculine independence. Above all, he demonstrates that he knows what he wants; he is critical, demanding, and free from the constraints of others. What he definitely does not want, and goes to some measure to avoid, is to appear less than masculine, in any way weak, frilly, feminine.

Avoiding the Feminine

Advertisers trying to develop male markets for products previously associated primarily with women must overcome the taboo that only women wear moisturizer, face cream, hair spray, or perfume. They do this by overt reference to masculine symbols, language, and imagery, and sometimes by confronting the problem head-on.

There is not so much of a problem in selling products to counteract balding—that traditionally has been recognized as a male problem (a bald woman is a sexual joke that is not particularly amusing to the elderly). But other hair products are another story, as the March 1987 *GQ* cover asks, "Are you man enough for mousse?" So the advertisements must make their products seem manly, as with S-Curl's "wave and curl kit" offering "The Manly Look" on its manly model dressed in business suit and carrying a hard hat (a nifty social class compromise), and as in college basketball sportscaster Al McGuire's testimonial for Consort hair spray:

> "Years ago, if someone had said to me, 'Hey Al, do you use hair spray?' I would have said, 'No way, baby!' "
> "That was before I tried Consort Pump."
> "Consort adds extra control to my hair without looking stiff or phony. Control that lasts clean into overtime and post-game interviews . . ."
> Grooming Gear for Real Guys. *Consort.*

Besides such "grooming gear" as perms and hair sprays, Real Guys use "skin supplies" and "shaving resources." They adopt a "survival strategy" to fight balding, and the "Fila philosophy"—"products with a singular purpose: performance"—for effective "bodycare." If they wear scent, it smells of anything *but* flowers: musk, woods, spices, citrus, and surf are all acceptable. And the names must be manly, whether symbolizing physical power ("Brut") or financial power ("Giorgio VIP Special Reserve," "The Baron. A distinctive fragrance for men," "Halston—For the privileged few").

As power/precision/performance runs as a theme throughout advertising to men, so too do references to the business world. Cars, as we have seen, promise to share their owner's professional attitude and aggressive drive to beat out the competition. Other products similarly reflect the centrality of business competition to the male gender role. And at the center of this competition itself, the business suit.

> At the onset of your business day, you choose the suit or sport coat that will position you front and center . . .
> The Right Suit can't guarantee he'll see it your way. The wrong suit could mean not seeing him at all.

Along with the Right Suit, the right shirt. "You want it every time you reach across the conference table, or trade on the floor, or just move about. You want a shirt that truly fits, that is long enough to stay put through the most active day, even for the taller gentleman." The businessman chooses the right cologne—Grey Flannel, or perhaps Quorum. He wears a Gucci timepiece as he conducts business on a cordless telephone from his poolside—or prefers the "dignity in styling" promised by Raymond Weil watches, "a beautiful way to dress for success."

Men's products connect status and success; the right products show that you have the right stuff, that you're one of them. In the 1950s C. Wright Mills[10] described what it took to get ahead, to become part of the "power elite":

> The fit survive, and fitness means, not formal competence . . . but conformity with the criteria of those who have already succeeded. To be compatible with the top men is to act like them, to look like them, to think like them: to be of and for them—or at least to display oneself to them in such a way as to create that impression. This, in fact, is what is meant by "creating"—a well-chosen word—"a good impression." This is what is meant—and nothing else—by being a "sound man," as sound as a dollar.[11]

Today, having what it takes includes knowing "the difference between dressed, and well dressed" (Bally shoes). It is knowing that "what you carry says as much about you as what you put inside it" (Hartmann luggage). It is knowing enough to imitate Doug Fout, "member of one of the foremost equestrian families in the country."

> Because of our adherence to quality and the natural shoulder tradition, Southwick clothing was adopted by the Fout family years ago. Clearly, they have as much appreciation for good lines in a jacket as they do in a thoroughbred.

There it is, old money. There is no substitute for it, really, in business or in advertising, where appeals to tradition form one of the mainstays guaranteeing men that their choices are not overly fashionable or feminine, not working class or cheap, but, rather, correct, in good form, above criticism. If, when, they achieve this status of gentlemanly perfection, then, the advertisement suggests, they may be invited to join the club.

> When only the best of associations will do.
>
> Recognizing style as the requisite for membership, discerning men prefer the natural shoulder styling of Racquet Club. Meticulously tailored in pure wool, each suit and sportcoat is the ultimate expression of the clubman's classic good taste.

Ralph Lauren has his Polo University Club, and Rolex picks up on the polo theme by sponsoring the Rolex Gold Cup held at the Palm Beach Polo and Country Club, where sixteen teams and sixty-four players competed for "the pure honor of winning, the true glory of victory":

> It has added new lustre to a game so ancient, its history is lost in legend. Tamerlane is said to have been its patriarch. Darius's Persian cavalry, we're told, played it. It was the national sport of 16th-century India, Egypt, China, and Japan. The British rediscovered and named it in 1857.
>
> The linking of polo and Rolex is uniquely appropriate. Both sponsor and sport personify rugged grace. Each is an arbiter of the art of timing.

In the spring of 1987, there was another interesting club event—or nonevent. The prestigious New York University Club was ordered to open its doors to women. This brought the expected protests about freedom of association—and of sanctuary. For that has been one of the points of the men's club. It wasn't open to women. Members knew women had their place, and everyone knew it was not there. In the advertisements, as in the world of reality, there is a place for women in men's lives, one that revolves around:

Sex and Seduction

The growing fascination with appearances, encouraged by advertising, has led to a "feminization" of culture. We are all put in the classic role of the female: manipulable, submissive, seeing ourselves as objects. This "feminization of sexuality" is clearly seen in men's advertisements, where many of the promises made to women are now made to men. If women's advertisements cry, "Buy (this product) and he will notice you," men's advertisements similarly promise that female attention will follow immediately upon purchase, or shortly thereafter. "They can't stay away from Mr. J." "Master the Art of Attracting Attention." She says, "He's wearing my favorite Corbin again." Much as in the advertisements directed at women, the advertisements of men's products promise that they will do the talking for you. "For the look that says come closer." "All the French you'll ever need to know."

Although many advertisements show an admiring and/or dependent female, others depict women in a more active role. "I love him—but life in the fast lane starts at 6 A.M.," says the attractive blonde tying on her jogging shoes, with the "him" in question very handsome and very asleep on the bed in the background. (Does this mean he's in the slow lane?) In another, the man slouches silhouetted against a wall; the woman leans aggressively toward him. He: "Do you always serve Tia Maria . . . or am I special?" She: "Darling, if you weren't special . . . you wouldn't be here."

The masculine role of always being in charge is a tough one. The blunt new honesty about sexually transmitted diseases such as AIDS appears in men's magazines as in women's, in the same "I enjoy sex, but I'm not ready to die for it" condom advertisement. But this new fear is accompanied by old fears of sexual embarrassment and/or rejection. The cartoon shows a man cringing with embarrassment in a pharmacy as the pharmacist yells out, "Hey, there's a guy here wants some information on Trojans." ("Most men would like to know more about Trojan brand condoms. But they're seriously afraid of suffering a spectacular and terminal attack of embarrassment right in the middle of a well-lighted drugstore.") Compared with such agony and responsibility, advertisements promising that women will *want* whatever is on offer, and will even meet the male halfway, must come as blessed relief. Men can finally relax, leaving the courting to the product and seduction to the beguiled woman, which, surely, must seem nice for a change.

Masculine Homilies

A homily is a short sermon, discourse, or informal lecture, often on a moral topic and suggesting a course of conduct. Some of the most intriguing advertisements offer just that, short statements and bits of advice on what masculinity is and on how real men should conduct themselves. As with many short sermons, many of the advertising homilies have a self-congratulatory air about them; after all, you do not want the consumer to feel bad about himself.

What is it, then, to be a man? It is to be *independent*. "There are some things a man will not relinquish." Among them, says the advertisement, his Tretorn tennis shoes.

It is to *savor freedom*. "Dress easy, get away from it all and let Tom Sawyer paint the fence," advises Alexander Julian, the men's designer. "Because man was meant to fly, we gave him wings" (even if only on his sunglasses).

It is to live a life of *adventure*. KL Homme cologne is "for the man who lives on the edge." Prudential Life Insurance preaches, "If you can dream it, you can do it." New Man sportswear tells the reader, "Life is more adventurous when you feel like a New Man."

It is to *keep one's cool.* "J. B. Scotch. A few individuals know how to keep their heads, even when their necks are on the line."

And it is to stay one step *ahead of the competition.* "Altec Lansing. Hear what others only imagine." Alexander Julian again: "Dress up a bit when you dress down. They'll think you know something they don't."

What is it, then, to be a woman? It is to be *dependent.* "A woman needs a man," reads the copy in the Rigolletto advertisement showing a young man changing a tire for a grateful young woman.

The American cowboy as cultural model was not supposed to care for or about appearances. He was what he was, hard-working, straightforward, and honest. He was authentic. Men who cared "too much" about how they looked did not fit this model; the dandy was effete, a European invention, insufficient in masculinity and not red-blooded enough to be a real American. The other cultural model, imported from England, was the gentleman. A gentleman did care about his appearance, in the proper measure and manifestation, attention to tailoring and to quality, understatement rather than exaggeration.[12]

From the gray flannel suit of the 1950s to the "power look" of the 1980s, clothes made the man fit in with his company's image. Sex appeal and corporate correctness merged in a look that spelled success, that exuded confidence.

Whether or not a man presumed to care about his appearance, he did care about having "the right stuff," as Tom Wolfe and *Esquire* call it, or "men's toys," as in a recent special issue of *M* magazine. Cars, motorcycles, stereos, sports equipment: These are part of the masculine appearance. They allow the man to demonstrate his taste, his special knowledge, his affluence: to extend his control. He can be and is demanding, for only the best will do.

He also wants to be loved, but he does not want to appear needy. Advertisements suggest the magic ability of products ranging from cars to hair creams to attract female attention. With the right products a man can have it all, with no strings attached: no boring marital ties, hefty mortgages, corporate compromises.

According to sociologist Barbara Ehrenreich, *Playboy* magazine did much to legitimate this image of male freedom. The old male ethos, up to the post-war period, required exchanging bachelor irresponsibility for married responsibility, which also symbolized entrance into social adulthood.[13] The perennial bachelor, with his flashy cars and interchangeable women, was the object of both envy and derision; he had fun, but . . . he was not fully grown up. There was something frivolous in his lack of purpose and application.

This old ethos has lost much of its legitimacy. Today's male can, as Baudrillard suggests, operate in both modes: the feminine mode of indulging oneself and being indulged and the masculine mode of exigency and competition. With the right look and the right stuff, he can feel confident and manly in boardroom or suburban backyard. Consumer society thus invites both men and women to live in a world of appearances and to devote ever more attention to them.

Notes

1. Katz and Katz, *Magazines*, pp. 703–5.
2. Ibid.
3. John Gagnon, "Physical Strength: Once of Significance," in Joseph H. Pleck and Jack Sawyer, eds., *Men and Masculinity* (Englewood Cliffs, N.J.: Prentice-Hall, 1974), pp. 139–49.
4. Jean Baudrillard (b. 1929)   French semiologist.—EDS.
5. Baudrillard, *La société de consommation*, pp. 144–47.
6. Ibid.
7. Ibid.
8. Todd Gitlin, "We Build Excitement," in Todd Gitlin, ed., *Watching Television* (New York: Pantheon, 1986), pp. 139–40.
9. Ibid.
10. C. Wright Mills (1916–1962)   American sociologist.—EDS.
11. C. Wright Mills, *The Power Elite* (New York: Oxford University Press, 1956), p. 141.
12. See Diane Barthel, "A Gentleman and a Consumer: A Sociological Look at Man at His Best," paper presented at the annual meeting of the Eastern Sociological Society, March 1983, Baltimore.
13. Barbara Ehrenreich, *The Hearts of Men: American Dreams and the Flight from Commitment* (New York: Anchor Books, 1983).

READING REFLECTIONS

1. According to Barthel, how are appearance-oriented products, such as clothing and cologne, marketed differently to men and women?
2. Barthel suggests that much advertising has portrayed men as all-powerful, yet some people have commented society should also emphasize more nurturing, communal, and cooperative activities for men. Try to find images in the media that extend the image of men beyond the traditional tough guy persona. How do these images reveal the cultural assumptions about what it means to be a man today?
3. What is a homily, and what are the homilies Barthel outlines about masculinity within advertising and mass culture?
4. Although Barthel focuses more on male rather than female homilies within advertising, what would homilies about femininity entail? With such homilies in mind, compare these to your reading of Gould's "X: A Fabulous Child's Story." Are there similar homilies that Gould wished to avoid?
5. After reading Barthel's article, is there hope that advertising can go beyond its portrayal of traditional gender roles? Try to find at least one ad that subverts male and female homilies to share with your classmates.

"Appearances versus Realities" Activities

READING REACTIONS

1. bell hooks' "Straightening Our Hair" and Alisa Valdes' "Looking Good, Feeling Scared" take the notion of social acceptance to another dimension, based on standards of appearance. Write an essay describing something you have done in the past for social acceptance, on the basis of class, gender, race, or age. What forces encouraged you or discouraged you from undertaking such a process?

2. Both Lois Gould and Marge Piercy suggest the limited nature of child's play and toys in fostering nontraditional gender roles. Based on their critique, develop a proposal for a gender-neutral toy or game appealing to both boys and girls. How will you attempt to market this new product?

3. Although many discussions of gender appearance focus on femininity, Alisa Valdes and Diane Barthel suggest that men are under equal pressure to "put on an appearance." Test such an assertion by interviewing several men of varying ethnicities and age groups, and share your results with your classmates.

CLASSROOM REACTIONS

1. Several of the readings and texts in this chapter focus on body and body images of both men and women. Share several images and your written commentary on them with your classmates, comparing and contrasting them and explaining what cultural assumptions these images portray about the way men and women should "look." How might such looks privilege or alienate some groups over others?

2. Katharine Greider traces the popularity of "shapewear" from the corset to the Wonderbra, suggesting a consistent body image for women to adhere to. But has the "American" standard of beauty been consistent throughout the years? Research what previous generations have considered to be "beautiful" bodies, and write an article describing the difference between those times and today's images.

3. Interview an equal number of men and women in your class about their ideal man or woman, including people from cultural backgrounds other than your own. Based on your results, write a commentary on the gender images valued by both women and men. Do women and men have the same ideals, and how do such ideas change between cultures?

MEDIA CONNECTIONS

1. Look for a representative film genre—horror, romance, action adventure— in your video store or in your library to analyze gender roles within particular genres. Then write a movie review describing how the film goes about

portraying these characters (i.e., does it do so stereotypically or with more depth and quality?).

2. Watch the morning news for several days and examine the difference between what kinds of stories male anchors report and female anchors report. How balanced are the stories between genders?

3. Select a series of World Wide Web sites to analyze the gendered or nongendered nature of these online sources. Then write a report to your classmates providing a commentary on the ethics and implications of these gender assumptions and images as they manifest themselves in a new medium.

COMMUNITY INTERACTIONS

1. Lois Gould's Baby X places emphasis on gender-neutral play for children. Visit a local video-game room and survey the various games and images of men and women within them, as well as the general plot or narrative of the game. Who does the game assume to be its primary audience, if any? Observe the difference between the number of boys and girls who enter the video arcade and the types of games they play, and then write an analysis about gender and video games. How might your observation support Gould's call for eliminating gender-restrictive play?

2. Observe, interview, or work with someone who has a job that has been typically gender specific, such as a male auto mechanic or a female nurse. Or observe, interview, or work with someone who has a job that is not traditionally done by someone of his or her gender, perhaps a male nurse. Write a detailed profile of your subject. Then collaborate with members of your group and collect the articles into a group booklet profiling local career opportunities that are open to both men and women.

3. Photograph a series of both women and men, attempting to represent a range of ethnic, age, and body types, and a variety of social roles. Compare your daily images with the images of women and men in a series of magazines aimed at both genders. Do your real subjects embody the homilies of femininity and masculinity, as suggested by Diane Barthel's article? How does this impact your understanding of the relationship between gender images in mass media versus gender images in daily life?

Net Nanny.
Net Nanny Software International, Inc. Copyright © 1994–1999. Courtesy Net Nanny.

The metaphor of the Net Nanny is a powerful one for parents' concerns about their children's access to objectionable material on-line. Likewise, the readings in this chapter focus primarily on the issue of media morality, media monitoring, and the protection of children, questioning the extent to which such protection is necessary or even possible in today's media-saturated world.

Join a media watchdog newsgroup on one of the various on-line chat services or on a Usenet group. Who are the typical members of such a group, and what types of media are considered to be problematic for the members of this group? How do you fit in in terms of the group's demographics and values? Given the impact of the Internet on daily life, how necessary are "protection" sites like Net Nanny?

5

Media Morals

With the advent of the V-chip and the recent move toward a television rating system, it is difficult to remember when sex and violence in the media have not been concerns of parents and educators alike. Indeed, from the Hays Production Code for Motion Pictures (introduced in 1934 and finally abolished in the late 1960s), which limited the representations of sexuality and violence in early twentieth-century film, to the early television portrayals of the married couple sleeping in separate beds, society has long feared the role of the media in shaping and even perhaps corrupting the moral fabric of society. Yet the conflict over the coverage of Barbara Eden's navel in the 1960s show *I Dream of Jeannie* seems trivial in light of today's concern with violent content and its impact on adolescent behavior, as teenagers represent a vast majority of the movie-going, television-viewing, music-listening, and Internet-surfing public.

In the 1980s, Tipper Gore, spouse of then Senator, now Vice President, Albert Gore, began a crusade against the lyrics in popular music, advocating and being largely responsible for the parental advisory labeling of albums, tapes, and CDs deemed to have themes and language unsuitable for the contemporary youth of America. Although Gore's initial campaign in the 1980s was often ridiculed in the mainstream media, it is clear from such incidents as the censorship trial of rap group 2 Live Crew or the trial against heavy metal group Judas Priest, in which their lyrics were said to be responsible for the joint suicide of two Nevada teenagers in 1985 (the case was later dismissed in 1990), that many communities and the parents within them have come to recognize the important influence of music in the lives of young people, with its ability to shape and reflect values. Whereas some educators, such as the late Allan Bloom, criticize contemporary music and its supposedly negative influence, still others point to the violent life and death of rapper Tupac Shakur, whose gangsta rap lyrics are said to have imitated his all too brief life. Yet for many commentators, rap and other forms of popular music have become a scapegoat, because, as Jill Nelson contends, rap music reflects a larger pattern of violence in the inner city, a violence that existed and continues to exist beyond the lyrics of both living and dead rappers. As a result, various social and political groups have come out against rap: Robert Dole, the 1996 GOP presidential hopeful, singled out Time Warner as a promoter of gangsta rap recordings that extol violence against police, and the Nation of Islam's "Hip Hop Day of Atonement" was a careful indictment of Death Row Records and the gangsta culture allegedly promoted by its artists. Moreover, the controversy caused by opposition to gangsta rap that was promoted by Time Warner almost brought down the world's largest media conglomerate, with protesters such as civil rights activist C. DeLores Tucker leading the campaign against what she considered dangerous lyrics.

If media of all kinds can have such an impact on the lives of the young, what is to be done, given that today's children are reared in much more media-saturated households than their parents could have imagined even a decade ago? From the plethora of cable channels for both adults and children, from video games that have migrated from the arcade to the home computer, and from Internet chat groups in which parents have little to no control over the public actions and interactions involving their own children, there is a distrust of all this media saturation. Although the Internet is seen to have its back alleys in which children should "not chat with strangers," how is the potential for Internet violence any different from the types of perils facing children in an increasingly violent American culture, where kidnappings take place anywhere and at any time of day? Nevertheless, Adrian McLeish, an English Catholic priest who has admitted to sexually abusing boys and exchanging pornography on the Internet, was jailed for six years, whereas Jake Baker, a University of Michigan student who created and transmitted a computer message about the rape and torture of a female classmate, was ultimately exonerated on the basis of no actual harm done to the female classmate, a ruling that for many was questionable. Still, because of Oliver Jovanovic's sexual assault of a college student he approached on-line, the media coverage of this particular criminal case, as Thomas Goetz contends, has focused on the negative impact of the Internet on issues of privacy and public safety.

As a result, although sex and sports represented much of the first wave of content on the World Wide Web, Web publishers are producing fare that is decidedly more family-oriented as the Internet becomes more mainstream for parents and children alike. Indeed, because Howard Stern's radio and television shows are known for their adult-oriented commentary, a Web site promoting his 1997 film *Private Parts* was registered with several on-line parental monitoring sites, including Net Nanny. A recent report from the American Medical Association urges doctors to take a more active role in educating young people and their parents about media violence. Among the AMA's media-use suggestions for parents are being alert to the shows that children view and limiting the use of media in general.

Much like those arguments supporting pornography as a form of free speech, debates over censorship of media come and go in our culture, with the First Amendment usually winning out, despite the supposedly objectionable content of many of today's films, television shows, magazines, CDs, and Web sites. John Davidson, in "Menace to Society" notes that an overlooked culprit may be the Saturday morning cartoon. Many of these debates have revolved around the following question: Is media violence a creator or reflection of violence in our culture? The readings in this chapter address this question in a way that suggests that the influence of mass media and the newest technologies is still subject to debate about media's reflection of mere violence, or of social commentary about such issues. Very often, those films, television programs, and recordings are labeled controversial in terms of their content: in particular, television shows such as Comedy Central's nighttime cartoon *South Park*, targeted at adult audiences despite the fact that almost a quarter of its audience is under eighteen. Recently, a nightly news story profiled a school's attempt to discourage parents from allowing their children to watch the cartoon about the fictional Colorado town, which airs at 10 P.M. weekly and is generally considered offensive. Meanwhile, as Rick Marin's story "The Rude Tube" chronicles, advertisers that include AT&T, Calvin Klein, and Snapple are paying twenty times the normal cost for a thirty-second commercial spot during what is now being termed a "pop-cult obsession."

Regardless of the varying opinions about media morals in all forms, it is clear that the issue that has been around since the early twentieth century will be around in the twenty-first. William Bennett's Empower America, which has had success in taking on advertisers of daytime TV talk shows, is also taking aim at more media targets, including music lyrics, TV violence, and pornography on the Internet. Although future attempts at censorship seem potentially unsuccessful, the use of technology in the name of parental control seems likely to develop further, from everything from the existing 1-900 number blocks on telephone systems, prohibiting young children from accessing adult and other forms of commercial entertainments, to the V-Chip, to Web services such as Net Nanny, which, for a fee, will disable links to Web sites containing content inappropriate for children. Just as children's exposure to media of all kinds is at an all-time high, "media violence" is beginning to emerge as the next frontier in the ever-expanding realm of social responsibility among parents, educators, and even the media conglomerates themselves, a point that Ellen Wartella stresses in "Electronic Childhood."

To what extent is one person's identification of objectionable content another person's form of entertainment? How much control should the government, schools, and parents have over children's and the general public's access to media technologies and the messages that circulate through them, good or bad? Some might argue, for example, that the evening news is scarier than the long list of Stephen King horror novels that have become feature films and are so widely popular with the viewing and reading public. Ironically, many television and print news organizations are taking to censoring themselves, noting that hard news stories that feature "bad news"—the homeless, wars abroad, gang activity in the inner city—are not the type of news people are interested in as they sit down to dinner after a long day at work.

Not unlike the calls for a return to family values profiled in Chapter 3, some concern about media violence or the general lack of intellectual value of popular media has a nostalgic tone to it, a hearkening back to the days when reading books and telling stories were common forms of entertainment. Yet even books are a form of media subject to scrutiny by teachers and parents alike, and there have been numerous cases of banned books and official reading lists in school districts across the country. For many educators, despite the desire to offer more cultural diversity in the curriculum, the use of profanity and sex in literary texts is problematic and cannot be ignored in the name of social realism, as Cynthia Hallen implies in her discussion of educational materials ranging from Kevin Costner's production of *Robin Hood* to Maya Angelou's widely read *I Know Why the Caged Bird Sings*.

To what extent are today's media bad for children? Are there instances of good media, taking in the education of children? How can television networks, for example, reconcile their goals of entertaining to win the ratings war with a culture in which children's access to technology, or depending on your perspective, technology's access to children, is drawing increasing concern from parents, educators, and politicians alike? We live in a culture where children are more media literate than they have ever been, and where parents are often criticized for using the television as a baby-sitter in a household when children are increasingly "home alone." As several of the readings and issues we profile in this chapter debate the relative role of various media genres on the social development of today's youth, we encourage you to think about the types of music, television, and advertisements you prefer and your perception of their influence on you. Are there some instances, such as the recent debate over cigarette advertisements' potential impact on adolescents, in which limits are needed? Or should we adopt the slogan of those opposing gun control and remind ourselves that people, not television shows, are responsible for their actions? Although every generation has had its genres that parents disapprove of, musical genres in particular, what compromises can be reached in the ongoing debate about the power of media messages?

MUSIC

Allan Bloom

───────────────────────────

Within the late 1980s' call from parents and pundits for a rating system of compact discs and cassettes, Allan Bloom's message about the denigrating influence of rock music on today's youth garnered support from educators devoted to the preservation of a Great Ideas tradition. Yet Bloom's overarching claim about the "masturbatory" nature of both pop-

───────────────────────────

ular music and the MTV generation sparked heated charges of cultural elitism and misunderstanding of contemporary music as a social and emotional force in the lives of adolescents.

Allan Bloom (1930–1992), a professor at the University of Chicago, will be best remembered for his controversial best-seller The Closing of the American Mind *(1987), a call to return to an educational tradition of great books and philosophy, as opposed to more contemporary manifestations of mass culture, particularly rock music. This excerpt from Bloom's chapter on music reveals his belief that modern music is largely responsible for the corruption of the minds of today's students.*

Though students do not have books, they most emphatically do have music. Nothing is more singular about this generation than its addiction to music. This is the age of music and the states of soul that accompany it. To find a rival to this enthusiasm, one would have to go back at least a century to Germany and the passion for Wagner's[1] operas. They had the religious sense that Wagner was creating the meaning of life and that they were not merely listening to his works but experiencing that meaning. Today, a very large proportion of young people between the ages of ten and twenty live for music. It is their passion; nothing else excites them as it does; they cannot take seriously anything alien to music. When they are in school and with their families, they are longing to plug themselves back into their music. Nothing surrounding them—school, family, church—has anything to do with their musical world. At best that ordinary life is neutral, but mostly it is an impediment, drained of vital content, even a thing to be rebelled against. Of course, the enthusiasm for Wagner was limited to a small class, could be indulged only rarely and only in a few places, and had to wait on the composer's slow output. The music of the new votaries, on the other hand, knows neither class nor nation. It is available twenty-four hours a day, everywhere. There is the stereo in the home, in the car; there are concerts; there are music videos, with special channels exclusively devoted to them, on the air nonstop; there are the Walkmans so that no place—not public transportation, not the library—prevents students from communing with the Muse, even while studying. And, above all, the musical soil has become tropically rich. No need to wait for unpredictable genius. Now there are many geniuses, producing all the time, two new ones rising to take the place of every fallen hero. There is no dearth of the new and the startling.

The power of music in the soul—described to Jessica marvelously by Lorenzo in the *Merchant of Venice*—has been recovered after a long period of desuetude. And it is rock music alone that has effected this restoration. Classical music is dead among the young. This assertion will, I know, be hotly disputed by many who, unwilling to admit tidal changes, can point to the proliferation on campuses of classes in classical music appreciation and practice, as well as performance groups of all kinds. Their presence is undeniable, but they involve not more than 5 to 10 percent of the students. Classical music is now a special taste, like Greek language or pre-Columbian archeology, not a common culture of reciprocal communication and psychological shorthand. Thirty years ago, most middle-class families made some of the old European music a part of the home, partly because they liked it, partly because they thought it was good for the kids. University students usually had some early emotive association with Beethoven, Chopin, and Brahms, which was a permanent part of their makeup and to which they were likely to respond throughout their lives. This was probably the only regularly recognizable class distinction between educated and uneducated in America. Many, or even most, of the young people of that generation also swung with Benny Goodman,[2] but with an element of self-consciousness—to be hip, to prove they weren't snobs, to show solidarity with the democratic ideal of a pop culture out of which would grow a new high culture. So there remained a class distinction between high and low, although private taste was beginning to create doubts about whether one really liked the high very much. But all that has changed. Rock music is as unquestioned and unproblematic as the air the students breathe, and very few have any acquaintance at all with classical music. This is a constant surprise to me. And one of the strange aspects of my relations with good students I come to know well is that I frequently introduce them to Mozart. This is a pleasure to me, inasmuch as it is always pleasant to give people gifts that please them. It is interesting to see whether and in what ways their studies are complemented by such music. But this is something utterly new to me as a teacher; formerly my students usually knew much more classical music than I did.

Music was not all that important for the generation of students preceding the current one. The romanticism that had dominated serious music since Beethoven appealed to refinements—perhaps overrefinements—of sentiments that are hardly to be found in the contemporary world. The lives people lead or wish to lead and their prevailing passions are of a different sort than those of the highly educated German and French bourgeoisie, who were avidly reading Rousseau and Baudelaire, Goethe and Heine,[3] for their spiritual satisfaction. The music that had been designed to produce, as well as to please, such exquisite sensibilities had a very tenuous relation to American lives of any kind. So romantic musical culture in America had had for a long time the character of a veneer, as easily susceptible to ridicule as were Margaret Dumont's displays of coquettish chasteness, so aptly exploited by Groucho Marx in *A Night at the Opera*. I noticed this when I first started teaching and lived in a house for gifted students. The "good" ones studied their physics and then listened to classical music. The students who did not fit so easily into the groove, some of them just vulgar and restive under the cultural tyranny, but some of them also serious, were looking for things that really responded to their needs. Almost always they responded to the beat of the newly emerging rock music. They were a bit ashamed of their taste, for it was not respectable. But I instinctively sided with the second group, with real, if coarse, feelings as opposed to artificial and dead ones. Then their musical sans-culotteism won the revolution and reigns unabashed today. No classical music has been produced that can speak of this generation.

Symptomatic of this change is how seriously students now take the famous passages on musical education in Plato's *Republic*. In the past, students, good liberals that they always are, were indignant at the censorship of poetry, as a threat to free inquiry. But they were really thinking of science and politics. They hardly paid attention to the discussion of music itself and, to the extent that they even thought about it, were really puzzled by Plato's devoting time to rhythm and melody in a serious treatise on political philosophy. Their experience of music was as an entertainment, a matter of indifference to political and moral life. Students today, on the contrary, know exactly why Plato takes music so seriously. They know it affects life very profoundly and are indignant because Plato seems to want to rob them of their most intimate pleasure. They are drawn into argument with Plato about the experience of music, and the dispute centers on how to evaluate it and deal with it. This encounter not only helps to illuminate the phenomenon of contemporary music, but also provides a model of how contemporary students can profitably engage with a classic text. The very fact of their fury shows how much Plato threatens what is dear and intimate to them. They are little able to defend their experience, which has seemed unquestionable until questioned, and it is most resistant to cool analysis. Yet if a student can—and this is most difficult and unusual—draw back, get a critical distance on what he clings to, come to doubt the ultimate value of what he loves, he has taken the first and most difficult step toward the philosophic conversion. Indignation is the soul's defense against the wound of doubt about its own; it reorders the cosmos to support the justice of its cause. It justifies putting Socrates to death. Recognizing indignation for what it is constitutes knowledge of the soul, and is thus an experience more philosophic than the study of mathematics. It is Plato's teaching that music, by its nature, encompasses all that is today most resistant to philosophy. So it may well be that through the thicket of our greatest corruption runs the path to awareness of the oldest truths.

Plato's teaching about music is, put simply, that rhythm and melody, accompanied by dance, are the barbarous expression of the soul. Barbarous, not animal. Music is the medium of the *human* soul in its most ecstatic condition of wonder and terror. Nietzsche,[4] who in large measure agrees with Plato's analysis, says in *The Birth of Tragedy* (not to be forgotten is the rest of the title, *Out of the Spirit of Music*) that a mixture of cruelty and coarse sensuality characterized this state, which of course was religious, in the service of gods. Music is the soul's primitive and primary speech and it is *alogon*, without articulate speech or reason. It is not only not reasonable, it is hostile to reason. Even when articulate speech is added, it is utterly subordinate to and determined by the music and the passions it expresses.

Civilization or, to say the same thing, education is the taming or domestication of the soul's raw passions—not suppressing or excising them, which would deprive the soul of its energy—but forming and informing them as art. The goal of harmonizing the enthusiastic part of the soul with what develops later, the rational part, is perhaps impossible to attain. But without it, man can never be whole. Music, or poetry, which is what music becomes as reason emerges, always involves a delicate balance between passion and reason, and, even in its highest and most developed forms—religious, warlike, and erotic—that balance is always tipped, if ever so slightly, toward the passionate. Music, as everyone experiences, provides an unquestionable justification and a fulfilling pleasure for the activities it accompanies: the soldier who hears the marching band is enthralled and reassured; the religious man is exalted in his prayer by the sound of the organ in the church; and the lover is carried away and his conscience stilled by the romantic guitar. Armed with music, man can damn rational doubt. Out of the music emerge the gods that suit it, and they educate men by their example and their commandments.

Plato's Socrates disciplines the ecstasies and thereby provides little consolation or hope to men. According to the Socratic formula, the lyrics—speech and, hence, reason—must determine the music—harmony and rhythm. Pure music can never endure this constraint. Students are not in a position to know the pleasures of reason; they can only see it as a disciplinary and repressive parent. But they do see, in the case of Plato, that that parent has figured out what they are up to. Plato teaches that, in order to take the spiritual temperature of an individual or a society, one must "mark the music." To Plato and Nietzsche, the history of music is a series of attempts to give form and beauty to the dark, chaotic, premonitory forces in the soul—to make them serve a higher purpose, an ideal, to give man's duties a fullness. Bach's religious intentions and Beethoven's revolutionary and humane ones are clear enough examples. Such cultivation of the soul uses the passions and satisfies them while sublimating them and giving them an artistic unity. A man whose noblest activities are accompanied by a music that expresses them while providing a pleasure extending from the lowest bodily to the highest spiritual, is whole, and there is no tension in him between the pleasant and the good. By contrast a man whose business life is prosaic and unmusical and whose leisure is made up of coarse, intense entertainments, is divided, and each side of his existence is undermined by the other.

Hence, for those who are interested in psychological health, music is at the center of education, both for giving the passions their due and for preparing the soul for the unhampered use of reason. The centrality of such education was recognized by all the ancient educators. It is hardly noticed today that in Aristotle's *Politics* the most important passages about the best regime concern musical education, or that the *Poetics* is an appendix to the *Politics*. Classical philosophy did not censor the singers. It persuaded them. And it gave them a goal, one that was understood by them, until only yesterday. But those who do not notice the role of music in Aristotle and despise Plato went to school with Hobbes, Locke, and Smith,[5] where such considerations have become unnecessary. The triumphant Enlightenment rationalism thought that it had discovered other ways to deal with the irrational part of the soul, and that reason needed less support from it. Only in those great critics of Enlightenment and rationalism, Rousseau and Nietzsche, does music return, and they were the most musical of philosophers. Both thought that the passions—and along with them their ministerial arts—had become thin under the rule of reason and that, therefore, man *himself* and what he sees in the world have become correspondingly thin. They wanted to cultivate the enthusiastic states of the soul and to reexperience the Corybantic[6] possession deemed a pathology by Plato. Nietzsche, particularly, sought to tap again the irrational sources of vitality, to replenish our dried-up stream from barbaric sources, and thus encouraged the Dionysian[7] and the music derivative from it.

This is the significance of rock music. I do not suggest that it has any high intellectual sources. But it has risen to its current heights in the education of the young on the ashes of classical music, and in an atmosphere in which there is no intellectual resistance to attempts to tap the rawest passions. Modern-day rationalists, such as economists, are indifferent to it and what it represents. The irrationalists are all for it. There is no need to fear that "the blond beasts" are going to come forth from the bland souls of our adolescents. But rock music has one appeal only, a barbaric appeal, to sexual desire—not love, not *eros*, but sexual desire undeveloped and untutored. It acknowledges the first emanations of children's emerging sensuality and addresses them seriously, eliciting them and legitimating them, not as little sprouts that must be carefully tended in order to grow into gorgeous flowers, but as the real thing. Rock gives children, on a silver platter, with all the public authority of the entertainment industry, everything their parents always used to tell them they had to wait for until they grew up and would understand later.

Young people know that rock has the beat of sexual intercourse. That is why Ravel's[8] *Bolero* is the one piece of classical music that is commonly known and liked by them. In alliance with some real art and a lot of pseudo-art, an enormous industry cultivates the taste for the orgiastic state of feeling connected with sex, providing a constant flood of fresh material for voracious appetites. Never was there an art form directed so exclusively to children.

Ministering to and according with the arousing and cathartic music, the lyrics celebrate puppy love as well as polymorphous attractions, and fortify them against traditional ridicule and shame. The words implicitly and explicitly describe bodily acts that satisfy sexual desire and treat them as its only natural and routine culmination for children who do not yet have the slightest imagination of love, marriage, or family. This has a much more powerful effect than does pornography on youngsters, who have no need to watch others do grossly what they can so easily do themselves. Voyeurism is for old perverts; active sexual relations are for the young. All they need is encouragement.

The inevitable corollary of such sexual interest is rebellion against the parental authority that represses it. Selfishness thus becomes indignation and then transforms itself into morality. The sexual revolution must overthrow all the forces of domination, the enemies of nature and happiness. From love comes hate, masquerading as social reform. A worldview is balanced on the sexual fulcrum. What were once unconscious or half-conscious childish resentments become the new Scripture. And then comes the longing for the classless, prejudice-free, conflictless, universal society that necessarily results from liberated consciousness—"We Are the World," a pubescent version of *Alle Menschen werden Brüder*,[9] the fulfillment of which has been inhibited by the political equivalents of Mom and Dad. These are the three great lyrical themes: sex, hate, and a smarmy, hypocritical version of brotherly love. Such polluted sources issue in a muddy stream where only monsters can swim. A glance at the videos that project images on the wall of Plato's cave since MTV took it over suffices to prove this. Hitler's image recurs frequently enough in exciting contexts to give one pause. Nothing noble, sublime, profound, delicate, tasteful, or even decent can find a place in such tableaux. There is room only for the intense, changing, crude, and immediate, which Tocqueville[10] warned us would be the character of democratic art, combined with a pervasiveness, importance, and content beyond Tocqueville's wildest imagination.

Picture a thirteen-year-old boy sitting in the living room of his family home doing his math assignment while wearing his Walkman headphones or watching MTV. He enjoys the liberties hard won over centuries by the alliance of philosophic genius and political heroism, consecrated by the blood of martyrs; he is provided with comfort and leisure by the most productive economy ever known to mankind; science has penetrated the secrets of nature in order to provide him with the marvelous, lifelike electronic sound and image reproduction he is enjoying. And in what does progress culminate? A pubescent child whose body throbs with orgasmic rhythms; whose feelings are made articulate in hymns to the joys of onanism or the killing of parents; whose ambition is to win fame and wealth in imitating the drag-queen who makes the music. In short, life is made into a nonstop, commercially prepackaged masturbational fantasy.

This description may seem exaggerated, but only because some would prefer to regard it as such. The continuing exposure to rock music is a reality, not one confined to a particular class or type of child. One need only ask first-year university students what music they listen to, how much of it, and what it means to them, in order to discover that the phenomenon is universal in America, that it begins in adolescence or a bit before and continues through the college years. It is *the* youth culture and, as I have so often insisted, there is now no other countervailing nourishment for the spirit. Some of this culture's power comes from the fact that it is so loud. It makes conversation impossible, so that much of friendship must be without the shared speech that Aristotle asserts is the essence of friendship and the only true common ground. With rock, illusions of shared feelings, bodily contact and grunted formulas, which are supposed to contain so much meaning beyond speech, are the basis of association. None of this contradicts going about the business of life, attending classes, and doing the assignments for them. But the meaningful inner life is with the music.

This phenomenon is both astounding and indigestible, and is hardly noticed, routine and habitual. But it is of historic proportions that a society's best young and their best energies should be so occupied. People of future civilizations will wonder at this and find it as incomprehensible as we do the caste system, witch-burning, harems, cannibalism, and gladiatorial combats. It may well be that a society's greatest madness seems normal to itself. The child described has parents who have sacrificed to provide him with a good life and who have a great stake in his future happiness. They cannot believe that the musical vocation will contribute very much to that happiness. But there is nothing they can do about it. The family spiritual void has left the field open to rock music, and they cannot possibly forbid their children to listen to it. It is everywhere; all children listen to it; forbidding it would simply cause them to lose their children's affection and obedience. When they turn on the television, they will see President Reagan warmly grasping the daintily proffered gloved hand of Michael Jackson and praising him enthusiastically. Better to set the faculty of denial in motion—avoid noticing what the words say, assume the kid will get over it. If he has early sex, that won't get in the way of his having stable relationships later. His drug use will certainly stop at pot. School is providing real values. And popular historicism provides the final salvation; there are new lifestyles for new situations, and the older generation is there not to impose its values but to help the younger one to find its own. TV, which compared to music plays a comparatively small role in the formation of young people's character and taste, is a consensus monster—the Right monitors its content for sex, the Left for violence, and many other interested sects for many other things. But the music has hardly been touched, and what efforts have been made are both ineffectual and misguided about the nature and extent of the problem.

The result is nothing less than parents' loss of control over their children's moral education at a time when no one else is seriously concerned with it. This has been achieved by an alliance between the strange young males who have the gift of divining the mob's emergent wishes—our versions of Thrasymachus, Socrates' rhetorical adversary—and the record-company executives, the new robber barons, who mine gold out of rock. They discovered a few years back that children are one of the few groups in the country with considerable disposable income, in the form of allowances. Their parents spend all they have providing for the kids. Appealing to them over their parents' heads, creating a world of delight for them, constitutes one of the richest markets in the postwar world. The rock business is perfect capitalism, supplying to demand and helping to create it. It has all the moral dignity of drug trafficking, but it was so totally new and unexpected that nobody thought to control it, and now it is too late. Progress may be made against cigarette smoking because our absence of standards or our relativism does not extend to matters of bodily health. In all other things the market determines the value. (Yoko Ono is among America's small group of billionaires, along with oil and computer magnates, her late husband having produced and sold a commodity of worth comparable to theirs.) Rock is a very big business, bigger than the movies, bigger than professional sports, bigger than television, and this accounts for much of the respectability of the music business. It is difficult to adjust our vision to the changes in the economy and to see what is really important. McDonald's now has more employees than U.S. Steel, and likewise the purveyors of junk food for the soul have supplanted what still seem to be more basic callings.

This change has been happening for some time. In the late fifties, De Gaulle gave Brigitte Bardot[11] one of France's highest honors. I could not understand this, but it turned out that she, along with Peugot, was France's biggest export item. As Western nations became more prosperous, leisure, which had been put off for several centuries in favor of the pursuit of property, the means to leisure, finally began to be of primary concern. But, in the meantime, any notion of the serious life of leisure, as well as men's taste and capacity to live it, had disappeared. Leisure became entertainment. The end for which they had labored for so long has turned out to be amusement, a justified conclusion if the means justify the ends. The music business is peculiar only in that it caters almost exclusively to children, treating legally and naturally imperfect human beings as though they were ready to enjoy the final or complete satisfaction. It perhaps thus reveals the nature of all our entertainment and our loss of a clear view of what adulthood or maturity is, and our incapacity to conceive ends. The emptiness of *values* results in the acceptance of the natural *facts* as the ends. In this case infantile sexuality is the end, and I suspect that, in absence of other ends, many adults have to agree that it is.

It is interesting to note that the Left, which prides itself on its critical approach to "late capitalism" and is unrelenting and unsparing in its analysis of our other cultural phenomena, has in general given rock music a free ride. Abstracting from the capitalist element in which it flourishes, they regard it as a people's art, coming from beneath the bourgeoisie's layers of cultural repression. Its antinomianism and its longing for a world without constraint might seem to be the clarion of the proletarian revolution, and Marxists certainly do see that rock music dissolves the beliefs and morals necessary for liberal society and would approve of it for that alone. But the harmony between the young intellectual Left and rock is probably profounder than that. Herbert Marcuse[12] appealed to university students in the sixties with a combination of Marx and Freud. In *Eros and Civilization* and *One Dimensional Man* he promised that the overcoming of capitalism and its false consciousness will result in a society where the greatest satisfactions are sexual, of a sort that the bourgeois moralist Freud called polymorphous and infantile. Rock music touches the same chord in the young. Free sexual expression, anarchism, mining of the irrational unconscious and giving it free rein are what they have in common. The high intellectual life . . . and the low rock world are partners in the same entertainment enterprise. They must both be interpreted as parts of the cultural fabric of late capitalism. Their success comes from the bourgeois's need to feel that he is not bourgeois, to have undangerous experiments with the unlimited. He is willing to pay dearly for them. The Left is better interpreted by Nietzsche than by Marx. The critical theory of late capitalism is at once late capitalism's subtlest and crudest expression. Antibourgeois ire is the opiate of the Last Man.

This strong stimulant, which Nietzsche called Nihiline, was for a very long time, almost fifteen years, epitomized in a single figure, Mick Jagger. A shrewd, middle-class boy, he played the possessed lower-class demon and teen-aged satyr up until he was forty, with one eye on the mobs of children of both sexes whom he stimulated to a sensual frenzy and the other eye winking at the unerotic, commercially motivated adults who handled the money. In his act he was male and female, heterosexual and homosexual; unencumbered by modesty, he could enter everyone's dreams, promising to do everything with everyone; and, above all, he legitimated drugs, which were the real thrill that parents and policemen conspired to deny his youthful audience. He was beyond the law, moral and political, and thumbed his nose at it. Along with all this, there were nasty little appeals to the suppressed inclinations toward sexism, racism, and violence, indulgence in which is not now publicly respectable. Nevertheless, he managed not to appear to contradict the rock ideal of a universal classless society founded on love, with the distinction between brotherly and bodily blurred. He was the hero and the model for countless young persons in universities, as well as elsewhere. I discovered that students who boasted of having no heroes secretly had a passion to be like Mick Jagger, to live his life, have his fame. They were ashamed to admit this in a university, although I am not certain that the reason has anything to do with a higher standard of taste. It is probably that they are not supposed to have heroes. Rock music itself and talking about it with infinite seriousness are perfectly respectable. It has proved to be the ultimate leveler of intellectual snobbism. But it is not respectable to think of it as providing weak and ordinary persons with a fashionable behavior, the imitation of which will make others esteem them and boost their own self-esteem. Unaware and unwillingly, however, Mick Jagger played the role in their lives that Napoleon played in the lives of ordinary young Frenchmen throughout the nineteenth century. Everyone else was so boring and unable to charm youthful passions. Jagger caught on.

In the last couple of years, Jagger has begun to fade. Whether Michael Jackson, Prince, or Boy George can take his place is uncertain. They are even weirder than he is, and one wonders what new strata of taste they have discovered. Although each differs from the others, the essential character of musical entertainment is not changing. There is only a constant search for variations on the theme. And this gutter phenomenon is apparently the fulfillment of the promise made by so much psychology and literature that our weak and exhausted Western civilization would find refreshment in the true source, the unconscious, which appeared to the late romantic imagination to be identical to Africa, the dark and unexplored continent. Now all has been explored; light has been cast everywhere; the unconscious has been made conscious, the repressed expressed. And what have we found? Not creative devils, but show business glitz. Mick Jagger tarting it up on the stage is all we brought back from the voyage to the underworld.

My concern here is not with the moral effects of this music—whether it leads to sex, violence, or drugs. The issue here is its effect on education, and I believe it ruins the imagination of young people and makes it very difficult for them to have a passionate relationship to the art and thought that are the substance of liberal education. The first sensuous experiences are decisive in determining the taste for the whole of life, and they are the link between the animal and spiritual in us. The period of nascent sensuality has always been used for sublimation, in the sense of making sublime, for attaching youthful inclinations and longings to music, pictures, and stories that provide the transition to the fulfillment of the human duties and the enjoyment of the human pleasures. Lessing, speaking of Greek sculpture, said "beautiful men made beautiful statues, and the city had beautiful statues in part to thank for beautiful citizens." This formula encapsulates the fundamental principle of the esthetic education of man. Young men and women were attracted by the beauty of heroes whose very bodies expressed their nobility. The deeper understanding of the meaning of nobility comes later, but is prepared for by the sensuous experience and is actually contained in it. What the senses long for as well as what reason later sees as good are thereby not at tension with one another. Education is not sermonizing to children against their instincts and pleasures, but providing a natural continuity between what they feel and what they can and should be. But this is a lost art. Now we have come to exactly the opposite point. Rock music encourages passions and provides models that have no relation to any life the young people who go to universities can possibly lead, or to the kinds of admiration encouraged by liberal studies. Without the cooperation of the sentiments, anything other than technical education is a dead letter.

Rock music provides premature ecstasy and, in this respect, is like the drugs with which it is allied. It artificially induces the exaltation naturally attached to the completion of the greatest endeavors—victory in a just war, consummated love, artistic creation, religious devotion, and discovery of the truth. Without effort, without talent, without virtue, without exercise of the faculties, anyone and everyone is accorded the equal right to the enjoyment of their fruits. In my experience, students who have had a serious fling with drugs—and gotten over it—find it difficult to have enthusiasms or great expectations. It is as though the color has been drained out of their lives and they see everything in black and white. The pleasure they experienced in the beginning was so intense that they no longer look for it at the end, or as the end. They may function perfectly well, but dryly, routinely. Their energy has been sapped, and they do not expect their life's activity to produce anything but a living, whereas liberal education is supposed to encourage the belief that the good life is the pleasant life and that the best life is the most pleasant life. I suspect that the rock addiction, particularly in the absence of strong counterattractions, has an effect similar to that of drugs. The students will get over this music, or at least the exclusive passion for it. But they will do so in the same way Freud says that men accept the reality principle—as something harsh, grim, and essentially unattractive, a mere necessity. These students will assiduously study economics or the professions and the Michael Jackson costume will slip off to reveal a Brooks Brothers suit beneath. They will want to get ahead and live comfortably. But this life is as empty and false as the one they left behind. The choice is not between quick fixes and dull calculation. This is what liberal education is meant to show them. But as long as they have the Walkman on, they cannot hear what the great tradition has to say. And, after its prolonged use, when they take it off, they find they are deaf.

Notes

1. Richard Wagner (1813–1883), famous German composer, primarily noted for grand opera.
2. American jazz clarinetist and band leader (1909–1986).
3. Prominent French and German literary figures of the eighteenth and nineteenth centuries; the French philosopher Jean-Jacques Rousseau, the French poet Charles Baudelaire, the German man of letters Johann Wolfgang von Goethe, and the German lyric poet Heinrich Heine.
4. Friedrich Nietzsche (1844–1900), German philosopher.
5. Major British political and moral philosophers of the seventeenth and eighteenth centuries: Thomas Hobbes, John Locke, and Adam Smith.
6. From Greek mythology, referring to a spirit of wild music and dance.
7. From Greek mythology, relating to Dionysus, the god of wine. The word refers to frenzied, uninhibited behavior.
8. Maurice Ravel (1875–1937), French composer.
9. German song: "All Men Will Be Brothers."
10. Alexis de Tocqueville (1805–1859). French statesman and author of an influential foreign assessment of American life, *Democracy in America*.
11. Popular French movie actress of the 1950s and 60s, known mainly for sexually provocative roles.
12. German philosopher who taught in American universities (1898–1979).

READING REFLECTIONS

1. What are the problems Allan Bloom has with popular music and its impact on young people?
2. What evidence does Bloom site to support his position, and what are the features of contemporary rock music that make Bloom take this position?
3. Critiques such as Bloom's often blast popular cultural forms, including contemporary music, which Bloom describes as "commercially prepackaged masturbational fantasy." Bloom is correct in recognizing the importance of rock, rap, and other musical genres in the lives of adolescents and young adults. Keeping Bloom's argument in mind, select a contemporary musical piece and use it to show the extent to which you support or refute Bloom's argument.
4. At the time Bloom wrote his discussion of rock music, he relied on such figures as Mick Jagger and Michael Jackson. If Bloom were writing this piece today, what rock and roll figures might he rely on to make his point?
5. What role does Plato play in Bloom's argument?

WHOLE LOTTA LOVE GOIN ON IN THE MIDDLE OF HELL
Public Enemy

Although many have blasted rap music for its violent content, Public En-emy's "Whole Lotta Love Goin On in the Middle of Hell" chronicles the day-to-day realities of violence in urban communities where poverty and crime abound and tensions among and between cultures have reached riot proportions. This leaves Public Enemy to echo the question "Can't we all just get along?" Yet as a musical genre, rap may speak these urban reali-ties with more complexity than other media forms can, a concern Jill Nel-son raises in her featured editorial on the death of rapper Tupac Shakur.

Public Enemy is a renowned rap group whose members include Chuck D, Terminator X, and Flavor Flav. The group has released several albums rang-ing from its 1987 debut Yo! Bum Rush the Show *to its platinum-selling* It Takes a Nation of Millions to Hold Us Back *and* Fear of Black Planet, *which featured the controversial "911 Is a Joke." The group has also contributed to the soundtracks for Spike Lee's* Do the Right Thing *and* He Got Game.

Whole lotta love goin on
In da middle of what?
Say what?
What's goin on?

I leave em home alone
Dey turned into danger zones
Studio shootouts, leavin no doubt
In da eyes of the wise
About the other guys

Fantasi n gettin nat rep
Makin you move
While they disturb the groove
Now the partys over ooops!
Outta time
Yo my brother can—you—spare a crime
Some wanna take me out
I even call em my own
(Can't we all just get along?)
Rap iz a contact sport
Can I get support

Public Enemy, "Whole Lotta Love Goin On in the Middle of Hell" (James Henry Boxley III, Carlton Douglas Ridenhour, Eric T. Sadler). From the album *Yo! Bum Rush the Show.* Def Jam, 1987. Released on Muse Sick-N-Hour Message, Def Jam, 1994. Reprinted by permission of DEF American Songs, Inc.

When I hum to da maximum
What I talk is straight
From da sidewalk strong

The velt New York
112 beatz a minute
An I'm flowin in it
Have no mercy
On da ones that curse me

And when I'm in da paint
The feuding might be over
But the fussin aint
Some hate the way I say em
Cause I block em like
Zo to da am
Beginning of an end of an error
Incredible shrinking race

Fiend without a face
Still got love for em
But some aint got love
For the rest of us

So my boys get iller than
Illinois (Terminator)
Return to da noise

I'd rather fall off
Than fall victim of crime
And a low percentage rhyme
If I go down they goin wit me
So come & get me . . . c'mon

READING REFLECTIONS

1. Rap music is commonly associated with violence. Test this assumption by obtaining some lyrics from several rap and hip-hop groups either online or from CDs of various rap artists. After listening to lyrics such as Public Enemy's "Whole Lotta Love Goin On in the Middle of Hell," compare them to lyrics of other musical genres for similarities and differences.
2. Based on your analysis, to what extent is rap any different from other genres? Could rap be getting a bad rap?
3. What is the significance of Public Enemy's including police brutality victim Rodney King's statement "Can't we all just get along?" in its song?
4. Considering that Public Enemy also has a song titled "911 Is a Joke," how would you describe its attitude toward the police?
5. Research the lyrics of another Public Enemy song. How are these lyrics similar to or different from "Whole Lotta Love Goin On in the Middle of Hell"?

THE RAP ON TUPAC

Jill Nelson

Jill Nelson asserts that in their "live by the gun, die by the gun" coverage of the death of rapper Tupac Shakur, the media once again failed to put his violent murder in a broader context. For Nelson, this larger cultural context would have illuminated the circumstances of "poverty, unemployment, and despair" that made such a life and death possible.

As a journalist, Jill Nelson has blended her experiences as an African American woman into her social commentary in such books as Straight, No Chaser: How I Became a Grown-Up Black Woman *(1997) and* Volunteer Slavery: My Authentic Negro Experience *(1993). "The Rap on Tupac" is an editorial that appeared in* The Nation *on the larger cultural forces contributing to the death of rapper Tupac Shakur in 1996 and its impact on the African American community.*

On Sunday, September 22, I stood in the rain along with several thousand other people on a street in Harlem, hoping to gain entry to what had been advertised as a "Hip-Hop Day of Atonement," following the death of rapper Tupac Shakur. The line undulated and thickened but did not move forward. Always in motion, still there was no movement.

On Friday, September 13, when I heard the news that the 25-year-old Shakur had died as a result of gunshot wounds suffered a week before, I wasn't surprised. He'd been playing out his death for several years in his music, films and public actions. Anyone who cared to look could watch the spectacle of an intelligent, talented and destructive young man roar to embrace his own demise. Still, I was saddened by yet another young man dying in a hail of bullets. His life, music and death reflected the lives of many young black men who grow up poor, fatherless, jobless and, most devastating of all, hopeless, in ghettos customized for their containment. That Shakur was successful, sold millions of dollars' worth of records, wasn't enough to erase the damage that had already been done. The role of the media was to put Shakur's death in a broader context, to give the larger background story that would illuminate not just one individual but the circumstances that made such a life and death possible, not only for him but for thousands of others like him. Once again, for the most part, the media failed.

Too often, instead of context we got condemnation. Mainstream media seized on "Live by the gun, die by the gun," words painted on a memorial to Shakur by artist Andre Charles the night he died, to sum up his life and explain his death. "Tupac Shows How Rage Can Backfire," "The End of Gangsta Rap," "Violence Was a Career Plus for Rapper Tupac Shakur," "All He Is Now Is Dead," "Shakur Encouraged Violent Culture That Led to His Death by Violence," "Shakur Lived Thug Life, Died Thug Life," read headlines in newspapers across the country. For the most part, the articles that followed were summaries of Shakur's rap sheet: an altercation in 1992 in California in which a gun went off, leaving a 6-year-old boy dead; a charge in 1993 of shooting two off-duty police officers in Atlanta; a 1994 conviction in New York for sexual assault (during the trial he was ambushed, robbed and shot five times); convictions in New York and Michigan for assault and battery; and more. But the more I heard, read and watched, the question that kept on presenting itself to me was, Why? Why was Shakur driven to seek his own violent death? Why was he killed? Why did no one intervene before it was too late? Why are Time Warner and Interscope, distributors of Shakur's music, and Marion "Suge" Knight, chief executive of Death Row Records—all of whom made millions off Shakur—not being held accountable for the violence and negativity of gangsta rap? But perhaps the real question is, how did we as a culture get to the point where we no longer notice or question the proliferation of guns, unemployment, violence and despair in black and poor communities until someone famous dies, and then only for a moment?

For the most part, the alternative and hip-hop media were no better at setting context, instead going into high romanticization mode, pronouncing Shakur a "martyr" or "his generation's Malcolm X" or "a revolutionary," as if simply saying it makes it so. With few exceptions, notably Hot 97 radio's opening the air to callers for hours after Shakur's death and Michel Marriott's reporting in *The New York Times*, most media seemed to be looking for a quick wrap-up: He's a devil/He's an angel. He's a thug/He's a martyr. He got what he wanted/He got what he deserved.

What was missing was the larger context. It's not enough to quote a few lyrics. Or to tell us that his mother, Afeni Shakur, a former Black Panther, was pregnant with him while she was incarcerated. Or that he grew up fatherless. Outside the context of what it means to be young, black, poor and male in America, these facts reveal little. They do not begin to explain the depth of Shakur's pain, rage and self-destructiveness. To suggest they do is to reduce his life and the lives of thousands of young black men whose existence he reflected and articulated to stereotype. The attitude that some in our society are inherently dangerous, expendable and no good is itself dangerous. It is surprising that so few who are perceived and treated as menaces to society act out this ruinous prophecy.

Shakur's life and death became a big story once he was dead—not only for the media but for political ambulance-chasers who use media attention to position themselves as black leaders. Oldsters' opportunism aside, the truth is that young black people have no leaders and no movement. They don't even have, as their parents' generation does, memories of a movement. One of the reasons hip-hop is so important to them is that they confuse the music with a politics. Who is there to caution them not to mistake motion for movement? Rather than its hasty assembly in Harlem on September 22, the Nation of Islam could have provided context and proved its sincerity by offering to provide security and a larger venue for a meeting at a future date. The focus of such a meeting would not be quickie atonement but serious discussion of the need to build an activist movement through which black youth can address the crises they are facing.

Most of the women in line in the rain that day are young; the median age is probably 17. They are there in search of something: comfort, understanding, context, guidance. As they talk, their conversation is more about their own lives than about Tupac. "I feel bad about Tupac, but that's not why I'm here," a young sister tells me. "I'm here because I've been to ten funerals in four years. I'm here because this killing has to stop. I'm worried about my son."

"How old is he?"

"Four," she says. We huddle together in the cold rain, always in motion, still waiting for some movement.

READING REFLECTIONS

1. According to Jill Nelson, how is the death of Tupac Shakur reflective of the larger problems in our society?
2. What role have the news media played in addressing these issues, or in attributing blame for such problems?
3. Why does Nelson contend that "hip-hop" is so important to today's African American youth? What type of tone does she take as she makes this point, and why?
4. Conduct an experiment in which several people of various ages, genders, and ethnicities listen to the same musical lyrics from different genres: rap, rock, country, but with similar themes. Do they identify one as more "violent" than the other? Do certain groups feel more or less offended by various lyrics? On what basis?
5. What is the significance of the image with which Nelson begins and ends her article: "always in motion, still waiting for some movement"?

MENACE TO SOCIETY

John Davidson

In a culture where all media are said to have a negative impact on children, John Davidson stresses the flawed nature of research about the relationship between violence in the media and the level of aggression in children. Although the National Coalition on Television Violence states that children in television-rich households will see about 32,000 murders before they are 18, Davidson urges that we consider other forms of media violence that may have just as much of an impact—the Saturday morning cartoon, itself a genre that many parents fail to consider "violent."

John Davidson is a freelance writer living in Texas whose articles on topics such as technology, family relationships, and urban life have appeared in Self, Working Woman, *and* GQ: Gentleman's Quarterly. *His commentary on the violent content of various media originally appeared in* Rolling Stone.

With three-quarters of Americans surveyed convinced that movies, television and music spur young people to violence, and politicians on the left and right blasting the entertainment industry for irresponsibility, the debate over violence in popular culture [was] a key issue in the presidential campaign. Republican presidential front-runner Bob Dole, conservative guru William Bennett, black activist C. DeLores Tucker and liberal Democrat Sen. Paul Simon all . . . attacked portrayals of violence, treating the link between art and reality as gospel truth. They've found support for their claims from the American Psychological Association and the American Psychiatric Association, which have both issued reports stating that television violence causes aggression.

And a new controversy surrounding video games has been sparked by Lt. Col. Dave Grossman, a psychologist and Army Ranger. In his book *On Killing*, he claims that these games function like firing ranges, using the same type of conditioning employed to overcome soldiers' built-in inhibition to killing in the Vietnam War. The research, however, is less clear. Most experts who have studied the issue believe there is some link—indirect, perhaps—between seeing violence and committing it, but there is no agreement on how strong that link is or how to measure it. What's more, even those who argue most persuasively that there is a case to be made for connecting violence and culture agree that the biggest problem may not be teenagers seeing *Natural Born Killers* or listening to the Geto Boys but small children watching Saturday morning cartoons.

For the last 40 years, social scientists have attempted to measure how media violence affects people, with the bulk of the research focused on television. One of the most influential studies was directed by George Gerbner. Beginning in 1967, Gerbner, who at that time was dean of the Annenberg School for Communication at the University of Pennsylvania, and his colleagues created a violence index that is still used to measure the percentage of network programs that have violence, the number of violent acts, the percentage of characters involved in violence and the percentage involved in killing. Their index doesn't reflect the increased amount of violent material made available through cable television and VCRs. (That count, according to the National Coalition on Television Violence, is that children in homes with cable TV and/or a VCR will see about 32,000 murders and 40,000 attempted murders by the time they're 18.)

Gerbner's group concluded that television acts as an electronic melting pot, which creates a national culture. Part of that culture is "the mean-world syndrome," which leads people to believe that they are more likely to be victims of violence than they are in reality. "People who watch the most television are usually, the ones who have fewer options, less money and less education," says Nancy Signorielli, a professor of communication at the University of Delaware who worked on the Gerbner study. Their views of the world reflect what they see on television, and they overestimate their chances of being involved in violence." Like the man in Louisiana who in 1992 shot and killed a Japanese exchange student looking for a Halloween party, people overreact to perceived threats and act violently.

Remarkably, Gerbner found that the indexes have remained relatively constant during the past two decades. Nonetheless, he's been accused of exaggerating the amount of violence by not taking context into consideration. A poke in the eye, as far as he's concerned, is basically a poke in the eye; his group counts The Three Stooges and Road Runner cartoons as violent programming.

A landmark study funded by the four major networks in response to congressional pressure and released this past fall attempted to correct that deficiency and qualify different types of violence by looking at time slot, parental advisory, duration, explicitness, relation to the story and consequences. Researchers at the Center for Communication Policy at the University of California at Los Angeles confirmed that context is crucial. In other words, a TV program that shows kids beating up a fellow student with impunity could have a more harmful effect than one that shows a couple of murderers who end up in jail. Even Signorielli acknowledges that context is important: "What we have in the U.S. is happy violence. In Japan, violence is much more graphic and much more realistic," she says. "There, television violence may actually work as a deterrent. But here, if someone's shot we don't see the wound. There's not much bleeding on U.S. television."

Leonard Eron, a research scientist at the University of Michigan, has taken another approach. He began by studying how aggression develops in children, never considering television to be important. "I thought television was just another version of the sort of things children were exposed [to] in the past—fairy tales, stories and movies," says Eron. "But television is different, if in no other way than that programs are repeated over and over again."

Eron and his colleagues tested 875 third-graders in New York's Columbia County and interviewed about 80 percent of their parents. To relieve tension in the interviews, Eron threw in a question about television viewing. What surprised him was the correlation between aggression and viewing habits. Children whose parents said they watched a lot of violent television turned out to be aggressive in school, and 10 years later, in the first of the follow-up studies, Eron discovered that what a child watched at 8 years old was one of the best predictors of adult aggression—more important than the parents' child-rearing habits or socioeconomic factors. "I could compare children over time," says Eron. "At 8, if the less aggressive of two children was watching more television violence, at 18, he would be the more aggressive of the two."

Eron's findings correspond with what psychologists believe about child development: Children are most vulnerable to television from ages 2 to about 8, when they become more capable of distinguishing what they see on the screen from reality. The conclusions also conform to what we know about the development of a child's moral sense: It is developed by age 9 at the latest.

Just how children learn from the media is the subject of competing theories. According to the simplest, the viewing of aggressive material triggers aggressive thoughts that influence subsequent actions. Kids imitate what they see, just as adults emulate styles of dress and behavior observed in movies and TV shows.

The theory is fine as far as it goes but doesn't take into account the child's expectations and comprehension—nor does it explain the cumulative effects of watching violence. Educators theorize that a child's response depends upon five variables: the child's intellectual achievement, social popularity, identification with television characters, belief in the realism of the violence and the amount of fantasizing about aggression. If a child identifies with the characters, for instance, then he tends to internalize scripts for future aggressive behavior. As a child becomes more aggressive, he becomes less popular and more troublesome in school. The more trouble he has with teachers and friends, the more likely he will turn to aggressive television for affirmation thus establishing a vicious cycle.

What's turned out to be the most startling result of Eron's study, however, was that a child's viewing beyond the age of 8 seems to have virtually no effect on his level of aggression: Once an 8-year-old's level of aggression is established, it tends to remain stable. If this is true, then most of the attacks on media are far off base. Children under the age of 8 are exposed to feature films but even with VCRs and cable, Hollywood movies are not staples in children's media diets in the same way that Mighty Morphin Power Rangers or Teenage Mutant Ninja Turtles are. In fact, the UCLA study singled out seven Saturday morning network shows including Power Rangers and Ninja Turtles for containing "sinister combat violence" or "violence for the sake of violence." The report warned that "the dark overtones and unrelenting combat in these shows constitute a fairly recent trend, which appears to be on the rise."

Of course, Eron's work is the subject of controversy. There are experts who warn against linking culture and violence at all. Jonathan Freedman, a psychology professor at the University of Toronto, says that after thoroughly reviewing all the existing studies on television and violence, he had to conclude that there was no convincing evidence that the media have an influence on real violence. "You always hear that there are 3,000 studies that prove that television contributes to violence," says Freedman, "but that's absolutely false. There are maybe 200 pertinent studies, and almost no one has read the literature. It sounds plausible that television causes violence, and everyone takes the word of the so-called experts. I was amazed at how different the studies were from what was being said about them."

Of those 200 studies, Freedman says, about 160 are lab studies, which he dismisses as "not totally irrelevant but not very meaningful." In typical lab studies, subjects are shown violent films, and then an attempt is made to measure their response. In one study, increased aggression was measured by showing children a balloon and asking if it would be fun to break it. In others, children were given plastic Bobo dolls that are designed to be hit. Freedman says that most experimenters get positive results because violent programs are simply more arousing than neutral programs and because children respond in the way they think the researchers expect them to. "All that these experiments show is potential effect," says Freedman. "But what is the real effect? In lab experiments they expose children to one kind of media, but in the real world no one watches just violence. You watch lots of different kinds of television. There's lots of different mediating stimuli."

Freedman finds the field studies equally disappointing. He thinks that Eron and his colleagues are true believers because they've devoted their careers to and built their reputations on the damaging effects of television violence. "Most people don't have the statistical and methodological expertise to read and evaluate the studies," Freedman explains, "Since these study committees all base their conclusions on the words of these few experts, naturally . . . they all conclude that television violence is harmful.

"People say that children are more aggressive," Freedman continues. "More aggressive than when? Not more than 1880. Somalia and Bosnia are worse than here, and Somalia doesn't have television."

The research on video games and rap music is even more inconclusive. A 1993 study of 357 seventh- and eighth-graders, for instance, found that 32 percent said fantasy violence was their favorite game category, while 17 percent chose human violence. But the study is small and doesn't draw conclusions between the games and aggression. As for rap, Peter Christiansen, a professor of communication at Lewis and Clark College, in Portland, Ore., says, "Seventy-six percent of rap is purchased by middle-class kids. For them, rap is a kind of cultural tourism . . . They aren't turned on by the explicit lyrics."

Poverty, the easy accessibility of guns, domestic abuse, social instability and the like may all contribute more than the media do to the level of violence. Even researchers like Signorielli warn against drawing cause-and-effect conclusions. "You can't just blame TV for the problems of society," she says. "Television contributes to children's aggressiveness, but it's only one of the factors."

Unfortunately, the political debate tends to ignore the nuances and uncertainties contained in the research. In reaction to the wave of political pressure, Time Warner sold its interest in Interscope, which distributed some of rap's most inflammatory artists, and Time Warner Chairman Gerald Levin agreed to develop standards for the distribution and labeling of potentially objectionable music. Meanwhile, Jack Valenti, the president of the Motion Picture Association of America, has commented that the entertainment industry "must . . . act as if TV is indeed a factor in anti-social behavior," adding that the industry "has to be more responsible." Valenti, however, still questions the link between media and violence. A sociopath could be triggered by reading a Bible verse as easily as by watching a film. As Valenti says, "We can't create movies that are safe for deviants. Anything can set them off. We can't function at their level."

Fortunately, even the most fervent critics, like William Bennett, still shy away from advocating legislative remedies; Bennett declares he hopes to shame the industry into taking a more responsible stand. Meanwhile, the Democrats are still pushing for a federal law that will create a ratings system for all programs and require new TVs to have a V chip, which gives parents the power to shut off certain pornographic or violent channels.

With the presidential race heating up, however, the rhetorical battle isn't likely to cool down any time soon. Dole . . . demanded in his campaign ads that "Hollywood stop corrupting our children." He . . . said on the Senate floor: "Those who continue to deny that cultural messages can and do bore deep into the hearts and minds of our young people are deceiving themselves and ignoring reality."

Yet if Saturday morning cartoons are more a problem than Hollywood blockbusters or rap music, who's ignoring reality?

READING REFLECTIONS

1. What are some of the ways Davidson indicates that children learn from the media?
2. In what ways does Davidson suggest that cartoons are more prone to stimulate violence than Hollywood blockbusters or rap music, the latter genres commonly cited as instigating violence?

3. According to Davidson and some of the researchers he cites, what are some of the flaws of studies on the impact of media violence on children?
4. At what point do children supposedly develop their "level of aggression," and how does this contribute to the reliability of such studies?
5. Why do you think this particular essay is published in *Rolling Stone?* In what ways does Davidson's essay appeal to this readership?

ELECTRONIC CHILDHOOD

Ellen Wartella

Is it the responsibility of entertainment executives to make children's "electronic childhood" more safe and caring? Because today's children grow up in households that are more media-rich than were those of their parents, Ellen Wartella calls for better awareness not only of the violent nature of television and video games but also of the increasingly commercial nature of much children's entertainment.

Ellen Wartella is a dean of the College of Communication at the University of Texas-Austin. Her scholarship has focused upon the role of the mass media in children's cognitive and social development. Her work includes the co-authored American Communication Research: The Remembered History *(1996) and the edited collection* Children Communicating: Media and the Development of Thought, Speech, Understanding *(1979). "Electronic Childhood" appeared in the scholarly* Media Studies Journal *and overviews the pros and cons of child development in an information age.*

My children are living an electronic childhood. And they are not alone. Channel surfing on cable, computer games, videos, e-mail and Internet are features of a world often alien to adults, but as familiar as the backyard to my sons, 11 and 6. As parents, teachers and television producers observe our children in this electronic world, we are both awed by their agility with media that sometimes intimidate us, and fearful of the ways those new media are changing the nature of children's lives and the society in which they grow up.

Ellen Wartella, "Electronic Childhood," *Media Studies Journal* 8, no. 4 (Fall 1994): 33–43. Reprinted with the permission of the author. The author adapted this essay from her remarks at the Cologne Conference, Germany, June 1994.

Indeed, concerns about the social effects of media on children and youth are echoed everywhere, and this shared worry can only accelerate as the marketplace for media products becomes ever more global and homogenized across national boundaries. Critics complain that young people spend too much time with media products that are too violent, commercialized and of inappropriate quality. But proponents of television, as well as champions of some of the newer interactive technologies such as video and computer, argue that such media enhance children's education.

Although several countries (such as France and Canada) limit importation of foreign films or television programs, a global cultural marketplace now exists in which media fare created in, say, Ireland, are marketed elsewhere in Europe as well as in the Americas, Asia and Australia. Throughout much of the global marketplace, the standards of aesthetic tastes or expectations for television dramatic content, films, popular music and videos are also increasingly homogenized. Like the armies of old, cultural products, created and distributed by multinational media conglomerates, now traverse industrialized democracies. And such a global international media market finds some of its most avid audiences among children.

What is this international electronic media environment for children?

In both Europe and the United States, children are heavy users of television and, increasingly, of all television programs accessed via the television set (i.e., videos, computer games). Children's television habits in Europe and the United States have been found to follow a similar pattern: Children are early users of television, showing a steady increase in viewing time from about age 2 until middle childhood (about age 8 or 9). Between the ages of 8 and 12, television viewing seems to level off at about two-and-three-quarter hours per day and then actually starts to decrease through adolescence, with the least amount of television viewing occurring among 14- to 19-year-olds, who watch about two hours per day.

But the TV set now makes available more than terrestrial television channels for children to watch: Cable, satellites and video-cassettes have now made considerable inroads into children's viewing of over-the-air television. In the United States, more than 60 percent of households now have cable and nearly three-quarters have VCRs. The most recent statistics I have seen on video-game usage suggest that one out of every three U.S. homes has a video game. Personal computers and CD-ROMs are less common, being newer, more expensive technologies, but are increasingly widespread every year.

In Europe, video and satellite penetration is more variable across countries. In 1988–89, for instance, the proportion of Italian households with a video recording machine was 19 percent, but 54 percent in Great Britain. And, as in the United States, in Europe households with children are more likely to own a VCR than are households without children. One British industry report found in 1990 that 22 percent of the population aged 7 and over had watched video during the previous week. The frequency of satellite TV viewing lies somewhere between terrestrial TV use and video use.

Without question, children today grow up in much more media-rich households than their parents' and, importantly, with more uses for the television set.

What do we know about what children watch on television? It's mostly adult fare. Children do not by any means watch only programs intended specifically for them. Horst Stipp, director of social and development research at NBC, recently pointed out that U.S. commercial television executives are fully aware that America's children prefer situation comedies to children's educational programs. Stipp says most of the programs that U.S. children watch are neither specially created for children nor shown in what is known as children's TV time—Saturday mornings.

A second noteworthy characteristic of children's viewing is that it roams across a range of live-action and animated fare that appears on cable or in syndication on local stations, not just on America's four commercial over-the-air networks. A third factor worth noting is that not one educational children's television show appears in the top-viewed programs, although if we looked at the ratings for children aged 2 to 5 separately from those aged 6 to 11, "Sesame Street," a widely acclaimed educational program for preschoolers, would make that list.

These data are not unique to the United States. When examining the listings of the top 10 programs for children in Great Britain, Switzerland, West Germany, France and the Netherlands, the most popular shows are comedies, game shows and soap operas. While preschool-aged children may start watching television by attending to children's programs, by the time they reach age 6 or 7 they watch more adult fare than children's programming.

Clearly, part of the explanation of children's viewing preferences may be the range of choices offered. Certainly, in the United States, the diversity and variety of entertaining fare specifically produced for children is limited, even with a proliferation of media and channels. In a 1990 study, I examined the variety and diversity of children's programming available in one Midwestern community. The question raised was whether children had access to both over-the-air broadcasts, cable and videocassette rentals of children's programming and whether that content included a range of genres for children to watch. In particular, I was interested in gauging the extent to which children's offerings provided them with informational or educational options (a particular concern of American public policy-makers).

We found that while the children in this community lived in homes with a variety of media available, including cable television and videocassette recorders, neither traditional broadcast television nor videocassette recorders provided much diversity of content for children. There were few informational or educational children's shows on broadcast television at the time, and most of those were dominated by toy-related animated programs—"Teenage Mutant Ninja Turtles" and the like. Similarly, most of the video rental fare was either adult-oriented or the same animated TV programs. The major exceptions to these were recycled Disney movies and some public broadcasting educational series such as "Sesame Street." Only households with cable were offered both variety and diversity of children's programming: Channels such as Nickelodeon, a commercial enterprise, offer a range of programming genres, quiz shows, game shows, drama, animated cartoons and variety shows, thus adding to the diversity of children's program options.

Since that 1990 study, there is now more competition in production of children's television and more program diversity in the United States. Much of this has been prompted by passage of the Children's Television Act of 1990, intended to increase the amount of educational and informational broadcast television programming available to children. Two of its provisions are important for the future of American children's television: that broadcasters must provide television programming that serves the educational and informational needs of children, and that, if they do not, broadcasters may be held accountable in license reviews every five years; second, the Act established a National Endowment for Children's Educational Television, a vehicle through which new programming ventures can be funded.

In addition to that important step, Congress in summer 1993 enacted the National Ready to Learn Act, which sets the goal of having all U.S. children prepared and ready to learn when they enter public school, and includes the use of television as part of the mandate. This year, money was funneled into public television to achieve this goal. Indeed, a few months ago, the U.S. public television system announced a renewed commitment to air an expanded block of nine hours a day of educational and informational children's programming this fall.

It may well be that the United States is approaching a renaissance in television programming for children. Even this year, one can point to a much larger diversity of programming genres for children on U.S. commercial television than was present a few years ago, in particular, renewed interest in science programs and quiz and game shows. The impact of privatized television on Europe's far more developed tradition of public broadcasting is less clear, although increasing amounts of U.S. animated children's programming now appear worldwide, so content improvements in the United States may have a positive global impact.

Concern about what children see and assimilate from television and videos is rooted in an assumption that the impact of television and other media is heavily determined by their content. Two aspects of content that have received most research and comment involve the violence and commercialization of much of commercial TV fare.

Violence in the media has been a topic for public debate and academic research since the film era in the 1920s, at least in the United States, where media violence has always seemed of more concern than in other areas of the world. In part this may be because American cultural products seem more violent than those of other countries. Yet, increasingly, media violence also transverses the globe, as the recent British outcry over "video nasties" demonstrates. Several major reviews of the predominantly U.S. research on violence effects have been issued over the past several years, converging on the conclusion that media violence is one environmental factor contributing to the maintenance of a stable pattern of aggressive behavior in children and adults. However, these studies conclude, media violence does constitute a threat to public health.

Partly because of such research and partly because of the political pressures to "do something" about violence in American life, U.S. cultural industries are responding. This year, the networks and the cable industry announced mechanisms to self-regulate their violent content, including the establishment of independent monitors to measure the amount of violence on television. In May 1994, the National Cable Television Association announced that it would contract with a consortium of four universities under the auspices of Mediascope (a not-for-profit organization in Hollywood organized to bring academics and industry people together around social issues of concern) to conduct TV violence monitoring over the next three years.

The second issue of public concern about television—commercialization—is exacerbated by the rise of privatized television in Europe and elsewhere in competition with public broadcasting, which has raised the stakes of a commercialized childhood. Around the world, for example, children now have access to the "Teenage Mutant Ninja Turtles" (or "Teenage Mutant Hero Turtles," as they are known in Great Britain) via television, video, books, interactive video games, movies and a whole host of toy products, comic books, clothing and children's furnishings. Programs that link television characters to toy products—termed program-length commercials in the United States—are of increasing concern around the globe.

The fact that television program characters are created with an eye toward their marketing potential as toys or other consumer items is only part of an entire marketing strategy that has evolved over a decade. Starting from the premise that children like the familiar and recognizable, the creation of children's programming (once based on children's books or films) is an elaborate manifestation of providing children with something familiar. Today, simultaneous production of a children's TV show and its toy-related characters is an assumed part of the package, with the relationship between media and merchandise reinforced via product licensing (such as for backpacks, sheets, towels, clothing and lunch boxes), cereal products (e.g., breakfast boxes featuring "Ghostbusters" and "The Addams Family"), character appearances at shopping malls and holiday events, movie appearances ("Batman: The Animated Movie" is based on Fox's kidshow, which in turn was issued after the success of the live-action [adult] "Batman" films), and, of course, a host of new-technology toys including arcade and home video games, story tapes and home-computer software. These characters and products range widely around the world—it is difficult to escape purple dinosaurs or talking fire engines anywhere.

What is emerging is unique to the new electronic age, what Marsha Kinder in her book on video games calls a "supersystem: a network of interrelated narrative texts or media products constructed around a pop cultural figure or group of figures." In addition to the Turtles, there are the characters from the "Star Wars" movies, the Simpsons, the Smurfs, the Muppets of "Sesame Street," Batman and, born-again through Hollywood's magic and eagerness to recycle proven vehicles, the Flintstones. Sometimes, pop cultural icons are real people too—Madonna, Michael Jackson and even the (apparently) dead Elvis Presley. "In order to be a supersystem," writes Kinder, "the network must cut across several modes of image production; must appeal to diverse generations, classes, ethnic subcultures, who in turn are targeted with diverse strategies; must foster 'collectibility' through a proliferation of related products; and must undergo a sudden increase in commodification, the success of which reflexively becomes a 'media event' that dramatically accelerates the growth curve of the system's commercial success."

Indeed, the notion of "interactive" media is a double entendre—not only are users interacting with the images on screens, but one media outlet is interacting with others in one large consumerist dance. And children—even preschoolers—are at its center, by being educated to become part of the consumer group of children around the world (and certainly at their preschools and in their neighborhoods) who together can play with the Turtles, Barney or other cultural icons.

If I am engaging the old arguments about marketplace constraints on the quality of cultural products, I do so with an awareness of the higher stakes involved in global markets saturated with a handful of cultural supersystems. The concern, of course, is that marketing will outweigh any concern with aesthetics. Moreover, I fear we are developing a generation of cynical consumers.

Beyond the pitfalls of commercialization, a media system of interrelated products has implications for the potential of new electronic media to enhance children's lives. Indeed, there are high hopes that the active nature of children's interactions with video games and computers, as well as the other newer electronic audio and video products, will help children learn about the world and themselves.

Many of the production principles that have governed children's television are being carried over into other interactive media. And no wonder. Many of the same production houses are moving into multiple technologies for delivering media products and, as discussed, cultural icons across media are often part of the same supersystem. These principles are rooted in observations of what engages and interests children as media users.

One principle that should be incorporated into production of all children's media is that repetition is a key to both educating and entertaining children. Just as children like to have the same stories read to them over and over, they enjoy the same television programs and videos. Repetition is not just important but essential to video games, since practice leads to mastery. Repetition both entertains and hones new skills: In video games as in life, once children learn to master one sort of obstacle, whenever it arises again, they are prepared.

A second principle is that children want recognizable characters and stories. And the supersystem of cultural production ensures that children can find favorite characters across a range of media technologies. In the future, recycling children's stories from television to video to CD-ROM to computer games and back again is likely to be the norm, not the exception. As discussed, this principle is very effective in developing marketing strategies for children, but only in the short term: Supersystems of image marketing quickly lead to cynicism among the older child audience members.

A third principle is that gender differences survive into this new electronic world. The common assumption among U.S. children's TV producers, for instance, is that boys like fast-paced action, adventure and superheroes, while girls take to fantasy, soft, cuddly characters and slower-paced television. Action, and often violence (good vs. evil, heroic feats, technical wizardry and male-dominated characters) are all marks of boys' television best typified by the Ninja Turtles' success. Girls' programming is dominated by sugary-sweet programs about cute, doll-like characters who demonstrate good pro-social qualities of caring and helpfulness (e.g., Ariel in "The Little Mermaid"). This expectation of male bias towards action and superheroes has carried over from movies and television into the video-game industry. As Kinder reports, the vast majority of video-game players are boys; when surveyed, both girls and boys as young as 5 and 6 see video games as more appropriate for boys than girls. Manufacturers see that, of course, so it is no surprise that current video-game products are more boy-oriented than girl-oriented, which clearly may have repercussions if such interactive media do, as some observers claim, have an impact on children's cognitive development.

Fourth, an implication of new media for children is that the nature of the visual-spatial interactivity of media such as video games and computers may have a positive impact on cognitive development. Psychologist Patricia Greenfield, for instance, suggests in her book *Mind and Media* that video-game playing does offer important cognitive benefits. The very structure of video games fosters the use of an inductive reasoning process, provides a means of verifying hypotheses, improves eye-hand coordination and the processing of visual information from multiple perspectives and helps develop skills in iconic-spatial representation. But video games tend to be based on boy-oriented television and video narratives; if video games are a gateway into greater comfort with computer use, then girls quite clearly are disadvantaged in entering the increasingly computerized work world. When transplanted to newer technologies, the gendered world of children's television may have serious consequences for future generations of workers.

On the other hand, there is something of a blurring of age distinctions in children's use of interactive technologies. I have observed boys as young as 3 and 4 rally round my 11-year-old when he's playing with his video games. In many ways, video games, computers and other new media can draw children and adolescents together around their interactive technology; sometimes only parents feel left out. Part of this observation is rooted in the way television is programmed for children. If, for instance, children "watch up"— that is, watch the programs that attract older siblings—it is no surprise that programmers seek to develop shows for an elastic age group of 5- to 13-year-olds. One beneficial result of this blurring of age-group interest in new media is that it may indeed lead to children of different ages, perhaps even with adults, gathering round interactive technologies together. I know that my children and their friends like to play video games together, the group watching while one tries his hand at the game. Contrary to many fears that video games and computers will lead to greater individual and social isolation, it may be that at least some of these technologies have inherent social aspects that have been thus far ignored.

The potential for new interactive media to change the nature of children's leisure time is enormous. Already, children are faced with a dizzying array of high-tech activities that fill their electronic childhoods, as well as with traditional printed media. Harnessing the potential of these old and new media to create entertaining as well as educationally beneficial cultural products, and to do so without further commercialization of our youth, is the challenge we all face. If history is a guide, great expectations of the transformatory power of new media to wonderfully enhance children's cognitive and emotional lives probably will fall short. On the other hand, if we do produce the very best products possible, perhaps those goals will move closer. In much of the world, children already live an electronic childhood. Can we make it a healthy, safe and caring one?

READING REFLECTIONS

1. Outline Wartella's discussion of the pros and cons of children's constant exposure to all forms of media, from television to video games.
2. If you were or are a parent, what media would you want your children to avoid and why? How capable would you be of "censoring" media images?
3. What is the Children's Television Act and what has been its impact on American television?
4. In addition to the warning labels on tapes and CDs, several cable and network stations have been using programming codes, such as PG in the corner of television screens, in a process similar to the rating system long in place for feature films. How seriously do you think people pay attention to such labels? Interview several adults with children for their opinions about the need for and effectiveness of such ratings.
5. Explain the concept of "watching up" among children and how it contributes to television programming for children.

THE RUDE TUBE

Rick Marin

With quotes from parents and children alike, "The Rude Tube" profiles the conflict over issues of censorship as the nighttime cartoon South Park *continues to be a big hit with kids and a big miss with their parents and teachers, many of whom have resorted to banning the show not only within individual homes but also within entire communities.*

Rick Marin is a senior writer for Newsweek. *He was previously a contributing editor of* TV Guide *and a frequent contributor to the* New York Times. *He has also written about television and pop culture for* Mademoiselle, GQ, Vogue, *the* Los Angeles Times, Interview, Rolling Stone, *and* Spin. *Marin holds an M.S. from Columbia University's Graduate School of Journalism as well as an M.A. in English from the University of Toronto and a B.A. in English from McGill. Born in Toronto, he currently lives in Manhattan.*

Visitors to the Los Angeles Headquarters of the cult cable hit "South Park" sit on an absurdly low, turquoise velour sofa and gaze up at a poster above the reception desk. It features four cartoon kids, cute as "Peanuts," and reads, "Alien Abductions, Anal Probes & Flaming Farts. South Park. Why They Created the V-Chip."

Comedy Central printed the ad when this weekly animated series about four flatulent third graders and their paranormal Colorado town went on the air eight months ago. Last week the up-yours slogan proved prophetic. The Federal Communications Commission issued technical guidelines for V-chips to be built into all new TV sets. The handy home-censor chip will empower parents to block the very anal probes and flaming farts that have catapulted "South Park" to the coolest schoolyard craze since MTV's "Beavis and Butt-head" introduced eight-letter words like "ass-munch" into the prepubescent vernacular. As in the heyday of "B&B," some grown-ups think that the cartoon is not appropriate for youngsters. Or, in the words of Action for Children's Television founder Peggy Charren, it is "dangerous to the democracy."

The difference between the last time the democracy was in danger and now is that, while "B&B" was a kid show with grown-up appeal, "South Park"

---

is a grown-up show with irresistible kid appeal. It airs at 10 P.M. and carries a TV-MA warning, but 23 percent of the audience is under 18. In the last two weeks of February, 5.2 million viewers watched, huge by cable standards. One Wednesday night it even beat ABC's "PrimeTime Live." Blue-chip advertisers like AT&T, Calvin Klein and Snapple are paying as much as $80,000 for a 30-second spot, 20 times the network's original rate-card cost. T-shirt sales have topped $30 million, and the merchandising mayhem has barely begun.

Using artfully artless cutout animation, "South Park" storyboards childhood through the eyes of two creatively dysfunctional adults: Trey Parker, 28, and Matt Stone, 26. Their colorful brood of minimally altered egos—Stan, Kyle, Cartman and Kenny—are foulmouthed li'l "bastards" (Stone and Parker's favorite description of 9-year-old boys) who abuse each other, delight in dissing authority figures and yet possess a dumb innocence that makes their bad behavior forgivable to anyone with an honest memory of third grade.

The adult population of this snowbound mountain hamlet—named after a real Colorado county notorious for alien sightings and other rural myths—is far more troubling. Stan's Uncle Jimbo is a gun nut with a Vietnam-vet sidekick. Mr. Garrison, the disturbed teacher, has a sidekick, too: a hand puppet named Mr. Hat. On the plus side, Jesus Christ, a guy in a white robe and sandals who hosts a local cable-access show, is a force of holy goodness. So is Chef, the town's singing school cook and only black soul (voiced by Isaac Hayes), who keeps an eye on the children as vigilantly as he does on the ladies.

Gleefully offensive and profoundly silly, the show revels in juxtaposing cute and crude, jaded and juvenile. In an episode called "Big Gay Al's Big Gay Boat Ride," Stan learns about tolerance after discovering that his dog is gay and suffering merciless "Stan's dog's a homo," taunts from his friends. Another favorite, titled "Mr. Hankey the Christmas Poo," is simply one long potty joke. And yet the cliffhanger episode, Cartman's quest to find his father, is almost poignant. Almost. The episode is called "Cartman's Mom Is a Dirty Slut."

Parker stresses that nasty gets boring fast. "People think the show is just fart jokes," he says, as we head to their new expanded production space in Marina del Rey. "I wish. It wouldn't be so hard to find writers." Anne Garefino, 37, a co-executive producer and den mother to its postcollegiate staff of 35 animators and production slaves, says, "Trey and Matt both have a sweetness that balances out the grossness."

Trey (the voice of Stan and Cartman) is the one people call the "genius" of the pair, the self-directed hustler who won a Student Academy Award and, while still in school, raised $125,000 for his feature, "Cannibal: The Musical." Matt (who does Kyle and Kenny) is more practical and business-savvy. But both still come off like dorks whose vocabulary is dominated by the words "rad" (cool), "lame" (uncool) and "dude" (dude).

They're smart guys—Stone majored in math—who love acting stupid. "Girls are so dumb!" says Stone, complaining about a frustrating conversation the previous night with his significant other. Parker, recently broken up from his girlfriend, sympathizes. "Talking's dumb," he says. One rad thing about

Matt and Trey is that they still haven't hired a publicist. Why bother? The story of how this goofball duo made it writes itself. They met at the University of Colorado-Boulder, and bonded because "we were the only ones who didn't want to make black-and-white films about lesbians," says Parker. Stone graduated, Parker cut too many classes to get his degree. Their professor Bruce Kawin is not a fan. "Trey doesn't remember anyone who helped him," Kawin says. "So he's not my favorite person." Stone's response: "We hate Kawin."

In 1995 they hit L.A., sharing a dump in Playa del Rey and peddling an animated short about Frosty the Snowman terrorizing some mountain-town kids until a dashboard-size Jesus vanquishes him. Brian Graden—then a Fox development exec, now head of programming at MTV—liked their twisted little fable and ponied up $1,200 of his own money for a holiday video for his industry pals. They came up with "The Spirit of Christmas," a refined version of "Frosty," only with Santa and Jesus kung-fu fighting while the kids cheer on.

The video became an underground bootleg obsession. George Clooney alone duped dozens of copies, and later offered to record the "Grrrs" of Stan's gay dog. By this time, Stone and Parker had William Morris agents and many offers, among them "Barney: The Movie." They chose Comedy Central because, Parker says, "when we asked, 'How do you feel about talking poo?' they said, 'Love it!' " Another historic moment in the annals of American culture.

After the show premiered in August the virus kept spreading, well beyond the 47 million households wired for Comedy Central. More than 250 unofficial Web sites have sprung up devoted to news, gossip and general worship. The largest site (at www.beef-cake.com) has received more than 2 million hits since a 21-year-old engineering student at Caltech started it almost a year ago. The show's stop-motion style makes it a natural to download. Comedy Central encourages the sites, since many cable systems (including the Colorado-based TCI) don't carry the channel. "Without the Internet I doubt I would have ever even heard about it," e-mail's Oskar Horyd, 15, from Troy, Mich., a Detroit suburb.

The availability of "South Park" on the Internet is another pesky issue for grown-ups worried about whether kids are or should be watching. Take Canton, Ga. Two weeks ago the principal of the town's Hickory Flat Elementary School banned the wearing of "South Park" gear on school property. That made Donna Beavers, a hairdresser and PTA co-president, very happy. She says the show is off-limits to her two boys, Mark, 11, and Wade, 8: "I want to keep them innocent as long as I can."

But keeping kids innocent is like squeezing toothpaste back into the tube. One 15-year-old Canton freshman sneaks her weekly fix. "When my dad comes in I change channels," she says. "He's, like, all Christian and stuff, and one time he gave me a big lecture about how bad the show was for me." But some parents are cooler about it. "I understand that kids have to learn to filter things for themselves," says Deborah Redford, whose 14-year-old son Blair is in middle school. "Hopefully it's not going to corrupt him." Besides, Blair chimes in, "it's just a cartoon!"

Saying the show corrupts young minds is selling short the show and the young minds. Underage fans grasp that the selfish, racist fat kid Cartman is not a role model. "We got a letter from a kid in Mississippi who said he was in a school play about Rosa Parks and played the bus driver as Cartman," Parker says. "Which shows how kids get it." Cartman dressing up as Hitler for Halloween might have alarmed some parents, but New York seventh grader Nick Farrar says, "With Cartman, you know he's just a complete idiot and you should sort of do the opposite of everything he does." As for the bleepable expletives that fly out of the mouths of Kyle, Kenny & Co., an 8-year-old boy from Larchmont, N.Y., says they weren't new to him: "My daddy says them every single day."

The kid's on to something. As trippy as some of the show's plots can get—like Barbra Streisand's transforming into a giant robot—they're grounded in reality. "It isn't a comedy, it's a documentary," B. J. Macumber, a sheriff's deputy in the real-life South Park county town of Alma, recently told an AP reporter after a local resident trashed government buildings with a front-end loader and killed an ex-mayor. Another docu-dramatic truth is that kids have foul mouths and *can* be total bastards. Like real third graders might, Stan and Kyle make fun of Cartman because his mother is on the cover of Crack Whore magazine, without really knowing what a crack whore is. They're raunchy but naively presexual.

Don't think the "South Park" guys haven't thought this stuff through. When they were developing the pilot, Brian Graden says, "we went away for a whole day and said, 'Who is Cartman? Who is Kenny?' We decided Kyle is the Jewish kid (like Matt) who's a bit smarter. Trey was the group leader, a B student who was good at football and probably the first one to get a girlfriend—and that's Stan." Kenny is the poor kid in every group—except he dies violently every week.

For all the noise about "South Park" and kids, it's worth remembering that the show's core viewers are of voting age. Almost 60 percent of them are 18 to 34. But Generation X's attention span is as fleeting as Generation Y's. So how long before the backlash? Now that "Oh my God, they killed Kenny!" has spread from subculture password to catchphrase, some hard-core fans are worried. "It seems like it's gonna start selling out soon," says Noah Gordon, a 14-year-old Boston devotee. May could be the watershed. The next season of 20 more "South Park" episodes starts then (after an April 1 teaser). . . . At a comedy festival in Aspen, Colo., two weeks ago, Parker had a recurring nightmare. "People kept surrounding my bed asking for autographs," he says. "But I'm sure some of that stems from being really, really drunk."

The price of fame. Parker just bought a $1.2 million house in Bel Air, Calif., "with a hot tub overlooking the city." But he's quick to complain that he and Matt are only seeing a fraction of the "South Park" profits. "I have a friend who writes for 'Just Shoot Me' who makes more a week than I do." he says. "Thirty million in T-shirt sales, and I got a check for $7,000." They might have thought twice about doing "Dumb & Dumber" except "it came at a time when we were getting really bitter about how little we were making off 'South

Park,' " says Parker. William Morris is renegotiating their deal, and Comedy Central wants to keep its star attractions happy.

The five remaining members of Monty Python were also in Aspen. "I wrote Terry Jones's home phone number on a napkin!" says Matt, as if he'd snagged the Shroud of Turin. "I'm gonna frame it." During their reunion show at the festival, the Pythons reminisced about how when their "Flying Circus" debuted in 1969, the BBC was saturated with political satire, which is why they wanted to do "something completely different." It's no accident that "South Park" has also taken off at a time when Monica Lewinsky jokes have overloaded our humor receptors. New York Times columnist Frank Rich explained the boys' appeal as "post-ideological."

That analysis may be too meta for the throng of raucous twentysomethings crowding the Bulldog bar in New Orleans last Wednesday night. Barkeep Billy Norris, 29, followed his weekly custom by turning the jukebox off and "South Park" on at 9. "It's the exact opposite of politically correct," Norris says, noting approvingly that the characters "show no sensitivity at all." Proving Parker's theory that offensiveness isn't enough, Norris adds that the writing is "subtle and clever" and that "the characters are all different and you can see them develop." How many TV shows can that be said of?

Comedy Central president Doug Herzog explains his hit not as a political but as a pop phenomenon. "It's dangerous comedy, and I think the rebellious nature of the show is really speaking to the audience. Pop music gets packaged so quickly now that the spirit of rebellion gets left out." In this age of poser punks, Trey and Matt truly are, in the words of their idols, something completely different. Rude bastards.

READING REFLECTIONS

1. Why would Action for Children's Television founder Peggy Charren deem the show *South Park* as "dangerous to the democracy"?
2. Is such a statement warranted? On what basis?
3. Among its attempts to provide cautionary warnings to parents about the adult content of *South Park*, the Comedy Central Network airs the show at 10 o'clock in the evening and flashes a TV-MA (mature audiences) rating before each episode. Yet statistics show that 23 percent of the viewing audience is under the age of 18. What do these facts suggest about the role and impact of such warnings?
4. What makes programs such as Comedy Central's *South Park*, Fox Network's *The Simpsons*, and MTV's *Daria* popular with young viewers? Watch an episode of each, noting similarities and differences in theme and tone.
5. *South Park* has generated a love-hate relationship with some parents and their children. Interview a parent who refuses to allow his or her children to watch the show, and one who allows viewings. How do their rationales connect to issues raised by parents quoted in the article?

CYBERSTALKER, QU'EST-CE-QUE C'EST?

Thomas Goetz

Are virtual "pick ups" any more or less safe than face-to-face ones? Thanks to the bizarre details of Oliver Jovanovic's sexual assault of a college student, the media coverage, as Thomas Goetz notes, personifies society's fears about technology, a paranoia that has led to the birth of the "cyberstalker." Because Jovanovic arranged his date by computer, Goetz questions the demonization of the Internet and associated technologies.

Thomas Goetz is a regular contributor to the Village Voice, *in which his commentary "Cyberstalker, Qu'est-ce-que c'est?" first appeared. Here, Goetz questions the extent to which the Internet has become a scapegoat, a supposed contributor to crime that somehow exceeds the violent impact of other electronic media, including something as basic as the telephone.*

Seven days after Oliver Jovanovic went on his alleged date turned torture session, computer programmer Michael Sperko had a date, too. At 7 P.M. on November 29, a female escort went to Sperko's downtown office for an appointment. He allegedly raped and beat her so severely that she slipped into a coma. Like Jovanovic, Sperko has been charged with rape. Like Jovanovic, he's been described by police as a computer geek."

So why has no one heard of Michael Sperko, when Jovanovic earns front-page tabloid coverage as a "cyberspace sex fiend"? Because for all his technical prowess, Sperko arranged his date with a phone call, where Jovanovic sent an e-mail. With that one click, he went from being yet another accused predator to a tabloid demon, embodying all our technological apprehensions. The consequent stories about Jovanovic's case may say more about us then about him.

It's safe to say that Oliver Jovanovic knows computers. As the *Post* and *Daily News* have feverishly reported, he was a frequent visitor to America Online chat rooms; scheduled to defend his microbiology dissertation at Columbia last week, he'd planned on moving to Seattle to start a computer firm with his brother.

But what does all this have to do with the assault? The papers have been free with speculation but short on answers. Only the *Times* suggested a causal link: that the ARREST AT COLUMBIA SHOWS RISKS IN ON-LINE DATING. The same, of course, could be said of coffee shops or singles bars. But that sort of risk-taking doesn't sell papers like the dangers of a new technology.

"The police don't bust dirty bookstores anymore, and nobody would care if they did," says Mike Godwin, staff counsel for the Electronic Frontier Foundation. "But if they shut down a BBS [bulletin-board service] or Web page with the same sort of content—or even milder stuff—it's guaranteed the front page. People are anxious about technology, and it's reflected in this unthinking focus on the computer angle."

Consider the following *Post* headlines:

INTERNET RAPE SCANDAL AT COLUMBIA, CYBER SUSPECT SAYS I'M NOT A SEX FIEND, and PLUGGED IN TO CYBER PSYCHE. The less adept *Daily News* first described Jovanovic as a lowly "Ph.D. student," but soon it too had taken to calling Jovanovic an ACCUSED CYBERSEX FIEND and the "cyberstalker."

Thanks to its other bizarre details, the Jovanovic case is a surprisingly rich reservoir for our fears. What with the alleged 20-hour torture session, complete with ropes, candle wax, and a martial-arts baton, the story is pure tabloid; all the better that the victim, a 20-year-old Barnard student, at first called it "kinky" and "weird" rather than rape, as the *Post* reported.

The scenario being constructed here is easy to see: the cyberstalker, who knows the technology better than his victim, uses it to lure her into his home, where he can act out the wicked fantasies he's devised in the hours spent online.

The Internet isn't the first technology to be so demonized. When they debuted, both radio and television came in for this sort of hysteria; you still hear that too much television causes cancer—not to mention juvenile delinquency and out-of-wedlock births. But both of these pale next to cyberspace. "TV and radio are passive; the Internet is active, interactive," says Godwin. "It's the most empowering communications medium the world has ever seen. That scares people. So when something bad happens, like this case, it's a chance for all those fears and all that anxiety to get brought to the surface."

Cyberstalkers have walked among us since 1994, when a hate-e-mailer known as Vito threatened Prodigy users with rape and violence. CBS's Connie Chung devoted an Eye to Eye segment to Vito, and the "cyberstalker" was born. Months later, the movie *Cyberstalker* appeared, in which a female computer nerd becomes obsessed with a humble cartoonist. The movie became the first downloadable feature film when Internet America put it online.

Ironically, that company's CEO, Robert Maynard, and his wife claim they became the target of computerized harassment earlier this year, when an ex-con named Kevin Massey posted comments about the company and death threats against the couple. Massey says it was more like ordinary flaming. Still, in a flurry of press releases hyping their torment, the Maynards secured a restraining order against Massey, who began calling himself "the cyberstalker" and tried to get on Howard Stern's radio show.

Such incidents not only make for good stories—they can easily become the basis for dubious law. On the heels of the newly formed Internet Content

Coalition and the Communications Decency Act, the U.S. Parole Commission approved restrictions on December 16 denying computer and Internet access to "certain high-risk parolees." Noting a "surge in 'how-to' information on child molestation" and bomb making online, commission chairman Edward Reilly said, "We cannot ignore the possibility that such offenders may be tempted to use computer services to repeat their crimes."

Even as Internet activists like Godwin argue that no such "surges" have been documented, or point out that bomb-making information is already available in libraries, groups like the CyberAngels are out to expose and magnify Internet crimes. An offshoot of the Guardian Angels, they've been monitoring the Net for harassment, software piracy, and child porn, turning some 5000 cases over to law enforcement in the past year. A list distributed by the CyberAngels, of cautions Internet users should take, has now been posted around the Barnard campus.

But even the hypervigilant CyberAngels aren't upset by the Jovanovic case. "People become hysterical when anything has to do with the Internet," says director Gabriel Hatcher. "But the percentage of crime online is basically the same as in real life. In fact, this story has very little to do with the Internet."

Except that everyone seems to think it does.

READING REFLECTIONS

1. According to Thomas Goetz, what accounts for the birth of the "cyberstalker"?
2. Why does Goetz feel that the Internet is being "demonized" in the media?
3. Test Goetz's position by surveying several news stories, print or television, about the role of the Internet in people's lives and report your results to your classmates.
4. How do cases like the Oliver Jovanovic sexual assault of a college student on a date arranged via computer affect the public's perception of the Internet?
5. How might public perception impact usage of the Internet for people less familiar with this newest information technology?

CENSORSHIP AND SENSITIVITY
Understanding Community Standards

Cynthia L. Hallen

Is censorship ever justified in the classroom? Cynthia Hallen acknowledges that students have as much right to say "no" to textual intercourse as they do to sexual intercourse, as some art forms, however historically or culturally relevant, can trigger anxiety in the lives of children suffering from numerous forms of abuse, a sadly increasing trend in our society.

Cynthia Hallen is a professor of linguistics and English at Brigham Young University. In this editorial for The Council Chronicle, *a newsletter of the National Council of Teachers of English, Hallen argues that some portrayals of sex and violence in contemporary literature and film may be offensive and detrimental to students based on students' religion or on their own histories of abuse. Ultimately, Hallen stresses that concerns about decency are as important as concerns about diversity.*

The National Council of Teachers of English has established firm guidelines on avoiding sexist language in NCTE conferences and publications, including a long list of appropriate substitutions for banned terms such as "mankind" and the generic "he." While many of the "correct" NCTE forms may be preferable, the arguments used to justify NCTE restrictions on "incorrect" forms seem strained, especially when every recent NCTE conference has had sessions on how to counteract censorship. The NCTE guidelines explain that they are not trying to create a new dogmatism, rather they just want to avoid the subtle conditioning that male-dominated language may impose in our minds. However, the NCTE guidelines do not mention the subtle conditioning of other forms of aggressive language such as profanity and obscenity. If a generic "he" pronoun can subtly influence our attitudes about women, then what about the influence of profanity on our attitudes about religion, and the influence of violent sexual expletives on our attitudes about human intimacy?

Many educators object to male-generic pronouns and other forms of sexist language, but they overlook the negative effects of profanity and obscenity in the media forms they require students to read or view. Educators who are anxious to ensure that each student has the "right to read" (or "right to view") must also realize that students have the right *not* to read texts that are personally painful or texts that violate their moral standards. Some educators seem to feel that it is their job to raise the consciousness of students so that they will be "mature" enough to handle the "real world." But some of our students have already experienced more than their share of harsh realities.

For example, students who are survivors of abuse may find it particularly difficult to partake of texts (or other art forms) that contain offensive language, graphic violence, or explicit sex scenes. Art forms containing such things may trigger memories that lead to anxiety, flashbacks, nightmares. The source of offensive language is often rooted in violence and abuse. In fact, Anne L. Horton, Byron J. Marquez, and others list vulgarity, profanity, degrading sexual jokes, embarrassing sexual comments, humiliation, and swearing as types of verbal abuse in *Confronting Abuse* (12–14, 159, 161–65).

Victims of assault are especially sensitive and should be warned in advance of materials that portray intense violence. Suanna Davis has conducted research which shows that victims of sexual assault often cannot endure exposure to explicit media forms. To avoid harming vulnerable people, a teacher who wants to show Kevin Costner's film "Robin Hood" would need to alert students about the attempted-rape scene and allow those who feel uncomfortable to be excused. Because of their background, some students may not be able to read certain scenes in the popular work *I Know Why the Caged Bird Sings* by Maya Angelou; such students should be allowed to choose an alternative text.

Students have just as much right to say "no" to textual intercourse as they do to say "no" to sexual intercourse. Nevertheless, some teachers may feel it is their duty to require students to read certain texts or watch certain videos. Such a duty needs to be tempered by affirmative action principles that protect the rights of students not only in terms of race and sex but also in terms of religion and creed. Students from some religious backgrounds have made covenants of moral cleanliness; their commitments may include avoiding art forms that are obscene, suggestive, and needlessly violent. Such religious covenants and moral commitments can be as sacred as Navajo sandpaintings in restoring or maintaining harmony in our communities. Some educators may mock standards of chastity and fidelity and purity of mind. But educators and citizens in a community have a responsibility to protect the innocent, the vulnerable, and the wounded; to promote respect in relationships; to establish peace; and to stop violence.

I once had a roommate from Poland who explained that under the Communist system, it was harder to do evil but it was also harder to do good. She noticed that there was more crime and corruption in the United States but that there was also more charity and compassion. She took advantage of the freedoms in America to perform many loving acts of service that would have been impossible in Poland. The same basic principle could apply to freedom of expression in art, language, and literature: communities that avoid censorship may have more smut and moral pollution, but such communities may also have more opportunities for creating and appreciating works that are exquisitely beautiful and moral. A friend once pointed out that those who would ban salacious texts in a community might also ban sacred texts such as the *Bible*, the *Koran*, or the *Book of Mormon*. No wonder most people feel instinctively threatened by any mention of censorship.

However, we all practice censorship, publicly and privately. Tom Loveridge, an administrator at the University of Utah, once taught students in a Philosophy of Education class that all communities practice some form of censorship. Professor Loveridge had students work in small groups until each group had arrived at a consensus on the topic of censorship. In our group, a few people expressed a desire to regulate pornographic materials, but those concerns were overruled by the group opinion. When called upon to report, every group leader announced that their group had decided that censorship was always bad. Dr. Loveridge listened patiently and then pointed out that removing racial and sexual stereotypes from textbooks is a form of censorship. Eyes opened and jaws dropped as people realized that concerns about decency can be just as vital and valid as concerns about equality.

In *After Babel*, George Steiner discusses the role of taboo topics in language and society (182–85). Steiner warns that communities that diminish the force of taboo forms will lose the ability to relate as intimate individuals:

> Over the past forty years, the vocabulary of sex has been massively publicized. It has been all but neutralized by constant exploitation on the stage, in print and in emancipated colloquialism. . . . Social psychologists welcome this change. They see it as a liberation from needless shadows. I wonder . . . the capacity of words to be at once devalued, loudly demeaned, and magical points to a dynamic poise between private and public aspects of language. These delicate strengths have been eroded. Moreover, the imaginative and expressive resources of most men and women are limited. . . . Being today, so loud and public.

Some people think that educators, authors, and artists should have the right to speak openly about anything, yet they object when vulnerable people speak openly about words or works that are harmful to them. Freedom of speech and freedom of expression need to include the rights of sensitive people to complain about vulgarity, violence, and violation.

In any community, but especially in a community that espouses peace education, some jokes should not be told; some scenes should not be shown; some words should not be spoken; some books should not be read; some stories should not be told.

Works Cited

Angelou, Maya. *I Know Why the Caged Bird Sings.* New York: Bantam, 1993.

Davis, Suanna Haston. "A Linguistic Interpretation of the Language of Rape Survivors." Paper given at the Deseret Language and Linguistics Symposium, Brigham Young University, April 2, 1993.

Horton, Anne L., B. Kent Harrison, and Barry L. Johnson, eds. *Confronting Abuse: An LDS Perspective on Understanding and Healing Emotional, Physical, Sexual, Psychological, and Spiritual Abuse.* Salt Lake City: Deseret Book Company, 1993.

Steiner, George. *After Babel: Aspects of Language and Translation.* New York: Oxford UP, 1992.

READING REFLECTIONS

1. Under what circumstances does Cynthia Hallen suggest that educational and community censorship is undertaken in the name of "peace education"?
2. How does Hallen's essay challenge those who consider any form of censorship bad?
3. Interview teachers in your major to determine whether controversies about censorship of material exist in disciplines other than English literature, the subject of Hallen's article.
4. In what ways does Hallen claim "we all practice censorship, publicly and privately"? What are ways in which you practice censorship, or whether you feel your parents or teachers have engaged in such practice?
5. Conduct a research study of some historical or contemporary attempts at censorship in the public school system. What has been the rationale for such attempts, whether it be for books, films, school news reporting, even hairstyle or clothing? Analyze the values or belief systems that led to such censorship efforts and any opposing efforts.

"Media Morals" Activities

READING REACTIONS

1. Preview a video game currently popular on the market. Based on the positions of John Davidson and Ellen Wartella, establish some criteria for what might be considered objectionable content. Use that criteria to determine how these games or shows compare to the more commonly cited culprits of sexual and violent content, such as television shows, films, or music videos and lyrics.
2. Share the Public Enemy lyrics with students outside your class and from varying social groups. Compare their responses toward these lyrics and any others with Allan Bloom's general attitude toward contemporary music to assess the support his argument receives among the young people he critiques.
3. Compare the points about literary and media texts made by Cynthia Hallen, Rick Marin, Allan Bloom, Ellen Wartella, and others in the chapter. Classify

these varying positions, determining who would seem to be more pro or con about the issue of media regulation and censorship.

CLASSROOM REACTIONS

1. In 1985, the rock group Judas Priest was sued by parents of two Nevada teenagers who committed suicide, having been influenced, the lawsuit claimed, by the group's allegedly satanic themes in various song lyrics. Searching library databases and on-line sites, write a research paper chronicling the specific instances in which the media have been said to contribute to specific crimes or violent acts. What were the arguments and evidence both for and against the accusation? Determine the strengths and weaknesses of both sides.
2. While many people cite the media as being irresponsible in privileging commercialization over conscience, how responsible should the media, television, music and film producers, as well as video-game manufacturers, have to be for the content of their material in light of free speech, censorship, and public decency issues? After an initial debate in class, write a response for publication in your student paper.
3. Given that so many made-for-television movies are "based on a true story," what does that say about the role of violence as a creator or reflection of violence in the media? Do the media create problems or reflect existing trends in our culture? Cite specific examples to prove your point. What would be the result if violent or other questionable content were taken out of all forms of media? Write a proposal for a television show as if you were "pitching it" to network executives on the basis of what you feel is an "acceptable" level of violence or adult content.

MEDIA CONNECTIONS

1. In groups, conduct a survey of television programming on the major networks for one week, assessing the types of shows: comedy, drama, news magazine. Watch episodes of the same shows in different genres, and write an analysis of the level of violence or adult content within each show. What types of activities occur on various shows that might be considered objectionable to parents concerned about their children's viewing habits?
2. Many news stations have been accused of commodifying violence for the purpose of ratings. Watch your community's local news program and survey the amount of coverage devoted to violence. How does your local news channel cover crime and other hard news? If you were a news programmer, what reporting strategies would you feel appropriate employ-

ing? Should the community have any say in this process? Write a broadcast editorial in response to your station's news coverage.

3. Conduct an experiment in which several people watch a series of films or television programs purported to contain content requiring restricted viewing or parental guidance, while several other people watch films or shows purported to have little "objectionable" content. What were each group's reactions? Will they continue to watch such shows? What might this say about the public perception of the significance of television violence?

COMMUNITY INTERACTIONS

1. Visit a local video store and survey patrons or employees about selection habits. Do films with purportedly more violent content do well in your community? What new releases seem to be most popular with viewers from varying age groups within your community? Write an informative feature article aimed at your newspaper's entertainment section.

2. Allan Bloom's excerpt from *The Closing of the American Mind* presents American teenagers as devoted to rock music above all else. As such characterizations suggest, people are often judged on the basis of musical preference; for example, a heavy metal person as opposed to an opera buff, a rap person as opposed to an easy listening person. It is important to understand why people like the music they do. What pleasure or sense of identification does it provide? Survey a series of people from differing age brackets and cultural backgrounds. What music do they listen to and what values, social or psychological, are behind those musical choices?

3. Observe the reactions of a child as he or she watches a Saturday morning cartoon show. Then compare this reaction to the same child as he or she reads a children's book. How are the reactions similar or different? How do your findings compare to the thesis about cartoons and violence made by John Davidson?

Thach Bui, "PC and Pixel."
From the *Corpus Christi Caller-Times*, May 26, 1997. Copyright © 1997 by T. Bui.
Reprinted with the permission of The Washington Post Writers Group.

Cartoons, which have a rich history in American culture, often provide us a humorous window into our daily lives. Thach Bui's "PC and Pixel" cartoon, which is syndicated and has appeared in newspapers across the country, is a relatively new one that addresses the changing computer technology.

Besides computers, are there any other technological advances that you think some children are more adept at than some adults? Why are some children better than some adults at these tasks? Write dialogue for a cartoon that addresses another computer problem that individuals commonly face.

6

Literacies and Learning

The one activity in your lifetime in which you have probably spent the greatest amount of time has been getting an education. In fact, you might think of yourself as a kind of expert student. This chapter is about stepping back from being inside the process of getting an education to examine what it means to be an educated person. By doing this kind of analyzing we are practicing a form of education itself, called critical literacy, a theme of *Cultural Attractions/ Cultural Distractions.* At the same time you are practicing critical literacy, you will be exploring other kinds of literacy:

- Cultural—what information you should know to be considered educated and who should decide that information
- Computer—what the technology means for getting an education today
- Functional—the fundamental ability to read and write to get along in society

Not everyone will agree on what it takes to be literate in any of these areas, but the purpose is to raise questions and issues for you to think and debate about. Some ideas may be uncomfortable to you but that is to be expected. Education is about grappling with ideas and opinions that may or may not be to your liking.

Cultural Literacy

Our first stop is a group of readings about cultural literacy. It begins with "Cultural Literacy," an excerpt from E. D. Hirsch's book *Cultural Literacy: What Every American Needs to Know.* For a high school graduate to be considered literate, says Hirsch, he or she needs to know a core of information from which to draw to understand material in any field, directed to a general reader. In *Cultural Literacy,* Hirsch provides a list of names and facts illustrating the nature of the shared knowledge he thinks literate Americans should know. An excerpt of the list is your first reading selection for the chapter. Hirsch's list has created great controversy among educators because some support his position and others argue that Hirsch's list has largely ignored the accomplishments of women and minorities and the value of popular American culture.

As a counterpart to Hirsch's list, the next reading, "Teleliteracy Pretest," is by television critic David Bianculli, who says the quiz is to test your fluency in the language and content of TV. It is set against more traditional educational facts, much like Hirsch's list. Another reading that offers an alternate view of Hirsch's list is "The Case for Multiculturalism" by Rodney D. Smith. This is a schoolteacher's personal testimony about how he decided to use multicultural literature in his classroom because it touched the life of one of his own students.

Computer Literacy

An obvious missing piece from Hirsch's list is many computer terms, which brings us to the second kind of literacy: computer literacy. Take a look at the "PC and Pixel" cartoon at the beginning of the chapter. Out of the impishness and ironic humor of the cartoon—that an adult would need a nine-year-old to solve a computer problem—is a much larger message: A child would be more knowledgeable, more skilled, and therefore more literate in undertaking the task than an adult. Does that strike you as unusual? Why?

Your next reading, Jay David Bolter's "The Network Culture," discusses how the change from the printed word to the electronic word is affecting almost all aspects of our lives, including how we learn. Do you think technology has changed what it means to be literate or educated? How so? To stretch your thinking even further, consider what some may see as a preposterous claim by technologist Seymour Papert in the "Obsolete Skill Set: The 3 Rs." He foresees a time when reading and writing may not even be necessary to be educated. How might Hirsch react to Papert's proposal?

Functional Literacy

For some futurists the possibility of a formal education without needing to know how to read and write may become a reality. In the meantime, however, learning to read and write, referred to as functional literacy, is a fundamental part of a formal education. But what may seem cut and dried, whether an individual can read and write, is far more complex. For instance, how well does a person have to be able to read or write to get his or her needs met every day? Do you know someone who cannot read? Or write? Or both? How well does this person get along daily? Does he or she feel stigmatized? Or, perhaps, he or she not only feels illiterate but moreover is seen by others as dumb or lazy. Your next reading selection, "Dyslexia," is a personal story by Eileen Simpson, a psychotherapist, about her struggle with learning to read because she is dyslexic. Dyslexia—a developmental disorder affecting how an individual sees letters in words—brings another perspective to the debate about the causes of illiteracy. Simpson suggests that because people with dyslexia cannot see letters correctly to sound out words, they frequently memorize the word or story as a coping strategy. To get the full impact of her points, be sure to read aloud Simpson's examples of how a person with dyslexia sees words.

Whether attempting to overcome a disability or other difficulties in life, some people develop keen coping strategies; we often say these individuals have street smarts. This exemplifies the type of person with political and social savvy who may go outside formal education and learn through the school of hard knocks. These people make paths by carefully listening, observing, and seeking advice from other people who know the ropes.

Your reading "Dropout Aces GED Test, Now Dreams of College" tells the story of fifteen-year-old Jessica Long's rise from abject poverty to win an award from the American Council on Education for getting the ninth highest score in the nation on the GED test. Aside from this obvious achievement, what people say about her and what she says about herself reveal a person who has learned to survive and succeed against all odds. The last two readings touch on the subjects of taking advice, learning from mistakes, and honing listening skills. In "To Err Is Wrong," creativity consultant Roger von Oech uses an analogy from baseball to show how an educational system based on teaching that you are good if you get only right answers is making us afraid to take risks, think creatively, and learn from our mistakes. Then well-known southern fiction writer Eudora Welty, in "Learning to Listen," recalls how she learned things and extols the power of listening to learn to find your own voice in writing.

As you consider all the readings in this chapter, you can be making your own mind up about what you believe constitutes literacy or education. Keep in mind that there may be more than one right answer or more than one perspective from which to view these issues. Ultimately, though, you will be deciding whether you and others are, want to be, or need to be conversant with literate people in this group.

CULTURAL LITERACY

E. D. Hirsch, Jr.

E. D. Hirsch, Jr.'s Cultural Literacy, *published in 1987, proposes that for someone to be considered a literate person in America today he or she needs to know a core of information from which to draw to understand material in any field, directed to a general reader. A best-seller, the book brought to the forefront a national debate about what it means to be an educated person while it fueled a firestorm of controversy. Some educators side with Hirsch and others disagree, pointing out that the list disregards many accomplishments of women and minorities. The excerpt here is edited from the text and from the list itself.*

A prominent literary critic, E. D. Hirsch, Jr., the William R. Kean Professor of English at the University of Virginia, has also published several books describing what elementary schoolchildren should know.

During the period 1970–1985, the amount of shared knowledge that we have been able to take for granted in communicating with our fellow citizens has also been declining. More and more of our young people don't know things we used to assume they knew.

A side effect of the diminution in shared information has been a noticeable increase in the number of articles in such publications as *Newsweek* and the *Wall Street Journal* about the surprising ignorance of the young. My son John, who recently taught Latin in high school and eighth grade, often told me of experiences which indicate that these articles are not exaggerated. In one of his classes he mentioned to his students that Latin, the language they were studying, is a dead language that is no longer spoken. After his pupils had struggled for several weeks with Latin grammar and vocabulary, this news was hard for some of them to accept. One girl raised her hand to challenge my son's claim. "What do they speak in Latin America?" she demanded.

At least she had heard of Latin America. Another day my son asked his Latin class if they knew the name of an epic poem by Homer. One pupil shot up his hand and eagerly said, "The Alamo!" Was it just a slip for *The Illiad?* No, he didn't know what the Alamo was, either. To judge from other stories about information gaps in the young, many American schoolchildren are less well informed than this pupil. The following, by Benjamin J. Stein, is an excerpt from one of the most evocative recent accounts of youthful ignorance.

I spend a lot of time with teenagers. Besides employing three of them part-time, I frequently conduct focus groups at Los Angeles area high schools to learn about teenagers' attitudes towards movies or television shows or nuclear arms or politicians. . . .

I have not yet found one single student in Los Angeles, in either college or high school, who could tell me the years when World War II was fought. Nor have I found one who could tell me the years when World War I was fought. Nor have I found one who knew when the American Civil War was fought. . . .

A few have known how many U.S. senators California has, but none has known how many Nevada or Oregon has. ("Really? Even though they're so small?") . . . Only two could tell me where Chicago is, even in the vaguest terms. (My particular favorite geography lesson was the junior at the University of California at Los Angeles who thought that Toronto must be in Italy. My second-favorite geography lesson is the junior at USC, a pre-law student, who thought that Washington, D.C. was in Washington State.) . . .

Only two could even approximately identify Thomas Jefferson. Only one could place the date of the Declaration of Independence. None could name even one of the first ten amendments to the Constitution or connect them with the Bill of Rights. . . .

On and on it went. On and on it goes. I have mixed up episodes of ignorance of facts with ignorance of concepts because it seems to me that there is a connection. . . . The kids I saw (and there may be lots of others who are different) are not mentally prepared to continue the society because they basically do not understand the society well enough to value it.

My son assures me that his pupils are not ignorant. They know a great deal. Like every other human group they share a tremendous amount of knowledge among themselves, much of it learned in school. The trouble is that, from the standpoint of their literacy and their ability to communicate with others in our culture, what they know is ephemeral and narrowly confined to their own generation. Many young people strikingly lack the information that writers of American books and newspapers have traditionally taken for granted among their readers from all generations. For reasons explained in this book, our children's lack of intergenerational information is a serious problem for the nation. The decline of literacy and the decline of shared knowledge are closely related, interdependent facts.

The evidence for the decline of shared knowledge is not just anecdotal. In 1978 NAEP [National Assessment of Educational Progress] issued a report which analyzed a large quantity of data showing that our children's knowledge of American civics had dropped significantly between 1969 and 1976. The performance of thirteen-year-olds had dropped an alarming 11 percentage points. That the drop has continued since 1976 was confirmed by preliminary results from a NAEP study conducted in late 1985. It was undertaken both because of concern about declining knowledge and because of the growing evidence of a causal connection between the drop in shared information and in literacy. The Foundations of Literacy project is measuring some of the specific information about history and literature that American seventeen-year-olds possess.

Although the full report will not be published until 1987, the preliminary field tests are disturbing. If these samplings hold up, and there is no reason to think they will not, then the results we will be reading in 1987 will show that two thirds of our seventeen-year-olds do not know that the Civil War occurred between 1850 and 1900. Three quarters do not know what *reconstruction* means. Half do not know the meaning of the *Brown decision* and cannot identify either Stalin or Churchill. Three quarters are unfamiliar with the names of standard American and British authors. Moreover, our seventeen-year-olds have little sense of geography or the relative chronology of major events. Reports of youthful ignorance can no longer be considered merely impressionistic.

My encounter in the seventies with this widening knowledge gap first caused me to recognize the connection between specific background knowledge and mature literacy. The research I was doing on the reading and writing abilities of college students made me realize two things. First, we cannot assume that young people today know things that were known in the past by almost every literate person in the culture. For instance, in one experiment conducted in Richmond, Virginia, our seventeen- and eighteen-year-old subjects did not know who Grant and Lee were. Second, our results caused me to realize that we cannot treat reading and writing as empty skills, independent of specific knowledge. The reading skill of a person may vary greatly from task to task. The level of literacy exhibited in each task depends on the relevant background information that the person possesses.

The Decline of Teaching Cultural Literacy

Why have our schools failed to fulfill their fundamental acculturative responsibility? In view of the immense importance of cultural literacy for speaking, listening, reading, and writing, why has the need for a definite, shared body of information been so rarely mentioned in discussions of education? In the educational writings of the past decade, I find almost nothing on this topic, which is not arcane. People who are introduced to the subject quickly understand why oral or written communication requires a lot of shared background knowledge. It's not the difficulty or novelty of the idea that has caused it to receive so little attention.

Let me hazard a guess about one reason for our neglect of the subject. We have ignored cultural literacy in thinking about education—certainly I as a researcher also ignored it until recently—precisely because it was something we have been able to take for granted. We ignore the air we breathe until it is thin or foul. Cultural literacy is the oxygen of social intercourse. Only when we run into cultural illiteracy are we shocked into recognizing the importance of the information that we had unconsciously assumed.

To be sure, a minimal level of information is possessed by any normal person who lives in the United States and speaks elementary English. Almost everybody knows what is meant by *dollar* and that cars must travel on the right-hand side of the road. But this elementary level of information is not sufficient for a modern democracy. It isn't sufficient to read newspapers (a sin against Jeffersonian democracy), and it isn't sufficient to achieve economic fairness and high productivity. Cultural literacy lies *above* the everyday levels of knowledge that everyone possesses and *below* the expert level known only to specialists. It is that middle ground of cultural knowledge possessed by the "common reader." It includes information that we have traditionally expected our children to receive in school, but which they no longer do.

During recent decades Americans have hesitated to make a decision about the specific knowledge that children need to learn in school. Our elementary schools are not only dominated by the content-neutral ideas of Rousseau and Dewey, they are also governed by approximately sixteen thousand independent school districts. We have viewed this dispersion of educational authority as an insurmountable obstacle to altering the fragmentation of the school curriculum even when we have questioned that fragmentation. We have permitted school policies that have shrunk the body of information that Americans share, and these policies have caused our national literacy to decline.

At the same time we have searched with some eagerness for causes such as television that lie outside the schools. But we should direct our attention undeviatingly toward what the schools teach rather than toward family structure, social class, or TV programming. No doubt, reforms outside the schools are important, but they are harder to accomplish. Moreover, we have accumulated a great deal of evidence that faulty policy in the schools is the chief cause of deficient literacy. Researchers who have studied the factors influencing educational outcomes have found that the school curriculum is the most important controllable influence on what our children know and don't know about our literate culture.

It will not do to blame television for the state of our literacy. Television watching does reduce reading and often encroaches on homework. Much of it is admittedly the intellectual equivalent of junk food. But in some respects, such as its use of standard written English, television watching is acculturative. Moreover, as Herbert Walberg points out, the schools themselves must be held partly responsible for excessive television watching, because they have not firmly insisted that students complete significant amounts of homework, an obvious way to increase time spent on reading and writing. Nor should our schools be excused by an appeal to the effects of the decline of the family or the vicious circle of poverty, important as these factors are. Schools have, or should have, children for six or seven hours a day, five days a week, nine months a year, for thirteen years or more. To assert that they are powerless to make a significant impact on what their students learn would be to make a claim about American education that few parents, teachers, or students would find it easy to accept.

Just how fragmented the American public school curriculum has become is described in *The Shopping Mall High School*, a report on five years of first-hand study inside public and private secondary schools. The authors report that our high schools offer courses of so many kinds that "the word 'curriculum' does not do justice to this astonishing variety." The offerings include not only academic courses of great diversity, but also courses in sports and hobbies and a "services curriculum" addressing emotional or social problems. All these courses are deemed "educationally valid" and carry course credit: Moreover, among academic offerings are numerous versions of each subject, corresponding to different levels of student interest and ability. Needless to say, the material covered in these "content area" courses is highly varied.

Cafeteria-style education, combined with the unwillingness of our schools to place demands on students, has resulted in a steady diminishment of commonly shared information between generations and between young people themselves. Those who graduate from the same school have often studied different subjects, and those who graduate from different schools have often studied different material even when their courses have carried the same titles.

The inevitable consequence of the shopping mall high school is a lack of shared knowledge across and within schools. It would be hard to invent a more effective recipe for cultural fragmentation.

The formalistic educational theory behind the shopping mall school (the theory that any suitable content will inculcate reading, writing, and thinking skills) has had certain political advantages for school administrators. It has allowed them to stay scrupulously neutral with regard to content. Educational formalism enables them to regard the indiscriminate variety of school offerings as a positive virtue, on the grounds that such variety can accommodate the different interests and abilities of different students. Educational formalism has also conveniently allowed school administrators to meet objections to the traditional literate materials that used to be taught in the schools. Objectors have said that traditional materials are class-bound, white, Anglo-Saxon, and Protestant, not to mention racist, sexist, and excessively Western. Our schools have tried to offer enough diversity to meet these objections from liberals and enough Shakespeare to satisfy conservatives. Caught between ideological parties, the schools have been attracted irresistibly to a quantitative and formal approach to curriculum making rather than one based on sound judgments about what should be taught.

Some have objected that teaching the traditional literate culture means teaching conservative material. Orlando Patterson answered that objection when he pointed out that mainstream culture is not the province of any single social group and is constantly changing by assimilating new elements and expelling old ones. Although mainstream culture is tied to the written word and may therefore seem more formal and elitist than other elements of culture, that is an illusion. Literate culture is the most democratic culture in our land: it excludes nobody; it cuts across generations and social groups and classes; it is not usually one's first culture, but it should be everyone's second, existing as it does beyond the narrow spheres of family, neighborhood, and region.

The following list of items has been excerpted from "What Literate Americans Know: A Preliminary List," published in *Cultural Literacy*. Compiled by Hirsch and his colleagues Dr. Joseph Kett and Dr. James Trefil, the full list of nearly 4500 entries was "intended to illustrate the character and range of the knowledge literate Americans tend to share."

Bunker Hill, Battle of	burn the midnight oil	bust (economic)
Bunyan, Paul	burn with a hard,	buy a pig in a poke
Burke, Edmund	gemlike flame	buyer's market
Burma	Burr, Aaron	Byron, Lord
Burns, Robert	Burr-Hamilton duel	Byronic
burnt child fears the	bury the hatchet	byte
fire, The	business before	Byzantine (complexity)
burn the candle at	pleasure	Byzantine empire
both ends	business cycle	cabinet (government)

cadre
Caesar, Julius
Caesar Augustus
Caesarean section
Cain and Abel
Cairo
calculus
Calcutta
Calder
fossil fuel
fossil record
Foster, Stephen
Founding Fathers
Four Freedoms
four-letter words
Fourteen Points
Fourteenth
    Amendment
fourth estate, the
Fourth of July
France
franchise (economics)
franchise (politics)
Francis Ferdinand,
    Archduke
Francis of Assisi, Saint
Franco
Frankenstein's
    monster
Frankfurt
Franklin, Benjamin
freedom of religion
freedom of speech
freedom of the press
Freedom Riders
free enterprises
free fall
free trade
free verse
free will
freezing point
French and Indian
    Wars
French châteaux
French horn

French Impressionism
French Revolution
frequency modulation
    (FM)
fresco
Fresno, California
Freud, Sigmund
Mars (Ares)
Mars (planet)
Marseilles
Marshall, Chief
    Justice John
Marshall, General
    George C.
Marshall Plan
Martha's Vineyard,
    Massachusetts
Marx, Karl
Marx Brothers
Marxism
Marxism-Leninism
Mary
Mary had a little lamb
    (text)
Maryland
Mary Magdalene
Mary, Mary, Quite
    Contrary (text)
masochism
Mason-Dixon line
Masons, Freemasons
mass (physics)
Mass (religion)
Massachusetts
massive resistance
massive retaliation
mass media
mass production
Mata Hari
materialism
mathematical
    induction
Mather, Cotton
Matisse, Henri
matriarchy

matrilineal
Matterhorn
Matthew, Saint,
    Gospel according to
Maxwell, James Clerk
Vinci, Leonardo da
viola
violin
VIP (very important
    person)
Virgil
Virginia
Virgin Islands
Virgin Mary
virtual image
vis-à-vis
visual aid
visual field
vital statistics
vitamin
vivisection
V-J Day
voilà
volcano
Volga River
Volstead Act
volt
voltage
Voltaire
Voting Rights Act of
    1965
vowel
Vox populi vox Dei.
voyeurism
Vulcan
vulcanization
Vulgate Bible
wage scale
Wailing (Western)
    Wall
wake (Irish)
Walden (title)
walkie-talkie
walking papers
walk on water

READING REFLECTIONS

1. How does Hirsch define *cultural literacy*? What are Hirsch's main reasons for asserting that education no longer teaches the type of literacy he considers important?
2. Do you agree or disagree with Hirsch's notion of cultural literacy? Do you agree that a well-educated person should know the kinds of facts and information on his list? Why or why not?
3. In reading through Hirsch's list, how did you fare in knowing who the people were and the information about the facts?
4. Look up three terms you didn't recognize on Hirsch's list, and write a sentence or two to define them. Do you think these terms are as important as Hirsch claims them to be?
5. Did you notice any pattern in the names and facts you could identify and those you didn't recognize on Hirsch's list? (What names and facts did you think you did well on and which were ones you did not?) How do you account for your strengths and weaknesses?
6. Hirsch's list contains thousands of cultural terms, but it is surprisingly lacking in such fields as television, toys/games, and multimedia. Give an example of five items you would add to the list and explain why each of these items should be included in a list of what literate Americans should know.

TELELITERACY PRETEST

David Bianculli

Rather than shamefully admit that we really know more about television "classics" than arts and literature "classics," we should consider our knowledge of television a type of literacy that is an integral part of our lives in America as the twenty-first century unfolds. So contends TV critic David Bianculli. In this "Teleliteracy Pretest" from Bianculli's book, Teleliteracy: Taking Television Seriously *(1992), the quiz juxtaposes questions on the classics in arts and literature with those from television.*

David Bianculli, "Teleliteracy Pretest," in *Teleliteracy: Taking Television Seriously* (New York: Continuum, 1992), pp. 7–22. Copyright © 1992 by David Bianculli. Reprinted with the permission of The Continuum Publishing Group.

David Bianculli, a TV critic for the New York Daily News, *also writes for the* Philadelphia Inquirer *and does reviews for National Public Radio. His book* Dictionary of Teleliteracy: Television's 500 Biggest Hits, Misses, and Events (The Television Series) *was published in 1997.*

Let's get right to the point: what is *Teleliteracy,* and how can we combat it? Basically, teleliteracy is the demonstration of fluency in the language and content of TV—and there's no reason to fight or fear it. In fact, teleliteracy is something to be embraced, not denounced, and this book sets out to explain why. From *Sesame Street* to *60 Minutes,* from the PBS documentary *The Civil War* to the TV coverage of the Gulf War, television is too important and pervasive a mass medium to be dismissed as a crass medium.

That's the pretext. Now for a pretest.

Are *you* teleliterate? *You Bet Your Life*—and if you just thought of Groucho Marx's quiz show of the same name, you've proven my point. To demonstrate that teleliteracy exists, and that a *Bonanza* of TV knowledge has been absorbed even by those who snobbishly maintain they watch little or no television and are much more comfortable discussing the classics, I've prepared a simple quiz—well, half simple, anyway. On one side is the "classics" portion, asking questions about famous works of art and literature; on the other side is the "teleliteracy" portion, asking parallel questions about famous works of . . . television. On one side, Milton; on the other, Milton Berle.

TV or not TV? That is the question. Well, that's *one* question. Here are 150 others.

CLASSICS LITERACY QUIZ

Section I. Lyric Poetry.
Provide the next line from the following poems. (One point for each correct answer.)

1) "In Xanadu did Kubla Khan / A stately pleasure-dome decree . . ."
_____

2) "Theirs not to reason why / theirs but to do or die . . ."
_____

3) "Laugh, and the world laughs with you / weep, and you weep alone . . ."
_____

4) "Under the spreading chestnut tree / the village smithee stands . . ."
_____

TELELITERACY QUIZ

Section I. Lyric Poetry.
Provide the next line from the following TV themes. (One point for each correct answer.)

1) "Come listen to a story / 'bout a man named Jed . . ."
_____

2) "Green Acres is the place to be . . ."
_____

3) "It's a beautiful day in this neighborhood/a beautiful day for a neighbor . . ."
_____

4) "Hey, hey, we're the Monkees / And people say we monkey around . . ."
_____

5) "Death, be not proud . . ."

_____

6) "I think that I shall never see / a poem lovely as a tree . . ."

_____

7) "Gather ye rosebuds while ye may . . ."

_____

8) "By the shores of Gitche Gumee / By the shining Big-Sea-Water . . . "

_____

9) "Beware the Jabberwock, my son! / The jaws that bite, the claws that catch! . . ."

_____

10) "It takes a heap o'livin' / in a house t' make it home . . ."

_____

5) "Here's the story / of a lovely lady / who was bringing up three very lovely girls . . ."

_____

6) "The house is a museum / when people come to see 'em . . ."

_____

7) "Rollin', rollin', rollin' / though the streams are swollen / Keep them doggies rollin' . . ."

_____

8) "M-I-C / See you real soon / K-E-Y / Why? Because we *like* you! . . ."

_____

9) "I'm so glad we had this time together . . ."

_____

10) "The weather started getting rough / The tiny ship was tossed . . ."

_____

Section II. Body of Work.

Put the following works by each artist in their related chronological order—'1' being the earliest, '3' being the latest. (One point for each correctly arranged trio.)

	1	2	3
11) Aristophanes			
a) *The Birds*	—	—	—
b) *The Frogs*	—	—	—
c) *Lysistrata*	—	—	—
12) Beethoven, Ludwig van			
a) *Pathetique Sonata*	—	—	—
b) Sonata in F Minor (*Appassionata*)	—	—	—
c) Symphony No. 6 (*Pastorale*)	—	—	—
13) Da Vinci, Leonardo			
a) *The Adoration of the Magi*	—	—	—
b) *The Last Supper*	—	—	—
c) *Mona Lisa*	—	—	—
14) Dickens, Charles			
a) *A Christmas Carol*	—	—	—
b) *Great Expectations*	—	—	—
c) *Life and Adventures of Nicholas Nickleby*	—	—	—

Section II. Body of Work.

Put the following works by each artist in their related chronological order—'1' being the earliest, '3' being the latest. (One point for each correctly arranged trio.)

	1	2	3
11) Arthur, Beatrice			
a) *All in the Family*	—	—	—
b) *The Golden Girls*	—	—	—
c) *Maude*	—	—	—
12) Ball, Lucille			
a) *Here's Lucy*	—	—	—
b) *I Love Lucy*	—	—	—
c) *Life with Lucy*	—	—	—
13) Cosby, Bill			
a) *Cos*	—	—	—
b) *The Cosby Show*	—	—	—
c) *I Spy*	—	—	—
14) Dey, Susan			
a) *Emerald Point N.A.S.*	—	—	—
b) *L. A. Law*	—	—	—
c) *The Partridge Family*	—	—	—

15) Dostoyevsky, Fyodor
   a) *The Brothers Karamazov*   ___ ___ ___
   b) *Crime and Punishment*   ___ ___ ___
   c) *Notes from the Underground*   ___ ___ ___

16) Eliot, T. S.
   a) *Murder in the Cathedral*   ___ ___ ___
   b) *Old Possum's Book of Practical Cats*   ___ ___ ___
   c) *The Waste Land*   ___ ___ ___

17) Hemingway, Ernest
   a) *For Whom the Bell Tolls*   ___ ___ ___
   b) *The Old Man and the Sea*   ___ ___ ___
   c) *The Sun Also Rises*   ___ ___ ___

18) Mozart, Wolfgang Amadeus
   a) *The Marriage of Figaro*   ___ ___ ___
   b) *Requiem*   ___ ___ ___
   c) *Symphony No. 41 (Jupiter)*   ___ ___ ___

19) O'Neill, Eugene
   a) *Ah! Wilderness*   ___ ___ ___
   b) *The Emperor Jones*   ___ ___ ___
   c) *The Iceman Cometh*   ___ ___ ___

20) Stravinsky, Igor
   a) *The Firebird*   ___ ___ ___
   b) *Five Easy Pieces*   ___ ___ ___
   c) *The Rite of Spring*   ___ ___ ___

15) Field, Sally
   a) *The Flying Nun*   ___ ___ ___
   b) *Gidget*   ___ ___ ___
   c) *Sybil* (miniseries)   ___ ___ ___

16) Griffith, Andy
   a) *The Andy Griffith Show*   ___ ___ ___
   b) *Matlock*   ___ ___ ___
   c) *The New Andy Griffith Show*   ___ ___ ___

17) Landon, Michael
   a) *Bonanza*   ___ ___ ___
   b) *Highway to Heaven*   ___ ___ ___
   c) *Little House on the Prairie*   ___ ___ ___

18) Morgan, Harry
   a) *AfterMASH*   ___ ___ ___
   b) *Dragnet*   ___ ___ ___
   c) *M*A*S*H*   ___ ___ ___

19) Serling, Rod (writer/producer)
   a) *Night Gallery*   ___ ___ ___
   b) *Requiem for a Heavyweight* (drama)   ___ ___ ___
   c) *The Twilight Zone*   ___ ___ ___

20) Wagner, Robert
   a) *Hart to Hart*   ___ ___ ___
   b) *It Takes a Thief*   ___ ___ ___
   c) *Switch*   ___ ___ ___

Section III. Classic Quotes.
   Match each quotation to its proper source. (One point for each correct match.)

21) "Better late than never."   ___ a. René Descartes
22) "Look homeward, Angel, now, and melt with ruth."   ___ b. Euripides
     ___ c. Ben Franklin

Section III. Classic Quotes.
   Match each quotation to its proper source. (One point for each correct match.)

21) "Baby, you're the greatest."   ___ a. Archie Bunker (*All in the Family*)
22) "Live long and prosper."

23) "Rome was not built in one day." ___ d. John Heywood

24) "A mighty fortress is our God." ___ e. Omar Khayyám

25) "I think; therefore I am." ___ f. Titus Livius

26) "The gods visit the sins of the fathers upon the children." ___ g. Martin Luther

27) "O Brave New World that has such people in't." ___ h. John Milton

___ i William Shakespeare

28) "A rolling stone gathers no moss." ___ j. Publilius Syrus

29) "A Jug of Wine, a Loaf of Bread—and Thou."

30) "There are no Gains, without Pains."

23) "Na-noo, na-noo." ___ b. Bart (*The Simpsons*)

24) "Don't have a cow, man." ___ c. Fernando (*Saturday Night Live*)

25) "Solid."

26) "Sorry about that, Chief." ___ d. Linc Hayes (*Mod Squad*)

27) "Stifle it, dingbat." ___ e. Ralph Kramden (*The Honey-mooners*)

28) "Warning! Warning! Danger! Danger!"

29) "Who loves ya, baby?" ___ f. Kojak (*Kojak*)

30) "You look mah-velous!" ___ g. Mork (*Mork & Mindy*)

___ h. Robot (*Lost in Space*)

___ i. Maxwell Smart (*Get Smart!*)

___ j. Mr. Spock (*Star Trek*)

Section IV. Character Studies.

In the following sets of matching questions, match the characters to the work in which they appear. (One point for each correct match.)

31) Aase ___ a. *The Faerie Queen*, Edmund Spenser

32) Alceste

33) Cleonice

34) Gloriana ___ b. *Lysistrata*, Aristophanes

35) Sir Toby Belch and Sir Andrew Aguecheek ___ c. *The Misan-thrope*, Molière

36) Benedick and Claudio ___ d. *Peer Gynt*, Henrik Ibsen

37) Quince and Bottom ___ a. *Much Ado about Nothing*, Shakespeare

___ b. *A Midsummer Night's Dream*, Shakespeare

___ c. *Twelfth Night*, Shakespeare

Section IV. Character Studies.

In the following sets of matching questions, match the characters to the work in which they appear. (One point for each correct match.)

31) Abby ___ a. *Dallas*

32) Alexis ___ b. *Dynasty*

33) Maddie ___ c. *Knots Landing*

34) Sue Ellen ___ d. *Moonlighting*

35) Gomer and Goober ___ a. *The Andy Griffith Show*

36) Larry, Darryl, & Darryl ___ b. *Laverne & Shirley*

37) Lenny and Squiggy ___ c. *Newhart*

Section V. Love and Death.

Mark an *X* next to the loving couples who were still alive, and together, at the end of their story. (One point for each correct answer, whether a mark or a blank.)

Section V. Love and Death.

Mark an *X* next to the loving couples who were still alive, and together, at the end of their story. (One point for each correct answer, whether a mark or a blank.)

38) ___ Jude Fawley and Sue Bridehead, Thomas Hardy's *Jude the Obscure*.
39) ___ Lenina Crowne and John, Aldous Huxley's *Brave New World*.
40) ___ Pierre and Natasha, Leo Tolstoy's *War and Peace*.
41) ___ Porgy and Bess, Gershwin's *Porgy and Bess*.
42) ___ Wilfred and Rowena, Sir Walter Scott's *Ivanhoe*.

38) ___ Archie and Edith, *Archie Bunker's Place*.
39) ___ Sam and Diane, *Cheers*.
40) ___ Sonny and Caitlin, *Miami Vice*.
41) ___ Jim and Margaret, *Father Knows Best*.
42) ___ Mr. and Mrs. Richard Kimble, *The Fugitive*.

Section VI. Loving Couples.

Match the men in the left column to the women on the right. (One point for each correct match.)

43) Almaviva   ___ a) Ada
44) Clyde   ___ b) Carmen
45) Jeeter   ___ c) Penelope
46) José   ___ d) Rosina
47) Odysseus   ___ e) Sondra

Section VI. Loving Couples.

Match the men in the left column to the women on the right. (One point for each correct match.)

43) Dan   ___ a) Hot Lips
44) Frank   ___ b) Laura
45) Luke   ___ c) Lucy
46) Norton   ___ d) Roseanne
47) Ricky   ___ e) Trixie

Section VII. Mythological Deaths.

(One point for each correct answer.)
Who killed . . .

48) Achilles? _____
49) Narcissus? _____
50) Remus? _____

Section VII. Televisual Deaths and Near-Deaths.

(One point for each correct answer.)
Who killed . . .

48) Mrs. Kimble on *The Fugitive?* _____
49) Laura Palmer on *Twin Peaks?* _____

Who shot . . .

50) J. R. Ewing on *Dallas* (that famous first time)? _____

Section VIII. Visual Aids, Nineteenth Century.

Match the work of nineteenth-century art to the decade in which it was produced. (One point for each correct match.)

51) *The Dead Toreador*,   ___ a) forties
    Édouard Manet
52) *Mother of the*   ___ b) fifties
    Artist, James
    McNeill Whistler
53) *The Peaceable*   ___ c) sixties
    Kingdom, Edward
    Hicks
54) *Starry Night*,   ___ d) seventies
    Vincent van Gogh
55) *Washington*   ___ e) eighties
    Crossing the
    Delaware, Emanuel
    Leutze

Section VIII. Visual Aids, Twentieth Century.

Match the work of twentieth-century TV to the decade in which it was introduced. (One point for each correct match.)

51) *Charlie's Angels*,   ___ a) forties
    ABC.
52) *Hill Street Blues*,   ___ b) fifties
    NBC.
53) *I Love Lucy*, CBS.   ___ c) sixties
54) *The Smothers*   ___ d) seventies
    Brothers Comedy
    Hour, CBS.
55) *Texaco Star*   ___ e) eighties
    Theater (Milton
    Berle), NBC.

Section IX. Numbers.

With one point for each correct name, identify the following:

Alexandre Dumas's Three Musketeers

56) _____
57) _____
58) _____

Chekhov's Three Sisters

59) _____
60) _____
61) _____

Book of Revelation's Four Horsemen of the Apocalypse

62) _____
63) _____
64) _____
65) _____

Dostoyevsky's Brothers Karamazov

66) _____
67) _____
68) _____
69) _____

Section X. Miscellaneous.

For each correct answer to the following questions, you earn one point.

What was the name of the dog . . .
70) In Washington Irving's "Rip Van Winkle"?

_____

71) That guards the gates of Hades (and had three heads)?

_____

Identify the son of . . .
72) Sir Lancelot in Sir Thomas Malory's *Le Morte d'Arthur.*

_____

Identify the daughter of . . .
73) Satan in John Milton's *Paradise Lost.*

_____

Identify the captain and first mate of the *Pequod* in Herman Melville's *Moby-Dick.*
74) Captain: _____
75) First mate: _____

Section IX. Numbers.

With one point for each correct name, identify the following:

Steve Douglas's *My Three Sons* (any three of four)

56) _____
57) _____
58) _____

The four *Golden Girls*

59) _____
60) _____
61) _____
62) _____

The two men from *U.N.C.L.E.*

63) _____
64) _____

The two astronauts on *I Dream of Jeannie*

65) _____
66) _____

Bonanza's brothers Cartwright

67) _____
68) _____
69) _____

Section X. Miscellaneous.

For each correct answer to the following questions, you earn one point.

What was the name of the dog . . .
70) That Jeff, then Timmy, played with for years?

_____

What was the name of the dolphin . . .
71) That headlined its own TV series?

_____

Identify the son of . . .
72) Cliff and Clair Huxtable on *The Cosby Show.*

_____

73) Lucy and Ricky Ricardo on *I Love Lucy.*

_____

Identify the captain and first mate of the *Minnow* in *Gilligan's Island.*
74) Captain: _____
75) First mate: _____

ANSWERS:

Section I. Lyric Poetry.

1) "Where Alph, the sacred river, ran / Through caverns measureless to man / down to a sunless sea." ("Kubla Kahn," Samuel Taylor Coleridge)
2) "Into the valley of death / Rode the six hundred." ("Charge of the Light Brigade," Alfred, Lord Tennyson)
3) "For the sad old earth must borrow its mirth / But has trouble enough of its own." ("Solitude," Ella Wheeler Wilcox)
4) "The smith, a mighty man is he / with large and sinewy hands." ("The Village Blacksmith," Henry Wadsworth Longfellow)
5) ". . . though some have called thee mighty and dreadful / For thou art not so." ("Death," John Donne)
6) "A tree whose hungry mouth is prest / Against the earth's sweet flowing breast." ("Trees," Joyce Kilmer)
7) "Old time is still a-flying." ("To the Virgins, to Make Much of Time," Robert Herrick)
8) "Stood the wigwam of Nokomis / Daughter of the moon, Nokomis." ("Hiawatha's Childhood," Henry Wadsworth Longfellow)
9) "Beware the Jubjub bird, and shun / The frumious Bandersnatch." ("Jabberwocky," Lewis Carroll)
10) "A heap o' sun an' shadder, / an' ye sometimes have t' roam." ("Home," Edgar A. Guest)

ANSWERS:

Section I. Lyric Poetry.

1) "A poor mountaineer, / barely kept his family fed." (*The Beverly Hillbillies*)
2) "Faaaarm livin' is the life for me." (*Green Acres*)
3) "Would you be mine? / Could you be mine?" (*Mister Rogers' Neighborhood*)
4) "But we're too busy singin' / to put anybody down." (*The Monkees*)
5) "All of them had hair of gold / like their mother / the youngest one in curls." (*The Brady Bunch*)
6) "They really are a scre-am / The Addams family." (*The Addams Family*)
7) "Rawhide." (*Rawhide*)
8) "M-O-U-S-E." (*The Mickey Mouse Club*)
9) "Just to have a laugh and sing a song." (*The Carol Burnett Show*)
10) "If not for the courage of the fearless crew / The *Minnow* would be lost." (*Gilligan's Island*)

Section II. Body of Work.

11) Aristophanes:	a-1 (414 B.C.), b-3 (405 B.C.), c-2 (411 B.C.).
12) Beethoven:	a-1 (1799), b-2 (1804–7), c-3 (1809).
13) Da Vinci:	a-1 (1481–82), b-2 (1495–97), c-3 (1504).
14) Dickens:	a-2 (1843), b-3 (1860–61), c-1 (1838–39).
15) Dostoyevsky:	a-3 (1879–80), b-2 (1866), c-1 (1864).
16) Eliot:	a-2 (1935), b-3 (1939), c-1 (1922).

Section II. Body of Work.

11) Arthur:	a-1 (1971–72), b-3 (1985–92), c-2 (1972–78).
12) Ball:	a-2 (1968–74), b-1 (1951–57), c-3 (1986–87).
13) Cosby:	a-2 (1976), b-3 (1984–92), c-1 (1965–68).
14) Dey:	a-2 (1983–84), b-3 (1986–92), c-1 (1970–74).
15) Field:	a-2 (1967–70), b-1 (1965–66), c-3 (1976).
16) Griffith:	a-1 (1960–68), b-3 (1986–91), c-2 (1971).

17) Hemingway: a-2 (1940), b-3 (1952), c-1 (1926).

18) Mozart: a-1 (1786), b-3 (1791), c-2 (1788).

19) O'Neill: a-2 (1933), b-1 (1922), c-3 (1946).

20) Stravinsky: a-1 (1909–10), b-3 (1916–17), c-2 (1911–13).

17) Landon: a-1 (1959–73), b-3 (1984–1990), c-2 (1974–82).

18) Morgan: a-3 (1983–84), b-1 (1967–70), c-2 (1975–83).

19) Serling a-3 (1970–73), b-1 (1956), c-2 (1959–64).

20) Wagner: a-3 (1979–84), b-1 (1968–70), c-2 (1975–78).

Section III. Classic Quotes.

21) f.
22) h.
23) d.
24) g.
25) a.
26) b.
27) i.
28) j.
29) e.
30) c.

Section III. Classic Quotes.

21) e.
22) j.
23) g.
24) b.
25) d.
26) i.
27) a.
28) h.
29) f.
30) c.

Section IV. Character Studies.

31) d.
32) c.
33) b.
34) a.
35) c.
36) a.
37) b.

Section IV. Character Studies.

31) c.
32) b.
33) d.
34) a.
35) a.
36) c.
37) b.

Section V. Love and Death.

40) and 42) get the *X*. Every other couple, in one way or another, got the shaft.

Section V. Love and Death.

Only 41) gets the *X*. Sam and Diane split up, and the other wives died.

Section VI. Loving Couples.

43) d. Almaviva and Rosina, Rossini's *The Barber of Seville.*
44) e. Clyde Griffiths and Sondra Finchley, Theodore Dreiser's *An American Tragedy.*
45) a. Jeeter and Ada Lester, Erskine Caldwell's *Tobacco Road.*
46) b. José and Carmen, Bizet's *Carmen.*
47) c. Odysseus and Penelope, Homer's *The Odyssey.*

Section VI. Loving Couples.

43) d. Dan and Roseanne, *Roseanne.*
44) a. Frank Burns and "Hot Lips" Houlihan, *M*A*S*H.*
45) b. Luke and Laura, *General Hospital.*
46) e. Ed Norton and Trixie, *The Honeymooners.*
47) c. Ricky and Lucy Ricardo, *I Love Lucy.*

Section VII. Mythological Deaths.

48) Achilles was killed by Paris (shot in the heel).
49) Narcissus was killed by himself—by his own vanity (he starved to death gazing at his reflection).
50) Remus was killed by Romulus.

Section VII. Televisual Deaths and Near-Deaths.

48) The one-armed man.
49) Leland Palmer (under the influence of Killer Bob).
50) Kristin Shepard.

Section VIII. Visual Aids, Nineteenth Century.

51) c. *The Dead Toreador*, Édouard Manet, 1864.
52) d. *Mother of the Artist*, James McNeill Whistler, 1872.
53) a. *The Peaceable Kingdom*, Edward Hicks, 1845.
54) e. *Starry Night*, Vincent van Gogh, 1889.
55) b. *Washington Crossing the Delaware*, Emanuel Leutze, 1851.

Section IX. Numbers.

56–58) Athos, Porthos, and Aramis.
59–61) Masha (Kuligin), and Olga and Irina Prozorov.
62–65) Conquest, Slaughter, Famine, Death. (Because of varying interpretations, credit is also given for such synonymous descriptions as War, Plague, and Hunger.)
66–69) Dmitri, Ivan, Alyosha, and Smerdyakov the bastard.

Section X. Miscellaneous.

70) Wolf.
71) Cerberus.
72) Sir Galahad.
73) Sin (who, with an incestuous union with her father, gave birth to Death).
74) Ahab.
75) Starbuck.

Section VIII. Visual Aids, Twentieth Century.

51) d. *Charlie's Angels*, ABC, premiered 1976.
52) e. *Hill Street Blues*, NBC, premiered 1981.
53) b. *I Love Lucy*, CBS, premiered 1951.
54) c. *The Smothers Brothers Comedy Hour*, CBS, premiered 1967.
55) a. *Texaco Star Theater* (Milton Berle), NBC, premiered 1948.

Section IX. Numbers.

56–58) Mike, Robbie, Chip, and eventually the adopted Ernie.
59–62) Dorothy, Rose, Blanche, and Sophia.
63–64) Napoleon Solo and Illya Kuryakin.
65–66) Tony Nelson and Roger Healey.
67–69) Adam, Hoss, and Little Joe.

Section X. Miscellaneous.

70) Lassie, on *Lassie*.
71) Flipper, on *Flipper*.
72 Theo.
73) Little Ricky.
74) Skipper.
75) Gilligan.

EUGENE O'NEILLSEN RATINGS

CLASSICS LITERACY	Score	TELELITERACY
Rhodes scholar. (Good as it gets.)	62–75	*Rhoda* scholar. Totally teleliterate.
Peabody award. (Amazing.)	48–61	Sherman and Peabody award. (Your knowledge goes Wayback.)
Honorary doctorate. (Born to be Wilde.)	34–47	Honorary *Daktari*. (Born to be wild.)
Captain Courageous. (Classic scholar.)	20–33	Captain Video. (Classy viewer.)
Classically literate. (You made the cut.)	6–19	Tele-illiterate. (You missed the cut.)
Turn on your mind.	0–5	Turn on your set.

READING REFLECTIONS

1. Take Bianculli's quiz and rate your performance according to his scale.
2. Analyze Bianculli's quiz. What factors would you cite as reasons for performing well or performing poorly on the test? How would you account for your strengths and weaknesses?
3. As a cultural studies professor at a university, you are asked to evaluate the validity of this test. Write an argument justifying the use or the uselessness of this test.
4. If you were to have a conversation with Bianculli, what would you tell him about the list?
5. In your opinion, how does the list compare with Hirsch's?
6. When Bianculli states, "I've prepared a simple quiz—well, half simple anyway," he is obviously referring to the television part of the quiz. Did you find the television part that much easier? Were the levels of difficulty for the literature side too difficult? Was the quiz fair in comparing works of literature with television counterparts?

THE CASE FOR MULTICULTURALISM

Rodney D. Smith

In a previous article, we read how some educators such as E. D. Hirsch, Jr. think students need to know a certain set of facts and information to be considered literate Americans. In the following article, "The Case for Multiculturalism," a schoolteacher explains how he learned the value of adding new and different types of literature in his classroom than the conventional types of readings that someone like Hirsch would want in a classroom. Is this personal testimony a valuable counterargument to Hirsch or not?

Rodney D. Smith is a writer and teacher in the San Francisco area.

Piedmont, Calif.—It took one journal entry written by Consuella Lopez, a student in my ninth-grade English class, to convince me that multiculturalism belongs in every American classroom.

Consuella is a gangbanger. Every day she struts into my class wearing baggy jeans and an oversized flannel shirt in her gang's color: black.

While taking roll, I easily spy the 3-inch wall of hair that rises defiantly off the top of her forehead as she slouches in the back row. Thick black eyeliner surrounds her brown eyes; dark burgundy lipstick covers her mouth. Silver hoops dangle from her ears.

So far this quarter she's been tardy five times and suspended once for being disrespectful to another teacher. After filling out her detention slip, I ask about her weekend. "Hey, Mr. Smith," she says. "Like I was kickin' it with my homeys. Ya know."

I don't.

I know virtually nothing about home girls or gangbangers or the fierce pride that burns within this Latina girl.

I'm an Anglo, born in Wisconsin, teaching in a California school where Asians, African-Americans, Pacific Islanders and Latinos all together make up the majority of the student body.

Consuella's life, like that of so many of my students, differs radically from my own.

And yet, until this year, I have taught the exact same books I was given when I attended my predominantly white high school: "The Great Gatsby," "Huckleberry Finn," "To Kill a Mockingbird," etc.

This year, however, I am teaching Sandra Cisneros' "The House on Mango Street."

The book, written by a Latina, tells the story of a 12-year-old girl who comes of age in a predominantly Hispanic neighborhood in Chicago.

Before adding this book to the curriculum, my colleagues and I had to overcome criticism against multiculturalism from parents, school board members and fellow teachers.

They asked: Were we instituting multicultural texts for the sake of multiculturalism, regardless of literary merit?

Wouldn't this "affirmative action" in English classes come at the expense of great literature?

What multicultural author—whatever his or her race, sexual preference, or gender—could match or excel the works of F. Scott Fitzgerald, Mark Twain or William Shakespeare?

"The House on Mango Street" dispels these criticisms.

The book's use of voice, theme and symbolism, as well as the honesty and clarity of its writing, rival that of the best novels I have ever taught.

While teaching "The House on Mango Street," I often rely on some of my Latino students for further clarification of the book's content.

I know nothing of private Catholic schools, but a few of my Latino students, including Consuella, added their experiences to what the main character described.

When I read *"Esta muerto," "los esperitus"* and the word that made most of my Latino students giggle, *"mamasota,"* some of my Latino students helped me define and pronounce these words correctly.

After a character died, some of my Latino and Filipino students explained to the rest of the class what the "Day of the Dead" meant to them.

Consuella began to attend class regularly after we read and discussed the chapter entitled "Those Who Don't." This chapter includes the lines, "Those who don't know any better come into our neighborhood scared . . . But we aren't afraid . . . All brown all around, we are safe. But watch us drive into a neighborhood of another color and our knees go shakity-shake . . . Yeah. That is how it goes and goes."

From then on, whenever I'd stop reading to begin a lesson, Consuella pleaded, "Don't stop. Let's keep reading." Normally, I'm the one who pleads with my students to read and finish our book.

If I had any doubts about the importance of multiculturalism in my classroom, Consuella eliminated them with a journal entry she handed in late.

Consuella, the gangbanger, the girl with "13" tattooed in black numerals between her right thumb and forefinger, wrote this:

"My favorite chapter in 'The House on Mango Street' is 'Hips.' The reason why is because when I was little I use to jump rope with my friends and make up weard songs to jump to. And my favorite part that she wrote was 'All brown all around.'

"I don't know why but that just got to me. Sometime I think back when we read this book and pitcher me being the main character. I like this book alot. It is like here is this Latina girl writing a book that I really like. I never have gotten in to a book like I do now. And that is the truth."

READING REFLECTIONS

1. Like Consuella, have you ever read a story that changed your life, or a story in which you "found yourself" because you could relate to what happened to one of the characters? What was the story, and how or why did it affect you?

2. What types of criticism did Smith have to face when he proposed adding *The House on Mango Street* to his curriculum? How did he respond?

3. What convinced Smith that multiculturalism should be "in every American classroom"? Based on his article, write a paragraph where you agree or disagree with his viewpoint.

4. Smith argues that there is not enough multiculturalism in present-day education. How can this deficiency be improved?

5. Provide an example of any multicultural work you encountered when growing up. How did that work affect you? (If you weren't exposed to any multicultural readings, how do you think that may have affected you?)

6. In his article, Smith describes how he went against his school's traditional curriculum to reach out to his students. Can you think of a teacher who used unorthodox methods or materials to reach out to the students? Describe what the teacher did and why it did or did not work.

THE NETWORK CULTURE

Jay David Bolter

Today computers, technology, and hypertext help students learn not only from their teacher but also with others inside and outside their classrooms. What is happening in classrooms is just one example of what Jay David Bolter argues is going on in society at-large. Bolter says, "our culture is moving from a hierarchical social order to what we might call a 'network culture.' " The characteristics of this new social order is a flattening of authority with people less dependent on institutions that have traditionally held authority and more focus on individual responsibility and freedom. Is Bolter's vision of the change in society the same as or different from yours?

Jay David Bolter, a professor in the school of literature, communication, and culture at the Georgia Institute of Technology, has lectured and written on the computer technology and its influence on society. This excerpt is originally from Writing Space: The Computer, Hypertext and the History of Writing, *published in 1991.*

Our culture is itself a vast writing space, a complex of symbolic structures. Just as we write our minds, we can say that we write the culture in which we live. And just as our culture is moving from the printed book to the computer, it is also in the final stages of the transition from a hierarchical social order to what we might call a "network culture." For decades all forms of hierarchy have been disintegrating, as greater and greater freedom of action is granted to the individ-

Jay David Bolter, "The Network Culture," in *Science and Technology Today: Readings for Writers*, ed. Nancy R. Mackenzie (New York: St. Martin's, 1995), pp. 212–19. Originally published in *Writing Space: The Computer, Hypertext, and the History of Writing* (Hillsdale, N.J.: Laurence Erlbaum Associates, 1991), pp. 231–40. Copyright © 1991 by Laurence Erlbaum Associates, Inc., Publishers. Reprinted with the permission of the publishers.

ual. Much of this disintegration accords with the goals of liberal democracy: the diminishing of racial and religious segregation, for example. But whatever one thinks of the trend, no one can deny that an extremely powerful leveling force is at work in our society. It can be said that this leveling has always been a feature of American culture, that Tocqueville remarked on it one hundred and fifty years ago. The authors of *Habits of the Heart* see today's "separation and individuation" as the culmination of a long historical process.

> [T]he colonists [to America] brought with them ideas of social obligation and group formation that disposed them to recreate in America structures of family, church, and polity that could continue . . . the texture of older European society. Only gradually did it become clear that every social obligation was vulnerable, every tie between individuals fragile. Only gradually did what we have called ontological individualism, the idea that the individual is the only firm reality, become widespread. (Bellah et al., 1985, p. 276)

Today the leveling has gone further than perhaps even Tocqueville could have imagined. Hierarchies in government, church, and family may retain status in law, but they have almost no moral authority. The vestigial hierarchies in our society, like the Catholic Church, are tolerated because they are completely misunderstood. (Thus many American Catholics seem to regard their hierarchy either as their representative government or as a quaint, decorative motif in their religious tradition.) The only great hierarchical force left is money, and today the possession of money creates and depends on no other distinctions. Among the richest people in America are athletes and celebrities who are often indistinguishable in education and tastes from the poorest Americans. We certainly do not think of rich people as better people. Instead, we use money to play at class, at hierarchical organizations that no one now takes seriously. However, the end of hierarchy is not the end of social structure. The individual may now be "the only firm reality," but that does not mean that individuals no longer form groups. They may well form more groups than ever, because they are free to associate and break off their associations as they please. Individuals now regularly join and quit jobs, neighborhoods, clubs, political parties and action committees, and even churches several times in their lives. These affiliations are all seen as voluntary, and they are horizontal rather than vertical. The network has replaced the hierarchy.

Sociologists may disagree over the causes of the networking of American culture. The point here is that our culture of interconnections both reflects and is reflected in our new technology of writing. With all these transitions, the making and breaking of social links, people are beginning to function as elements in a hypertextual network of affiliations. Our whole society is taking on the provisional character of a hypertext: it is rewriting itself for each individual member. We could say that hypertext has become the social ideal. No one now holds as an ideal the proposition that a child, if male, should follow his father into his profession or, if female, should emulate her mother, stay home, and raise a family. Instead the message is that a child (as an ontological individual) should be free to choose what he or she wishes to do in life. That freedom of choice includes everything: profession, family, religion, sexual preference, and above all the ability to change any of the options (in effect to rewrite one's life story) at almost any time. Admittedly, for many Americans this ultimate freedom is not available. But the ideal remains, and it is the ideal of a network culture.

When critics complain of a decline in social and political values, they are often complaining about the loss of hierarchy. What Christopher Lasch identifies as the "culture of narcissism" or Allan Bloom calls the "closing of the American mind" are manifestations of the breakdown of traditions in which civic duty was placed above radical individualism and in which certain kinds of learning were regarded as more important than others. What has been lost is the belief in the legitimacy of hierarchy itself. The critics' complaints are as predictable as are the forces that incline our society to ignore the complaints and continue to replace hierarchies with networks. The development of electronic writing can only serve both to clarify and to accelerate the present impulse for change.

Cultural Unity

One consequence of the networking of culture is the abandonment of the ideal of high culture (literature, music, the fine arts) as a unifying force. If there is no single culture, but only a network of interest groups, then there is no single favored literature or music. Nor is there a single standard of grammar or diction in writing. Elizabeth Eisenstein has argued convincingly that printing was a force for cultural unification during the centuries when the modern nation states were being formed. "Typography arrested linguistic drift, enriched as well as standardized vernaculars, and paved the way for the more deliberate purification and codification of all major European languages" (Eisenstein, 1979, vol. 1, p. 117). As we have seen, electronic writing has just the opposite effect. It opposes standardization and unification as well as hierarchy. It offers as a paradigm the text that changes to suit the reader rather than expecting the reader to conform to its standards.

This attitude is already widespread among readers in the late age of print. As our written culture becomes a vast hypertext, the reader is free to choose to explore one subnetwork or many, as he or she wishes. It is no longer convincing to say that one subject is more important than another. Today even highly educated readers, especially but not exclusively scientists, may know only one or a few areas well. Such ignorance of the shared textual tradition is in part the result of the specialization of the sciences that has been proceeding since the 17th century. But even the humanities are now utterly fragmented, so that a student of Latin literature may know nothing about Renaissance poetry or the 20th-century novel. Throughout the late age of print, however, there has been a lingering feeling of guilt about this situation—a call somehow to reestablish a core of textual knowledge that everyone must possess. The last vestige of this guilt can be heard in pleas for a canon of great authors, which we discussed in an earlier chapter. But the specialization has gone far too far to be recalled. In the sciences it is indispensable. In the humanities and social sciences it is institutionalized. The intellectual world is now defined by numerous "special interest groups" pulling this way and that—Marxists, neo-Freudians, deconstructionists, cognitive scientists, phenomenologists. All the groups are interconnected: some grew out of others, and each sends outrunners (links) into other camps. Thus, there are Christian Marxists, Marxist deconstructionists, phenomenological anthropologists, Lacanian psychoanalysts who write on literature, and so on. But an over-arching unification is no longer even the goal. In *After Virtue* Alasdair MacIntyre (1981), complaining about the fragmented state of moral philosophy, drew the following compelling analogy. Imagine an environmental catastrophe that causes human society to turn against modern science. Scientists are persecuted, and science texts are torn up or destroyed. Then imagine a later generation trying to reassemble these fragments ("half-chapters from books, single pages from articles, not always fully legible because torn and charred") into a single system. The result would be a mish-mash of incoherent theories and misunderstood facts. Of course, this disaster has not happened to modern science, but it is according to MacIntyre exactly what has happened to the great systems of moral philosophy (MacIntyre, 1981, pp. 2–3). For MacIntyre the disaster was the Enlightenment.

MacIntyre's analogy can be extended beyond moral philosophy to almost all fields today: each is an incomplete and disorganized hypertext that no one knows how to read in its entirety. But to call this fragmentation a disaster is to assume that unity is an achievable goal. What MacIntyre does not admit is that there is now no way out of this impasse. (It is certainly not possible to forget the lessons of the Enlightenment.) In fact, the fragmentation of our textual world is only a problem when judged by the standards of print technology, which expects the humanities, including metaphysics and ethics, to be relatively stable and hierarchically organized. What we have instead in the sciences is fruitful specialization and in the humanities a noisy collision of conflicting groups who in the end must agree to disagree. Anyone can enter or leave any group at any time or maintain a combination of interests and positions that characterize two or more camps.

In the late age of print, this situation must appear as chaos, because print holds up stability and order as its ideals. Even though printed materials are still the medium of expression for all these conflicting views, the unwritten assumption is that the disorder can eventually be set right. But in the context of electronic writing, nothing is more natural than the centrifugal disorder of our present cultural life. There is no conceptual problem (though many technical ones) in feeding all these conflicting texts into the computer and generating one vastly reticulated, self-contradictory hypertext. The computer provides the only kind of unity now possible in our culture: unity at the operational level.

Hypertextual publication can accommodate all the mutually incomprehensible languages that the intellectual world now speaks, and this unification of technique must serve as the consolation for the lost unity of purpose.

Within the hypertextual libraries that are now being assembled, individual intellectual communities can retreat into their subnetworks and operate with as much or as little connection to each other as they desire. These communities may be large or small. Contemporary art, music, and literature have divided into several tiny elites and several huge popular movements, while most of the liberal arts are now pursued by relatively small groups of professionals. We have come to accept the fact that a new painting, a novel, or an essay will appeal only to one group of viewers or readers—that each person is free not only to dislike a new work, but simply to ignore it as irrelevant to his or her needs. Individuals today wander through an aesthetic supermarket picking out what interests them—atonal music, concrete poetry, science fiction films, situation comedies on television, or paperback romances. We are hard put to criticize any of these choices: they are simply questions of taste.

In the United States, the most thoroughly networked society, the distinction between high culture and popular culture has all but vanished. In place of the hierarchical organization in which high culture (poetry, "serious" novels, scholarly monographs) is valued above popular culture (doggerel, genre literature, how-to books), we have simply different subnetworks that appeal to different readers. None of the familiar indications of quality apply. In the age of print, a classic might be presented on high-quality paper and bound in cloth or leather, whereas a popular romance would appear in paperback with a suitably gaudy cover. In the electronic writing space, both texts will likely arrive on a diskette. The software for the romance may well be more sophisticated than the software that presents the "serious" fiction—for the same economic reasons that Hollywood's popular movies are often technologically more polished than European art films. The refusal to distinguish between high art and popular entertainment has long been a feature of American culture, but the computer as hypertextual network both ratifies and accelerates this trend. We can now see that American culture has been working for decades against the assumptions of the printed book and toward the freedom from top-down control provided by electronic writing. The computer is the ideal technology for the networking of America, in which hierarchical structures of control and interpretation break down into their component parts and begin to oscillate in a continuously shifting web of relations.

Cultural Literacy

Because of this shift from hierarchy to network, the debate over cultural unity takes its strangest turns here in the United States. Recent examples are the discussion of Allan Bloom's *The Closing of the American Mind* (Bloom, 1987) and E. D. Hirsch's *Cultural Literacy*. Hirsch's book is a particularly instructive case. Many readers took it as a call to return to the classics, to a fixed curriculum of works and authors that would make one culturally literate. But this was a misreading, as anyone can see from the first sentences of the Preface:

> To be culturally literate is to possess the basic information needed to thrive in the modern world. The breadth of that information is great, extending over the major domains of human activity from sports to science. It is by no means confined to "culture" narrowly understood as an acquaintance with the arts. Nor is it confined to one social class. (Hirsch, 1987, p. xiii)

Hirsch is no champion of culture in the traditional sense. For him cultural literacy is the ability to function effectively in our current world of reading and writing. His is an operational definition of literacy—what one needs to get by. Hirsch never demands deep knowledge of any subject: a literate person simply needs to touch the surface of a broad range of topics. At the end of his book, Hirsch gives a list of hundreds of topics that exemplifies the range needed for cultural literacy in contemporary America. Here is a passage from the t's: "Tutankhamen; Twain, Mark; Tweed, Boss; Tweedledum and Tweedledee; Twenty-third Psalm (text); Twinkle, Twinkle Little Star (text)" (p. 210). Here is the beginning of the v's: "vaccine, vacuum, vagina, valence, Valhalla, Valley Forge, valley of the shadow of death, value judgement, Van Allen Belt, Vancouver" (p. 211). Clearly Hirsch's definition of culture has nothing to do with high culture: it is simply anything that a reader might expect to encounter in a newspaper or magazine. Elements in Hirsch's list shoot off in all directions; they are linked not by any hierarchy of values, but by shared associations. Hirsch's alphabetized list reminds us of the eclecticism of the local bookstore, where in the section marked "Philosophy" Hegel is shelved next to Kahlil Gibran, Shirley MacLaine next to John Locke. A visit to the bookstore reminds us that there are no longer accepted principles by which pop culture and high culture can be separated. As in Hirsch's list, there is no hierarchy; all these printed products are of value simply because they will appeal to some group of paperback consumers.

From this perspective, cultural literacy does not require a knowledge of traditional texts; instead, it means access to the vocabulary needed to read and write effectively. And in fact this operational definition is now making cultural literacy almost synonymous with computer literacy. Both cultural and computer literacy simply mean access to information and the ability to add to the store of information. Increasingly, cultural literacy will require working with the computer, as the computer becomes the most important writing space in our culture. The cultural literates will be those who can use this new medium either for their work or for personal communication and expression. By this measure traditional scholars, who are at home in the world of printed books and conventional libraries, are relatively illiterate: they may not know how to work their way through an electronic network of information, certainly not how to write electronically for a contemporary audience.

This new definition of cultural literacy brings us back to the question of the canon of important works and authors. The idea of a relatively stable canon made sense in a culture dominated by printed books. The canon was also appropriate to a centralized educational system, in which everyone studied the same subjects and the same texts in order to be introduced into the standards of cultural life. But the notion of a standard has now collapsed, and the collapse is mirrored in the shift from the printed to the electronic writing space, in which a stable canon of works and authors is meaningless. No wringing of hands and no proposals for a renewed emphasis on the great authors of the past can do much to counter the trend toward a network culture, which is fostered not only by social preference, but also by the very medium of reading and writing that is coming to dominate the literacy of our society.

This prediction must seem bleak to those who still feel allegiance to the traditional culture of printed books. The loss is real; the hope for a cultural center based upon traditional texts must now be abandoned. But much of the loss has already occurred in the late age of print. The computer is only reinforcing the effects of centrifugal forces in the 20th century. More important, as we have seen from the outset, the end of traditional print literacy is not the end of literacy. The computer is simply the technology by which literacy will be carried into a new age.

The Electronic Hiding Place

There is another, more positive way to view the loss of a stable core for our culture. Although we do lose the satisfaction of belonging to a coherent cultural tradition, we gain the freedom to establish our own traditions in miniature. The computer offers people the opportunity to build liaisons with other readers and writers and to work in relative isolation from other such groups. A group does not need to convince a major publishing house of its importance or saleability; it can use electronic mail and diskettes to disseminate its materials. A group does not need to feel answerable to a cultural norm, but can pursue its own definition of literacy. This feature of electronic writing will be as useful to traditionalists as to the avant-garde. Scholars in esoteric subjects will be able to communicate and publish their results by fax machine or electronic mail. Unlike television, which promotes uniformity (even through the apparent diversity of cable and satellite stations), the microcomputer and the phone network really do permit special literacies to survive.

The computer is an ideal writing space for our networked society, because it permits every form of reading and writing from the most passive to the most active. A large group of users (perhaps the largest) will use the resources of the machine to shop, read the weather report, and play fantastic video games under the rubric of virtual reality. There will be a large market for the electronic equivalents of how-to books and interactive romances, science fiction, and the other genres. Small groups will read and write "serious" interactive fiction and non-fiction. Tiny networks of scholars will conduct esoteric studies in ancient and modern literature and languages. Hundreds or thousands of different interest groups from fundamentalist religion to space exploration will publish and read each other's messages and hypertexts—on commercial, academic, or governmental communication networks. Government and business will produce electronic documents by the billions. All these groups will be in contact at various levels for various purposes. In other words, the chaos of publication and communication in the late age of print will continue. The ideal of stability and cultural cohesion will largely disappear. Few will feel the need to assert such cohesion, since even the smallest group of writers and readers can function happily in its niche in the electronic network. The computer can in fact provide a quiet place for readers and writers to pursue such interests, relatively secure from the noise of what remains of shared cultural elements. The computer as a writing space can also be a place to hide from the sensory overload of the daily world of work and leisure and the other electronic media. In this space, all the various definitions of cultural literacy can survive, but no single definition can triumph at the expense of all others.

References

Bellah, Robert N., Madsen, Richard, Sullivan, William M., Swidler, Ann, & Tipton, Steven M. (1985) *Habits of the heart: Individualism and commitment in American life.* Berkeley: University of California Press.

Bloom, Allan D. (1987) *The closing of the American mind.* New York: Simon and Schuster.

Eisenstein, Elizabeth. (1979) *The printing as an agent of change: Communications and cultural transformations in early-modern Europe* (Vols. 1–2). Cambridge: Cambridge University Press.

Hirsch, E. D., Jr. (1987) *Cultural literacy: What every American needs to know.* Boston: Houghton Mifflin.

MacIntyre, Alasdair. (1981) *After virtue: A study in moral theory.* Notre Dame, IN: University of Notre Dame Press.

READING REFLECTIONS

1. Do you agree with Bolter's observations about the fragmentation of culture? Provide an example of a general field of study that has become specialized and its specializations.

2. Bolter states that there is not one common canon of important works in any given field. Do you agree or disagree? Write an argument where you defend or attack his position.

3. Bolter claims that there is little distinction between cultural elements that are regarded as high culture and popular culture. Create a list of cultural elements and classify them as either high culture, popular culture,

or miscellaneous. Explain your classification system. For example, is it based on finances, intellectual content, and so on?

4. How does the availability of so many cultural elements change our cultural unity according to Bolter?
5. What advantages does hypertext have over traditional printed text? Include examples.

OBSOLETE SKILL SET
The 3 Rs

Seymour Papert

In what many may see as a preposterous notion, Seymour Papert envisions a time in the near future when one will not necessarily need to read and write in order to learn. Instead learning could be done via a "knowledge machine," where an individual could be virtually transported to any place and time to learn whatever he or she needed to learn, a kind of virtual learning environment. Such an environment, says Papert, would enable people with all kinds of learning styles to reach their learning potential. How does this proposal strike you?

Seymour Papert holds the Lego Chair for Learning Research at MIT, where he studies, writes, and lectures on the computer's role in children's education. Papert contends that traditional teaching methods are not responsive to the interests and cultures of most children. The article here is from Wired *magazine, an international technology magazine directed toward young computer entrepreneurs, which includes articles on philosophical, educational, and societal aspects of computer technology.*

The facetious old turn of phrase that identifies schooling with the three Rs—reading, 'riting, and 'rithmetic—may express the most obstinate block to change in education. The central role of these "basics" is never discussed; it is considered obvious. Thus the most important consequences of new technologies are not recognized by education policy-makers.

The role of the Rs in elementary education used to be beyond question. How effectively could one teach geography, history, and science to students who could not read? Looking back, we cannot seriously fault these arguments—within their historical context.

But looking forward, we can formulate new arguments beyond the imagination of 19th century thinkers, who could hardly have conjured images of media that would provide modes of accessing and manipulating knowledge radically different than those offered by the Rs. Nor could they have formulated what I see as the deep difference between education past and future: In the past, education adapted the mind to a very restricted set of available media; in the future, it will adapt media to serve the needs and tastes of each individual mind.

In my forthcoming book, *The Children's Machine: Rethinking School in the Age of the Computer*, I use as a thematic image an encounter with a four-year-old girl who heard that I grew up in Africa and asked if I knew how giraffes sleep. I did not. But the ensuing conversation led me to pursue the question when I got home. Reference books were scattered all over my floor as I jumped from one to another in an exciting exploration of the giraffe's world. As I enjoyed the chase I pondered the unfairness of being able to get all this fun out of the girl's question—why couldn't she do what I was doing?

Not long ago the answer would have been obvious: She can't read. But today, there is no technical obstacle to creating a "Knowledge Machine" that would allow a girl of four to navigate through a virtual knowledge space where she could see for herself how giraffes live. It will take time for the vast quantities of information available in print to be recast for such a machine. But it will happen; and when it does, the Knowledge Machine (a metaphor for much more varied forms of media) will provide easier access to richer and fuller bodies of knowledge than can be offered by any printed encyclopedia.

Admitting the prospect of Knowledge Machines does not imply that people will no longer need to read. But reading will no longer be the unique primary access road to knowledge and learning, and it should therefore no longer be the dominant consideration in the design of School.

Demoting reading from its privileged position in the school curriculum is only one of many consequences of Knowledge Machines. A child who has grown up with the freedom to explore provided by such machines will not sit quietly through the standard curriculum dished out in most schools today. Already, children are made increasingly restive by the contrast between the slowness of School and the more exciting pace they experience in videogames and television. But the restiveness is only a pale precursor to what will come when they can freely enter virtual realities of animals in Africa or wars in ancient Greece.

What follows from imagining a Knowledge Machine is a certainty that School will either change very radically or simply collapse. It is predictable (though still astonishing) that the Education Establishment cannot see farther than using new technologies to do what it has always done in the past: teach the same curriculum. I have suggested that new media radically change the concept of curriculum by demoting its core elements. But I would go further:

The possibility of freely exploring worlds of knowledge calls into question the very idea of an administered curriculum.

When knowledge had to be handed out to children, it was necessary to break it up into pre-digested units that could be passed out in a systematic way. Thus the definition of knowledge by subjects, children by grades, and achievement by test scores. But the success with which they learn to speak (and manipulate parents) in their pre-school years attests to the fact that they learn very well from direct interaction with knowledge. The existence of media that could give children direct access to knowledge leads me to question much that is taken for granted in the organizational structure of school. But organizational issues are only at the surface of the rethinking. Deeper rethinking focuses on the nature of knowledge and the learner's relationship to it.

To illustrate this idea, I go back to the story about the child and the giraffes. I may have adopted an adult approach to the question by using books. But more important, I pursued the question by exploring in the way that children explore the immediate world around them. When I looked up giraffes in the encyclopedia I did not find out how they sleep, but I did learn a lot about giraffes, which led to new searches. I went from article to article and then from book to book following associations. I was playing. But as I played, I built a web of knowledge that could not always be described, even though it came from the medium of print.

When I went to bed I still had not found a direct answer. But by then I knew enough about giraffes to think about the question in an informed way, and to figure out that they probably sleep standing up. My activity followed a pattern very reminiscent of a child at play. And the knowledge I gained was not the collection of propositions I read in the books, but the web of intuitive connections that formed as my mind bounced here and there in a non-linear fashion.

Babies begin to build their knowledge by exploration of everything they can see and touch. When they become more mobile, their exploration is widened, but the mode is the same. My young friend came to me at a point of transition when the questions that arose in her immediate world—which might have included pictures of giraffes or a local zoo—could not be answered in her accustomed immediate way. Her acquisition of knowledge was shifting to a more mediated form, more dependent on the narrow bandwidth of verbal communication. The only way she could bring her inner speculations in contact with an outer reality was through the highly unreliable and usually not very interactive method of asking an adult. The transition is not clear-cut: Children ask questions even when they can barely talk, and nobody ever entirely abandons active exploration as a way of acquiring knowledge. But by the time they move into school, mediated acquisition has become the dominant form.

After mastering the Rs, the print medium gave me an "extended immediacy"—a larger world I could explore in a freely interactive spirit. But thanks to an archaic school system, many children lose the taste for immediate exploration long before they acquire the mastery of book skills needed to find that extended immediacy. This is the real tragedy of dropping out: Whether or not

they put in the requisite number of years in the classroom, many (or even most)
children emerge without the intellectual spark with which all are born.

I see then a pattern of intellectual development that I shall oversimplify
by casting it in three distinct phases. The first phase is one of universally successful learning. All children show a passion for interactive exploration of their
immediate world. The diversity of possible activity is great enough for different individuals to find their own styles. The third phase is seen in intellectually awake adults. Here too we see a great diversity of styles. But not everyone
gets there. The second phase is the narrow and dangerous passage in which
many factors conspire to undermine the continuation of phase one. School is
often blamed for imposing on children a uniformity that suffocates those who
have developed markedly different intellectual styles; much as it used to suf-
focate left-handed people by forcing them to "write properly." Most of the
blame is well-founded. But in these practices, schools reflect (and amplify) the
poverty of media that has plagued society in the past. As long as writing was
the only medium in town, schools did not have many choices.

The early and massive imposition on children of what I call "letteracy"
carries risk not only because it suppresses diversity of style, but because it
forces an abrupt break with the modes of learning shared by the first and
third phases. New media promise the opportunity to offer a smoother transition to what really deserves to be called "literacy." Literacy should not
mean the ability to decode strings of alphabetic letters. Consider a child who
uses a Knowledge Machine to acquire a broad understanding of poetry (spoken), history (perhaps relived in simulations), and art and science (through
computer-based labs), and thus draws on this knowledge to conduct a well-
informed, highly persuasive campaign to preserve the environment. All this
could happen without being letterate. If it does, should we say that the child
is illiterate?

The use of the same word to mean both the mechanical ability to read as
well as a rich connection with culture is one more reflection of today's paucity
of media. As we enter an age in which diversity of media will allow individuals to choose their own routes to literacy, that dual meaning will pass away. For
the next generation or two one must expect literacy to include some letteracy,
since our culture's past is so connected with expression through writing. But
even if a truly literate person of the future will be expected to know how to read
books as well as understand the major trends in art history or philosophy, via
whatever other media become available, it will not follow that learning the letters should be the cornerstone of elementary education.

My Knowledge Machine is a metaphor for things close enough in the future to demand serious consideration now. Although the software that can be
purchased today gives only an inkling of what is to come, it should be seen in
the same light as the first flight of the Wright Brothers' machine: Its importance for the future was not measured by its performance in feet of flight, but
its ability to fuel the well-informed imagination. There are very few school environments in which the idea of the illetterate but literate child is plausible.

The pundits of the Education Establishment have failed to provide leadership in this area. Perhaps the readers of *Wired*, who can see farther into the future, have a profoundly important social role in stirring up such debate.

READING REFLECTIONS

1. Papert contends that the basics of reading and writing will someday be obsolete. What does he use for evidence? How realistic is Papert's proposal to you?
2. What is the "knowledge machine"? Does something like this excite or frighten you? Why? Write an essay on why it either excites or frightens you, or both.
3. If such a machine were created, who should decide what kinds of knowledge should be programmed into it? (Can you foresee any problems with a uniform "knowledge machine"?)
4. To replace reading and writing, what other media does Papert propose as learning tools? Write about a teaching strategy that uses media other than reading or writing to teach.
5. Papert's plans to restructure education by eliminating the need to learn reading and writing are very radical. Imagine you must present his ideas to a school board for consideration. Write a proposal to convince the school board to adopt his system.

DYSLEXIA

Eileen Simpson

In a society where literacy is gauged by how well you read, for 10 percent of Americans who struggle with reading because of a developmental disorder called dyslexia, the ongoing need to read is an often painful and frustrating experience. In the following autobiographical selection, Eileen Simpson demonstrates the reality of the dyslexic's life.

Eileen Simpson is a psychologist and author of fiction and nonfiction in-cluding Poets in Their Youth *(1982), a memoir of poet John Berryman, from whom Simpson was divorced in 1956. Her most recent book,* Late Love: A Celebration of Marriage After 50, *is in the self-help sections of bookstores and libraries. The excerpt here is originally from her own story,* Reversals: A Personal Account of Victory over Dyslexia, *published in 1979.*

Dyslexia (from the Greek, *dys*, faulty, + *lexis*, speech, cognate with the Latin *legere*, to read), developmental or specific dyslexia as it's technically called, the disorder I suffered from, is the inability of otherwise normal children to read. Children whose intelligence is below average, whose vision or hearing is defective, who have not had proper schooling, or who are too emotionally disturbed or brain-damaged to profit from it belong in other diagnostic categories. They, too, may be unable to learn to read, but they cannot properly be called dyslexics.

For more than seventy years the essential nature of the affliction has been hotly disputed by psychologists, neurologists, and educators. It is generally agreed, however, that it is the result of a neurophysiological flaw in the brain's ability to process language. It is probably inherited, although some experts are reluctant to say this because they fear people will equate "inherited" with "untreatable." Treatable it certainly is: not a disease to be cured, but a malfunction that requires retraining.

Reading is the most complex skill a child entering school is asked to develop. What makes it complex, in part, is that letters are less constant than objects. A car seen from a distance, close to, from above, or below, or in a mirror still looks like a car even though the optical image changes. The letters of the alphabet are more whimsical. Take the letter *b*. Turned upside down it becomes a *p*. Looked at in a mirror, it becomes a *d*. Capitalized, it becomes something quite different, a *B*. The *M* upside down is a *W*. The *E* flipped over becomes Ǝ. This reversed *E* is familiar to mothers of normal children who have just begun to go to school. The earliest examples of art work they bring home often have I LOVE YOU written on them.

Dyslexics differ from other children in that they read, spell, and write letters upside down and turned around far more frequently and for a much longer time. In what seems like a capricious manner, they also add letters, syllables, and words, or, just as capriciously, delete them. With palindromic words (was–saw, on–no), it is the order of the letters rather than the orientation they change. The new word makes sense, but not the sense intended. Then there are other words where the changed order—"sorty" for story—does not make sense at all.

The inability to recognize that g, g, and G are the same letter, the inability to maintain the orientation of the letters, to retain the order in which they appear, and to follow a line of text without jumping above or below it—all the results of the flaw—can make of an orderly page of words a dish of alphabet soup.

Also essential for reading is the ability to store words in memory and to retrieve them. This very particular kind of memory dyslexics lack. So, too, do they lack the ability to hear what the eye sees, and to see what they hear. If the eye sees "off," the ear must hear "off" and not "of," or "for." If the ear hears "saw," the eye must see that it looks like "saw" on the page and not "was." Lacking these skills, a sentence or paragraph becomes a coded message to which the dyslexic can't find the key.

It is only a slight exaggeration to say that those who learned to read without difficulty can best understand the labor reading is for a dyslexic by turning a page of text upside down and trying to decipher it.

While the literature is replete with illustrations of the way these children write and spell, there are surprisingly few examples of how they read. One, used for propaganda purposes to alert the public to the vulnerability of dyslexics in a literate society, is a sign warning that behind it are guard dogs trained to kill. The dyslexic reads:

<blockquote align="center">

Wurring

Guard God

Patoly

</blockquote>

for

<blockquote align="center">

Warning

Guard Dog

Patrol

</blockquote>

and, of course, remains ignorant of the danger.

Looking for a more commonplace example, and hoping to recapture the way I must have read in fourth grade, I recently observed dyslexic children at the Educational Therapy Clinic in Princeton, through the courtesy of Elizabeth Travers, the director. The first child I saw, eight-year-old Anna (whose red hair and brown eyes reminded me of myself at that age), had just come to the Clinic and was learning the alphabet. Given the story of "Little Red Riding Hood," which is at the second grade level, she began confidently enough, repeating the title from memory, then came to a dead stop. With much coaxing throughout, she read as follows:

> Grandma you a top. Grandma [looks over at picture of Red Riding Hood]. Red Riding Hood [long pause, presses index finger into the paper. Looks at me for help. I urge: Go ahead] the a [puts head close to the page, nose almost touching] on Grandma

for

> Once upon a time there was a little girl who had a red coat with a red hood. Etc.

"Grandma" was obviously a memory from having heard the story read aloud. Had I needed a reminder of how maddening my silences must have been to Miss Henderson, and how much patience is required to teach these children, Anna, who took almost ten minutes to read these few lines, furnished it. The main difference between Anna and me at that age is that Anna clearly felt no need to invent. She was perplexed, but not anxious, and seemed to have infinite tolerance for her long silences.

Toby, a nine-year-old boy with superior intelligence, had a year of tutoring behind him and could have managed "Little Red Riding Hood" with ease. His text was taken from the *Reader's Digest's Reading Skill Builder*, Grade IV. He read:

> A kangaroo likes as if he had but truck together warm. His saw neck and head do not . . . [Here Toby sighed with fatigue] seem to feel happy back. They and tried and so every a tiger Moses and shoots from lonesome day and shouts and long shore animals. And each farm play with five friends . . .

He broke off with the complaint, "This is too hard, Do I have to read any more?"

His text was:

> A kangaroo looks as if he had been put together wrong. His small neck and head do not seem to fit with his heavy back legs and thick tail. Soft eyes, a twinkly little nose and short front legs seem strange on such a large strong animal. And each front paw has five fingers, like a man's hand.

An English expert gives the following bizarre example of an adult dyslexic's performance:

> An the bee-what in the tel mother of the biothodoodoo to the majoram or that emidrate eni eni Krastrei, mestriet to Ketra lotombreidi to ra from treido as that.

His text, taken from a college catalogue the examiner happened to have close at hand, was:

> It shall be in the power of the college to examine or not every licentiate, previous to his admission to the fellowship, as they shall think fit.

That evening when I read aloud to Auntie for the first time, I probably began as Toby did, my memory of the classroom lesson keeping me close to the text. When memory ran out, and Auntie did not correct my errors, I began to invent. When she still didn't stop me, I may well have begun to improvise in the manner of this patient—anything to keep going and keep up the myth that I was reading—until Auntie brought the "gibberish" to a halt.

READING REFLECTIONS

1. How does Simpson help define dyslexia? Provide examples.
2. According to Simpson, what are some of the different ways in which dyslexics read aloud? For instance, how does she contrast her reading as a child to that of eight-year-old Anna?
3. Has Simpson's article helped you understand dyslexia better? How?
4. What analogy does Simpson use to describe the difficulty of seeing letters as opposed to objects?
5. According to Simpson, why are experts hesitant to label dyslexia as an inherited problem?
6. What does Simpson claim is the problem with literature that shows what dyslexics read as opposed to how they read? What does Simpson ask normal readers to do in order to better understand what dyslexics see when they read?

DROPOUT ACES GED TEST, NOW DREAMS OF COLLEGE

Marsha King

Being a teen in America today is not easy for anyone. But imagine being a homeless teen? What kind of life and future would that hold? The following newspaper story tells the account of a teenager who not only pulled herself out of poverty but moreover aced the GED and is headed toward college. At a time when most media stories about teens involve drugs and violence, this story tells another side. What kinds of stories do you think the media ignore about teens? How does that affect how people see teens?

Marsha King, staff writer for the Seattle Times, *the largest newspaper in Washington State, has written numerous features about people's lives. This article, which appeared in the newspaper's local section in 1996, was later published on the newspaper's Web site.*

Five years ago, Jessica Long was a homeless 15-year-old, a high-school dropout who slept in abandoned buildings and panhandled in the University District. Today, she's working two jobs, and hunting for a good college, after getting the ninth-highest score out of nearly 700,000 people who completed a high-school-equivalency exam in the United States and its territories.

At a ceremony this month, Long received a national award from the American Council on Education as one of the top scorers on the General Education Development (GED) test. Her next goal is to earn at least a master's degree in physical anthropology—if she's accepted to college and wins scholarship money. The GED test lasts 7 1/2 hours and covers what graduating high-school seniors are supposed to know in English, science, math, social studies, literature and the arts. Long did not study for the test. Her achievement is all the more unusual, because "the awards often go to students who've had every economic advantage," says Janet Anderson, with the Washington State Board for Community and Technical Colleges.

When Long dropped out of 10th grade in California, she was failing every class, though she'd been in programs for the intellectually gifted and played classical clarinet throughout elementary school. Things started to unravel when her mother, a single parent, was diagnosed with breast cancer—twice—and was forced to quit a good job. Without another source of income, Long and her mother faced poverty. "I was really having a lot of emotional problems at the time," Long recalled. "I was having family problems, and I was really bored in school. I'd been bored for a long time."

Soon after, she and her mother moved to the Seattle area. Long applied to a public high school but didn't enroll. Then, at age 15, she left her mom and moved to the streets. "I was really depressed for a long time," she says. "It was a mutual decision. She didn't throw me out. It was just like we couldn't live together at that point in time." In retrospect, "it was a good decision," says Long. The experience helped her discover herself, what she wanted out of life and that "I could do whatever I wanted to do and that I didn't need to be walked through it." She survived on "whatever"—free food programs, friends' help, panhandling, finding things and selling them.

Meanwhile, her mother "was doing her own soul searching" and also became homeless. When the two reunited, the YWCA found them a place to live, through its Homeless Intervention Program. That was when Long enrolled in NOVA, an alternative public high school in Seattle. The opportunity for intellectual freedom and creativity was overwhelming. She wrote plays, painted and sculpted but totally neglected academics. After a year, she dropped out again and went to work.

For the past three years, Long has been an outreach worker for the 45th Street Clinic several nights a week. She finds homeless youth, wins their trust and steers them to medical help at the clinic when appropriate. "She's a very unique individual," says Paul Barry, her supervisor at the clinic. "She really has a mature understanding of how society is made up and how it results that some people are homeless." And, he adds, "She's entertaining and vivacious. She's a scream." Long also has been employed at the Seattle Infant Development Center and Preschool the past 15 months. "The kids just love her. The parents love her," said Executive Director Marna Towle.

Ever since that year on the streets, the young woman has hung out off and on at the Orion Center for homeless youth. One of the components of Orion's program is a classroom that's part of Interagency School, a Seattle public school. Staffers there counseled her about everything from self-esteem to study skills and paid her $25 fee to take the GED test. "It felt like God just put her in here and we were supposed to say something to her and she just spread her wings and, bam!" recalls teacher Lynn Bier. "We just sat back with our mouths open and said 'Gee.' "

Long and her mother are close again. Her mom encouraged her to take the GED test and now hopes her daughter might attend prestigious Smith College in Northampton, Mass. The two also plan to attend the National College Fair, Nov. 8–9, at the Washington State Convention and Trade Center, to find out about different schools and financial aid. Long settled on anthropology as a major because ever since she was a little kid she has been trying to figure out why people act the way they do.

And why do kids drop out of high school and end up on the street? For a million different reasons, she says. One of the biggest: "Life around you gets way too crazy to be able to be just a teenager." Anything can throw it off— death, drugs, alcohol, abuse or emotional problems just a little bit heavier than other people's adolescent stuff. What's her advice for parents? Encourage teens to think about themselves and what they want to do. With a belief in themselves, they'll have no problem succeeding, she says.

And, maybe, people also need to change their idea of success. "I consider myself a success," says Long, who still looks the part of a punk rocker with a ring in her nostril, a piece of jewelry that looks like a tiny barbell piercing her tongue, and a shaved head except for bangs and springy little pigtails dyed to match in yellow, blue, purple and green. "I make $6.50 an hour as a day-care-center teacher," she says. "I enjoy what I do every day, and I go home feeling good about myself. I'm teaching 3-year-olds to be nice to each other and to love themselves. I'm a success right now even if I never get a Ph.D."

READING REFLECTIONS

1. King considers "street smarts" to be a type of literacy. Would you agree? Why or why not?
2. What quotes from people interviewed in this article demonstrate the street smarts of Jessica Long?
3. Keeping in mind how King describes Jessica Long, do you know someone you consider street smart? What characteristics does that person have to make you believe she or he is street smart?

4. Perhaps you have a different definition of someone who is street smart or the circumstances that make someone street smart than the one discussed by King. What is it? If you agree with King, outline her main points for defining a street-smart person.

5. From the description of Jessica given in the article, what type of prejudice do you think she encounters despite her obvious intelligence?

6. If you were a counselor, how would you have advised someone in Jessica's situation? What kind of advice and guidance would you have given her?

TO ERR IS WRONG

Roger von Oech

Students often believe there are two kinds of people—those who can write and those who cannot. But most writers will tell you that, like learning to play an instrument or play a sport, the more you practice writing, the better you become at it. But learning to write well, like so many things in life, comes from the bumps, the errors, you make along the way. In "To Err Is Wrong," von Oech uses an analogy from the popular sport of baseball to spin out his lesson about how learning from our mistakes helps us to become successful.

With a doctorate from Stanford University in a self-conceived program in the history of ideas, Roger von Oech is the president of Creative Think, a California consulting business. He has conducted creative seminars with organizations as diverse as Apple Computer, CBS, and NASA, and the U.S. Olympic Swimming Team. The excerpt here is originally from A Whack on the Side of the Head: How You Can Be More Creative *(1983), a book that has become a creativity classic. In its preface, von Oech comments, "I think the real need for creativity is in our basic institutions—especially in the family and the schools. That's where it needs to be cultivated."*

Hits and Misses

In the summer of 1979, Boston Red Sox first baseman Carl Yastrzemski became the fifteenth player in baseball history to reach the three thousand hit plateau. This event drew a lot of media attention, and for about a week prior to the attainment of this goal, hundreds of reporters covered Yaz's every move. Finally, one reporter asked, "Hey Yaz, aren't you afraid all of this attention will go to your head?" Yastrzemski replied, "I look at it this way: in my career I've been up to bat over ten thousand times. That means I've been unsuccessful at the plate over seven thousand times. That fact alone keeps me from getting a swollen head."

Most people consider success and failure as opposites, but they are actually both products of the same process. As Yaz suggests, an activity which produces a hit may also produce a miss. It is the same with creative thinking; the same energy which generates good creative ideas also produces errors.

Many people, however, are not comfortable with errors. Our educational system, based on "the right answer" belief, cultivates our thinking in another, more conservative way. From an early age, we are taught that right answers are good and incorrect answers are bad. This value is deeply embedded in the incentive system used in most schools:

Right over 90% of the time = "A"
Right over 80% of the time = "B"
Right over 70% of the time = "C"
Right over 60% of the time = "D"
Less than 60% correct, you fail.

From this we learn to be right as often as possible and to keep our mistakes to a minimum. We learn, in other words, that "to err is wrong."

Playing It Safe

With this kind of attitude, you aren't going to be taking too many chances. If you learn that failing even a little penalizes you (e.g., being wrong only 15% of the time garners you only a "B" performance), you learn not to make mistakes. And more important, you learn not to put yourself in situations where you might fail. This leads to conservative thought patterns designed to avoid the stigma our society puts on "failure."

I have a friend who recently graduated from college with a Master's degree in Journalism. For the last six months, she has been trying to find a job, but to no avail. I talked with her about her situation, and realized that her problem is that she doesn't know how to fail. She went through eighteen years of schooling without ever failing an examination, a paper, a midterm, a pop-quiz, or a final. Now, she is reluctant to try any approaches where she might fail. She has been conditioned to believe that failure is bad in and of itself, rather than a potential stepping stone to new ideas.

Look around. How many middle managers, housewives, administrators, teachers, and other people do you see who are afraid to try anything new because of this fear of failure? Most of us have learned not to make mistakes in public. As a result, we remove ourselves from many learning experiences except for those occurring in the most private of circumstances.

A Different Logic

From a practical point of view, "to err is wrong" makes sense. Our survival in the everyday world requires us to perform thousands of small tasks without failure. Think about it: you wouldn't last very long if you were to step out in front of traffic or stick your hand into a pot of boiling water. In addition, engineers whose bridges collapse, stock brokers who lose money for their clients, and copywriters whose ad campaigns decrease sales won't keep their jobs very long.

Nevertheless, too great an adherence to the belief "to err is wrong" can greatly undermine your attempts to generate new ideas. If you're more concerned with producing right answers than generating original ideas, you'll probably make uncritical use of the rules, formulae, and procedures used to obtain these right answers. By doing this, you'll by-pass the germinal phase of the creative process, and thus spend little time testing assumptions, challenging the rules, asking what-if questions, or just playing around with the problem. All of these techniques will produce some incorrect answers, but in the germinal phase errors are viewed as a necessary by-product of creative thinking. As Yaz would put it, "If you want the hits, be prepared for the misses." That's the way the game of life goes.

Errors as Stepping Stones

Whenever an error pops up, the usual response is "Jeez, another screwup, what went wrong this time?" The creative thinker, on the other hand, will realize the potential value of errors, and perhaps say something like, "Would you look at that! Where can it lead our thinking?" And then he or she will go on to use the error as a stepping stone to a new idea. As a matter of fact, the whole history of discovery is filled with people who used erroneous assumptions and failed ideas as stepping stones to new ideas. Columbus thought he was finding a shorter route to India. Johannes Kepler stumbled on to the idea of interplanetary gravity because of assumptions which were right for the wrong reasons. And, Thomas Edison knew 1800 ways *not* to build a light bulb.

The following story about the automotive genius Charles Kettering exemplifies the spirit of working through erroneous assumptions to good ideas. In 1912, when the automobile industry was just beginning to grow, Kettering was interested in improving gasoline-engine efficiency. The problem he faced was "knock," the phenomenon in which gasoline takes too long to burn in the cylinder—thereby reducing efficiency.

Kettering began searching for ways to eliminate the "knock." He thought to himself, "How can I get the gasoline to combust in the cylinder at an earlier time?" The key concept here is "early." Searching for analogous situations, he looked around for models of "things that happen early." He thought of historical models, physical models, and biological models. Finally, he remembered a particular plant, the trailing arbutus, which "happens early," i.e., it blooms in the snow ("earlier" than other plants). One of this plant's chief characteristics is its red leaves, which help the plant retain light at certain wavelengths. Kettering figured that it must be the red color which made the trailing arbutus bloom earlier.

Now came the critical step in Kettering's chain of thought. He asked himself, "How can I make the gasoline red? Perhaps I'll put red dye in the gasoline—maybe that'll make it combust earlier." He looked around his workshop, and found that he didn't have any red dye. But he did happen to have some iodine—perhaps that would do. He added the iodine to the gasoline and, lo and behold, the engine didn't "knock."

Several days later, Kettering wanted to make sure that it was the redness of the iodine which had in fact solved his problem. He got some red dye and added it to the gasoline. Nothing happened! Kettering then realized that it wasn't the "redness" which had solved the "knock" problem, but certain other properties of iodine. In this case, an error had proven to be a stepping stone to a better idea. Had he known that "redness" alone was not the solution, he may not have found his way to the additives in iodine.

Negative Feedback

Errors serve another useful purpose: they tell us when to change direction. When things are going smoothly, we generally don't think about them. To a great extent, this is because we function according to the principle of negative feedback. Often it is only when things or people fail to do their job that they get our attention. For example, you are probably not thinking about your kneecaps right now; that's because everything is fine with them. The same goes for your elbows: they are also performing their function—no problem at all. But if you were to break a leg, you would immediately notice all of the things you could no longer do, but which you used to take for granted.

Negative feedback means that the current approach is not working, and it is up to you to figure out a new one. We learn by trial and error, not by trial and rightness. If we did things correctly every time, we would never have to change direction—we'd just continue the current course and end up with more of the same.

For example, after the supertanker *Amoco Cadiz* broke up off the coast of Brittany in the spring of 1978, thereby polluting the coast with hundreds of thousands of tons of oil, the oil industry rethought many of its safety standards regarding petroleum transport. The same thing happened after the accident at the Three Mile Island nuclear reactor in 1979—many procedures and safety standards were changed.

Neil Goldschmidt, former Secretary of Transportation, had this to say about the Bay Area Rapid Transit (BART):

> It's gotten too fashionable around the country to beat up on BART and not give credit to the vision that put this system in place. We have learned from BART around the country. The lessons were put to use in Washington, in Atlanta, in Buffalo, and other cities where we are building mass transit systems. One of the lessons is not to build a system like BART.

We learn by our failures. A person's errors are the whacks that lead him to think something different.

Trying New Things

Your error rate in any activity is a function of your familiarity with that activity. If you are doing things that are routine and have a high likelihood of correctness, then you will probably make very few errors. But if you are doing things that have no precedence in your experience or are trying different approaches, then you will be making your share of mistakes. Innovators may not bat a thousand—far from it—but they do get new ideas.

The creative director of an advertising agency told me that he isn't happy unless he is failing at least half of the time. As he puts it, "If you are going to be original, you are going to be wrong a lot."

One of my clients, the president of a fast-growing computer company, tells his people: "We're innovators. We're doing things nobody has ever done before. Therefore, we are going to be making mistakes. My advice to you: make your mistakes, but make them in a hurry."

Another client, a division manager of a high-technology company, asked his vice president of engineering what percentage of their new products should be successful in the marketplace. The answer he received was "about 50%." The division manager replied, "That's too high. 30% is a better target; otherwise we'll be too conservative in our planning."

Along similar lines, in the banking industry, it is said that if the credit manager never has to default on any of his loans, it's a sure sign he's not being aggressive enough in the marketplace.

Thomas J. Watson, the founder of IBM, has similar words: "The way to succeed is to double your failure rate."

Thus, errors, at the very least, are a sign that we are diverging from the main road and trying different approaches.

Nature's Errors

Nature serves as a good example of how trial and error can be used to make changes. Every now and then genetic mutations occur—errors in gene reproduction. Most of the time, these mutations have a deleterious effect on the species, and they drop out of the gene pool. But occasionally, a mutation provides the species with something beneficial, and that change will be passed on to future generations. The rich variety of all species is due to this trial and error process. If there had never been any mutations from the first amoeba, where would we be now?

Summary

There are places where errors are inappropriate, but the germinal phase of the creative process isn't one of them. Errors are a sign that you are diverging from the well-traveled path. If you're not failing every now and then, it's a sign you're not being very innovative.

Tip #1:

If you make an error, use it as a stepping stone to a new idea you might not have otherwise discovered.

Tip #2:

Differentiate between errors of "commission" and those of "omission." The latter can be more costly than the former. If you're not making many errors, you might ask yourself, "How many opportunities am I missing by not being more aggressive?"

Tip #3:

Strengthen your "risk muscle." Everyone has one, but you have to exercise it or else it will atrophy. Make it a point to take at least one risk every twenty-four hours.

Tip #4:

Remember these two benefits of failure. First, if you do fail, you learn what doesn't work; and second, the failure gives you an opportunity to try a new approach.

READING REFLECTIONS

1. Von Oech uses a baseball analogy to make his point. Are there other analogies you can think of that make the same point?
2. What do you think about von Oech's notion that the education system is too focused on testing you to get the right answer rather than helping you develop creative thinking?
3. Besides the various examples provided in the article, think of other instances where a failure rate outweighs a success rate. Why is this the case for this situation?
4. At what thinking level does von Oech feel that it is necessary to make mistakes? Why does he choose this level?
5. What advice does von Oech offer to encourage good errors?

LEARNING TO LISTEN

Eudora Welty

When we interact with media and technology today, we learn not only by reading words but also through the variety of voices, sounds, and music that come from movies, video games, or telephone conversations. Although author Eudora Welty does not specifically address media and technology in this excerpt, she talks about the virtues of learning to listen—not just casually, but carefully hearing what people say, the stories being told, and what is going on around us. In addition Welty explains the importance of listening to the "inward voice," which to Welty is the beginning for developing one's voice as a writer.

Born in Jackson, Mississippi, in 1909, Eudora Welty received her B.A. from the University of Wisconsin in 1929. Early in her career, she worked in newspapers, radio, and as a publicity agent for the Works Project Administration (WPA). This autobiographical piece is an excerpt from her lecture series at Harvard published as One Writer's Beginnings *in 1984.*

Learning stamps you with its moments. Childhood's learning is made up of moments. It isn't steady. It's a pulse.

In a children's art class, we sat in a ring on kindergarten chairs and drew three daffodils that had just been picked out of the yard; and while I was drawing, my sharpened yellow pencil and the cup of the yellow daffodil gave off whiffs just alike. That the pencil doing the drawing should give off the same smell as the flower it drew seemed part of the art lesson—as shouldn't it be? Children, like animals, use all their senses to discover the world. Then artists come along and discover it the same way, all over again. Here and there, it's the same world. Or now and then we'll hear from an artist who's never lost it.

In my sensory education I include my physical awareness of the *word.* Of a certain word, that is; the connection it has with what it stands for. At around age six, perhaps, I was standing by myself in our front yard waiting for supper, just at that hour in a late summer day when the sun is already below the horizon and the risen full moon in the visible sky stops being chalky and begins to take on light. There comes the moment, and I saw it then, when the moon goes from flat to round. For the first time it met my eyes as a globe. The word "moon" came into my mouth as though fed to me out of a silver spoon. Held in my mouth the moon became a word. It had the roundness of a Concord grape Grandpa took off his vine and gave me to suck out of its skin and swallow whole, in Ohio.

This love did not prevent me from living for years in foolish error about the moon. The new moon just appearing in the west was the rising moon to me. The new should be rising. And in early childhood the sun and moon, those opposite reigning powers, I just as easily assume rose in east and west respectively in their opposite sides of the sky, and like partners in a reel they advanced, sun from the east, moon from the west, crossed over (when I wasn't looking) and went down on the other side. My father couldn't have known I believed that when, bending behind me and guiding my shoulder, he positioned me at our telescope in the front yard and, with careful adjustment of the focus, brought the moon close to me.

The night sky over my childhood Jackson was velvety black. I could see the full constellations in it and call their names; when I could read, I knew their myths. Though I was always waked for eclipses, and indeed carried to the window as an infant in arms and shown Halley's Comet in my sleep, and though I'd been taught at our diningroom table about the solar system and knew the earth revolved around the sun, and our moon around us, I never found out the moon didn't come up in the west until I was a writer and Herschel Brickell, the literary critic, told me after I misplaced it in a story. He said valuable words to me about my new profession: "Always be sure you get your moon in the right part of the sky."

My mother always sang to her children. Her voice came out just a little bit in the minor key. "Wee Willie Winkie's" song was wonderfully sad when she sang the lullabies.

"Oh, but now there's a record. She could have her own record to listen to," my father would have said. For there came a Victrola record of "Bobby Shafftoe" and "Rock-a-Bye Baby," all of Mother's lullabies, which could be played to take her place. Soon I was able to play her my own lullabies all day long.

Our Victrola stood in the diningroom. I was allowed to climb onto the seat of a diningroom chair to wind it, start the record turning, and set the needle playing. In a second I'd jumped to the floor, to spin or march around the table as the music called for—now there were all the other records I could play too. I skinned back onto the chair just in time to lift the needle at the end, stop the record and turn it over, then change the needle. That brass receptacle with a hole in the lid gave off a metallic smell like human sweat, from all the hot needles that were fed it. Winding up, dancing, being cocked to start and stop the record, was of course all in one the act of *listening*—to "Overture to *Daughter of the Regiment*," "Selections from *The Fortune Teller*," "Kiss Me Again," "Gypsy Dance from *Carmen*," "Stars and Stripes Forever," "When the Midnight Choo-Choo Leaves for Alabam," or whatever came next. Movement must be at the very heart of listening.

Ever since I was first read to, then started reading to myself, there has never been a line read that I didn't *hear*. As my eyes followed the sentence, a voice was saying it silently to me. It isn't my mother's voice, or the voice of any person I can identify, certainly not my own. It is human, but inward, and it is inwardly that I listen to it. It is to me the voice of the story or the poem itself. The cadence, whatever it is that asks you to believe, the feeling that resides in the printed word, reaches me through the reader-voice. I have supposed, but never found out, that this is the case with all readers—to read as listeners—and with all writers, to write as listeners. It may be part of the desire to write. The sound of what falls on the page begins the process of testing it for truth, for me. Whether I am right to trust so far I don't know. By now I don't know whether I could do either one, reading or writing, without the other.

My own words, when I am at work on a story, I hear too as they go, in the same voice that I hear when I read in books. When I write and the sound of it comes back to my ears, then I act to make my changes. I have always trusted this voice.

In that vanished time in small-town Jackson, most of the ladies I was familiar with, the mothers of my friends in the neighborhood, were busiest when they were sociable. In the afternoons there was regular visiting up and down the little grid of residential streets. Everybody had calling cards, even certain children; and newborn babies themselves were properly announced by sending out their tiny engraved calling cards attached with a pink or blue bow to those of their parents. Graduation presents to high-school pupils were often "card cases." On the hall table in every house the first thing you saw was a silver tray waiting to receive more calling cards on top of the stack already piled up like jackstraws; they were never thrown away.

My mother let none of this idling, as she saw it, pertain to her; she went her own way with or without her calling cards, and though she was fond of her friends and they were fond of her, she had little time for small talk. At first, I hadn't known what I'd missed.

When we at length bought our first automobile, one of our neighbors was often invited to go with us on the family Sunday afternoon ride. In Jackson it was counted an affront to the neighbors to start out for anywhere with an empty seat in the car. My mother sat in the back with her friend, and I'm told that as a small child I would ask to sit in the middle, and say as we started off, "Now *talk*."

There was dialogue throughout the lady's accounts to my mother. "I said" . . . "He said" . . . "And I'm told she very plainly said" . . . "It was midnight before they finally heard, and what do you think it *was!*"

What I loved about her stories was that everything happened in *scenes*. I might not catch on to what the root of the trouble was in all that happened, but my ear told me it was dramatic. Often she said, "The crisis had come!"

This same lady was one of Mother's callers on the telephone who always talked a long time. I knew who it was when my mother would only reply, now and then, "Well, I declare," or "You don't say so," or "Surely not." She'd be standing at the wall telephone, listening against her will, and I'd sit on the stairs close by her. Our telephone had a little bar set into the handle which had to be pressed and held down to keep the connection open, and when her friend had said goodbye, my mother needed me to prize her fingers loose from the little bar; her grip had become paralyzed. "What did she say?" I asked.

"She wasn't *saying* a thing in this world," sighed my mother. "She was just ready to talk, that's all."

My mother was right. Years later, beginning with my story "Why I Live at the P.O.," I wrote reasonably often in the form of a monologue that takes possession of the speaker. How much more gets told besides!

This lady told everything in her sweet, marveling voice, and meant every word of it kindly. She enjoyed my company perhaps even more than my mother's. She invited me to catch her doodlebugs; under the trees in her backyard were dozens of their holes. When you stuck a broom straw down one and called, "Doodlebug, doodlebug, your house is on fire and all your children are burning up," she believed this is why the doodlebug came running out of the hole. This was why I loved to call up her doodlebugs instead of ours.

My mother could never have told me her stories, and I think I knew why even then: my mother didn't believe them. But I could listen to this murmuring lady all day. She believed everything she heard, like the doodlebug. And so did I.

This was a day when ladies' and children's clothes were very often made at home. My mother cut out all the dresses and her little boys' rompers, and a sewing woman would come and spend the day upstairs in the sewing room fitting and stitching them all. This was Fannie. This old black sewing woman, along with her speed and dexterity, brought along a great provision of up-to-the-minute news. She spent her life going from family to family in town and worked right in its bosom, and nothing could stop her. My mother would try, while I stood being pinned up. "Fannie, I'd rather Eudora didn't hear that." "That" would be just what I was longing to hear, whatever it was. "I don't want her exposed to gossip"—as if gossip were measles and I could catch it. I did catch some of it but not enough. "Mrs. O'Neil's oldest daughter she had her wedding dress *tried on*, and all her fine underclothes featherstitched and ribbon run in and then—" "I think that will do, Fannie," said my mother. It was tantalizing never to be exposed long enough to hear the end.

Fannie was the worldliest old woman to be imagined. She could do whatever her hands were doing without having to stop talking; and she could speak in a wonderfully derogatory way with any number of pins stuck in her mouth. Her hands steadied me like claws as she stumped on her knees around me, tacking me together. The gist of her tale would be lost on me, but Fannie didn't bother about the ear she was telling it to; she just liked telling. She was like an author. In fact, for a good deal of what she said, I daresay she *was* the author.

Long before I wrote stories, I listened for stories. Listening *for* them is something more acute than listening *to* them. I suppose it's an early form of participation in what goes on. Listening children know stories are *there*. When their elders sit and begin, children are just waiting and hoping for one to come out, like a mouse from its hole.

It was taken entirely for granted that there wasn't any lying in our family, and I was advanced in adolescence before I realized that in plenty of homes where I played with schoolmates and went to their parties, children lied to their parents and parents lied to their children and to each other. It took me a long time to realize that these very same everyday lies, and the stratagems and jokes and tricks and dares that went with them, were in fact the basis of the *scenes* I so well loved to hear about and hoped for and treasured in the conversation of adults.

My instinct—the dramatic instinct—was to lead me, eventually, on the right track for a storyteller: the *scene* was full of hints, pointers, suggestions, and promises of things to find out and know about human beings. I had to grow up and learn to listen for the unspoken as well as the spoken—and to know a truth, I also had to recognize a lie.

It was when my mother came out onto the sleeping porch to tell me goodnight that her trial came. The sudden silence in the double bed meant my younger brothers had both keeled over in sleep, and I in the single bed at my end of the porch would be lying electrified, waiting for this to be the night when she'd tell me what she'd promised for so long. Just as she bent to kiss me I grabbed her and asked: "Where do babies come from?"

My poor mother! But something saved her every time. Almost any night I put the baby question to her, suddenly, as if the whole outdoors exploded, Professor Holt would start to sing. The Holts lived next door; he taught penmanship (the Palmer Method), typing, bookkeeping and shorthand at the high school. His excitable voice traveled out of their diningroom windows across the two driveways between our houses, and up to our upstairs sleeping porch. His wife, usually so quiet and gentle, was his uncannily spirited accompanist at the piano. "High-ho! Come to the Fair!" he'd sing, unless he sang "Oho ye oho ye, who's bound for the ferry, the briar's in bud and the sun's going down!"

"Dear, this isn't a very good time for you to hear Mother, is it?"

READING REFLECTIONS

1. What stories have you heard from a family member that taught you a lesson about how you should think or behave? How did Welty use the stories she heard as a child?
2. According to Welty, how important is learning to listen to being successful? What makes you think this?
3. Welty remarks that children and artists use all their senses to learn. Why does she compare these two groups?
4. What function does gossip serve in Welty's life? Why does her mother discourage anyone from gossiping in front of her?
5. Analyze a newspaper or television gossip segment considering Welty's emphasis on listening. What purpose does the gossip serve? Why is the information important enough to appear in the media? Who is the intended audience?
6. Why does Welty relate her story about the moon? What purpose does the story serve in advancing her narrative?

"Literacies and Learning" Activities

READING REACTIONS

1. What factors does Jay David Bolter say helped to change the notion of cultural literacy? Based on his article, what is Bolter's perspective on E. D. Hirsch's notion of cultural literacy?
2. The Hirsch, Bianculli, Smith, and Bolter articles have to do with what it means to be an educated person. What are the similarities and differences among the authors' perspectives? What do you think? Who is right or wrong? Or is there some middle ground?

3. Smith, Bianculli, Bolter, Papert, and von Oech are suggesting innovative ways of educating students. If you were a teacher, what kinds of innovative educational ideas would you employ to reach some students who resent being in school?

CLASSROOM REACTIONS

1. This chapter presents different kinds of literacies. Do you think these are literacies? Why or why not? Brainstorm with your classmates about other kinds of literacies. Are there other activities that youth are better at than adults? If so, name them, and offer your reasons for the differences in abilities. Report to your classmates about what your group decided.
2. Find a textbook from an English class from ten, twenty, or thirty years ago. Compare the content of the textbook with this one or another current English textbook. How are they alike or different in content? How would you account for these differences?
3. Make a shorter list from E. D. Hirsch's list of items that you think students in your generation *should know*. Then break into groups with your classmates and decide twenty things you all agree that students in your generation should know to be considered literate. Be prepared to explain why you chose each one.
4. Seymour Papert talks about a "Knowledge Machine." Design your own knowledge machine. Sketch out a picture of what it looks like and list the kinds of information you would choose to be in it.

MEDIA CONNECTIONS

1. Seymour Papert's article first appeared in *Wired* magazine. Find copies of the magazine and analyze its audience and purpose. Look for other articles like this in *Wired* and other magazines. Abstract at least three of the articles, and share them with your classmates.
2. Dyslexia is just one kind of learning problem. Research on-line for user groups, chat programs, and message boards about learning problems, and list the various coping strategies offered for learning from the sources you found. Then collaborate with your classmates to create a booklet with the information available and offer the booklet to your campus student services office.
3. Create a multimedia presentation, complete with animation and sound, about any kind of literacy you would like to present. It can be about functional, cultural, or computer literacy, or street smarts. Or it can be a kind of literacy you can think of. Then show your presentation to your classmates and friends.

COMMUNITY INTERACTIONS

1. Interview someone who is trained in teaching individuals with developmental disabilities. Then write an essay explaining what techniques the teacher uses to help these students overcome the disabilities.
2. Ask a teacher where he or she attended college and find out what the person thinks about the value of a liberal arts education. What does this person think a well-educated individual should know? Send out a questionnaire to other community leaders, asking them what they think is important for a well-educated person to know.
3. Find ethnic communities near your school or home, and make a cultural literacy list from items from that community, complete with a description of each item. Make the lists into a booklet and offer it to your local public library's section on local history.
4. Survey the different types of computers and software programs in your community's schools, and compare the facilities and educational opportunities among these schools. How would you account for the differences among these schools? Which students do you think will be better prepared for either college or jobs in the future? Why?

"On the Internet, nobody knows you're a dog."

Peter Steiner, *The New Yorker* Cartoon, "On the Internet, Nobody Knows You're a Dog."
From *The New Yorker* (1993). Copyright © 1993 by Peter Steiner. Reprinted with the permission of The Cartoon Bank, The New Yorker Collection. All rights reserved.

The New Yorker cartoon that begins this discussion of virtual communities is by Peter Steiner, a nationally famous cartoon artist who has contributed regularly to *The New Yorker* magazine for several years. The cartoon has become a touchstone for those heralding virtual forums as democratic and nondiscriminatory. As the readings we profile in this chapter suggest, the initial utopian flavor of virtual communities has given way to a more balanced understanding of the possibilities of establishing an on-line identity.

What is the point of the cartoon "On the Internet, nobody knows you're a dog"? What are the pros and cons of being "anonymous" on-line? Feel free to share any experience you've had on-line, or experiment with this process in some of your on-line class discussions by using pseudonyms.

7

Virtual Communities/ Virtual Selves

The media have made much these days of virtual communities—sites where people can find social and political solidarity, personal friendships, even romance—as people surf the Internet at work and at home. Whether you are a fan of Madonna or devoted to Russian politics, there is probably a group for you among the nearly 5,000 Usenet groups, or the various subcultures emerging on services such as America Online. As a result, this chapter questions the concept of community in the virtual age.

In the age of cyberspace, not only can you make friends and find lovers, you can also access information and people in a way not possible just five years ago. Who would have thought it possible to send the President of the United States an e-mail or to access the White House home page? As more and more people go on-line across the world, we now have new terms for the types of activities taking place in the *virtual community*, a term popularized by Howard Rheingold and other Internet enthusiasts. Indeed, many of us are familiar with the term *flaming*, in which someone uses overtly hostile language on-line, often in response to those new to the cybercommunity in question and not familiar with the communication conventions or acceptable list topics, a process described by Judy Anderson in "Not for the Faint of Heart: Contemplations on Usenet." To avoid such interchanges, many on-line communities now have lengthy guidelines called FAQs (Frequently Asked Questions), a long message of do's and don'ts available on many lists' archives or posted at the beginning of each month. Moreover, as Internet communities become consistent in their demographic or ideological makeup, advertisers have also found their way on to our bulletin boards, posting notes about everything from software to beauty products, often without regard to the protests of virtual citizens desiring to escape from the billboards and television commercials that bombard daily existence. Such mass advertising on-line has come to be known as *spamming*. In this sense, virtual communities are not all that different from our real-time neighborhoods.

Although news media frequently chronicle Internet addiction at the same time they encourage us to refer to their Web sites for more up-to-date coverage, what is it that is making us go on-line? Is there something more appealing, safer, more communal, or more immediate about our virtual connections, often made from the privacy of our own offices or houses? Is it more than convenience that we can conduct conversations or business early in the morning or late at night wearing pajamas and drinking hot chocolate? Or that we might save hundreds of dollars on phone bills by conversing via e-mail? What is the nature of the virtual experience that is drawing more and more of us away from our real-time friendships and into what Sherry Turkle refers to as a "life on the screen"?

Just how representative are virtual communities? Can they be as segregated as some of our real-time communities? John Perry Barlow stresses that "diversity is essential to a healthy community" but also notes that women, children, old people, and poor people are "mostly missing" from the virtual world. Reginald Stuart concludes that many African American families "just don't have enough fuel to travel the new highway." Although many real-time communities have circumvented access problems by establishing free-nets or by contributing a tax for a common Internet provider, computer use is still associated with household income. As Stuart's research shows, 4.8 percent of households with incomes of less than $15,000 own computers, a fact combined with that nearly one-third of African Americans lived at or below the poverty level as recently as 1990. Although those of us who work in university, government, or corporate systems often take free Internet access for granted, not everyone in all parts of the world is as fortunate, with the highest Internet access fees being charged in countries such as China or several in the Middle East, limiting equal access to the social solidarity and information the Internet can provide.

Yet as more and more writing courses are taught in electronic settings and more classes rely on the Internet as a resource and site of community building, we hope but do not necessarily assume your class is in an electronic environment or that you use a computer at home. Often teachers' and students' receptiveness to the Internet is based on the amount of access they have had to it; thus we encourage you to discuss with your peers and your teachers the role or lack of role the Internet plays in your daily life. As part of this, we encourage you to conduct a computer literacy autobiography, a writing activity at the end of the chapter that asks you to consider the way in which your access to computers in general has been impacted perhaps by your campus, your high school district, your cultural and economic background, even your major in school. Many students can feel a sense of anxiety about the changing technology and the need to learn technology as a means to academic and professional success, given the increasing role of electronic communication in the workplace. Despite this anxiety, however, many students become very familiar with computers in general and on-line dialogue systems in particular, becoming virtual citizens.

Although the majority of this chapter addresses e-mail communities, the advent of the World Wide Web has further complicated issues of access and representation on-line. The anonymity of e-mail pseudonyms or gender-neutral chat characters has in one sense allowed people to experiment with multiple personalities or behave in ways (some good and some bad) that perhaps they would not dare to consider in real-time interchanges. As Kara Swisher's discussion of the Buzbee family indicates, many families and many individuals have turned the Web into a family photo album or into a personal essay. How are Web pages an extension of the self, a projection of ideas and interests into the virtual community in ways that are empowering for some individuals or, in the case of some sites, alienating to others? Just as it is possible to find sites that are devoted to issues of domestic violence or the homeless, it is equally possible to find sites that are devoted to the Nazi party—information that exists, as we often experience in our real-time communities, whether we like it or not. For every utopic community on-line, there can exist a parallel universe of dark alleys and sidewalks where some people have more power than others.

Even as the now-famous cartoon parodies empowerment in its claim, "On the Internet, nobody knows you're a dog," there are times, as both Lindsy Van Gelder's "The Strange Case of the Electronic Lover" and Julian Dibbell's "A Rape in Cyberspace" chronicle, that some people feel free to use this sense of anonymity to violate the feelings and rights of others on-line. As you will read in Dibbell's article, one community took drastic measures to punish the perpetrator of such virtual violation. Although many people value on-line anonymity to speak in a way that in other forums we would perhaps be too shy to speak for fear of being judged by our peers, we also have the right to be "ourselves," just as we have that same right in face-to-face discussion. In this sense, the Internet can serve as a forum for voicing our beliefs in order to change the status quo.

Positive or negative, modern technology in general, and the Internet in particular, is a popular topic in our contemporary culture. Consider the film and recent television version of *The Net*, in which the material identity of Sandra Bullock's film character Angela Bennett is eliminated in favor of a virtual one, created and disseminated by the technology where one's social security number is a secret password to public and private lives. What are the dominant messages about technology and societies' increasingly virtual existence? Are the messages in our media, such as film or the nightly news, mostly positive or negative? What attracts us to this on-line existence: necessity, escape? How can the Internet serve as more than just an information or entertainment function in our lives? Overall, we hope the on-line communities you may be a part of, both in and out of class, as well as the readings and activities compiled in this chapter, will serve as a starting point to consider the role of these new forums in your personal and professional lives.

IS THERE A THERE IN CYBERSPACE?

John Perry Barlow

What is a community, anyway? For John Perry Barlow, the combination of television and suburban population patterns has destroyed the traditional American sense of community. As a result, the need to find that sense of community, of "home," has prompted many to go on-line, often with mixed results.

As his own Web biography reads, John Perry Barlow is a retired Wyoming cattle rancher, a lyricist for the Grateful Dead, and cofounder of the Electronic Frontier Foundation. Recognized as one of the leading voices on the virtual communities, Barlow's "Is There a There in Cyberspace?" is an analysis of the pros and cons of cyberspace, including Barlow's personal story of the loss of his fiancée and the sense of comfort he was able to find through an on-line forum.

I am often asked how I went from pushing cows around a remote Wyoming ranch to my present occupation (which *Wall Street Journal* recently described as "cyberspace cadet"). I haven't got a short answer, but I suppose I came to the virtual world looking for community.

Unlike most modern Americans, I grew up in an actual place, an entirely nonintentional community called Pinedale, Wyoming. As I struggled for nearly a generation to keep my ranch in the family, I was motivated by the belief that such places were the spiritual home of humanity. But I knew their future was not promising.

At the dawn of the 20th century, over 40 percent of the American workforce lived off the land. The majority of us lived in towns like Pinedale. Now fewer than 1 percent of us extract a living from the soil. We just became too productive for our own good.

Of course, the population followed the jobs. Farming and ranching communities are now home to a demographically insignificant percentage of Americans, the vast majority of whom live not in ranch houses but in more or less identical split-level "ranch homes" in more or less identical suburban "communities." Generica.

In my view, these are neither communities nor homes. I believe the combination of television and suburban population patterns is simply toxic to

John Perry Barlow, "Is There a There in Cyberspace?" *UTNE Reader*, no. 68 (March–April 1995): 53–56. Reprinted with the permission of the author.

the soul. I see much evidence in contemporary America to support this view.

Meanwhile, back at the ranch, doom impended. And, as I watched community in Pinedale growing ill from the same economic forces that were killing my family's ranch, the Bar Cross, satellite dishes brought the cultural infection of television. I started looking around for evidence that community in America would not perish altogether.

I took some heart in the mysterious nomadic City of the Deadheads, the virtually physical town that follows the Grateful Dead around the country. The Deadheads lacked place, touching down briefly wherever the band happened to be playing, and they lacked continuity in time, since they had to suffer a new diaspora every time the band moved on or went home. But they had many of the other necessary elements of community, including a culture, a religion of sorts (which, though it lacked dogma, had most of the other, more nurturing aspects of spiritual practice), a sense of necessity, and, most importantly, shared adversity.

I wanted to know more about the flavor of their interaction, what they thought and felt, but since I wrote Dead songs (including "Estimated Prophet" and "Cassidy"), I was a minor icon to the Deadheads, and was thus inhibited, in some socially Heisenbergian way, from getting a clear view of what really went on among them.

Then, in 1987, I heard about a "place" where Deadheads gathered where I could move among them without distorting too much the field of observation. Better, this was a place I could visit without leaving Wyoming. It was a shared computer in Sausalito, California, called the Whole Earth 'Lectronic Link, or WELL. After a lot of struggling with modems, serial cables, init strings, and other computer arcana that seemed utterly out of phase with such notions as Deadheads and small towns, I found myself looking at the glowing yellow word "Login:" beyond which lay my future.

"Inside" the WELL were Deadheads in community. There were thousands of them there, gossiping, complaining (mostly about the Grateful Dead), comforting and harassing each other, bartering, engaging in religion (or at least exchanging their totemic set lists), beginning and ending love affairs, praying for one another's sick kids. There was, it seemed, everything one might find going on in a small town, save dragging Main Street and making out on the back roads.

I was delighted. I felt I had found the new locale of human community—never mind that the whole thing was being conducted in mere words by minds from whom the bodies had been amputated. Never mind that all these people were deaf, dumb, and blind as paramecia or that their town had neither seasons nor sunsets nor smells.

Surely all these deficiencies would be remedied by richer, faster communications media. The featureless log-in handles would gradually acquire video faces (and thus expressions), shaded 3-D body puppets (and thus body language). This "space," which I recognized at once to be a primitive form of the cyberspace William Gibson predicted in his sci-fi novel *Neuromancer*, was still without apparent dimensions or vistas. But virtual reality would change all that in time.

Meanwhile, the commons, or something like it, had been rediscovered. Once again, people from the 'burbs had a place where they could encounter their friends as my fellow Pinedalians did at the post office and the Wrangler Cafe. They had a place where their hearts could remain as the companies they worked for shuffled their bodies around America. They could put down roots that could not be ripped out by forces of economic history. They had a collective stake. They had a community.

It is seven years now since I discovered the WELL. In that time, I cofounded an organization, the Electronic Frontier Foundation, dedicated to protecting its interests and those of other virtual communities like it from raids by physical government. I've spent countless hours typing away at its residents, and I've watched the larger context that contains it, the Internet, grow at such an explosive rate that, by 2004, every human on the planet will have an e-mail address unless the growth curve flattens (which it will).

My enthusiasm for virtuality has cooled. In fact, unless one counts interaction with the rather too large society of those with whom I exchange electronic mail, I don't spend much time engaging in virtual community at all. Many of the near-term benefits I anticipated from it seem to remain as far in the future as they did when I first logged in. Perhaps they always will.

Pinedale works, more or less, as it is, but a lot is still missing from the communities of cyberspace, whether they be places like the WELL, the fractious newsgroups of USENET, the silent "auditoriums" of America Online, or even enclaves on the promising World Wide Web.

What is missing? Well, to quote Ranjit Makkuni of Xerox Corporation's Palo Alto Research Center, "the *prāna* is missing," *prāna* being the Hindu term for both breath and spirit. I think he is right about this and that perhaps the central question of the virtual age is whether or not *prāna* can somehow be made to fit through any disembodied medium.

Prāna is, to my mind, the literally vital element in the holy and unseen ecology of relationship, the dense mesh of invisible life, on whose surface carbon-based life floats like a thin film. It is at the heart of the fundamental and profound difference between information and experience. Jaron Lanier has said that "information is alienated experience," and, that being true, *prāna* is part of what is removed when you create such easily transmissible replicas of experience as, say, the evening news.

Obviously a great many other, less spiritual, things are also missing entirely, like body language, sex, death, tone of voice, clothing, beauty (or homeliness), weather, violence, vegetation, wildlife, pets, architecture, music, smells, sunlight, and that ol' harvest moon. In short, most of the things that make my life real to me.

Present, but in far less abundance than in the physical world, which I call "meat space," are women, children, old people, poor people, and the genuinely blind. Also mostly missing are the illiterate and the continent of Africa. There is not much human diversity in cyberspace, which is populated, as near as I can tell, by white males under 50 with plenty of computer terminal time, great typing skills, high math SATs, strongly held opinions on just about everything, and an excruciating face-to-face shyness, especially with the opposite sex.

But diversity is as essential to healthy community as it is to healthy ecosystems (which are, in my view, different from communities only in unimportant aspects).

I believe that the principal reason for the almost universal failure of the intentional communities of the '60s and '70s was a lack of diversity in their members. It was a rare commune with any old people in it, or people who were fundamentally out of philosophical agreement with the majority.

Indeed, it is the usual problem when we try to build something that can only be grown. Natural systems, such as human communities, are simply too complex to design by the engineering principles we insist on applying to them. Like Dr. Frankenstein, Western civilization is now finding its rational skills inadequate to the task of creating and caring for life. We would do better to return to a kind of agricultural mind-set in which we humbly try to re-create the conditions from which life has sprung before. And leave the rest to God.

Given that it has been built so far almost entirely by people with engineering degrees, it is not so surprising that cyberspace has the kind of overdesigned quality that leaves out all kinds of elements nature would have provided invisibly.

Also missing from both the communes of the '60s and from cyberspace are a couple of elements that I believe are very important, if not essential, to the formation and preservation of real community: an absence of alternatives and a sense of genuine adversity, generally shared. What about these?

It is hard to argue that anyone would find losing a modem literally hard to survive, while many have remained in small towns, have tolerated their intolerances and created entertainment to enliven their culturally arid lives simply because it seemed there was no choice but to stay. There are many investments—spiritual, material, and temporal—one is willing to put into a home one cannot leave. Communities are often the beneficiaries of these involuntary investments.

But when the going gets rough in cyberspace, it is even easier to move than it is in the 'burbs, where, given the fact that the average American moves some 12 times in his or her life, moving appears to be pretty easy. You can not only find another bulletin board service (BBS) or newsgroup to hang out in, you can, with very little effort, start your own.

And then there is the bond of joint suffering. Most community is a cultural stockade erected against a common enemy that can take many forms. In Pinedale, we bore together, with an understanding needing little expression, the fact that Upper Green River Valley is the coldest spot, as measured by annual mean temperature, in the lower 48 states. We knew that if somebody was stopped on the road most winter nights, he would probably die there, so the fact that we might loathe him was not sufficient reason to drive on past his broken pickup.

By the same token, the Deadheads have the Drug Enforcement Administration, which strives to give them 20-year prison terms without parole for distributing the fairly harmless sacrament of their faith. They have an additional bond in the fact that when their Microbuses die, as they often do, no one but another Deadhead is likely to stop to help them.

But what are the shared adversities of cyberspace? Lousy user interfaces? The flames of harsh invective? Dumb jokes? Surely these can all be survived without the sanctuary provided by fellow sufferers.

One is always free to yank the jack, as I have mostly done. For me, the physical world offers far more opportunity for *prāna*-rich connections with my fellow creatures. Even for someone whose body is in a state of perpetual motion, I feel I can generally find more community among the still-embodied.

Finally, there is that shyness factor. Not only are we trying to build community here among people who have never experienced any in my sense of the term, we are trying to build community among people who, in their lives, have rarely used the word *we* in a heartfelt way. It is a vast club, and many of the members—following Groucho Marx—wouldn't want to join a club that would have them.

And yet . . .

How quickly physical community continues to deteriorate. Even Pinedale, which seems to have survived the plague of ranch failures, feels increasingly cut off from itself. Many of the ranches are now owned by corporate types who fly their Gulfstreams in to fish and are rarely around during the many months when the creeks are frozen over and neighbors are needed. They have kept the ranches alive financially, but they actively discourage their managers from the interdependence my former colleagues and I require. They keep agriculture on life support, still alive but lacking a functional heart.

And the town has been inundated with suburbanites who flee here, bringing all their terrors and suspicions with them. They spend their evenings as they did in Orange County, watching television or socializing in hermetic little enclaves of fundamentalist Christianity that seem to separate them from us and even, given their sectarian animosities, from one another. The town remains. The community is largely a wraith of nostalgia.

So where else can we look for the connection we need to prevent our plunging further into the condition of separateness Nietzsche called sin? What is there to do but to dive further into the bramble bush of information that, in its broadcast forms, has done so much to tear us apart?

Cyberspace, for all its current deficiencies and failed promises, is not without some very real solace already.

Some months ago, the great love of my life, a vivid young woman with whom I intended to spend the rest of it, dropped dead of undiagnosed viral cardiomyopathy two days short of her 30th birthday. I felt as if my own heart had been as shredded as hers.

We had lived together in New York City. Except for my daughters, no one from Pinedale had met her. I needed a community to wrap around myself against colder winds than fortune had ever blown at me before. And without looking, I found I had one in the virtual world.

On the WELL, there was a topic announcing her death in one of the conferences to which I posted the eulogy I had read over her before burying her in her own small town of Nanaimo, British Columbia. It seemed to strike a chord among the disembodied living on the Net. People copied it and sent it to one another. Over the next several months I received almost a megabyte of electronic mail from all over the planet, mostly from folks whose faces I have never seen and probably never will.

They told me of their own tragedies and what they had done to survive them. As humans have since words were first uttered, we shared the second most common human experience, death, with an openheartedness that would have caused grave uneasiness in physical America, where the whole topic is so cloaked in denial as to be considered obscene. Those strangers, who had no arms to put around my shoulders, no eyes to weep with mine, nevertheless saw me through. As neighbors do.

I have no idea how far we will plunge into this strange place. Unlike previous frontiers, this one has no end. It is so dissatisfying in so many ways that I suspect we will be more restless in our search for home here than in all our previous explorations. And that is one reason why I think we may find it after all. If home is where the heart is, then there is already some part of home to be found in cyberspace.

So . . . does virtual community work or not? Should we all go off to cyberspace or should we resist it as a demonic form of symbolic abstraction? Does it supplant the real or is there, in it, reality itself?

Like so many true things, this one doesn't resolve itself to a black or a white. Nor is it gray. It is, along with the rest of life, black/white. Both/neither. I'm not being equivocal or wishy-washy here. We have to get over our Manichean sense that everything is either good or bad, and the border of cyberspace seems to me a good place to leave that old set of filters.

But really it doesn't matter. We are going there whether we want to or not. In five years, everyone who is reading these words will have an e-mail address, other than the determined Luddites who also eschew the telephone and electricity.

When we are all together in cyberspace we will see what the human spirit, and the basic desire to connect can create there. I am convinced that the result will be more benign if we go there open-minded, open-hearted and excited with the adventure than if we are dragged into exile.

And we must remember that going to cyberspace, unlike previous great emigrations to the frontier, hardly requires us to leave where we have been.

Many will find, as I have, a much richer appreciation of physical reality for having spent so much time in virtuality.

Despite its current (and perhaps in some areas permanent) insufficiencies, we should go to cyberspace with hope. Groundless hope, like unconditional love, maybe the only kind that counts.

READING REFLECTIONS

1. Outline the concept of "community" as defined by Barlow.
2. How are on-line communities similar to and different from face-to-face communities in terms of the possibilities and constraints for those seeking personal and political solidarity?
3. What is *prāna*, and what role, according to Barlow, does it play in the formation of communities?
4. Barlow claims his "enthusiasm for virtuality has cooled." After reading his essay, why do you think this is?
5. Given Barlow's personal circumstances, to what extent does his waning enthusiasm about virtual communities seem contradictory?

HIGH-TECH REDLINING
Are African-Americans Being Frozen Out of the New Communications Network?

Reginald Stuart

Whose community is it? Whereas John Perry Barlow addresses the extent to which community is possible on the information superhighway, Reginald Stuart suggests that not all citizens are equally able to drive on it. As Stuart notes, it will take a concerted effort for African Americans not to be left behind. While computer use has dramatically increased, its use by African Americans continues to be minimal, suggesting an equally marginalized presence for this group within virtual communities.

Reginald Stuart, "High-Tech Redlining: Are African-Americans Being Frozen Out of the New Communications Network?" *Emerge* (November 1994). Reprinted in *UTNE Reader*, no. 68 (March–April 1995): 72–73. Copyright © 1994 by Reginald Stuart. Reprinted with the permission of the author.

Reginald Stuart has served as the president for the Society of Professional Journalists and is a regular contributor to the organization's national magazine, The Quill, *as well as* Emerge, *a magazine devoted to African American issues and the original source of this article. It was reprinted in the* UTNE Reader *in its special 1995 issue on virtual communities.*

In the embryonic days of the now 40,000-mile-plus interstate highway system, few black people actually knew of its potential to redefine or even destroy entire communities. Just as many blacks today still bear the scars of the interstate highway that many times plowed right through the heart of their communities a generation ago, African-Americans today are threatened by the so-called information superhighway.

When it is completed, the information superhighway will be a pipeline through which nearly every form of communication conceivable will pass. You name it and the highway most likely will carry it: love letters, business mail, televised telephone calls, newspaper stories, radio and TV shows, movies, educational programs, and even medical assistance. Jeff Chester, executive director of the Washington-based Center for Media Education, says that a new central nervous system is being built for our society, and that African-Americans in particular have a lot at stake. "I see this as *the* civil rights and economic rights issue of the 21st century," says Chester.

In many respects, the scenario for the development of the communications highway is evolving in much the same way the interstate highway system did. A handful of visionaries are working the halls of Congress to clear the legal obstacles, and in boardrooms across the nation grand ideas—how to pool big money to control positions in the information marketplace—are being explored. In this frenzied activity, African-Americans are being viewed as consumers, not directors.

"It is going to require a concentrated effort" on the part of African-Americans not to be left behind, says Larry Irving, an assistant secretary in the U.S. Department of Commerce and director of the National Telecommunications Information Administration. "We either have to get on it or be left behind," Irving says. "We have to get the technologies deployed in minority communities, make sure our children are technologically literate, and seize the entrepreneurial opportunities."

Things are off to a rocky start. A coalition of groups following developments in Washington have accused the nation's telephone companies of "electronic redlining" in planning a communications network. The Center for Media Education, the NAACP, the Office of Communication of the United Church of Christ, the Consumer Federation of America, and the Council of La Raza have joined together to warn that minority communities are being bypassed and have asked the Federal Communications Commission to investigate. (The phone companies strongly deny the claim.)

A 1989 report by the U.S. Census Bureau found computer use and ownership skyrocketing. But use and ownership by African-Americans was almost negligible. The report said that 26.9 million whites—but only 1.5 million blacks—used computers at home. Among children age 3 to 17, some 10.7 million white children used computers at home, compared with 806,000 black children. In school, the number of children using computers rises significantly for both groups, but the gap is just as profound: 17.4 million white students but only 2.4 million black students.

The same report found that owning a computer is closely associated with household income (and education) levels: 47.5 percent of households with annual incomes of $75,000 or more owned computers; 4.8 percent of households with incomes of $15,000 or less owned them. Combine that with the fact that nearly one-third of all black Americans lived in poverty in 1990, according to the census bureau (the government defines poverty as a two-person household making $9,165 or less a year, or a four-person household with an annual income of $13,924 or less). Many African-American families just don't have enough fuel to travel the new highway.

"When television sets were first introduced, very few blacks had them, but now they are in virtually every home," recalls Delores Davis-Penn, a gerontologist at Missouri's Lincoln University who has been sent to Washington twice by Southwestern Bell to argue for affordable phone service for minorities. "Looking into the future, [I believe] that computers will become like television sets in our homes," she says. Electronic innovations bring new job opportunities, not to mention new chances to create radio and television programming that is culturally sensitive to African-Americans, she adds. "It requires creativity to push our people to accept the challenge."

READING REFLECTIONS

1. What evidence does Reginald Stuart cite to suggest the gap between the numbers of computer users among white and black populations?
2. What factors account for this gap?
3. Why does Stuart feel it is important for African Americans to gain access to the information superhighway?
4. Stuart quotes a gerontologist who claims that just as televisions were once appliances for the few but now exist in almost every home, so too will be computers. If this is true, in what ways will virtual reality change our lives? Will all of the changes be positive? What will be missing?
5. Do an Internet search of African American–related sites. What types of services are directed at this particular on-line consumer group? What might Stuart have to say about such sites?

THERE'S NO PLACE LIKE A HOME PAGE

Kara Swisher

Be it ever so humble. . . . These days most people give out their Web URL or e-mail address as frequently as they do their phone number, with individuals and families hoping to establish an on-line identity, a place called home on the Internet. As Kara Swisher suggests, these virtual connections are not just wired ones but social ones, extending the boundaries of home in ways we never imagined possible a decade ago.

As a staff writer for the Washington Post, Kara Swisher's articles on cyberspace and other electronic media issues appear regularly on-line at http://www.washingtonpost.com. Her 1996 "There's No Place Like a Home Page" examines the growing importance of the web in connecting friends and family.

The Buzbee clan now has global reach.

Switch on a computer in Washington or Buenos Aires or Hong Kong, or any other spot that's linked to the World Wide Web, and you can summon images of John and Sally Buzbee to your screen. There they are enjoying a meal, mugging for the camera during a family celebration. You can read about the recent travels abroad of the District couple or their time as students at the University of Kansas.

It's a personal "home page" on the Web, a sort of electronic front porch to which the whole world is invited. But don't leave without meeting the rest of the far-flung family. On the Buzbees' page, you'll find highlighted words and symbols. "Click" on them with your computer's pointing device and you'll jump to the home pages of other Buzbees.

There's "Dad" Buzbee, actually Richard E. Buzbee of Hutchinson, Kan., who was a newspaperman, served in Korea during the war and has four sons and a wife named Marie. There's Jim Buzbee, John's brother, who lives outside Denver and loves bats so much that he built a bat house. His home page is devoted to the winged night creatures, complete with bat facts, bat advice, bat pictures and even bat jokes and bat poetry. And there's Jim's 8-year-old son, Tom, who has his own page made up of his reviews of R.L. Stine's "Goosebumps" book series for children.

Unusual, but not that unusual.

Across the nation, people are creating personal home pages to announce themselves to the world. At the Washington, D.C. Personal Home Page Registry, a Web site where Washington area residents post notice that they've created pages, more than 2,200 are listed.

All told, an estimated 11 million people use the World Wide Web these days. Some, like the Buzbees and their fellow personal home page creators, provide information. Most, however, come to consume it. Some consult the Web as casually as they do books, newspapers or television.

Of course, people who don't use the Web far outnumber those who do. And not a few users lose their excitement quickly, having been turned off by the confusion, the cost and the frequent mindlessness of what they find in cyberspace.

"I find you can dismiss 90 [percent] to 95 percent of Web sites," said Jack Cremeans, a sheep farmer in Howard County who uses the Web occasionally to find information on sheep, the economy and current events. Often, he said, you're "better going off to the corner library, where there's more discipline to the research."

Still, the numbers shift a bit in favor of the users each month.

"There's a lot to complain about and everyone does, but I have to tell you I love" the Web, said John Buzbee, a graduate student at Georgetown University's Center for Contemporary Arab Studies. "I use it extensively for school, doing research on government pages. . . . I also use it to keep up with my faraway sports teams and in weak moments I just wander. It's exciting not only because of what's available, but because it's getting better every hour."

For now, the typical on-line traveler isn't typical of the population at large. Forrester Research Inc. of Cambridge, Mass., estimates that 74 percent of the people on the Internet, the larger computer network of which the Web is a part, are men, 22 percent are women and about 4 percent are children.

But each day, as thousands of Americans join in, the on-line population is becoming a bit more like the country as a whole.

Children are signing on to visit sites related to TV shows they watch. Or to do homework—for many, the first step in an assignment to research a paper on, for example, abolitionist Harriet Tubman is to zip to a Web "search engine," type in the name and see what comes up. "You can get lots of information about the world, quickly," said 10-year-old Stephanie Tapiero, a Bethesda fifth-grader who uses the Web that way.

Eileen Betancourt, an aspiring romance novelist who lives in Gaithersburg, uses the Web to research settings for her writings. She couldn't find a map of the Maryland town of Frostburg at her local library; she found one on the Web. For her "pay the rent" job, telemarketing, she uses the Web to gather telephone numbers.

"I get on it with a purpose in mind," she said. "I'm on there to get information. I really fight the urge to surf; I don't think it would be that time-effective."

Multiply Betancourt by several thousand newcomers a day and you get an idea of the momentum the Web has built up.

"I don't think anybody had an idea of how big this thing would be," said James Barksdale, chief executive of Netscape Communication Corp., which makes the world's most popular software to navigate the Web. "Unlike a lot of passive mediums, this is a network that the mere mortal can effect, can jump on and ride to anywhere."

Carnival Atmosphere

Each of the millions of people who venture onto the Web is courted by providers of "content," which includes pictures, text and sounds. Like barkers at the doors of carnival tents, content creators must find ways to distinguish themselves from the great mass and get Web travelers to come and sample their wares.

Content is a dynamic, ever-changing work in progress. Just as the Web's circuits are not owned by any one party, content is a group effort. No one vets it for accuracy or taste. With a few exceptions, anything goes.

Some sites are pure labors of love. For the Buzbees, it's the sheer fun of knowing their tales are available to the world. "Yes, there's a bit of an ego thing," John Buzbee said. "It's nice to think you're writing for an audience, and on the Web it's possible to convince yourself of that whether anyone is reading it or not."

Other people find pleasure in maintaining unofficial sites devoted to the "Star Wars" films, actress Alicia Silverstone or computerized fortune-telling, to name a few.

There's even a site devoted to complaints that the Web's being corrupted. Called "suck," it's a soapbox from which a coterie of smart, young naysayers spew forth on various media deals and on-line developments.

Institutions with the purpose of serving the public also are well represented in the new medium. It's an obvious step for a library, for instance, to put material on-line, so as to expand the pool of people that it reaches. The Library of Congress has offered up its card catalogue and images and text from exhibits that it holds in its halls. So have universities, government agencies and nonprofit organizations.

Virginia Tech's Seismological Observatory in Blacksburg has a site with a handsome red-and-orange picture of Virginia and charts of recent seismic activity. There also is a lot of information about earthquakes in the region, which sits on the center of the North American plate. Included is the surprising fact that there have been 160 earthquakes in the region since 1977, 16 percent of which have been felt.

The Web lets the FBI circulate its wanted posters more widely than is possible through post office notice boards. Escaped bank robber Leslie Rogge, one of the bureau's "10 most wanted" fugitives, recently was arrested in Guatemala after being recognized by someone on the FBI's Web page.

As more Americans have entered the Web, politicians have followed. It now is fashionable for a presidential candidate to have a Web site. And their critics sometimes set up countersites to ridicule them, though sometimes it's not immediately clear which site is which.

Helping the newcomers find their footing, for a price, are companies like Electric Press Inc. of Reston, run by Duffy Mazan.

Formerly director of computers at the National Academy of Sciences, Mazan left the organization with three colleagues. They raised $100,000 and started the firm. Today it has about 100 clients, including the Kiplinger publications, and revenue that Mazan predicts will exceed $3 million this year. Its basic job is designing, creating and maintaining other people's Web sites. Like many people involved day to day in the Web, he's a bit breathless about it all. "It's such a huge cacophony that it's getting hard to rise above the noise," he said. "I never would have predicted it."

Profiting On-Line

Putting out information for free is one thing; more challenging is making money from it.

The Web has unleashed a burst of capitalistic energy that rivals anything seen on the floor of a commodity exchange at peak time. Companies are rushing to get on the Web and establish sites with addresses that end in ".com," indicating a commercial site. The new mantra: You're nobody if you're not somebody.com.

It's equally true that nobody is quite sure what to do once they get there.

Underlying all of these ventures is the conviction that the Web is just waiting to be turned into a global bazaar. On-line commerce will become as big if not bigger than the once-small business of selling things by catalogue over toll-free telephone lines, the pioneers said. It's cheap, it's efficient, it matches buyer and seller.

Big established corporations are trying it out as a new vehicle for ads. By posting electronic billboards at different sites where passers-by will see them, companies such as General Motors Corp. and Bell Atlantic Corp. hope to build brand recognition and image. One thing they like: The technology can measure precisely how many people visit a site and see the ad.

Others use the Web to complement their existing business. Federal Express Corp., for instance, has a Web site that customers can contact to check on the progress of specific packages. Other companies provide technical advice about their products on the Web. Record companies offer audio snippets of new songs in hopes that people will go out and buy the full compact disc or tape.

Microsoft Corp. is using the Web to deliver software that people otherwise would pick up on disks in a store. Newspapers, *The Washington Post* among them, are offering electronic versions on the Web. Catalogue firms offer on-line catalogues. You place the order on-line and it's delivered by courier.

Other owners of .com addresses are start-ups convinced that they can invent a new business based on the Web. A site called Amazon is selling books on the Web. Other services help people plan their gardens and road trips. Still another composes customized love poems—you type in the name of your beloved, his or her interests, the level of intensity you want in the finished product, and out comes a (generally laughable) poem.

The sex industry, never slow to pick up on technologies that help preserve customers' anonymity, is there too. The first electronic peep shows have appeared. Using the Web's developing though still primitive function as a video pipeline, customers pay money to watch images of sex acts that are transmitted live to their screens.

So far, none of this commerce has turned into anything resembling mass market. A recent survey by the firm Find/SVP found that only 19 percent of Web users have ever bought anything on-line. Those who did buy tended to be from a rather narrow group—men ages 30 to 49—and most were buying computer goods, music and adult-oriented books.

One big impediment: the basic question of whether people really want to shop this way. The Web remains agonizingly slow. Photos of summer blazers from a men's catalogue take a long time to move over the Web, and then they're not nearly as good as what is available in a catalogue of shiny paper.

Security is another concern. Though consumers in general think nothing of using credit cards in restaurants where numbers could be filched at will by waiters and clerks, many fear their credit card numbers will be intercepted by hackers.

Several companies, such as Cybercash Inc. of Reston have introduced technologies to protect customer's accounts from intruders. Other companies are functioning as validators, checking the bona fides of sites on the Web to assure that they are run by whom they claim to be. Those sites that check out get a validator code; software in the machines of visitors look for that code and flash a warning if they don't find it.

Often the technology turns out to be the easy part. By making new things possible, it rubs up against long-standing laws, practices and expectations.

Copyright law, for example. Owners of copyrighted material, such as newspapers, books, and records, are reflexively suspicious of a medium that allows wholesale, flawless copying of their material. Many have held back putting material on-line out of fear that its value would evaporate if one person copied it and sent it to multiple others.

Should libraries put books on-line? People who couldn't make it to one would no doubt benefit. But it might result in book sales declining. It's hard to copy a 400-page novel checked out from the library; it's not hard to copy one in electronic version. This issue is being hashed out. Some owners of copyrighted material put nothing up; others put a sample in hopes of getting people to buy the full product in a store.

The same holds true with on-line shopping. In theory, one great advantage is software that would automatically query different shopping services and seek out the lowest price on a given item. But retailers are loathe to allow that to happen because they want to "sell" you with soft words and pretty pictures and make you put aside the question of price. So many of them have fought use of software that sniffs out the lowest price.

The Cyber Fearful

These debates will last for years. In the meantime, people like the Buzbees will continue to log on, explore, try out this and abandon that.

They're a lot like most Americans. Take the Denver Buzbees. Judy, wife of Jim, doesn't venture into cyberspace at all. "I don't have a lot of free time," she said, "because I am pretty busy raising a family.

And it still seems a bit complex at this point.

Still, she was impressed at something that her husband recently accomplished on-line. He planned an entire vacation using the Web. First he used search engines to find a paradise isle in the Caribbean—Dominica. Then he researched it using a variety of Web pages and made reservations for the trip.

"This puts the tools in our hands rather than in somebody else's," Jim Buzbee said. "It is very empowering."

READING REFLECTIONS

1. Swisher quotes Richard Buzbee, who claims the Web to be very empowering. What do you think he means by this?
2. How might this statement connect to Swisher's comment that the Web is an "electronic front porch"?
3. To what extent have you found the Web to be empowering in your personal or academic life? How are your feelings similar to or different from those of the Buzbees?
4. What are some of the drawbacks to the Web, according to Swisher?
5. What is the overall tone of Swisher's article, and how might it reflect the media's attitude toward technology?

NOT FOR THE FAINT OF HEART
Contemplations on Usenet

Judy Anderson "yduJ"

Ever go to a party and feel like you didn't belong? As new e-mail lists and chat rooms crop up on a daily basis, the standards of community develop just as quickly and are not always clear to the "newbie," the recently connected newcomer. As Judy Anderson points out, just when you thought a

Judy Anderson "yduJ," "Not for the Faint of Heart: Contemplations on Usenet," in *wired-women: Gender and New Realities in Cyberspace*, ed. Lynn Cherney and Elizabeth Reba Weise (Seattle: Seal Press, 1996), pp. 126–38. Copyright © 1996 by Lynn Cherny and Elizabeth Weise. Reprinted with the permission of Seal Press, Seattle. This selection includes an illustration of a flamingo by Rowan Crawford. Reprinted with the permission of the artist.

face-to-face social gaffe was bad, on-line ones can be even worse, as many experienced users will tell you in no uncertain terms.

Judy Anderson is a Stanford University graduate with experience as a systems administrator at Hewlett-Packard. She currently works for Harlequin, Inc., in Cambridge, Massachusetts. This article, which appeared in wired-women: Gender and New Realities in Cyberspace *(1996), addresses the "netiquette" of virtual communities and the extent to which such communities are genuinely more open and democratic forums accepting of newcomers.*

While attending Stanford University, I witnessed the birth of the Internet, and have since watched its growth spurts and growing pains as connectivity has increased. I got my first email account in 1979 and joined my first netwide mailing list in 1980—in other words, I have seen a lot of different styles of email, mailing list and netnews messages. It has not been my perception that my gender was relevant to my participation in this new medium of computer-mediated communication: I offer you my thoughts, experiences and advice on the net as a *person*, not just as a "woman online."

Me and Ten Guys

I grew up in the heyday of Women's Lib. I didn't pay a whole lot of attention to it, really, I just went along with my life one day at a time. But my mother never said, "You can't do that—you're a girl," so I played with model railroads alongside my Barbie dolls, and felt no aversion to math and science classes. When I was in high school, I started to notice that most girls weren't like me. I still had a few female friends, though, so it wasn't blindingly obvious; enough men were also sufficiently different from me that I did not draw deep conclusions along gender lines. But by the time I got to college, girls (now women) had become an alien species. They cared about things I had no interest in, and vice versa. Hardly any of them were science fiction fans, and those that were preferred fantasy. I hung out at the computer center, and most of the time when a group of us would head out to grab a snack, it was me and ten guys.

My interests—science, science fiction, computers, technology, math—share something that's not offered by creative outlets such as art and literature or by descriptive studies such as history and some social sciences. I have a deep need for predictability. Not for things to be boring—just to understand how they came to be. If I hear a crash in my living room, I don't say, "Something must have fallen down," I go look to see what fell, and I feel some distress if I can't match the sound I heard with the state of the living room floor.

So it is with computer software. If my computer program doesn't work, I want to know why, how and what I can do about it. I build detailed models of the inner workings of the machine. Not the electrons in their quantum states, but at a logical level. I believe it is this personal requirement of consistency that makes me a skilled computer programmer. I have a sufficiently deep understanding of the machine at all levels that I can easily catch logical errors, and when I can't see a reason for some anomaly, I know how to proceed. Eventually I find a contradiction between my model and the real world; this discovery leads to a solution to the problem, and I update my model.

I don't think most people, either male or female, have this deep need for consistency and logical thinking, but I have noticed that those who do are more likely to be men than women. It is rare that I find a woman who thinks a lot like me. Although less rare, it is still uncommon that I find a man whose mind works like mine. But I still find myself in social groups consisting of me and ten guys. This frustrates me, and so I attempt to join with other women in social or professional contexts. Since the net is a large part of my life, it is an obvious place to seek such contacts.

The FIST Fiasco

A few years ago I joined an electronic mailing list called FIST, an acronym for Feminism in Science and Technology. It sounded like just the ticket; I thought I would be exposed to other women scientists and engineers, perhaps get to meet them in person and maybe establish some friendships with kindred spirits.

I was dismayed to learn that what many members of this list thought of as feminism and feminist thinking bore very little relation to my ideas. I am fond of the quote, "Feminism is the radical notion that women are people." I find no need to prove that women are different from men, that women's way of thinking is different (or better!) from men's, and so on. But the FIST list was full of messages decrying the sexism of scientific investigation, and not just "regular" sexism, that is, the difficulty women face in getting promotions, raises and other recognition in all fields. No, their messages declared that the scientific method itself was anathema to women.

I stayed on the FIST mailing list for a few months. I grew increasingly dismayed, and increasingly depressed, that I could not fit into the mold my body had given me—every time I read a FIST message I'd look for my penis! Eventually some women on the list proposed that the list should be closed to men. At the time, there was a lively debate going on about the feminist view of science, with a few men arguing what was also my point of view. I became outraged that these women would close themselves off because they could not stand to have their beliefs questioned. I resigned from the list.

Sometimes, it can be appropriate to close a list to unwanted outsiders. It is not immoral to have a small community or even a closed community. "Community" is lost at some size, and "politics" sets in. The Internet is not a community, it's a nation. There are things I want to discuss with my friends and neighbors; parties I want to hold without inviting the entire world. So it is with the net—small community mailing lists that do not grow without bound are not *a priori* a bad thing. There is a place both for small communities and for larger societies where any and all may join.

But I resist strongly the desire to close lists solely based on gender. Currently, the overwhelming majority of Internet users are men. Some people, like the FIST proponents, say that the masculine way is to speak without listening, and that the feminine way is to listen and speak only when needed. This is a generalization, and like all generalizations is true at best in the abstract; in the specific it is often false. Some men are considerate; some women are rude. Some men are quiet; some women are prolific. I disagreed with the FIST list's proposal to close its borders; it seemed like a bad reaction to what I felt was well-placed criticism. In contrast, Usenet, the collection of public newsgroups on many topics, provides lots of places for people to voice dissenting opinions without any fear of being kicked out. But there are different standards in each newsgroup, and you may be "flamed" if you don't fit in.

A Little Usenet Advice

Usenet (also called netnews) is an anarchy and is "run," therefore, by those with the loudest voices, or the most time to spend on an issue. There are no representatives on the net. The only way to have your issue raised or your opinion voiced is to speak out. Thus the net is run by those who are prolific, by those who primarily speak and only secondarily listen. Those who only listen are ignored, and those who rarely speak are drowned out. Some of the latter run away from the net after only a short experience, and only a few learn to participate in the net without fear.

Parts of the net can be pretty nasty places. Some people on the network seem to enjoy flaming other people for their views or their ineptness (real or imagined). These flames can be very blunt and insulting—things someone would never say in a telephone or face-to-face conversation. One can learn to accept such vicious abuse of one's intellect—but this may lead to joining in and returning fire. Far better, I think, is to avoid flaming others and inciting others to flame. The net is large enough for both flamers and those who wish to avoid them. I have been an active participant on Usenet for over a decade and have developed a number of techniques for approaching the net in general and Usenet in specific without getting burned. Here, I'll primarily discuss my experiences on Usenet, where messages and responses are available to be read by anyone anywhere on the net, thus amplifying both the highs and lows of communication.

I have frequently heard the advice, when in a classroom or lecture situation, that if I have a question, odds are someone else in the audience has the same question, so I should definitely ask it. This advice is intended to counteract the inherent shyness most people have in large groups. This advice does *not* hold for the net. It is easier to lose your shyness on the net than in a class-room—it feels intimate, since it's just you and the computer in the privacy of your own home or office. But, really, the lecture hall you are in is huge—much larger than any physical site you've ever been in! It is more likely that, if you have a question, someone else has *already* asked it. The answer will be wait-ing for you shortly. Indeed, some questions are so frequently asked that they have given rise to the FAQ—most informational, and some social, groups have lists of Frequently Asked Questions with answers. Asking something that's in the FAQ, if there is a FAQ for a group, can get you flamed way out of propor-tion to your transgression. Being the recipient of this sort of abuse can be very painful, especially since it generally occurs early in a netter's career. This is the nastiness that turns people off completely from the net—or encourages them to themselves *become* a flamer! Yet it can be alleviated by simply waiting for the FAQ to appear, which it will in due time.

Before posting, I always check out a group by reading it for a few weeks. It can be annoying to wait, but the emotional savings can be substantial, especially if a group of hotheads is dominating the group. Sometimes I'm just tapping into the collective wisdom of the net—to find out how to do something or to get ad-vice on some problem, whether it is with a computer issue, or some unrelated technical or recreational issue. Even if I'm not planning on becoming a long-term member of the group, simply by doing a little lurking in advance I can determine if my question is appropriate to the group, if it has already been asked and an-swered, and what sorts of replies I am likely to receive from my query.

Scuba Tanks, Motorcycles and Denizens of Doom

Some Usenet groups are community-oriented—that is, the group has gathered together to discuss a topic, and the population is more or less stable. Although the group's population may be increasing because of the general pop-ulation increase on the net, posters tend to stick around for significant periods of time and get to know one another. Other groups are more of a resource, and most participants are drop-ins or transients. A few regulars volunteer, in essence, to run a public service: for example, maintaining FTP-able archives of past postings and FAQs.[1] A terrific example of this type of group is *rec.scuba*. People post reviews of scuba service providers in locations around the globe. These reviews are collected into an FTP archive and made available via the FAQ. The posting population of *rec.scuba* tends to write in a fairly professional fashion, with a high signal-to-noise ratio, that is, the interesting or useful posts (signals) outnumber the boring, repetitive, flaming or just plain useless posts (noise). The questions are well-formed, and the answers are thoughtful. Indeed, I've found that most recreational groups targeted to real-life activities, as op-posed to online-based activities, contain serious enthusiasts who enjoy helping new people learn about their activity and enjoy talking about their experiences with related equipment and locales. It may appear otherwise to the dilettante:

All the posters seem to have so much experience and skill in the activity that they would not welcome a novice posting. I've generally found, though, that as long as I am polite and my question or comment is well-phrased, I will not be laughed off the group, but instead will receive helpful advice.

Noncontroversial topic-oriented groups, by definition, are less likely than controversial groups to be full of flames. Low-traffic groups will also be nicer. Generally in a low-traffic group fewer people post, fostering a sense of community and lowering the probability of a bad apple. In a small community, would-be flamers may come to respect the opinions of others in the group more and tone down their own messages. If a group is too large, a post is just one in a multitude, which is nearly equivalent to anonymity, and it's easier to be nasty when you're anonymous. In a huge group it's easy to feel that *they* don't care about *you* so why should *you* care about them? This lack of community reinforces itself, and pretty soon you have a group full of hate-filled messages far beyond reasonable expectations. But this is not a hard-and-fast rule: There *are* nice large groups. The best way to tell is to observe for a few weeks.

For example, *rec.motorcycles* is a high-volume community-oriented group where you will find folks who've been around since before Usenet posting right alongside folks who hadn't even heard of the net a year ago. *Rec.motorcycles* is quite nice, especially considering how the naive outsider might otherwise stereotype its posters. I've been active on and off for several years and am a member of the official *rec.motorcycles* motorcycle club, the Denizens of Doom. I'm not active now because of the volume; the group gets well over two hundred messages a day, and I simply haven't got the time. What I've found, though, is that *rec.motorcycles* is generally full of helpful people whenever you have a technical question about motorcycles and motorcycling. Denizens are tolerant of most frequently asked questions and proffer lots of useful advice in response to questions regardless of how trivial or technical they may be. Yet denizens can have a bite, should you trespass into one of the forbidden zones. There are a number of in-jokes, most having to do with the club, references to old posts or (sometimes apocryphal) stories about real-life gatherings. If you ask an obvious newbie-question about one of these in-jokes, you'll get bitten. The only way to enjoy them is to be patient; hints get dropped regularly that will give you a clue to what the jokes are about.

A lot of the social and recreational (*soc.* and *rec.*) groups have real-life get-togethers. For *rec.motorcycles*, there are organized group rides, and once while visiting California I was able to join local rec.motorcyclists for dinner. Attending even just one such get-together can be very helpful for a better understanding of people's messages. The printed (or displayed) word lacks a lot of expressive power that comes from facial expression and voice tone. Meeting other posters can compensate for those losses and soften what might otherwise seem harsh words. It gives you as reader a voice to hear, as though the poster were reading the post aloud, making it easier to imagine appropriate facial expression and tone of voice. Obviously it's not practical to meet everyone in a global network, but meeting even a few can help make Usenet seem more personal.

Warlording

Some groups on the net have nastiness and flaming almost built in. Certainly such groups as *alt.flame* are solely dedicated to flaming and have raised it to an art form: you get flamed if your flame isn't hot enough. But there are also many political groups you would hope would be a place for informed debate, yet which devolve into name-calling at the slightest provocation. *Talk.politics.abortion* is the canonical example of such a group. People have strong views, and they express those views in the strongest possible terms. To make matters worse, the attitude of "if you can't stand the heat, get out of the kitchen" prevails in many Usenet groups. Quiet, sensitive, thoughtful people are drowned out. I stay away from such places. Even if you too have strong feelings, there is little point in subjecting yourself to this sort of abuse in the vain (and it *is* vain) effort to change the minds of a few people. Far better to support the local real-life grassroots organization that promotes your point of view, or to write your government representatives, agencies or local or national news and educational media to express your views.

Some of the topic-oriented groups discuss an online topic rather than a real-life topic. It is much easier for one of these groups to develop a bad attitude or bad reputation—somehow grounding a topic in real life helps foster an attitude of friendliness or helpfulness.[2] And some of these online topic groups go out of their way to be unfriendly.

Besides *alt.flame*, another such group is *alt.fan.warlord*. The origins of the group's name may be obscure, but the group's purpose is very evident: to publicly ridicule a certain class of net newbie and net idiot—those with preposterous .signature files. Being "warlorded" is a not a pleasant experience.

Sigs

A .signature file automatically includes your contact information, email address, and so on into a posting, saving you the trouble of remembering to sign a message and preventing you from making embarrassing typos in your email address or other pertinent information. Signature files can be quite useful, and thus the feature is included in most posting programs. However, it opens up a whole world of potential silliness and abuse: Arbitrary text can be included in all of one's postings with nearly zero effort. When something is effortless to do, one doesn't necessarily take into account the impact one's actions have upon others. And when something is automatic, as is the inclusion of .signature files, one doesn't necessarily realize or remember that this is occurring, or even what the .signature file contains. This can have embarrassing results, for instance, when someone has edited their .signature to contain a joke and forgets to remove the joke while posting on a serious newsgroup, or if someone overreacts to the ability to have a .signature and creates a large, complex file full of difficult-to-decipher, allegedly artistically presented information, which keeps getting posted over and over, creating an eyesore for readers across the globe.

Let me include my own .signature file and explain why it collects compliments rather than flames. First, I have several signature files, all very similar, but slightly tailored to the group I'm posting to—I recommend this approach, as it permits you to make in-jokes for one group without forcing them upon another group that may not care or may deride you for it. Since I have more than one, I must choose which to use, and manually insert it, raising the effort level and thus the amount of thought required. Sure, computers are supposed to reduce effort, but they should not reduce effort so far as to eliminate thought! This is my *rec.motorcycles* signature:

```
Judy Anderson yclept yduJ        'yduJ' rhymes with 'fudge'
   yduJ@cs.stanford.edu                DoD #166
Join the League for Programming Freedom, lpf@uunet.uu.net
```

The good parts: It's very short, and it says clearly who I am and how to contact me. It has one cutesy thing ("yduJ rhymes with fudge"); I've been using this since I began posting on the net, and it has become a sort of trademark. Thus it lends consistency; people recognize me from one group to another by this phrase. It has one private reference, to my Denizens of Doom membership number, which is good as long as I confine myself to posts to *rec.motorcycles* and related groups with this signature, otherwise people don't have a clue what it means.

The bad parts: It contains an advertisement. The advertisement is short, though, which does alleviate it somewhat, and the League for Programming Freedom happens to be neutral or politically correct within most Usenet communities, so this hasn't gotten me flamed. It contains one archaic word (yclept).[3] This generates primarily queries rather than flames, but still it is the sort of thing that a good signature writer will think about carefully before including.

There are a lot of things this signature does not have: It does not have ascii art. It does not attempt to emphasize itself with a surrounding box of asterisks. It is written in mixed case. There are no spelling errors. It does not have a quote from some well-known personality, or worse yet, a quote from an obscure personality (a quote can be all right if it's short and sweet and useful as a trademark, but it's important to avoid long quotes. Allegedly funny quotes can be problematic as people's senses of humor are quite varied.)

The aforementioned *alt.fan.warlord* group is a reaction to the over-the-top signature, a network-wide blight afflicting all groups. But, as in many such things, warlorders can themselves go overboard, no holds barred and pulling no punches. It is not a newsgroup for the faint of heart, though when in the right mood I get a certain smug satisfaction from being a member of this "elite," laughing at the plebes with their pathetic attempts to be seen as different among the masses. But one definitely has to be in the right mood for it.

Brush Strokes in ASCII

A signature element participants in *al.fan.warlord* deride with vehemence is ascii art. Ascii art (really ASCII, American Standard Code for Information Interchange, the internal code of most computers which translates into ordinary text) is an art form in which the characters on the screen form the lines that make up the picture. For instance, one can make large "fonts" out of horizontal, vertical and diagonal lines from some punctuation characters. A lot of ascii art is schlock, but a talented and patient artist can do quite a lot with the medium. As one might expect, there is a newsgroup dedicated to ascii art. I have been a frequent contributor, not as an artist, but as a collector. I have been collecting ascii art since I saw my first picture, and my collection is now quite extensive. Even with more than fifteen years of collecting, I am constantly amazed at the variety and quality of art that can be created. As just one example, I show here a piece created by Rowan Crawford, a very prolific ascii artist from Australia.

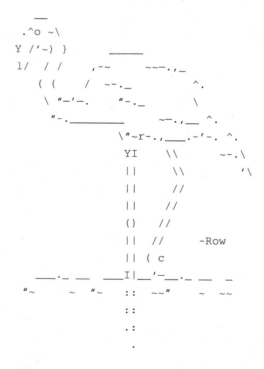

The choice of just a few individual letters, punctuation and spacing (which make up the brush strokes) can make the difference between a rough, ugly picture and an aesthetic one. Of course, more of the former gets posted, because not everyone is as talented as Rowan.

It is every *alt.* group's dream to upgrade to a mainstream group.[4] I helped in *alt.ascii-art*'s attainment of that goal: There is now also *rec.arts.ascii*, with primarily the same content, though a slightly different population and tone. To upgrade, one has to go through a fairly lengthy process of writing a proposal, participating in a discussion period and, finally, waiting out the voting period. I felt I had two jobs in this campaign: First, to help make sure the proposal was acceptable to the Usenet cabal, and second, to prevent young, bubbly *alt.ascii-artists* from inadvertently biasing the vote against the group by bringing their misplaced enthusiasm to older, more staid groups during the campaign. There isn't really a Usenet cabal, conspiracy theorists aside; it is simply that some people prefer to spend their recreational network time by commenting on all new group proposals. A lot of these people are smart and experienced and know what does and doesn't work in Usenet groups. Another group is made up of hot-heads who have strong opinions, whether right or wrong, on how the net should be run. It's not all that difficult to accept the advice of the experienced folks while dodging the flames of the hotheads, but it entails some careful wording of messages, and my experience at deflecting flames was helpful in this task.

Alt.ascii-art is a good beginner's group (for those interested in the subject). Where many people go wrong, though, is in bringing the lessons of the "good beginner's group" to the rest of the net. Ascii art gets its bad reputation because some of its fans tend to lose sight of the fact that it is inappropriate to post a three-screenful picture of a vaguely helical shape to *sci.med* on the grounds that it represents a strand of DNA.

The community of *alt.ascii-art* is very much the antithesis of *alt.fan.war-lord*. It is full of young, (usually overly) enthusiastic, would-be artists, who are prolific posters of primarily schlock (though, for a collector, the gems in there are definitely worth waiting for). They bubble about their own cool art and other people's cool art, they ask huge numbers of Frequently Asked Questions, they can't spell and they repost messages multiple times per week. In contrast, *alt.fan.warlord* members usually have several years' experience under their belt and have seen it all, over and over and over, so they make fun of everyone, even those whose transgressions are quite small. You might think it difficult to be a member of both communities, but by altering my frame of mind appropriately I find it possible to view the same .signature as beautiful on *alt.ascii-art* and laughably inappropriate when quoted on *alt.fan.warlord*.

What Really Counts

The phrase "On the Internet, no one knows you're a dog" appeared in *The New Yorker* in a P. Steiner cartoon in 1993. It is something that one should take to heart. Usenet, while it can be nasty, acerbic, uncaring and unsympathetic, is a truly nondiscriminatory society. It judges you only through your postings, not by what you look like, your marital status, whether you have a disability, or any of the other things that are traditionally used for discrimination. I have read *misc.handicap* postings written by a deaf-blind woman; nothing in the postings showed any sign of disability. If you have a cooperative administration, even your name (and thus presumed gender) can be masked or changed.

In general, it is your opinions and your manner of expression that really count. I like to think that people respect me; the responses I receive to my postings confirm that they do. My postings are not immune to being flamed, but usually I am expecting it, whether it is because of the opinion I express or the manner in which I express it. I feel I have a lot of control over how people perceive me. What works in one group may not work in another, but with careful reading, I've determined what will be accepted, appreciated and even admired. By paying attention to simple things such as using proper spelling and adequate grammar, as well as more subtle things such as the mood and traditions of the target group, you can become a well-respected poster, whether it be as an asker of intelligent questions or a good source of information.

Notes

1. FTP refers to File Transfer Protocol, a standard Internet protocol that allows a user to log on to a remote computer and transfer public files to their own computer.

2. A big exception to this generalization is *talk.politics.abortion*, which is completely flame-ridden.

3. *yclept* is the past participate of *clepe*, an archaic word meaning "to name or call."

4. Mainstream groups are *rec* (recreational), *soc* (social), *talk* (discussion), *sci* (scientific), *comp* (computer related), *news* (relating to Usenet itself) and *misc* (all other categories). *Alt* is a separate hierarchy with different politics and rules for group creation and propagation.

READING REFLECTIONS

1. What strategies does Judy Anderson suggest when joining virtual communities such as Usenet, and why are such strategies important for first-time participants in these forums?

2. Anderson claims that "Usenet, while it can be nasty, acerbic, uncaring and unsympathetic, is truly a nondiscriminatory society." Test this position by joining a new newsgroup you are not normally a part of and remaining on-line for several weeks. Contrast this to other on-line communities you may belong to. How do people respond to you on various lists? Consider responding in the form of a letter or posting to members of the community, or even as a Web page accessible to other members of your class and the group in question.

3. Explain the concept of "flaming" and what social factors may account for this particular on-line behavior.
4. Anderson notes that "It is easier to lose your shyness on the net than in a classroom." Why is this? Do you agree?
5. In what context does Anderson refer to the "On the Internet, nobody knows you're a dog" cartoon we profile at the beginning of this chapter? What point is she trying to make in this reference?

THE STRANGE CASE OF THE ELECTRONIC LOVER

Lindsy Van Gelder

Today, gender-bending abounds in on-line chat rooms. Although many Internet users tout the liberation of choosing to adopt male, female, or gender-neutral identity, questions of honesty and ethics have always been an issue, particularly in romantic relationships. Lindsay Van Gelder's experience as a participant on CompuServe is a case in point, as she reported in an early but now infamous case of gender deception.

Lindsy Van Gelder is a long-time contributor to Ms. *magazine whose most recent writings include* The Girls Next Door: Into the Heart of Lesbian America *(1996). In this article, which originally appeared in* Ms., *Van Gelder analyzes the ethical and moral implications of gender deception on-line in the case of a prominent male psychiatrist masquerading on-line as a disabled woman.*

I "met" Joan in the late spring of 1983, shortly after I first hooked my personal computer up to a modem and entered the strange new world of on-line communications. Like me, Joan was spending a great deal of time on the "CB" channel of the national network CompuServe, where one can encounter other modem owners in what amounts to a computer version of CB radio. I was writing an article for *Ms.* about modems and doing on-line interviews with CB regulars. Joan was already a sought-after celebrity among the hundreds of users who hung out on the channel—a telecommunications media star.

Her "handle" was "Talkin' Lady." According to the conventions of the medium, people have a (usually frivolous) handle when they're on "open" channels with many users; but when two people choose to enter a private talk mode, they'll often exchange real information about themselves. I soon learned that her real name was Joan Sue Greene, and that she was a New York neuropsychologist in her late twenties, who had been severely disfigured in a car accident that was the fault of a drunken driver. The accident had killed her boyfriend; Joan herself spent a year in the hospital, being treated for brain damage, which affected both her speech and her ability to walk. Mute, confined to a wheelchair, and frequently suffering intense back and leg pain, Joan had at first been so embittered about her disabilities that she literally didn't want to live.

Then her mentor, a former professor at Johns Hopkins, presented her with a computer, a modem, and a year's subscription to CompuServe to be used specifically doing what Joan was doing—making friends on-line. At first, her handle had been "Quiet Lady," in reference to her muteness. But Joan could type—which is, after all, how one "talks" on a computer—and she had a sassy, bright, generous personality that blossomed in a medium where physicality doesn't count. Joan became enormously popular, and her new handle, "Talkin' Lady," was a reflection of her new sense of self. Over the next two years, she became a monumental on-line presence who served both as a support for other disabled women and as an inspiring stereotype-smasher to the able-bodied. Through her many intense friendships and (in some cases) her on-line romances, she changed the lives of dozens of women.

Thus it was a huge shock early this year when, through a complicated series of events, Joan was revealed as being not disabled at all. More to the point, Joan, in fact, was not a woman. She was really a man we'll call Alex—a prominent New York psychiatrist in his early fifties who was engaged in a bizarre, all-consuming experiment to see what it felt like to be female, and to experience the intimacy of female friendships.

Even those who barely knew Joan felt implicated—and somehow betrayed—by Alex's deception. Many of us on-line like to believe that we're a utopian community of the future, and Alex's experiment proved to us all that technology is no shield against deceit. We lost our innocence, if not our faith.

To some of Alex's victims—including a woman who had an affair with the real-life Alex, after being introduced to him by Joan—the experiment was a "mind rape," pure and simple. (Several people, in fact, have tentatively explored the possibility of bringing charges against Alex as a psychiatrist—although the case is without precedent, to put it mildly.) To some other victims, Alex was not so much an impostor as a seeker whose search went out of control. (Several of these are attempting to continue a friendship with Alex—and, as one woman put it, "to relate to the soul, not the sex of the person. The soul is the same as before.")

Either way, this is a peculiarly modern story about a man who used some of our most up-to-date technology to play out some of our oldest assumptions about gender roles.

More than most stories, it requires a bit of background. A modem, of course, is the device that connects a computer to the phone and from there to any other similarly equipped computer. CompuServe is the largest of a number of modem networks; it charges its subscribers an initial small fee to open an account with a special ID number and then charges hourly fees for access to its hundreds of services, from stock reports to airline information. In addition to its business services, the network also offers a number of "social" services (including numerous Special Interest Groups—SIGs—and the CB channels) where users can mingle.

The unfolding of an on-line relationship is unique, combining the thrill of ultrafuturistic technology with the veneration of the written word that informed 19th-century friendships and romances. Most people who haven't used the medium have trouble imagining what it's like to connect with other people whose words are wafting across your computer screen. For starters, it's dizzyingly egalitarian, since the most important thing about oneself isn't age, appearance, career success, health, race, gender, sexual preference, accent, or any of the other categories by which we normally judge each other, but one's *mind*. My personal experience has been that I often respond to the minds of people whom, because of my own prejudices (or theirs), I might otherwise not meet. (For example, my best friend on-line is from Appalachia, which I once thought was inhabited only by Li'l Abner and the Dukes of Hazzard. My friend, in turn, had never had a gay friend before.)

But such mind-to-mind encounters presume that the people at both keyboards are committed to getting past labels and into some new, truer way of relating. In the wake of the Alex/Joan scandal, some on-line habitués have soberly concluded that perhaps there's a thin line between getting out of one's skin and getting into a completely false identity—and that the medium may even encourage impersonation. (One network, for example, has a brochure showing a man dressed up as Indiana Jones, Michael Jackson, and an Olympic athlete; the copy reads, "Be anything you want on American PEOPLE/LINK.") Still, when it works, it works. Disabled people are especially well represented on-line, and most of them say that it's a medium where they can make a first impression on their own terms.

Another positive consequence of the medium's mind-to-mind potential— and this is germane to Joan's story—is that it's powerfully conducive to intimacy. Thoughts and emotions are the coin of this realm, and people tend to share them sooner than they would in "real life" (what CBers refer to as "offline"). Some people, in fact, become addicted to computer relationships, per se. But most use the modem merely as a way to start relationships that way, in time, continue off-line. After several on-line conversations with someone who seems especially compatible, people commonly arrange to speak on the telephone, to exchange photographs, and eventually, to meet in person, either by themselves or at one of the regular "CB parties" held around the country. (Several marriages have resulted from on-line meetings on CompuServe CB alone.) I've met four good computer friends in person, and found them all much the same off-line as on. For me, the only odd thing about these relationships has been their chronology. It's a little surreal to know intimate details about someone's childhood before you've ever been out to dinner together.

One of the reasons that Joan's real identity went undetected for so long was that her supposed disability prevented her from speaking on the phone. (Several people did communicate with Joan on the phone, in one case because Joan had said that she wanted to hear the sound of the other woman's voice. Joan in turn "would make horrible noises into the receiver—little yelps and moans.") There was also the matter of Joan's disfigurement; she supposedly drooled and had a "smashed up" face, untreatable by plastic surgery. She was, she said, embarrassed to meet her computer friends in person. Those who wanted to be sensitive to disabled concerns naturally didn't push. It was an ingenious cover.

Alex supposedly began his dual identity by mistake. One of the social realities of the computing world is that the majority of its inhabitants are male; women usually get a lot of attention from all the men on-line. (Women who don't want to be continually pestered by requests from strange males to go into private talk mode often use androgynous handles.) Female handles also get attention from other women, since many women on-line are pioneering females in their fields and feminists. Alex apparently came on-line sometime in late 1982 or early 1983 and adopted the handle "Shrink, Inc." His epiphany came one evening when he was in private talk mode with a woman who for some reason mistook him for a female shrink. "The person was open with him in a way that stunned him," according to one of the women—let's call her Laura—who has maintained a friendship with Alex. "What he really found as Joan was that most women opened up to him in a way he had never seen before in all his years of practice. And he realized he could help them."

"He later told me that his female patients had trouble relating to him— they always seemed to be leaving something out," said Janis Goodall, a Berkeley, California, software firm employee who also knew both Joan and Alex. "Now he could see what it was." (Despite their similar recollections, Goodall is in the opposite camp from Laura, and says: "For someone supposedly dedicated to helping people, I think he rampaged through all of our feelings with despicable disregard.") At some point after "Shrink, Inc.'s" inadvertent plunge into sisterhood, Joan was born.

According to both Goodall and Laura (both of whom are disabled themselves), Alex has a back condition, "arthritis of the spine or a calcium deposit of some kind," according to Goodall, "which causes him discomfort, and has the potential, but *not* the probability of putting him in a wheelchair someday." Goodall added that Alex later defended his choice of a disabled persona by claiming that he "wanted to find out how disabled people deal with it." Others on-line believe that Joan's handicaps were a way both to shroud her real identity and aggrandize her heroic stature.

If Joan began spontaneously, she soon became a far more conscious creation, complete with electronic mail drop, special telephone line, and almost novelistically detailed biography (although she sometimes told different versions to different people). She was, by my own recollection and by the accounts of everyone interviewed, an exquisitely wrought character. For starters, she had guts. (She had once, before the accident, driven alone across the interior of Iceland as a way to cure her agoraphobia.) She had traveled everywhere, thanks to money left to her by her family's textile mill fortune. She lived alone (although neighbors checked on her and helped her with errands) and was a model independent female. In fact, Joan was quite a feminist. It was she who suggested the formation of a women's issues group within CompuServe, and she actively recruited members. Several women had relationships with Joan in which they referred to each other as "sister."

Joan was earthy, too, and spoke easily about sex. One woman remembers hearing at length about Joan's abortion at age 16; another recalls having a long conversation about Joan's decision not to embark on a particular course of spinal surgery that might relieve her leg pain, but "would also affect her clitoral nerve, and she wouldn't do that." She was bisexual. Although her family had been religious (she told some people that her parents were ministers), she herself was an ardent atheist who liked to engage religious people in debate. She was also a grass-smoker who frequently confessed to being a little stoned if you encountered her late at night. Her usual greeting was a flashy, flamboyant "Hi!!!!!!!!!!!!!"

Interestingly, the two people who knew Joan and also met Alex in person say that their surface personalities were opposite. Alex is Jewish. He almost never drinks or smokes pot (although one of his medical specialties is pharmacology). He is a workaholic whose American Psychiatric Association biography reports wide publication in his field. "Joan was wild and zingy and flamboyant and would do anything you dared her to," notes Laura. "A part of Alex wanted to be like that, but he's actually quite intellectual and shy." Adds Janis Goodall: "Alex has a great deal of trouble expressing his emotions. There are long silences, and then he'll say, 'uh-huh, uh-huh'—just like a shrink."

Above all, Joan was a larger-than-life exemplary disabled person. At the time of her accident, she had been scheduled to teach a course at a major New York medical school (in fact, the teaching hospital that Alex is affiliated with as a psychiatrist). Ironically, Joan noted, the course dealt with many of the same neurological impairments that she herself now suffered. One of Joan's goals was eventually to resume her career as if the accident had never happened—and when I first knew her, she was embarked on an ambitious plan to employ a computer in the classroom to help her teach. The idea was that Joan would type her lecture into a computer, which would then be either magnified on a classroom screen or fed into student terminals. To all of us techno-fans and believers in better living through computers, it was a thrilling concept.

Joan was also a militant activist against the dangers of drunken drivers. Early in her convalescence, when she was frequently half out of her mind with anger, she had on several occasions wheeled herself out of her apartment and onto the streets of Manhattan, where she would shout at passing motorists. On one such occasion, police officers in her precinct, upon learning her story, suggested that she put her rage and her talent to more productive use. Joan then began to go out on patrol with a group of traffic cops whose job it was to catch drunken drivers. Joan's role in the project was twofold: (1) as a highly credentialed neuropsychologist, she was better trained than most to detect cars whose drivers had reflex problems caused by too much drinking, and (2) she was willing to serve as an example to drunken drivers of what could befall them if they didn't shape up.

On one of Joan's forays, she met a young police officer named Jack Carr. As he and Joan spent more time together, he came to appreciate her spirit in much the same way the rest of us had. They fell in love—much to the distress of Jack's mother, who thought he was throwing his life away. (Joan's on-line friends were heartened to learn much later that Mrs. Carr had softened after Joan bought her a lap-top computer, and the two of them learned to communicate in the on-line world where Joan shone so brightly.) Jack occasionally came on-line with Joan, although I remember him as being shy and far less verbal than Joan.

Shortly after I met Joan, she and Jack got married. Joan sent an elaborate and joyous announcement to all her CB pals via electronic mail, and the couple held an on-line reception, attended by more than 30 CompuServe regulars. (On-line parties are not unusual. People just type in all the festive sound effects, from the clink of champagne glasses to the tossing of confetti.) Joan and Jack honeymooned in Cyprus, which, according to Pamela Bowen, a Huntington, West Virginia, newspaper editor, Joan said "was one of the few places she'd never been." Bowen and many of Joan's other on-line friends received postcards from Cyprus. The following year Joan and Jack returned to Cyprus and sent out another batch of cards.

"I remember asking Joan how she would get around on her vacation," recalls Sheila Deitz, associate professor of law and psychology at the University of Virginia. "Joan simply replied that if need be, he'd carry her. He was the quintessential caring, nurturing, loving, sensitive human being"—a Mr. Right who, Deitz adds, exerted enormous pull on the imaginations of all Joan's on-line female friends. In hindsight, Deitz feels, "he was the man Alex would have loved to be"—but in fact could only be in the persona of a woman.

Joan was extraordinarily generous. On one occasion, when Laura was confined to her bed because of her disability and couldn't use her regular computer, Joan sent her a lap-top model—a gift worth hundreds of dollars. On another occasion, when Laura mentioned that no one had ever sent her roses, Joan had two dozen delivered. Marti Cloutier, a 42-year-old Massachusetts woman with grown children, claims that it was Joan who inspired her to start college. "She made me feel I could do it at my age." When it came time for Cloutier to write her first term paper, she was terrified, but Joan helped her through it, both in terms of moral support and in the practical sense of sending her a long list of sources. (Ironically, Cloutier's assignment was a psychology paper on multiple personalities. She got an "A" in the course.) On another occasion, Joan told Cloutier that she was going out to hear the "Messiah" performed. When Cloutier enviously mentioned that she loved the music, Joan mailed her the tape. On still another occasion, when Cloutier and her husband were having difficulties over the amount of time that she spent on-line, Joan volunteered to "talk" to him. Cloutier's husband is also a part-time police officer, as Jack ostensibly was, and he and Joan easily developed a rapport. According to Marti Cloutier, Joan was able to persuade him that if his wife had her own friends and interests, it would ultimately be good for their marriage. "She was always doing good things," Cloutier recalls, and "and never asking anything in return."

My personal recollections are similar. Once, when Joan and I were chatting on-line late at night, I realized to my great disbelief that a bat had somehow gotten into my apartment and was flapping wildly about, with my cats in crazed pursuit. I got off the computer, managed to catch the bat and get it back out the window—but in the attendant confusion, the windowpane fell out of the window and onto my arm, slicing my wrist and palm. Needless to say, I ended up in the emergency room. Joan dropped me several extremely solicitous notes over the next few weeks, making sure that my stitches were healing properly and that I was over the scare of the accident. Even earlier, around the time I first met Joan, the child of two of my oldest friends was hit by a car and knocked into a coma that was to last for several weeks. Joan had a lot of thoughts about the physiology of comas, as well as about how to deal with hospital staffs, insurance companies, and one's own unraveling psyche in the midst of such a crisis. She offered to set up an on-line meeting with the child's mother. I later heard that Joan had also helped several women who had suicidal tendencies or problems with alcohol.

Still another way that Joan nurtured her friends—hilarious as it sounds in hindsight—was to try to keep CB free of impostors. Although Joan was probably the slickest and most long-lived impostor around, she was hardly the only one; they are a continuing phenomenon on CompuServe, and on every other network. Some lie about their ages, others about their accomplishments. Some appropriate the handles of established CB personae and impersonate them. (Unlike ID numbers, handles can be whatever you choose them to be.) There are also numerous other gender benders, some of them gay or bisexual men who come on in female guise to straight men. Most aren't hard to spot. Joan herself told several friends she had been fooled by a man pretending to be a gay woman, and she was furious. "One of the first things she ever told me," recalls Janis Goodall, "was to be terribly careful of the people you meet on CB—that things were not always as they seemed."

Sheila Deitz remembers meeting a man on-line who said he was single, but turned out to be not only married in real life, but romancing numerous women on-line. Deitz met the man off-line and realized that his story was full of holes. "Joan was very sympathetic when I told her about it, and we agreed that we didn't want this guy to have the chance to pull this on other women." At some later point, according to Deitz, "Joan created a group called the Silent Circle. It was sort of an on-line vigilante group. She'd ferret out other impostors and confront them and tell them they'd better get their act together."

All of Joan's helping and nurturing and gift-giving, in Deitz's opinion, "goes beyond what any professional would want to do. Alex fostered dependency, really." But at the time, especially among those of us who are able-bodied, there was a certain feeling that here was a person who needed all the support we could give her. Numerous disabled women have since rightly pointed out that our Take-a-Negro-to-Lunch-like attitudes were in fact incredibly patronizing.

The truth is that there was always another side to Joan's need to be needed. She could be obnoxiously grabby of one's time. Because she and I both lived in New York, she once suggested that we talk directly, modem to modem, over our phone lines—thus paying only the cost of a local call instead of CompuServe's $6 an hour connect charges. But as soon as I gave Joan my phone number, I was sorry. She called constantly—the phone would ring, and there would be her modem tone—and she refused to take the hint that I might be busy with work, lover, or children. "Everybody else had the same experience," according to Bob Walter, a New York publisher who also runs CompuServe's Health SIG, where Joan (and later Alex, too) frequently hung out. "She would bombard people with calls." Finally, I had to get blunt—and I felt guilty about it, since Joan, after all, was a disabled woman whose aggressive personality was probably the best thing she had going for her. (My first somewhat sexist thought, when I found out that Joan was really a man, was *Of course! Who else would be so pushy?*)

Joan was sexually aggressive. Every woman I interviewed reported—and was troubled by—Joan's pressuring to have "compusex." This is on-line sex, similar to phone sex, in which people type out their hottest fantasies while they masturbate. (In the age of herpes and AIDS, it has become increasingly popular.) According to one woman, "one time she said she and Jack had been smoking pot and then he'd gone off to work, but she was still high. She told me she had sexual feelings toward me and asked if I felt the same." (Joan's husband, who was conveniently off on undercover detail most nights, supposedly knew about these experiments and wasn't threatened by them, since Joan's partners were "only" other women.) Her m.o., at least with friends, was to establish an intense nonsexual intimacy, and then to come on to them, usually with the argument that compusex was a natural extension of their friendship. In one case, cited by several sources, a woman became so involved as Joan's compusex lover that she was on the verge of leaving her husband.

Interestingly, Joan never came on to me—or, to my knowledge, to any bisexual or gay women. Sheila Deitz is of the opinion that Alex only wanted to have "lesbian" compusex with heterosexual women, those whom he might actually be attracted to in real life. Some straight women apparently cooperated sexually not out of physical desire, but out of supportiveness or even pity—and this too might have been part of Alex's game. But it would be misleading to overemphasize Joan's sexual relationships, since compusex in general tends to be a more casual enterprise on-line than affairs of the heart and mind. Deitz estimates that at least 15 people were "badly burned" by the revelation that Joan was Alex, and that only a few were compusex partners. Lovers or not, most were caught in Joan's emotional web.

Janis Goodall was in a category all her own. Now 37 and cheerfully describing herself as "a semiretired hippie from 'Berserkeley,' California," Goodall met Joan at a time in her life "when I was a real sick cookie—an open raw wound." Goodall was herself coping with the emotional and physical aftermath of an automobile accident. (Although she can walk, Goodall's legs are badly scarred and she suffers from both arthritis and problems of the sciatic nerve.) Beyond her injuries, Goodall was also dealing with a recent separation from her husband and her brother's death. "It was Joan who helped me to deal with those things, and to make the transition into the life of a disabled person who accepts that she's disabled."

Joan and Goodall were "fixed up" by other CompuServe regulars after Goodall attended an on-line conference on pain management. When she and Joan arranged via electronic mail to meet in CB, "it was love at first sight. By the end of that first discussion, which lasted a couple of hours, we were honorary sisters. Later, I went around profusely thanking everyone who had told me to contact her."

The fact that Joan's disability was more severe than her own gave her an authority in Goodall's eyes, and her humor was especially therapeutic. "We used to make jokes about gimps who climb mountains. At the time, just to get through the day was a major accomplishment for me, and my attitude was screw the mountains, let me go to the grocery store." The two never became lovers, despite strenuous lobbying on Joan's part. ("I often found myself apologizing for being straight," said Goodall.) But they did become intense, close friends. "I loved her. She could finish my sentences and read my mind."

About a year ago, Joan began telling Goodall about "this great guy" who was also on-line. His name was Alex. He was a psychiatrist, very respected in his field, and an old friend of Joan's, an associate at the hospital. Largely on the strength of Joan's enthusiastic recommendation, Goodall responded with pleasure when Alex invited her into private talk mode. "During our second or third conversation, he began to get almost romantic. He clearly thought I was the greatest thing since sliced bread. I couldn't understand why an established Manhattan psychiatrist his age could be falling so quickly for a retired hippie—

although of course I was very flattered. Hey, if a shrink thought I was okay, I was okay!"

Alex told Goodall that he was married, but that his marriage was in trouble. Last winter he invited her to come visit him in New York, and when she said she couldn't afford it, he sent her a round-trip ticket. "He treated me like a queen for the four days I was there," Goodall remembers. "He put me up at a Fifth Avenue hotel—the American Stanhope, right across the street from the Metropolitan Museum. He took me to the Russian Tea Room for dinner, the Carnegie Deli for breakfast, Serendipity for ice cream, museums, everywhere—he even introduced me to his daughters." The two became lovers, although, Goodall says, his back problems apparently affected his ability and their sex life was less than satisfactory. Still, it seems to have been a minor off note in a fabulously romantic weekend. There were also many gifts. Once, Goodall says, "he went out to the corner drugstore to get cigarettes and came back with caviar. I went back to Berkeley on Cloud Nine."

Naturally, Goodall had also hoped that she might meet Joan during her New York holiday. None of Joan's other women friends had. Some of the able-bodied women, especially, were hurt that Joan still felt shame about her appearance after so many protestations of love and friendship. According to Sheila Deitz, several people were reported to have arranged rendezvous with Joan and were stood up at the last minute—"although you just know Alex had to be lurking about somewhere, checking them out." Joan would, in each case, claim to have gotten cold feet.

Marti Cloutier says that Joan told her that she had promised her husband that she would never meet any of her on-line friends, but "that *if* she ever changed her mind and decided to meet any of her on-line friends, I would be one of them." In fact, the only CB person who had ever seen Joan was her hospital colleague—Alex. Over the course of Goodall's four days in the city, she and Alex both tried to reach Joan by phone, but without success. Goodall had brought Joan a gift—a stylized, enameled mask of a smiling face. Alex promised to deliver it.

Back in Berkeley, Goodall resumed her on-line relationship with Joan, who had been out of town for the weekend. Joan, however, was anxious to hear every detail of Goodall's trip. Did she think she was in love with Alex? Was the sex good?

It was the disabled women on-line who figured it out first. "Some things about her condition were very farfetched," says one. Says another woman: "The husband, the accomplishments—it just didn't ring true from the beginning." But her own hunch wasn't that Joan was a male or able-bodied; she suspected that she was in fact a disabled woman who was pretending to have a life of dazzling romance and success.

Although such theories, however, ultimately ran up against the real postcards from Cyprus, people began to share their misgivings. "There were too many contradictions," says Bob Walter. "Here was this person who ran off to conferences and to vacations and did all these phenomenal things, but she wouldn't let her friends on-line even see her. After a while, it just didn't compute."

In hindsight, I wonder why I didn't question some of Joan's exploits more closely. As a journalist, I've dealt with the public relations representatives of both the New York City Police Department and the hospital where Joan supposedly taught—and it now seems strange to me that her exploits as drunk-spotter and handicapped professor weren't seized on and publicized. Pamela Bowen says she once proposed Joan's story to another editor, but urged him "to have somebody interview her in person because her story was too good to be true. So my instincts were right from the beginning, but I felt guilty about not believing a handicapped person. I mean, the story *could* have been true." It's possible that many of us able-bodied were playing out our own need to see members of minority groups as "exceptional." The more exceptional a person is, the less the person in the majority group has to confront fears of disability and pain.

Even with the contradictions, the game might have continued much longer if Joan hadn't brought Alex into the picture. According to both Goodall and Laura, Alex has, since his unmasking, said that he realized at some point that he had gotten in over his head, and he concocted a plan to kill Joan off. But after seeing how upset people were on one occasion when Joan was off-line for several weeks, supposedly ill, he apparently couldn't go through with it. "It would have been a lot less risky for him to let Joan die," according to Laura, "but he knew it would be cruel." (Meanwhile, someone had called the hospital where Joan was thought to be a patient and been told that no such person was registered.)

What Alex seems to have done instead of commit compu-murder was to buy a new ID number and begin his dual *on-line* identity. Joan increasingly introduced people to her friend Alex, always with great fanfare. We may never know what Alex intended to do with Joan eventually, but there's certainly strong evidence that he was now trying to form attachments as Alex, both off-line (with Goodall) and on.

One might imagine that The Revelation came with a big bang and mass gasps, but this was not the case. According to Walter, months and months went by between the time that some of Joan's more casual acquaintances (he among them) put it together and the time that those of her victims whom they knew heeded their warnings. "People were so invested in their relationships with the female persona that they often just didn't want to know," Walter said. And Joan was also a brilliant manipulator who always had an explanation of why a particular person might be trashing her. "If you ever questioned her about anything," Goodall recalls, "she would get so defensive and turn the topic into an argument about whether you really loved her."

Goodall now acknowledges that she and others ignored plenty of clues, but, as she says, "Let's remember one thing—it was a *pro* doing this."

Deitz, whose off-line work sometimes involves counseling rape victims, agrees that Alex's victims were caught in an intolerable psychological bind.

"Alex zeroed in on good people," she says, "although they were often good women at vulnerable stages of their lives." To admit that Joan was a phantom was, in many cases, also to assault the genuine support and self-esteem that they had derived from the relationship. In fact, with only two exceptions—pressuring for compusex, and, in Goodall's case, using the Joan persona to pump "girl talk" confidences about Alex—there seems to have been absolutely nothing that Joan did to inspire anyone's rancor. What makes people angry is simply that Joan doesn't exist. "And a lot of what a lot of people were feeling," Deitz adds, "is mourning."

Laura ultimately confronted Joan on-line. She had already "cooled off" her relationship with Joan because of all the inconsistencies in her persona, but while she was suspicious, she had failed to suspect the enormity of the imposture. In February, however, she called another woman close to Joan, who told her she was convinced that Joan was a man. When Laura found Joan on-line later that night, she immediately asked Joan about the charge. Joan at first denied it. It was only after Laura made it clear that "I believed that we're all created after the image of God, and that I loved the person, not the sex, and would continue to do so" that Alex came out.

Laura, who is Catholic and says that her decision to stick with Alex is partially motivated by principles of Christian love, admits that it took her several weeks to "make the transition." Since then, however, she's met Alex in person and come to love him "as my adopted brother instead of my adopted sister."

Marti Cloutier to this day hasn't confronted Alex, although she has talked with him by CB and phone. "I just haven't the courage. Once, when we were talking, he mentioned something about going for a walk that day, and I wrote back that it would be a lovely day for Joan to go for a walk. I was instantly sorry." Cloutier adds: "Joan was a very special person and I loved Joan. I feel as if she died. I can't really say that I love Alex, although maybe I could, in time. Maybe I wouldn't have given him a chance if I'd known from the beginning he was a male. I've tried to sort out my feelings, but it's hard. I know I don't feel like a victim, and I don't understand why some of these other women have gone off the deep end. I don't think he was malicious. What I can't get out of my mind was that he's the same person I've spent hours and hours with."

Sheila Deitz had been introduced on-line to Alex by Joan, but found him "not all that interesting" and never became close to him. But as a visible on-line person known to many as a psychologist, she heard from many of the victims—some of whom formed their own circle of support, and in Goodall's words, "sort of held each other together with bubble gum." Some victims, according to Deitz, were so upset by the chain of events that they stopped using their modems temporarily.

Janis Goodall heard it first over the telephone, from Alex himself who mistakenly assumed that Goodall already knew. "I had just come home from the doctor, and was incredibly frustrated at having just spent $155 to have some asshole neurosurgeon tell me I would have to live with what was bothering me.

The phone rang, and it was Alex. The first words out of his mouth were 'yep—it's me.' I didn't know what he was talking about. Then he said: 'Joan and I are the same person.' I went into shock. I mean, I really freaked out—I wanted to jump off a bridge."

Since then, she has communicated with Alex by letter but has refused to see him. She emphatically resents those on-line who have spent efforts trying to "understand" him. She agreed to speak for this interview in part because "although I think this is a wonderful medium, it's a dangerous one, and it poses more danger to women than men. Men in this society are more predisposed to pulling these kinds of con games, and women are predisposed to giving people the benefit of the doubt."

Laura thinks that CompuServe and other networks ought to post warnings to newcomers that they might, in fact, encounter impostors. Others believe that the fault doesn't lie with the medium or the network, but with human frailty. "Blaming CompuServe for impostors makes about as much sense as blaming the phone company for obscene calls," says Bob Walter. CompuServe itself has no official position on the subject, although CompuServe spokesman Richard Baker notes: "Our experience has been that electronic impersonators are found out about as quickly as are face-to-face impersonators. While face-to-face impersonators are found out due to appearance, on-line impersonators are found out due to the use of phrases, the way they turn words, and the uncharacteristic thought processes that go into conversing electronically. I also believe that people are angrier when they've been betrayed by an electronic impersonator."

It would have been nice to hear Alex's side of the story. The first time I called his office, I gave only my name (which Alex knows)—not my magazine affiliation or the information that I was working on an article about "our mutual friend Joan." The receptionist asked if I was a patient. Did I want to make an appointment? I had a giddy vision of impersonating one, but decided against it. Although I telephoned twice more and identified myself as a journalist, Alex never returned my calls. He has continued his presence on-line, however, even telling Deitz that he planned to form a SIG—on another network—for psychologists and mental health professionals.

Meanwhile, in the aftermath of the Joan/Alex case, soul-searching has run rampant on CompuServe's CB and in certain SIGs. One common thread was that of Eden betrayed. As one man wrote: "I guess I figured the folks here [on-line] were special . . . but this has certainly ruptured the 'pink cloud' of CompuServe." A woman wrote back: "The feelings remind me of the ending of my first love relationship. Before that, I didn't realize fully how much hurt could result from loving."

Some of the reactions were frankly conservative—people who were sickened simply by the notion of a man who wanted to feel like a woman. There was much talk of "latency." Others seemed completely threatened by the idea that they might ever have an "inappropriate" response to someone of the "wrong" gender on-line. One message left by a male gravely informed other users that he and his girlfriend had nearly been conned by a male pretending to be a swinging female—until the girlfriend was tipped off by the impersonator's "claiming to be wearing panty hose with jeans." The message prompted an indignant reply by someone who insisted: "I always wear heels with my jeans, and when I wear heels I wear panty hose, and I don't think that is odd, and I am all female!"

But Alex's story raises some other questions that have special resonance for feminists. Chief among them, for me, is why a man has to put on electronic drag to experience intimacy, trust, and sharing. Some women have suggested that the fault is partly ours as women—that if Alex had approached us as a male, with all of Joan's personality traits, we wouldn't have been open to him. I for one reject that notion—not only because I have several terrific male friends on-line but also because it presumes that men are too fragile to break down stereotypes about themselves. (After all, *we've* spent the last 15 years struggling to prove that we can be strong, independent, and capable.) On the other hand, in Alex's defense, I can't help but appreciate the temptation to experience life in the actual world from the point of view of the other sex. Think of "Tootsie" and "Yentl." Annie Lennox and Boy George. What Alex did was alien, taboo, weird . . . and yet the stuff of cosmic cultural fantasy. Haven't you ever wanted to be a fly on the locker room (or powder room) wall?

Sheila Deitz comments that some on-line transsexualism may be essentially harmless. Where she draws the line—and where I would also—is at the point that such experimentation starts impinging on other people's trust. Joan clearly stepped over that line years ago.

Maybe one of the things to be learned from Alex and Joan is that we have a way to go before gender stops being a major, volatile human organizing principle—even in a medium dedicated to the primacy of the spirit.

I personally applaud those souls on CB who, when asked "R u m or f?" [Are you male or female?], simply answer "yes."

READING REFLECTIONS

1. What was the reason behind Alex's dual identity of Joan, and why was it initially so easy for him to get away with his deception?
2. Why were people so upset about the gender misrepresentation of Alex/Joan? How is this situation more or less disturbing than a face-to-face misrepresentation?
3. How might Joan's "nurturing" personality have contributed to the sense of betrayal people felt?
4. Write a letter in which you take the position of Alex/Joan, trying to explain the nature of his actions, or as the one of participants, explaining this perspective.
5. What types of roles does the computer play throughout Van Gelder's narrative?

A RAPE IN CYBERSPACE

Julian Dibbell

Whether it be virtual or face-to-face, Julian Dibbell's "A Rape in Cyberspace" proves that all communities have their share of violence. While in our real-time lives, some of us fear walking down a poorly lit street at night, our personal safety on-line is at issue as well in that those with technological knowledge have the power to control others to the point of violating the virtual body in a public place where onlookers are powerless to intervene. Who protects the on-line citizen and punishes the on-line perpetrator? Dibbell's widely read chronicle questions the extent to and manner in which virtual justice can be served.

Julian Dibbell is a longtime contributor to the Village Voice, *where this article originally appeared in December 1993. As a participant and an observer in the actual Lambda MOO community in which the "rape" took place, Dibbell's article has continued to spark debate about on-line rights and the distinction between virtual and material rape. He continues to publish articles that problematize virtual communities, many of which can be found on-line.*

They say he raped them that night. They say he did it with a cunning little doll, fashioned in their image and imbued with the power to make them do whatever he desired. They say that by manipulating the doll he forced them to have sex with him, and with each other, and to do horrible, brutal things to their own bodies. And though I wasn't there that night, I think I can assure you that what they say is true, because it all happened right in the living room—right there amid the well-stocked bookcases and the sofas and the fireplace—of a house I came later to think of as my second home.

Call me Dr. Bombay. A good many months ago—let's say about halfway between the first time you heard the words *information superhighway* and the first time you wished you never had—I found myself tripping now and then down the well-traveled information lane that leads to LambdaMOO, a very large and very busy rustic mansion built entirely of words. On the occasional free evening I'd sit down in my New York City apartment and type the commands that called those words onto my computer screen, dropping me with what seemed a warm electric thud inside the house's darkened coat closet, where I checked my quotidian identity, stepped into the persona and appearance of a minor character from a long-gone television sitcom, and stepped out into the glaring chatter of the crowded living room. Sometimes, when the mood struck me, I emerged as a dolphin instead.

I won't say why I chose to masquerade as Samantha Stephens's outlandish cousin, or as the dolphin, or what first led me into the semifictional digital otherworlds known around the Internet as multi-user dimensions, or MUDs. This isn't quite my story yet. It's the story, for now, of an elusive congeries of flesh and bytes named Mr. Bungle, and of the ghostly sexual violence he committed in the halls of LambdaMOO, and most importantly of the ways his violence and his victims challenged the thousand and more residents of that surreal, magic-infested mansion to become, finally, the community so many of them already believed they were.

That I was myself already known to wander the mansion grounds from time to time has little direct bearing on the story's events. I mention it only as a warning that my own perspective may be, at this late date, too steeped in the surreality and magic of the place to serve as an altogether appropriate guide. For the Bungle Affair raises questions that—here on the brink of a future in which human existence may find itself as tightly enveloped in digital environments as it is today in the architectural kind—demand a clear-eyed, sober, and unmystified consideration. It asks us to shut our ears for the time being to techno-utopian ecstasies and look without illusion upon the present possibilities for building, in the on-line spaces of this world, societies more decent and free than those mapped onto dirt and concrete and capital. It asks us to behold the new bodies awaiting us in virtual space undazzled by their phantom powers, and to get to the crucial work of sorting out the socially meaningful differences between those bodies and our physical ones. And perhaps most challengingly it asks us to wrap our late-modern ontologies, epistemologies, sexual ethics, and common sense around the curious notion of rape by voodoo doll—and to try not to warp them beyond recognition in the process.

In short, the Bungle Affair dares me to explain it to you without resort to dime-store mysticisms, and I fear I may have shape-shifted by the digital moonlight one too many times to be quite up to the task. But I will do what I can, and can do no better than to lead with the facts. For if nothing else about Mr. Bungle's case is unambiguous, the facts at least are crystal clear.

The facts begin (as they often do) with a time and a place. The time was a Monday night in March, and the place, as I've said, was the living room—which, due largely to the centrality of its location and to a certain warmth of decor, is so invariably packed with chitchatters as to be roughly synonymous among LambdaMOOers with a party. So strong, indeed, is the sense of convivial common ground invested in the living room that a cruel mind could hardly imagine a better place in which to stage a violation of LambdaMOO's communal spirit. And there was cruelty enough lurking in the appearance Mr. Bungle presented to the virtual world—he was at the time a fat, oleaginous, Bisquick-faced clown dressed in cum-stained harlequin garb and girdled with a mistletoe-and-hemlock belt whose buckle bore the quaint inscription KISS ME UNDER THIS, BITCH! But whether cruelty motivated his choice of crime scene is not among the established facts of the case. It is a fact only that he did choose the living room.

The remaining facts tell us a bit more about the inner world of Mr. Bungle, though only perhaps that it wasn't a very cozy place. They tell us that he commenced his assault entirely unprovoked, at or about 10 p.m. Pacific Standard Time. That he began by using his voodoo doll to force one of the room's occupants to sexually service him in a variety of more or less conventional ways. That this victim was exu, a Haitian trickster spirit of indeterminate gender, brown-skinned and wearing an expensive pearl gray suit, top hat, and dark glasses. That exu heaped vicious imprecations on him all the while and that he was soon ejected bodily from the room. That he hid himself away then in his private chambers somewhere on the mansion grounds and continued the attacks without interruption, since the voodoo doll worked just as well at a distance as in proximity. That he turned his attentions now to Moondreamer, a rather pointedly nondescript female character, tall, stout, and brown-haired, forcing her into unwanted liaisons with other individuals present in the room, among them exu, Kropotkin (the well-known radical), and Snugberry (the squirrel). That his actions grew progressively violent. That he made exu eat his/her own pubic hair. That he caused Moondreamer to violate herself with a piece of kitchen cutlery. That his distant laughter echoed evilly in the living room with every successive outrage. That he could not be stopped until at last someone summoned Iggy, a wise and trusted old-timer who brought with him a gun of near wizardly powers, a gun that didn't kill but enveloped its targets in a cage impermeable even to a voodoo doll's powers. That Iggy fired this gun at Mr. Bungle, thwarting the doll at last and silencing the evil, distant laughter.

These particulars, as I said, are unambiguous. But they are far from simple, for the simple reason that every set of facts in virtual reality (or VR, as the locals abbreviate it) is shadowed by a second, complicating set: the "real-life" facts. And while a certain tension invariably buzzes in the gap between the hard, prosaic RL facts and their more fluid, dreamy VR counterparts, the dissonance in the Bungle case is striking. No hideous clowns or trickster spirits appear in the RL version of the incident, no voodoo dolls or wizard guns, indeed no rape at all as any RL court of law has yet defined it. The actors in the drama were university students for the most part, and they sat rather undramatically before computer screens the entire time, their only actions a spidery flitting of fingers across standard QWERTY keyboards. No bodies touched. Whatever physical interaction occurred consisted of a mingling of electronic signals sent from sites spread out between New York City and Melbourne, Australia. Those signals met in LambdaMOO, certainly, just as the hideous clown and the living room party did, but what was LambdaMOO after all? Not an enchanted mansion or anything of the sort—just a middlingly complex database, maintained for experimental purposes inside a Xerox Corporation research computer in Palo Alto and open to public access via the Internet.

To be more precise about it, LambdaMOO was a MUD. Or to be yet more precise, it was a subspecies of MUD known as a MOO, which is short for "MUD, Object-Oriented." All of which means that it was a kind of database especially designed to give users the vivid impression of moving through a physical space that in reality exists only as words filed away on a hard drive. When users dial into LambdaMOO, for instance, the program immediately presents them with a brief textual description of one of the rooms of the database's fictional mansion (the coat closet, say). If the user wants to leave this room, she can enter a command to move in a particular direction and the database will replace the original description with a new one corresponding to the room located in the direction she chose. When the new description scrolls across the user's screen it lists not only the fixed features of the room but all its contents at that moment—including things (tools, toys, weapons) and other users (each represented as a "character" over which the user has sole control).

As far as the database program is concerned, all of these entities—rooms, things, characters—are just different subprograms that the program allows to interact according to rules very roughly mimicking the laws of the physical world. Characters may not leave a room in a given direction, for instance, unless the room subprogram contains an "exit" at that compass point. And if a character "says" or "does" something (as directed by its user-owner via the *say* or the *emote* command), then only the users whose characters are also located in that room will see the output describing the statement or action. Aside from such basic constraints, however, LambdaMOOers are allowed a broad freedom to create—they can describe their characters any way they like, they can make rooms of their own and decorate them to taste, and they can build new objects almost at will. The combination of all this busy user activity with the hard physics of the database can certainly induce a lucid illusion of presence—but when all is said and done the only thing you *really* see when you visit LambdaMOO is a kind of slow-crawling script, lines of dialogue and stage direction creeping steadily up your computer screen.

Which is all just to say that, to the extent that Mr. Bungle's assault happened in real life at all, it happened as a sort of Punch-and-Judy show, in which the puppets and the scenery were made of nothing more substantial than digital code and snippets of creative writing. The puppeteer behind Bungle that night, as it happened, was a young man logging in to the MOO from a New York University computer. He could have been Al Gore's mother-in-law for all any of the others knew, however, and he could have written Bungle's script that night any way he chose. He could have sent a command to print the message *Mr. Bungle, smiling a saintly smile, floats angelic near the ceiling of the living room, showering joy and candy kisses down upon the heads of all below*—and everyone then receiving output from the database's subprogram #17 (a/k/a the "living room") would have seen that sentence on their screens.

Instead, he entered sadistic fantasies into the "voodoo doll," a subprogram that served the not-exactly kosher purpose of attributing actions to other characters that their users did not actually write. And thus a woman in Haverford,

Pennsylvania, whose account on the MOO attached her to a character she called Moondreamer, was given the unasked-for opportunity to read the words *As if against her will, Moondreamer jabs a steak knife up her ass, causing immense joy. You hear Mr. Bungle laughing evilly in the distance.* And thus the woman in Seattle who had written herself the character called exu, with a view perhaps to tasting in imagination a deity's freedom from the burdens of the gendered flesh, got to read similarly constructed sentences in which exu, messenger of the gods, lord of crossroads and communications, suffered a brand of degradation all-too-customarily reserved for the embodied female.

"Mostly voodoo dolls are amusing," wrote exu on the evening after Bungle's rampage, posting a public statement to the widely read in-MOO mailing list called *social-issues*, a forum for debate on matters of import to the entire populace. "And mostly I tend to think that restrictive measures around here cause more trouble than they prevent. But I also think that Mr. Bungle was being a vicious, vile fuckhead, and I . . . want his sorry ass scattered from #17 to the Cinder Pile. I'm not calling for policies, trials, or better jails. I'm not sure what I'm calling for. Virtual castration, if I could manage it. Mostly, [this type of thing] doesn't happen here. Mostly, perhaps I thought it wouldn't happen to me. Mostly, I trust people to conduct themselves with some veneer of civility. Mostly, I want his ass."

Months later, the woman in Seattle would confide to me that as she wrote those words posttraumatic tears were streaming down her face—a real-life fact that should suffice to prove that the words' emotional content was no mere fiction. The precise tenor of that content, however, its mingling of murderous rage and eyeball-rolling annoyance, was a curious amalgam that neither the RL nor the VR facts alone can quite account for. Where virtual reality and its conventions would have us believe that exu and Moondreamer were brutally raped in their own living room, here was the victim exu scolding Mr. Bungle for a breach of "civility." Where real life, on the other hand, insists the incident was only an episode in a free-form version of Dungeons and Dragons, confined to the realm of the symbolic and at no point threatening any player's life, limb, or material well-being, here now was the player exu issuing aggrieved and heartfelt calls for Mr. Bungle's dismemberment. Ludicrously excessive by RL's lights, woefully understated by VR's, the tone of exu's response made sense only in the buzzing, dissonant gap between them.

Which is to say it made the only kind of sense that *can* be made of MUDly phenomena. For while the *facts* attached to any event born of a MUD's strange, ethereal universe may march in straight, tandem lines separated neatly into the virtual and the real, its meaning lies always in that gap. You learn this axiom early in your life as a player, and it's of no small relevance to the Bungle case that you often learn it between the sheets, so to speak. Netsex, tinysex, virtual sex—however you name it, in real-life reality it's nothing more than a 900-line encounter stripped of even the vestigial physicality of the voice. And yet, as many a wide-eyed newbie can tell you, it's possibly the headiest experience the very heady world of MUDs has to offer. Amid flurries of even the most cursorily described caresses, sighs, or penetrations, the glands do engage, and often as throbbingly as they would in a real-life assignation—sometimes even more so, given the combined power of anonymity and textual suggestiveness to unshackle deep-seated fantasies. And if the virtual setting and the interplayer vibe are right, who knows? The heart may engage as well, stirring up passions as strong as many that bind lovers who observe the formality of trysting in the flesh.

To participate, therefore, in this disembodied enactment of life's most body-centered activity is to risk the realization that when it comes to sex, perhaps the body in question is not the physical one at all, but its psychic double, the bodylike self-representation we carry around in our heads—and that whether we present that body to another as a meat puppet or a word puppet is not nearly as significant a distinction as one might have thought. I know, I know, you've read Foucault and your mind is not quite blown by the notion that sex is never so much an exchange of fluids as it is an exchange of signs. But trust your friend Dr. Bombay, it's one thing to grasp the notion intellectually and quite another to feel it coursing through your veins amid the virtual steam of hot netnookie. And it's a whole other mind-blowing trip altogether to encounter it thus as a college frosh, new to the net and still in the grip of hormonal hurricanes and high-school sexual mythologies. The shock can easily reverberate throughout an entire young worldview. Small wonder, then, that a newbie's first taste of MUD sex is often also the first time she or he surrenders wholly to the quirky terms of MUDish ontology, recognizing in a full-bodied way that what happens inside a MUD-made world is neither exactly real nor exactly make-believe, but nonetheless profoundly, compellingly, and emotionally *true.*

And small wonder indeed that the sexual nature of Mr. Bungle's crime provoked such powerful feelings, and not just in exu (who, be it noted, was in real life a theory-savvy doctoral candidate and a longtime MOOer, but just as baffled and overwhelmed by the force of her own reaction, she later would attest, as any panting undergrad might have been). Even players who had never experienced MUD rape (the vast majority of male-presenting characters, but not as large a majority of the female-presenting as might be hoped) immediately appreciated its gravity and were moved to condemnation of the perp. exu's missive to *social-issues* followed a strongly worded one from Iggy ("Well, well," it began, "no matter what else happens on Lambda, I can always be sure that some jerk is going to reinforce my low opinion of humanity") and was itself followed by others from Zakariah, Wereweasel, Crawdaddy, and emmeline. Moondreamer also let her feelings ("pissed") be known. And even Xander, the Clueless Samaritan who had responded to Bungle's cries for help and uncaged him shortly after the incident, expressed his regret once apprised of Bungle's deeds, which he allowed to be "despicable."

A sense was brewing that something needed to be done—done soon and in something like an organized fashion—about Mr. Bungle, in particular, and about MUD rape, in general. Regarding the general problem, emmeline, who identified herself as a survivor of both virtual rape ("many times over") and real-life sexual assault, floated a cautious proposal for a MOO-wide powwow on the subject of virtual sex offenses and what mechanisms if any might be put in place to deal with their future occurrence. As for the specific problem, the answer no doubt seemed obvious to many. But it wasn't until the evening of the second day after the incident that exu, finally and rather solemnly, gave it voice:

"I am requesting that Mr. Bungle be toaded for raping Moondreamer and I. I have never done this before, and have thought about it for days. He hurt us both."

That was all. Three simple sentences posted to *social.* Reading them, an outsider might never guess that they were an application for a death warrant. Even an outsider familiar with other MUDs might not guess it, since in many of them "toading" still refers to a command that, true to the gameworlds' sword-and-sorcery origins, simply turns a player into a toad, wiping the player's description and attributes and replacing them with those of the slimy amphibian. Bad luck for sure, but not quite as bad as what happens when the same command is invoked in the MOOish strains of MUD: not only are the description and attributes of the toaded player erased, but the account itself goes too. The annihilation of the character, thus, is total.

And nothing less than total annihilation, it seemed, would do to settle LambdaMOO's accounts with Mr. Bungle. Within minutes of the posting of exu's appeal, HortonWho, the Australian Deleuzean, who had witnessed much of the attack from the back room of his suburban Melbourne home, seconded the motion with a brief message crisply entitled "Toad the fukr." HortonWho's posting was seconded almost as quickly by that of Kropotkin, covictim of Mr. Bungle and well-known radical, who in real life happened also to be married to the real-life exu. And over the course of the next 24 hours as many as 50 players made it known, on *social* and in a variety of other forms and forums, that they would be pleased to see Mr. Bungle erased from the face of the MOO. And with dissent so far confined to a dozen or so antitoading hardliners, the numbers suggested that the citizenry was indeed moving towards a resolve to have Bungle's virtual head.

There was one small but stubborn obstacle in the way of this resolve, however, and that was a curious state of social affairs known in some quarters of the MOO as the New Direction. It was all very fine, you see, for the LambdaMOO rabble to get it in their heads to liquidate one of their peers, but when the time came to actually do the deed it would require the services of a nobler class of character. It would require a wizard. Master-programmers of the MOO, spelunkers of the database's deepest code-structures and custodians of its day-to-day administrative trivia, wizards are also the only players empowered to issue the toad command, a feature maintained on nearly all MUDs as a quick-and-dirty means of social control. But the wizards of LambdaMOO, after years of adjudicating all manner of interplayer disputes with little to show for it but their own weariness and the smoldering resentment of the general populace, had decided they'd had enough of the social sphere. And so, four months before the Bungle incident, the archwizard Haakon (known in RL as

Pavel Curtis, Xerox researcher and LambdaMOO's principal architect) formalized this decision in a document called "LambdaMOO Takes a New Direction," which he placed in the living room for all to see. In it, Haakon announced that the wizards from that day forth were pure technicians. From then on, they would make no decisions affecting the social life of the MOO, but only implement whatever decisions the community as a whole directed them to. From then on, it was decreed, LambdaMOO would just have to grow up and solve its problems on its own.

Faced with the task of inventing its own self-governance from scratch, the LambdaMOO population had so far done what any other loose, amorphous agglomeration of individuals would have done: they'd let it slide. But now the task took on new urgency. Since getting the wizards to toad Mr. Bungle (or to toad the likes of him in the future) required a convincing case that the cry for his head came from the community at large, then the community itself would have to be defined; and if the community was to be convincingly defined, then some form of social organization, no matter how rudimentary, would have to be settled on. And thus, as if against its will, the question of what to do about Mr. Bungle began to shape itself into a sort of referendum on the political future of the MOO. Arguments broke out on *social and elsewhere that had only superficially to do with Bungle (since everyone seemed to agree he was a cad) and everything to do with where the participants stood on LambdaMOO's crazy-quilty political map. Parliamentarian legalist types argued that unfortunately Bungle could not legitimately be toaded at all, since there were no explicit MOO rules against rape, or against just about anything else—and the sooner such rules were established, they added, and maybe even a full-blown judiciary system complete with elected officials and prisons to enforce those rules, the better. Others, with a royalist streak in them, seemed to feel that Bungle's as-yet-unpunished outrage only proved this New Direction silliness had gone on long enough, and that it was high time the wizardocracy returned to the position of swift and decisive leadership their player class was born to.

And then there were what I'll call the technolibertarians. For them, MUD rapists were of course assholes, but the presence of assholes on the system was a technical inevitability, like noise on a phone line, and best dealt with not through repressive social disciplinary mechanisms but through the timely deployment of defensive software tools. Some asshole blasting violent, graphic language at you? Don't whine to the authorities about it—hit the @gag command and said asshole's statements will be blocked from your screen (and only yours). It's simple, it's effective, and it censors no one.

But the Bungle case was rather hard on such arguments. For one thing, the extremely public nature of the living room meant that gagging would spare the victims only from witnessing their own violation, but not from having others witness it. You might want to argue that what those victims didn't directly experience couldn't hurt them, but consider how that wisdom would sound to a woman who'd been, say, fondled by strangers while passed out drunk in the middle of a party and you have a rough idea how it might go over with a crowd of hard-core MOOers. Consider, for another thing, that many of the biologically female participants in the Bungle debate had been around long enough to grow lethally weary of the gag-and-get-over-it school of virtual-rape counseling, with its fine line between empowering victims and holding them responsible for their own suffering, and its shrugging indifference to the window of pain between the moment the rape-text starts flowing and the moment a gag shuts it off. From the outset it was clear that the technolibertarians were going to have to tiptoe through this issue with care, and for the most part they did.

Yet no position was trickier to maintain than that of the MOO's resident anarchists. Like the technolibbers, the anarchists didn't care much for punishments or policies or power elites. Like them, they hoped the MOO could be a place where people interacted fulfillingly without the need for such things. But their high hopes were complicated, in general, by a somewhat less thorough-going faith in technology (*Even if you can't tear down the master's house with the master's tools*—read a slogan written into one anarchist player's self-description—*it is a damned good place to start*). And at present they were additionally complicated by the fact that the most vocal anarchists in the discussion were none other than exu, Kropotkin, and HortonWho, who wanted to see Mr. Bungle toaded as badly as anyone did.

Needless to say, a pro–death penalty platform is not an especially comfortable one for an anarchist to sit on, so these particular anarchists were now at great pains to sever the conceptual ties between toading and capital punishment. Toading, they insisted (almost convincingly), was much more closely analogous to banishment; it was a kind of turning of the communal back on the offending party, a collective action which, if carried out properly, was entirely consistent with anarchist models of community. And carrying it out properly meant first and foremost building a consensus around it—a messy process for which there were no easy technocratic substitutes. It was going to take plenty of good old-fashioned, jawbone-intensive grassroots organizing.

So that when the time came, at 7 p.m. PST on the evening of the third day after the occurrence in the living room, to gather in emmeline's room for her proposed real-time open conclave, Kropotkin and exu were among the first to arrive. But this was hardly to be an anarchist-dominated affair, for the room was crowding rapidly with representatives of all the MOO's political stripes, and even a few wizards. Hagbard showed up, and Aurea and Quanto, Spaff, TomTraceback, Lithium and Bloof, ShermieRocko, Silver Surfer, MaoTse-Hedgehog, Toothpick—the names piled up and the discussion gathered momentum under their weight. Arguments multiplied and mingled, players talked past and through each other, the textual clutter of utterances and gestures filled up the screen like thick cigar smoke. Peaking in number at around 30, this was one of the largest crowds that ever gathered in a single LambdaMOO chamber, and while emmeline had given her place a description that made it *infinite in expanse and fluid in form*, it now seemed anything but roomy. You could almost feel the claustrophobic air of the place, dank and overheated by virtual bodies, pressing against your skin.

I know you could because I too was there, in one of those pivotal accidents of personal history one always wants later to believe were approached with a properly solemn awareness of the moment's portent. Almost as invariably, of course, the truth is that one wanders into such occasions utterly without a clue, and so it was with me that night. Completely ignorant of any of the goings-on that had led to the meeting, I showed up mainly to see what the crowd was about, and though I observed the proceedings for a good while, I confess I found it hard to grasp what was going on. I was still the rankest of newbies then, my MOO legs still too unsteady to make the leaps of faith, logic, and empathy required to meet the spectacle on its own terms. I was fascinated by the concept of virtual rape, but I was even more so by the notion that anyone could take it altogether seriously.

In this, though, I found myself in a small and mostly silent minority, for the discussion that raged around me was of an almost unrelieved earnestness, bent it seemed on examining every last aspect and implication of Mr. Bungle's crime. There were the central questions, of course: thumbs up or down on Bungle's virtual existence? And if down, how then to insure that his toading was not just some isolated lynching but a first step toward shaping LambdaMOO into a legitimate community? Surrounding these, however, a tangle of weighty side issues proliferated. What, some wondered, was the real-life legal status of the offense? Could Bungle's university administrators punish him for sexual harassment? Could he be prosecuted under California state laws against obscene phone calls? Little enthusiasm was shown for pursuing either of these lines of action, which testifies both to the uniqueness of the crime and to the nimbleness with which the discussants were negotiating its idiosyncracies. Many were the casual references to Bungle's deed as simply "rape," but these in no way implied that the players had lost sight of all distinctions between the virtual and physical versions, or that they believed Bungle should be dealt with in the same way a real-life criminal would. He had committed a MOO crime, and his punishment, if any, would be meted out via the MOO.

On the other hand, little patience was shown toward any attempts to downplay the seriousness of what Mr. Bungle had done. When the affable HerkieCosmo proposed, more in the way of an hypothesis than an assertion, that "perhaps it's better to release . . . violent tendencies in a virtual environment rather than in real life," he was tut-tutted so swiftly and relentlessly that he withdrew the hypothesis altogether, apologizing humbly as he did so. Not that the assembly was averse to putting matters into a more philosophical perspective. "Where does the body end and the mind begin?" young Quastro asked, amid recurring attempts to fine-tune the differences between real and virtual violence. "Is not the mind a part of the body?" "In MOO, the body IS the mind," offered HerkieCosmo gamely, and not at all implausibly, demonstrating the ease with which very knotty metaphysical conundrums come undone in VR. The not-so-aptly named Obvious seemed to agree, arriving after sufficient consideration of the nature of Bungle's crime at the hardly novel yet now somehow newly resonant conjecture that "all reality might consist of ideas, who knows."

On these and other matters the anarchists, the libertarians, the legalists, the wizardists—and the wizards—all had their thoughtful say. But as the evening wore on and the talk grew more heated and more heady, it seemed increasingly clear that the vigorous intelligence being brought to bear on this swarm of issues wasn't going to result in anything remotely like resolution. The perspectives were just too varied, the meme-scape just too slippery. Again and again, arguments that looked at first to be heading in a decisive direction ended up chasing their own tails; and slowly, depressingly, a dusty haze of irrelevance gathered over the proceedings.

It was almost a relief, therefore, when midway through the evening Mr. Bungle himself, the living, breathing cause of all this talk, teleported into the room. Not that it was much of a surprise. Oddly enough, in the three days since his release from Iggy's cage, Bungle had returned more than once to wander the public spaces of LambdaMOO, walking willingly into one of the fiercest storms of ill will and invective ever to rain down on a player. He'd been taking it all with a curious and mostly silent passivity, and when challenged face to virtual face by both exu and the genderless elder statescharacter PatSoftly to defend himself on *social, he'd demurred, mumbling something about Christ and expiation. He was equally quiet now, and his reception was still uniformly cool. exu fixed an arctic stare on him—*no hate, no anger, no interest at all. Just . . . watching.* Others were more actively unfriendly. "Asshole," spat Karl Porcupine, "creep." But the harshest of the MOO's hostility toward him had already been vented, and the attention he drew now was motivated more, it seemed, by the opportunity to probe the rapist's mind, to find out what made it tick and if possible how to get it to tick differently. In short, they wanted to know why he'd done it. So they asked him.

And Mr. Bungle thought about it. And as eddies of discussion and debate continued to swirl around him, he thought about it some more. And then he said this:

"I engaged in a bit of a psychological device that is called thought-polarization, the fact that this is not RL simply added to heighten the affect of the device. It was purely a sequence of events with no consequence on my RL existence."

They might have known. Stilted though its diction was, the gist of the answer was simple, and something many in the room had probably already surmised: Mr. Bungle was a psycho. Not, perhaps, in real life—but then in real life it's possible for reasonable people to assume, as Bungle clearly did, that what transpires between word-costumed characters within the boundaries of a make-believe world is, if not mere play, then at most some kind of emotional laboratory experiment. Inside the MOO, however, such thinking marked a person as one of two basically subcompetent types. The first was the newbie, in which case the confusion was understandable, since there were few MOOers who had not, upon their first visits as anonymous "guest" characters, mistaken the place for a vast playpen in which they might act out their wildest fantasies without fear of censure. Only with time and the acquisition of a fixed character do players tend to make the critical passage from anonymity to pseudonymity, developing the concern for their character's reputation that marks the attainment of virtual adulthood. But while Mr. Bungle hadn't been around as long as most MOOers, he'd been around long enough to leave his newbie status behind, and his delusional statement therefore placed him among the second type: the sociopath.

And as there is but small percentage in arguing with a head case, the room's attention gradually abandoned Mr. Bungle and returned to the discussions that had previously occupied it. But if the debate had been edging toward ineffectuality before, Bungle's anticlimactic appearance had evidently robbed it of any forward motion whatsoever. What's more, from his lonely corner of the room Mr. Bungle kept issuing periodic expressions of a prickly sort of remorse, interlaced with sarcasm and belligerence, and though it was hard to tell if he wasn't still just conducting his experiments, some people thought his regret genuine enough that maybe he didn't deserve to be toaded after all. Logically, of course, discussion of the principal issues at hand didn't require unanimous belief that Bungle was an irredeemable bastard, but now that cracks were showing in that unanimity, the last of the meeting's fervor seemed to be draining out through them.

People started drifting away. Mr. Bungle left first, then others followed—one by one, in twos and threes, hugging friends and waving goodnight. By 9:45 only a handful remained, and the great debate had wound down into casual conversation, the melancholy remains of another fruitless good idea. The arguments had been well-honed, certainly, and perhaps might prove useful in some as-yet-unclear long run. But at this point what seemed clear was that emmeline's meeting had died, at last, and without any practical results to mark its passing.

It was also at this point, most likely, that TomTraceback reached his decision. TomTraceback was a wizard, a taciturn sort of fellow who'd sat brooding on the sidelines all evening. He hadn't said a lot, but what he had said, there and elsewhere, indicated that he took the crime committed against exu and Moondreamer very seriously, and that he felt no particular compassion towards the character who had committed it. But on the other hand he had made it equally plain that he took the elimination of a fellow player just as seriously, and moreover that he had no desire to return to the days of wizardly intervention. It must have been difficult, therefore, to reconcile the conflicting impulses churning within him at that moment. In fact, it was probably impossible, for though he did tend to believe that the consensus on *social was sufficient proof of the MOO's desire to see capital justice done in the Bungle case, he was also well aware that under the present order of things nothing but his own conscience could tell him, ultimately, whether to ratify that consensus or not. As much as he would have liked to make himself an instrument of the MOO's collective will, therefore, there was no escaping the fact that he must in the final analysis either act alone or not act at all.

So TomTraceback acted alone.

He told the lingering few players in the room that he had to go, and then he went. It was a minute or two before ten. He did it quietly and he did it privately, but all anyone had to do to know he'd done it was to type the @*who* command, which was normally what you typed if you wanted to know a player's present location and the time he last logged in. But if you had run a @*who* on Mr. Bungle not too long after TomTraceback left emmeline's room, the database would have told you something different.

Mr. Bungle, it would have said, *is not the name of any player*.

The date, as it happened, was April Fool's Day, but this was no joke: Mr. Bungle was truly dead and truly gone.

They say that LambdaMOO wasn't really the same after Mr. Bungle's toading. They say as well that nothing really changed. And though it skirts the fuzziest of dream-logics to say that both these statements are true, the MOO is just the sort of fuzzy, dreamlike place in which such contradictions thrive.

Certainly the Bungle Affair marked the end of LambdaMOO's brief epoch of rudderless social drift. The rash of public-spiritedness engendered by the events might alone have led in time to some more formal system of communal self-definition, but in the end it was the archwizard Haakon who made sure of it. Away on business for the duration of the episode, Haakon returned to find its wreckage strewn across the tiny universe he'd set in motion. The death of a player, the trauma of several others, and the nerve-wracked complaints of his colleague TomTraceback presented themselves to his concerned and astonished attention, and he resolved to see if he couldn't learn some lesson from it all. For the better part of a day he puzzled over the record of events and arguments left in *social, then he sat pondering the chaotically evolving shape of his creation, and at the day's end he descended once again into the social arena of the MOO with another history-altering proclamation.

It was to be his last, for what he now decreed was the final, missing piece of the New Direction. In a few days, Haakon announced, he would build into the database a system of petitions and ballots whereby anyone could put to popular vote any social scheme requiring wizardly powers for its implementation, with the results of the vote to be binding on the wizards. At last and for good, the awkward gap between the will of the players and the efficacy of the technicians would be closed. And though some anarchists grumbled about the irony of Haakon's dictatorially imposing universal suffrage on an unconsulted populace, in general the citizens of LambdaMOO seemed to find it hard to fault a system more purely democratic than any that could ever exist in real life. A few months and a dozen ballot measures later, widespread participation in the new regime had already produced a small arsenal of mechanisms for dealing with the types of violence that called the system into being. MOO residents now had access to a @boot command, for instance, with which to summarily eject berserker "guest" characters. And players could bring suit against one another through an ad hoc mediation system in which mutually agreed-upon judges had at their disposition the full range of wizardly punishments—up to and including the capital.

Yet the continued dependence on extermination as the ultimate keeper of the peace suggested that this new MOO order was perhaps not built on the most solid of foundations. For if life on LambdaMOO began to acquire more coherence in the wake of the toading, death retained all the fuzziness of pre-Bungle days. This truth was rather dramatically borne out, not too many days after Bungle departed, by the arrival of a strange new character named Dr. Jest. There was a forceful eccentricity to the newcomer's manner, but the oddest thing about his style was its striking yet unnameable familiarity. And when he developed the annoying habit of stuffing fellow players into a jar containing a tiny simulacrum of a certain deceased rapist, the source of this familiarity became obvious:

Mr. Bungle had risen from the grave.

In itself, Bungle's reincarnation as Dr. Jest was a remarkable turn of events, but perhaps even more remarkable was the utter lack of amazement with which the LambdaMOO public took note of it. To be sure, many residents were appalled by the brazenness of Bungle's return. In fact, one of the first petitions circulated under the new voting system was a request for Dr. Jest's toading that almost immediately gathered several dozen signatures (but failed in the end to reach ballot status). Yet few were unaware of the ease with which the toad proscription could be circumvented—all the toadee had to do (all the ur-Bungle at NYU presumably had done) was to go to the minor hassle of acquiring a new Internet account, and LambdaMOO's character registration program would then simply treat the known felon as an entirely new and innocent person. Nor was this ease necessarily understood to represent a failure of toading's social disciplinary function. On the contrary, it only underlined the truism (repeated many times throughout the debate over Mr. Bungle's fate) that his punishment, ultimately, had been no more or less symbolic than his crime.

What *was* surprising, however, was that Mr. Bungle/Dr. Jest appeared to have taken the symbolism to heart. Dark themes still obsessed him—the objects he created gave off wafts of Nazi imagery and medical torture—but he no longer radiated the aggressively antisocial vibes he had before. He was a lot less unpleasant to look at (the outrageously seedy clown description had been replaced by that of a mildly creepy but actually rather natty young man, with *blue eyes . . . suggestive of conspiracy, untamed eroticism and perhaps a sense of understanding of the future*), and aside from the occasional jar-stuffing incident, he was also a lot less dangerous to be around. It seemed obvious, at least to me, that he'd undergone some sort of personal transformation in the days since I'd first glimpsed him back in emmeline's crowded room—nothing radical maybe, but powerful nonetheless, and resonant enough with my own experience, I felt, that it might be more than professionally interesting to talk with him, and perhaps compare notes.

For I too was undergoing a transformation in the aftermath of that night in emmeline's—and was increasingly uncertain what to make of it. As I pursued my runaway fascination with the discussion I had heard there, as I pored over the *social debate and got to know exu and some of the other victims and witnesses, I could feel my newbie consciousness falling away from me. Where before I'd found it hard to take virtual rape seriously, I now was finding it difficult to remember how I could ever *not* have taken it seriously. I was proud to have arrived at this perspective—it felt like an exotic sort of achievement, and it definitely made my ongoing experience of the MOO a richer one.

But it was also having some unsettling effects on the way I looked at the rest of the world. Sometimes, for instance, it grew difficult for me to understand why RL society classifies RL rape alongside crimes against person or property. Since rape can occur without any physical pain or damage, I found myself reasoning, then it must be classed as a crime against the mind—more intimately and deeply hurtful, to be sure, than cross burnings, wolf whistles, and virtual rape, but undeniably located on the same conceptual continuum. I did not, however, conclude as a result that rapists were protected in any fashion by the First Amendment. Quite the opposite, in fact: the more seriously I took the notion of virtual rape, the less seriously I was able to take the tidy division of the world into the symbolic and the real that underlies the very notion of freedom of speech.

Let me assure you, though, that I did not at the time adopt these thoughts as full-fledged arguments, nor am I now presenting them as such. I offer them, rather, as a picture of the sort of mind-set that my initial encounters with a virtual world inspired in me. I offer them also, therefore, as a kind of prophecy. For whatever else these thoughts were telling me, I have come to hear in them an announcement of the final stages of our decades-long passage into the Information Age, a paradigm shift that the classic liberal firewall between word and deed (itself a product of an earlier paradigm shift commonly known as the Enlightenment) is not likely to survive intact. After all, anyone the least bit familiar with the workings of the new era's definitive technology, the computer, knows that it operates on a principle impracticably difficult to distinguish from the pre-Enlightenment principle of the magic word: the commands you type into a computer are a kind of speech that doesn't so much communicate as *make things happen*, directly and ineluctably, the same way pulling a trigger does. They are incantations, in other words, and anyone at all attuned to the technosocial megatrends of the moment—from the growing dependence of economies on the global flow of intensely fetishized words and numbers to the burgeoning ability of bioengineers to speak the spells written in the four-letter text of DNA—knows that the logic of the incantation is rapidly permeating the fabric of our lives.

And it was precisely this logic, I was beginning to understand, that provided whatever real magic LambdaMOO had to offer—not the fictive trappings of voodoo and shapeshifting and wizardry, but the conflation of speech and act that's inevitable in any computer-mediated world, be it Lambda or the increasingly wired world at large. This was dangerous magic, to be sure, a potential threat—if misconstrued or misapplied—to our always precarious freedoms of expression, and as someone who lives by his words I dared not take the threat lightly. And yet, on the other hand, I could no longer convince myself that our wishful insulation of language from the realm of action had ever been anything but a valuable kludge, a philosophically imperfect stopgap against oppression that would just have to do till something truer and more elegant came along.

Was I wrong to think this truer, more elegant thing might be found on LambdaMOO? I did not know. I continued, in my now and then visits, to seek it there, sensing its presence just below the surface of every interaction, yet increasingly I sensed as well that if I really wanted to see what lay beneath those surfaces—to glimpse unveiled whatever there was of genuine historical novelty in VR's slippery social and philosophical dynamics—I was going to have to radically deepen my acquaintance with the MOO somehow.

For a time I considered the possibility, as I said, that discussing with Dr. Jest our shared experience of the workings of the place might be a step towards just such a breakthrough. But when that notion first occurred to me, I still felt somewhat intimidated by his lingering criminal aura, and I hemmed and hawed a good long time before finally resolving to drop him MOO-mail suggesting we get together. By then it appeared to be too late. For reasons known only to himself, Dr. Jest had stopped logging in. Maybe he'd grown bored with the MOO. Maybe the loneliness of ostracism had gotten to him. Maybe a psycho whim had carried him far away or maybe he'd quietly acquired a third character and started life over with a cleaner slate.

Wherever he'd gone, though, he left behind the room he'd created for himself—a treehouse *tastefully decorated* with rare-book shelves, an operating table, and a life-size William S. Burroughs doll—and he left it unlocked. So I took to checking in there occasionally, heading out of my own cozy nook (inside a TV set inside the little red hotel inside the Monopoly board inside the dining room of LambdaMOO) and teleporting on over to the treehouse, where the room description always told me Dr. Jest was present but asleep, in the conventional depiction for disconnected characters. The not-quite-emptiness of the abandoned room invariably instilled in me an uncomfortable mix of melancholy and the creeps, and I would stick around only on the off chance that Dr. Jest might wake up, say hello, and share his understanding of the future with me.

It happens, in fact, that Dr. Jest did eventually rise again from his epic sleep. But what wisdom he had to offer on that occasion I couldn't tell you, for I had given up the habit of my skittish stakeouts by then. Some final transformation had come over me between visits to that lonely place: the complex magic of the MOO grew gradually to interest me less and less as a way of understanding the future and more and more as a way of living the present, until one day I teleported home from Dr. Jest's treehouse for the last time, determined to wait no longer for a consultation with my fellow doctor to give me what I wanted from the MOO, but to wrest it instead from the very heart of the place. I was resolved now, in other words, to make a life there—to loosen for a while the RL ties that kept me still a sort of tourist on the MOO and to give in, body and soul, to the same powerful gravity that kept so many other MOOers logged on day after day and for hours at a time.

And in the end that's just what I did, so that for a brief, unforgettable season the buzzing haze of VR came at last to envelop my existence: my small daily dramas were absorbed into the MOO's teeming reservoir of small daily dramas, my labors were directed as much toward the ongoing construction of that virtual world as toward the quotidian maintenance of my stake in the material one, and my days were swept by the same broad currents of MOO history that gave rise to the Bungle Affair and the momentous social changes that followed on it.

That is all quite another story, of course. Yet as I said before, it begins where Mr. Bungle's ends, and there remains now only a very little of his to tell. Dr. Jest did finally reawaken, it's true, one late-December day—but he didn't even make it to January before he decided, for no apparent reason but old times' sake, to go on a late-night Bungle-grade rampage through the living room, thus all but formally requesting to be hauled before an official mediator and toaded with a vengeance. The new MOO polity promptly obliged, and I, still busily contriving to loosen those RL ties in preparation for my full-time residency, missed by days my last chance to hear the doctor's story from his own virtual mouth.

But this was no great loss, I suppose, for after all what more could I have learned? Dr. Jest's relapse into mindless digital violence, mocking as it did my wishful projection of hard-earned wisdom onto him, was lesson enough, driving home what Bungle's story in its fullest implications should have already taught me by then: that nothing in the MOO was ever quite what one imagined it to be.

I would still have to learn this lesson many times over, of course. I'd learn it again when on the eve of my immersion in VR two separate and credible sources revealed to me that the virtual psychosis of Mr. Bungle had been even starker than anyone guessed: that the Bungle account had been the more or less communal property of an entire NYU dorm floor, that the young man at the keyboard on the evening of the rape had acted not alone but surrounded by fellow students calling out suggestions and encouragement, that conceivably none of those people were speaking for Bungle when he showed up in emmeline's room to answer for the crime, that Dr. Jest himself, thought commonly to have reincarnated the whole Bungle and nothing but the Bungle, in fact embodied just one member of the original mob—just one scattered piece of a self more irreparably fragmented than any RL multiple personality could ever fear to be.

I don't know exactly how often it occurred to me, in the VR-saturated months to follow, that other such shards of Mr. Bungle's shattered identity might lurk among the ethereal population I moved through on a daily basis. But if they were there they never made themselves known, and I certainly never tried to sniff them out. It was far too late for that: the time had come for me to live in LambdaMOO, and I no longer sought the company of ghosts.

READING REFLECTIONS

1. What is a MOO? How is it different from other forms of on-line communication, such as e-mail?
2. In his article, Julian Dibbell uses the term *rape* to describe the experience of the female characters on LambdaMOO. Given this situation, do you

agree with his use of this term? In what ways would you argue that virtual rape is similar to or different from rape in the physical world?

3. How did the technology within the MOO allow the rape to take place? In what sense does the technology become a type of weapon?

4. At what point should on-line participants be punished for their actions, via banishment or, depending on the nature of the charge, through real-time justice, that is, arrest and prosecution? Summarize the debate about the nature of on-line rights and responsibilities as represented by the various participants within LambdaMOO. Engage in either a face-to-face or on-line discussion of this issue in order to brainstorm and write a classroom position statement regarding behavior and "netiquette" in your own on-line community.

5. Dibbell notes "They say that LambdaMOO wasn't really the same" since Mr. Bungle's demise. If this is true, what social factors account for the change?

"Virtual Communities/Virtual Selves" Activities

READING REACTIONS

1. In his article, John Perry Barlow states that cyberspace is a place where community is possible. However, Reginald Stuart's article states that this community isn't readily available to everyone. Taking this into consideration, create a list of people who you think would have limited or no access to cyberspace and state your reasons for these limits.

2. Lindsy Van Gelder and Julian Dibbell's articles are both case studies of conflict within virtual communities. Based on your own usage of on-line communication or any other media coverage, to what extent does such conflict seem common or unavoidable? Are you aware of more positive discussions or instances of virtual community?

3. Kara Swisher notes Judy Buzbee's reluctance to "go on-line." Although Buzbee's reasons appear to be both time and knowledge related, how do points made by Judy Anderson and Julian Dibbell suggest that females can be disadvantaged on-line? Does Swisher's discussion support this in any other way?

CLASSROOM REACTIONS

1. When did you first use a computer, and how did you learn more about computers? From work, school, home, friends? What advantages or disadvantages do you think you've had that have made the use of computers an easier or harder process for you? Some advantages may include types of schools or training received, whereas some disadvantages may include

financial situations, family circumstances, even such issues as gender or age. How might your own access to technology connect to issues raised by Reginald Stuart in his concerns about African American access?

2. Find an on-line article to use in a paper you are currently working on. How and where did you find it? Was it as easy to find as an article in a journal or magazine in your college library? What is the difference in format, style, and tone between the on-line source and another source from the library? Which information do you find to be more valuable or reliable to include in your paper?

3. Make a visual representation of your reliance upon technology during your daily life. How important are certain types of technologies in your personal and professional routines? How do these technologies help you interact with others or obtain information? As a class, debate whether or not we are overly dependent on technology.

MEDIA CONNECTIONS

1. Conduct an experiment on-line in which you or several participants go on-line as a woman for several weeks and then go on-line as a man. Are there differences in the way you or they are treated as one gender or the other? Explain. What might such interactions reveal about claims, such as those raised by Van Gelder, Anderson, and Dibbell, of virtual empowerment or virtual victimization for women?

2. Analyze a series of computer or virtual reality–oriented magazines, such as *Wired* or *Mondo 2000*. What dominant topics or messages are disseminated about technology? Who are the audiences for these technology-specific journals? How do you identify or not identify with these depictions of virtual life?

3. If your class has access to the Internet, work with your teacher to create a keypal system in which your class chats with another class, perhaps in a different region of the country. Your conversations can be related to the issues being discussed in the class—family, gender, and so forth—addressing the cultural or regional conflicts the two groups might have about these issues. At the end of the project, write an analysis of what you learned from these on-line dialogues, considering the assumptions of others and the ways in which such discussions altered your own opinions about the issues throughout the term.

COMMUNITY INTERACTIONS

1. Both John Perry Barlow and Kara Swisher chronicle the potential empowerment of on-line communities. Interview several people about their perceptions of their roles on a particular list. What types of reasons do they

have for going on-line? How frequently do they post or do they lurk? To what extent to they feel empowered or marginalized in their on-line communities as opposed to their real-time communities?

2. Conduct a study in which you look at the role electronic communication (e-mail) plays in a classroom or a business. What is e-mail used for? Who has access to on-line systems? Who controls what is discussed? Why do people in the class or business like or dislike e-mail? How does it improve or not improve communication? Write an informative report for the members of the community studied.

3. Investigate the role of the Internet in children's lives by surveying the types of sources available on-line for kids—the types of links, activities available. Are they commercial or nonprofit? Are any of them run by kids? Take several children, preferably ones who have not had much Internet access, to these sites to gauge their interest in what's out there. How do you evaluate the impact of these sources on either an educational or entertainment level?

Index of Authors and Titles

319